The Liberty Bell and Its Legacy

The Liberty Bell and Its Legacy

An Encyclopedia of an American Icon in U.S. History and Culture

John R. Vile

BLOOMSBURY ACADEMIC

NEW YORK · LONDON · OXFORD · NEW DELHI · SYDNEY

BLOOMSBURY ACADEMIC
Bloomsbury Publishing Inc
1385 Broadway, New York, NY 10018, USA
50 Bedford Square, London, WC1B 3DP, UK
29 Earlsfort Terrace, Dublin 2, Ireland

BLOOMSBURY, BLOOMSBURY ACADEMIC and the Diana logo are trademarks
of Bloomsbury Publishing Plc

First published in the United States of America by ABC-CLIO 2020
Paperback edition published by Bloomsbury Academic 2025

Library of Congress Cataloging-in-Publication Data

Names: Vile, John R., author.
Title: The Liberty Bell and its Legacy : An Encyclopedia of an American Icon in U.S.
History and Culture / John R. Vile.
Description: Santa Barbara, California : ABC-CLIO,
2020. | Includes bibliographical references
and index.
Identifiers: LCCN 2019026978 (print) | LCCN 2019026979
(ebook) | ISBN 9781440872907
(hardback) | ISBN 9781440872914 (ebook)
Subjects: LCSH: Liberty Bell—History—Encyclopedias.
Classification: LCC F158.8.I3 V55 2020 (print) | LCC F158.8.I3
(ebook) | DDC 974.8/11—dc23
LC record available at https://lccn.loc.gov/2019026978
LC ebook record available at https://lccn.loc.gov/2019026979

ISBN: HB: 978-1-4408-7290-7
PB: 979-8-7651-3829-8
ePDF: 978-1-4408-7291-4
eBook: 979-8-2161-1086-6

To find out more about our authors and books visit www.bloomsbury.com
and sign up for our newsletters.

To American Citizens and Leaders Who Believe in Ordered Liberty
Under Law for All Inhabitants of This Sweet Land.

Contents

Alphabetical List of Entries

Topical List of Entries

PHYSICAL ASPE CTS OF THE LIBERTY BELL

REPLICAS AND NAMESAKES ABROAD

REPLICAS AND NAMESAKES IN THE UNITED STATES

Preface

I am pleased to offer this work as the third consecutive encyclopedia that I have authored in the last two years. Those who are familiar with the previous two, one of which focuses on the U.S. flag and the other on the Declaration of Independence, will undoubtedly see connections among all three. All deal with symbols that express American identity. The last two deal with objects, in one case a parchment, and now a bell with a biblical inscription that is relatively self-explanatory, but only partially illuminates the object itself. These encyclopedias are, in turn, related to the largest encyclopedia that I have written, on the Constitutional Convention of 1787, as well as to encyclopedias that I have edited on the First and Fourth Amendments, civil rights and liberties, constitutional amendments and proposed amendments, and great American lawyers and judges.

I enjoy compiling and writing encyclopedia entries perhaps much as natural scientists might enjoy collecting and cataloguing species. Just as such scientists gain more knowledge about a species by identifying and collecting individual members, so too have I have gained a greater understanding of the history of the Liberty Bell as I've written and researched about it. As I near the process of identifying and describing all the individual essays, I generally begin to think of some summative essays that help put them in context. One of the joys of writing an encyclopedia on the Liberty Bell is finding how many replicas there are both in the United States and abroad. Although each has an individual story, the replicas as a whole, the reasons they were cast, and the ways that they have been interpreted paint a broader picture. Similarly, while it is exciting to research each of the seven trips that the Liberty Bell took from 1885 to 1915, it is also important to try to analyze the impact of these trips as a whole on the national consciousness.

As I describe in the Introduction, I began this work remembering the many questions that schoolchildren I gave guest talks to asked about the Liberty Bell/ on those occasions where I happened to mention the topic while discussing the Declaration of Independence and the U.S. Constitution. It was not until a month or two after I began research and writing that I was sure there was enough material for a book, and even as the project wound down, I found myself waking up in the early morning and wondering if there were any entries that I might have omitted. As assiduously as I canvassed the Internet and other resources, I suspect that there are some roadside replicas of the Liberty Bell that I have missed and some tidbits that will remain for future editions.

AUDIENCE

Although I would be flattered if readers (reviewers, perhaps) were to read the book from cover to cover, this book is primarily intended as a reference book, and it is accordingly written in an A to Z format. I have designed the Introduction and timeline to serve as historical overviews of the topic for novitiates, and I have provided generous cross-references throughout. I have provided sources in each entry for those who might want to do further research, and those wanting to dig further still will likely want to consult the topical table of contents and the index.

Having so many times profited from phone calls that I have made to reference librarians, I am particularly concerned with presenting them a volume that will meet their varying needs, from queries posed by elementary school teachers to those by college professors. As one who has served as a guide at tourist sites, I further hope that this book might prove to be a ready reference for those who interpret U.S. history at Independence Hall and related locations. Although my experience with grade school students is relatively limited, I have also tried to compose this book with a view to the kinds of questions that I was asked when I went to speak to them.

ENTRIES

All together, there are more than 180 entries in this book. They range from 200 or 300 words to 2,000 or 3,000. Generally, I have devoted more space to topics that I believe to be more consequential, but in some cases, there is simply more information about topics of comparable importance than about others, and I have tried to utilize all the information that I could find. I have devoted particular attention to celebrations and commemorations related to the Liberty Bell, to displays and locations of the Bell, to the journeys that the Bell has taken, to literary works and musical compositions that describe the Bell (with special attention to the covers of sheet music), to the replicas and namesakes of the Bell both at home and abroad, and to political and social movements that have utilized it.

The difficulty of writing about the Liberty Bell, similar to that which surrounds the U.S. flag, is that the symbolic significance goes far beyond the physical object, or even the words that are inscribed on the Bell. I doubt seriously that any volume can fully capture the emotional resonance that the Bell invokes in many people, but I have included some entries specifically on the symbolism of the Bell, and many others, such as the entry on kissing the Bell, that attempt to demonstrate this emotional link by providing concrete examples of such feelings in action. The fact that there are so many replicas of the Bell is, I believe, further testimony to its ability to evoke deep sentiments.

I once recall a colleague in another academic field who, perhaps trying to demonstrate his sophistication, said that he had read the U.S. Constitution once and didn't think much of it. When I repeated the story to another colleague, he observed that this reminded him of the reported rube who went to a museum to see the *Mona Lisa* and could not understand what all the fuss was about. As American symbols go, the Liberty Bell joins a select number of other icons, such as the U.S. flag, the Statue of Liberty, and core documents, that are the historical counterparts to works of art such as the *Mona Lisa.* There has often been a disparity between the ideal that the inscription on the Bell announces, and the reality of American life. This was especially true of the American tolerance of slavery in the country's early years, which is now reflected in an exhibit as one approaches the Liberty Bell Center, but the disparity has also been evident through much of U.S. history in the status of women and other groups.

As the Introduction to this book reveals, the Liberty Bell, like Independence Hall with which it is so closely associated, is clearly situated in U.S. history, but the shades differ from one era to another. One of the aspects that I most enjoyed while preparing this book was the manner in which the Liberty Bell spans colonial history, early American history, the antebellum period, U.S. participation in foreign imperialism after the Spanish-American War, two world wars, the Cold War, and modern reform movements. Although its position near Independence Hall, which has been painstakingly reconstructed, probably leads most visitors to think back to revolutionary times, the symbol has evolved with the nation. I'm sure that this is true of other symbols, such as how the U.S. flag marks national progress in part through the process of adding new stars, but few are as old as the Bell.

I hope that this book, the subject of which has become a virtual obsession, will stimulate renewed interest and affection not only in the symbol, but for the principle of equal liberty to all that it has increasingly come to represent.

Acknowledgments

I have encountered many helpful people in the process of research and writing this book. I owe special thanks to the following:

Karie Diethorn, Chief Curator at Independence National Historical Park, for help in locating a critical resource;

Tyler Love, Archivist and Library Manager at the Independence National Historical Park, for helping to arrange a visit and locate relevant information in the archives;

Robert Giannini, Associate Curator, Independence National Historical Park, for locating valuable information and answering queries;

Tim Verdin and Pat Bradley of the Verdin Bell Company in Cincinnati, Ohio;

Jim Lewis, with the Park Service at the Stones River Battlefield National Park in Murfreesboro, Tennessee, for help in locating a critical resource;

Pam Middleton, at the Middle Tennessee State University Inter-Library Loan Office, for ordering numerous outside resources, and Sharan Parente, at the Reference Desk, for helping with queries;

Dr. Mary Evins of Middle Tennessee State University, for referring me to an important index;

Professor Charlene Mires, at Rutgers University at Camden, for answering a query;

Dr. Philip Phillips, Associate Dean of the Honors College, and Carolle Morini, at the Boston Athenaeum, for helping me to track down the identity of a nineteenth-century poet;

Professor Miles Orvell, Professor of English and American Studies at Temple University, for providing helpful information regarding a source;

Rachel K. Morris, of the Middle Tennessee State University Center for Popular Music, for helping me to locate sheet music and images of the Liberty Bell;

Linda C. Vile, who faithfully accompanied me to the Independence National Historical Park and helped complete the chart documenting cities and towns that the Liberty Bell visited; Morgan Murphy and Susan Lyons, who helped with formatting this manuscript, and Jeffrey Summers, who helped retrieve information from the Internet.

Although I have never met them, I owe special thanks to John C. Paige and David C. Kimball, who wrote and edited *The Liberty Bell: A Special Study,* respectively; to Gary B. Nash, who wrote *The Liberty Bell*; and to Victor Rosewater, who wrote *The Liberty Bell: Its History and Significance*. All engaged in primary historical research, which has been invaluable.

I continue to be grateful for the supportive environment at Middle Tennessee State University and to my friends and colleagues who serve as sounding boards. As always, my wife, Linda, has been another critical sounding board who has gone to sleep at nights and awakened in the mornings over the past few months to conversations about my most recent discoveries about the Liberty Bell. I owe special thanks to the many children who have questioned me about the Liberty Bell and helped me to understand that it has an emotional resonance that may well transcend its historical significance.

Introduction

This encyclopedia has grown out of two of the last several books that I have written. I wrote the first on the U.S. flag at the request of a publisher, but I became increasingly enamored with the topic as I proceeded. I especially enjoyed the way that the flag was so entwined with other American institutions and symbols, including in art, music, sports, collecting, comic books, advertising, and other aspects of popular culture. That book, in turn, motivated me to do another tome on the Declaration of Independence, which, like the flag, is a ubiquitous part of American culture; but it also has the advantage of being a seminal text, which my background in political theory helped me to assess.

As I wrote each book, I tried to think of comparable topics that could be appropriate for encyclopedic coverage. As I did so, I recalled talks that I have given to elementary school students, typically during Constitution Week (the seven-day period each year beginning on September 17, when delegates signed the historic document). One of the lessons I quickly learned in explicating the Declaration of Independence, the Constitution, and the modern U.S. government was that if I mentioned that the Declaration and Constitution were debated and signed in the same building that had housed the Liberty Bell, children almost invariably pelted me with many questions. They wanted to know how much it weighed, haw tall it is, why it cracked, when it cracked, who made it, what it said, who cracked it, what it was made of, and a seemingly endless set of other questions. It was as though I had sparked an interest (indeed, what sometimes appeared to be obsession) that I could not comprehend, but, which reminded me, as I wrote this volume, that I needed a specific entry on children and the Liberty Bell.

I remembered back to my own childhood when a dear great aunt, Evelyn Vile, who never forgot our birthdays, sent a small metal replica of the Liberty Bell, which I loved to ring. My wife recalls that her parents saved money for Christmas in a small Liberty Bell bank similar to one that we now display on our own bedroom dresser. As if to confirm that the topic might be choosing me as much as I was choosing the topic, I also recalled that the first book that I published for my father was a book of his poetry, the title of which I drew from one of his poems: "Let the Bells Ring Out on Christmas Morning."

I have long collected American memorabilia, generally focusing on commemorations of American independence. One of the joys of writing this book was searching our cupboards, walls and cabinets, to find plates, bowls, bookends, trays, prints, ribbons, pictures, and other objects depicting the Liberty Bell, many of which we didn't even realize contained this iconography. It is almost enough to make me wonder whether I have overcompensated for my Protestant heritage, which looks with general disfavor on statues and relics from the saints, by collecting relics from America's founding fathers instead.

Although our church did not feature a bell, it was located in Luray, Virginia, which remains notable for the Luray Singing tower. This is a beautiful stone structure not far from the Luray Caverns, with its own stalactite organ, which was constructed in 1937 to honor the memory of Belle Brown Northcott, the wife of Colonel T. C. Northcott. The tower, which remains the site of concerts, especially in the summer months, has 47 bells, the largest of which weighs almost four tons and is six feet in diameter ("The Luray Singing Tower," n.d.).

I attended the College of William and Mary as an undergraduate and recall the ringing of the bell in the historic Wren building. During one of the days that I attended, the bell tolled, in what I believe to be either a protest against, or a commemoration of all who had died in, the Vietnam War. I have since learned that this bell, of about 650 pounds, is the sixth in the school's history and dates to 1889. Graduating seniors are now permitted to ring the bell and often wait in long lines to do so (Ducibella, 2017). As I have researched this book, I find that there are other historic bells in Williamsburg, one sometimes designated as the "Liberty Bell of Virginia," which is in the tower of the Bruton Parish Church, and another at the First Baptist Church. The latter was recently used to ring in the opening of the new African American Museum in Washington, D.C.

Although our bells are much newer, Middle Tennessee State University, where I have long taught and where I now proudly serve as dean of our University Honors College, has a somewhat similar tradition to that of William and Mary. Our undergraduate students defend their theses in a room in the Paul W. Martin, Sr. Honors College Building, located immediately under our bell tower. If they successfully pass their defense (as most do), we allow them to ring the bells in celebration. Consistent with the times, they do so by pushing a button rather than by pulling on a rope.

After some negotiation over whether I should write about the Liberty Bell or the Statue of Liberty, another American icon with a similar name and with surprising popular resonance, I finally launched into this volume. I did so knowing that the symbol was firmly rooted in more than 250 years of American history and public consciousness and that by explicating the Bell, I might also be explicating larger currents of American political life and thought.

LANDSCAPES AND THE LIBERTY BELL

One of the aspects of the Liberty Bell that appeals to me is that it takes my imagination back to the time before the cacophonous sounds of telephones, steam engines, radios, televisions, and even typewriters and keyboards. Having lived in the country and in small towns, I know that even colonial days must have been alive with the sound of poultry, other livestock, and wild animals. I also know that in many towns and cities, the bell served much like modern mass media and cell phones. As I detail in an extended essay in this book, bells were part of many landscapes, often mystically bridging the gap between heaven and Earth, not only on the Sabbath, when they called people to worship, but on other occasions of joy and grief, alarm and rejoicing. There is even the story of a Florentine peasant who rang his village bell, more than 400 years ago, to announce that justice was dead, after the local lord had moved the boundary stones so that there was no land left for the peasants (Saramago, 2002).

Particularly in rural areas, dinner bells, which were sometimes no more than triangular pieces of metal, called workers in from the fields for hot meals. Our language is still rife with references of bells tolling for funerals (as John Donne said in his poem "For Whom the Bell Tolls," "never send to know for whom the bell tolls; it tolls for thee"); ringing for weddings and births; clamoring out alarms; and even, with nine successive rings, announcing public executions. Paul Revere, who was a bell ringer at the Old North Church in Boston as a youth and who, with his sons, later cast many bells, some of which still ring, was known for inscribing his bells with the words "THE LIVING TO THE CHURCH I CALL AND TO THE GRAVE I SUMMON ALL" ("Ring Those Bells: Paul Revere, Bell Maker," n.d.). The classic movie *It's a Wonderful Life* claimed, "Every time a bell rings, an angel gets its wings." Much like modern sirens, the ringing of bells often raised people from reveries and sound sleep, and at other times may have lulled people to sleep. What one bell could not do on its own, multiple bells sometimes did together. It is easy to understand how they came to symbolize the many events that they had announced.

THE LIBERTY BELL AS SACRED SYMBOL

Although there are many reproductions, some life-size and others designed to sit on a shelf, there is only one true Liberty Bell. After taking several trips, the last to San Francisco and San Diego, it has, at least since 1915, been firmly rooted in one city. Unlike the flag, which can be flown on sea or on land, the Bell remains stationary, although over the past 50 years, it has been moved from Independence Hall to first one pavilion or center, and then another. Some years ago, I was overcome with awe as I revisited Independence Hall, shortly after I had completed a two-volume encyclopedia on the Constitutional Convention of 1787. It seemed more like a holy place than a historical site, although there is certainly no reason that it cannot be both.

Few religious analogies are perfect. However, in a nation that since the Pilgrim Fathers has been regarded as a shining city on a hill and as a new Zion, it doesn't seem far afield to suggest that Philadelphia (the famed "City of Brotherly Love" so often epitomized, as in Edward Hicks's paintings, as the land of the Peaceable Kingdom) remains a type of Jerusalem, and Independence Hall a type of secular temple (Shalev, 2014). The Bell, and the two pavilions that have been built to house it, in turn highlight the origins of the nation's two greatest documents, the Declaration of Independence and the U.S. Constitution. The Bell symbolizes not only the birth of the new Israel, but the spread of liberties to African Americans, women, and other disenfranchised groups.

Just as the Ten Commandments are associated with Moses, Israel's greatest lawmaker, the Liberty Bell is associated with George Washington, Thomas Jefferson, James Madison, and other early American statesmen. As if to validate this analogy, the Bell, like the Ten Commandments, contains a passage from the Torah—in this case Leviticus 25:10: "Proclaim LIBERTY throughout all the land unto all the inhabitants thereof."

THE MEANING OF LIBERTY

While few Americans would denigrate the value of liberty, they might vary in how they interpret the concept and how they would rank its importance against other values. If the Liberty Bell were celebrating the liberty of Pennsylvania, it most certainly would have included religious liberty within its ambit. That colony, which was largely founded by Quakers, offered religious freedoms not only to various Protestant sects, but also to Roman Catholics, Jews, and others. Colonists might have distinguished liberty from license, or licentiousness, much as modern judges might talk about "liberty under law," or as the Fifth and Fourteenth Amendments would permit deprivations of "life, liberty, and property," albeit only with "due process of law."

During the Revolutionary period, Patriots often associated liberty with independence from the rule and taxation of a Parliament in which Americans were not physically represented. Citizens gathered in protests under "liberty trees" and beside "liberty poles." One of John Hancock's ships that the British had confiscated was named *Liberty,* and an early Revolutionary song was John Dickinson's "Song of Liberty."

Those in bondage knew that their own involuntary servitude contradicted not only the words on the Liberty Bell, but American protestations, like those in the Declaration of Independence, that all men were created equal and entitled to the rights of life, liberty, and the pursuit of happiness. Women like Abigail Adams would urge their husbands to "Remember the Ladies," as they planned for independence for American men. Delegates who gathered in Philadelphia to write a new Constitution in 1787 in turn envisioned themselves as "securing the blessings of liberty" to themselves and their posterity, just as modern-day Americans pledge allegiance to a flag "with liberty and justice for all." One beauty of the term is that, although it has a solid core of historical associations and meaning, it can be extended not only to the abolition of slavery, but also to the expansion of opportunities for other groups that were long treated as second-class citizens.

COLONIAL TIMES

The Liberty Bell was ordered by the Pennsylvania Assembly in 1751. It was apparently designed to replace a much smaller bell, probably brought to the colony by William Penn. It had hung in a tree near the Pennsylvania State House (today's

Independence Hall) and called sessions of the Assembly to order. As Philadelphia expanded, the smaller bell could no longer be heard throughout the city. The most notable aspect of the bell that the Assembly ordered is that, at the request of House Speaker Isaac Norris II, it contained the inscription from Leviticus. Because this is from a passage that talks about making every 50th year a Year of Jubilee, where lands would be restored to their original families and slaves would be freed, it is widely believed that, in addition to its practical functions, the Bell designed another Year of Jubilee—namely, the 50th year of religious freedom under the Pennsylvania Charter of Privileges that William Penn had issued to the colony in 1701. Cast by Thomas Lister, of the Whitechapel Foundry in London, which only closed its doors in recent years, the bronze bell weighing about 2,080 pounds appears to have made it across the sea successfully, only to crack when first tested in Pennsylvania.

This left leaders of the Pennsylvania Assembly with a choice. They could either try to send the Bell back to England for recasting or try to recast it in the colony. At least initially, the first option was blocked when the captain of the next ship headed to England was unable to take the Bell aboard. This played into the hands of two local foundry workers, John Pass and John Stow, whose own last names would become immortalized on a new Bell that they agreed to cast. Their own first production was judged as beautiful to the eye but lacking the sweetness of sound that the colonists desired. Pass and Stow recast their own recasting, and the new Bell was rehung in the steeple prior to the receipt of yet another bell from the Whitechapel Foundry. The colonists decided to connect this bell to a clock in the building, the face of which was to be displayed on the side of the State House.

THE REVOLUTIONARY YEARS

One of the earliest descriptions of the Bell refers to it as the "Old Bell" because it was hung before the new Bell from England arrived to be connected to the clock in the tower, and in its early years, the first bell was sometimes called the State House Bell or even the "Grand Bell," probably because of its size. The 25 years after it was initially hung were among the most seminal in American history and marked increasing colonial protests against the imposition of British taxes. During this time, the Bell not only called the Pennsylvania Assembly members to gather, but it also announced mass protests against British policies, as well as sounding alarms for fires, tolling the deaths of famous people and pealing for good news.

The Bell soon became identified with the Revolutionary cause when its ringing became associated with the announcement of colonial independence in July of 1776. Ironically, the wooden steeple in which it was housed was in a state of disrepair, so it is not altogether certain that it actually rang for independence. Yet if it could be rung for the occasion, it undoubtedly was. The date it rang would not have been on July 2, 1776, when delegates actually voted for Richard Henry Lee's resolution declaring independence, or on July 4, 1776, when they finally voted to accept Thomas Jefferson's amended Declaration of Independence to explain this action to a waiting world. Instead, it would have rung on July 8, when John Nixon first publicly read the Declaration from a platform in front of the State House.

The next year, Patriots in Pennsylvania were on the run as British forces approached, and Patriots removed the Liberty Bell and church bells that the British might have been melted down for shot or cannon to Allentown. They were hidden in the basement of the Zion Reformed Church, to be later restored to the State House in the sturdy brick tower rather than the decaying steeple from which it had formerly hung. It is known that for some of this time, the Bell was actually used to ring for classes at the University of Pennsylvania that were being taught in nearby Philosophical Hall. It likely rang in 1787 to summon delegates each day to the Constitutional Convention and perhaps to announce its ratification, as well as the ratification of a new state constitution, the convention for which had been housed in the same building.

YEARS OF NEGLECT

The new U.S. Congress met from 1780 to 1800 in the State House, but in 1799, the state capital moved to Lancaster (and later still to Harrisburg). The State House became best known as the site of Charles Willson Peale's natural history museum. Despite the role that the building had played in so much of early American history, Pennsylvania had considered selling the State House and surrounding properties to be subdivided in 1816, but Philadelphia took its offer to purchase the buildings for $70,000.

Somewhat fortuitously, a visit from the Marquis de Lafayette in Philadelphia in 1824 began to rekindle interest in the site where the Declaration of Independence and the U.S. Constitution had been written. As the lower floor was transformed into a reception area, it became known as "Independence Hall," the name that was soon applied to the building as a whole. The Old Bell continued to ring on important occasions, including Lafayette's visit, and in 1828, the newer bell that had been used in conjunction with the clock was replaced by a larger bell manufactured by John Wilbank.

The most obvious feature of today's Liberty Bell is that it has a large crack. Unfortunately, it is hard to say with certainty when it cracked. Some damage may have been done on the journey to Allentown and back. Some believe it was damaged during Lafayette's visit to Philadelphia in 1824. Others believe that it may have cracked on Washington's birthday in 1835 or during the tolling of the bells after the death of Chief Justice John Marshall later that year. It is known that attempts were made to repair the Bell, but in 1846, it was not functional during a tribute to George Washington's birth. Aside from some ceremonial tapping, it has largely been silent ever since.

THE BELL BECOMES AN ABOLITIONIST SYMBOL

Although it lost its musical voice, the Liberty Bell was elevated as a symbol. For so much of its history, the inscription has been largely out of sight, but one can only imagine the glee with which abolitionists must have seized its phraseology to extend liberty "unto all the inhabitants" of the land. Indeed, the abolitionists appear to be the first to speak specifically of a "liberty bell." Although historians continue to dispute whether they were referring to *a* liberty bell or *the* Liberty Bell, abolitionists clearly evoked the inscription of the Liberty Bell to argue that African Americans deserved to enjoy the same political liberties as white Americans, and the *Liberty Bell Gift Books* that the abolitionists published continued to use verse to urge the nation to live up to its unrealized commitment to liberty. In 1844, the Hutchinson family sang a song called "Get Off the Track! (A Song for Emancipation)," in which they announced that the train of liberty was coming, and vacillating preachers and politicians needed to get off the track and prepare the way for emancipation. In the song, the sound of the whistle on the emancipation train blends with that of the newly dubbed Liberty Bell. In 1850, African Americans in Pittsburgh sent a replica of the Liberty Bell to Buxton, Canada, which was receiving fugitive slaves who could find no justice under American law. Escaped fugitives wrote a letter back to an African American congregation in Pittsburgh that had supplied them with a bell, saying that they were pleased to have been able to leave "a land of pretend freedom."

At about the same time, the process of mythologizing the Liberty Bell began with the publication of George Lippard's "The Fourth of July, 1776," in 1847. Going back to the time of the Revolution, Lippard told a dramatic story in which an aged sexton waited in the tower for news of whether the delegates to the Second Continental Congress were going to vote for independence or not. In time, a flaxen-haired lad brought the joyful news, which the sexton rang out, proclaiming that the colonies would no longer be under the thumb of the king. This story seemed to become more exaggerated and emotional on each retelling, and it was embodied in verses that were distributed in elementary school texts throughout the land, inextricably tying the Bell to American independence at a time when much of the population remained in bondage.

Slavery was hardly the nation's only problem. Despite William Penn's commitment to religious liberty, the American Nativist movement became active in the 1840s and 1850s. Indeed, a riot in 1844 resulted in the burning of St. Augustine's Roman Catholic Church in Philadelphia, where the "sister" bell to the Liberty Bell that had been used to strike in conjunction with the clocks, was heavily damaged. For his part, Abraham Lincoln announced that he could no more accept the proposition that Catholics and immigrants should have variable rights than he could accept the idea that rights were limited to whites. Notably, as Abraham Lincoln came to Washington, D.C., for his inauguration as president, he stopped at Independence Hall and proclaimed that he had taken his most fundamental political principles from the Declaration of Independence. He came to the capital as the first elected Republican president to prevent the further spread of slavery.

As Southern states announced their intention to secede, Lincoln reaffirmed his intention to preserve the Union. As the war progressed, he increasingly realized that if the nation were to survive, it could no longer be half free and half slave. At the war's end, three amendments were proposed and ratified that sought to provide guarantees of liberty that the *Dred Scott* Supreme Court decision of 1857 had claimed were only reserved for white people. The Thirteenth Amendment (1865) extended Lincoln's Emancipation Proclamation, a military measure that applied only behind enemy lines, and abolished involuntary servitude. The Fourteenth Amendment extended the rights of citizenship to all persons born or naturalized in the United States and sought to guarantee to all the privileges and immunities of citizenship, the equal protection of the law, and due process of the law to all. Although it would long be evaded, the Fifteenth Amendment prohibited denial of the franchise on the basis of race or previous condition of servitude. After the period of congressional Reconstruction from 1865–1877, when whites who had fought on the Confederate side regained control of Southern governments, the nation retreated from concern for African Americans, who largely lost their voting rights, and encountered from 1896 to 1954 a period in which American courts specifically justified an apartheid policy of "separate but equal."

YEARS ON THE ROAD

As Reconstruction was coming to an end, there were efforts to reunite North and South. In 1876, Philadelphia hosted the nation's first World's Fair, which coincided with the centennial of the nation's independence. Although the fair was not held at Independence Hall, many visitors went to that building, where the Bell had been placed on an elaborate platform and mounted with a stuffed American bald eagle. In time, it would be hung from the bell tower by a chain of 13 links and moved to yet another platform.

The Liberty Bell took seven train tours to various fairs and expositions throughout the nation beginning in 1885, and continuing intermittently until 1915. The first, and one of the clearest attempts at reconciliation, was the trip of the Liberty Bell to the World's Industrial and Cotton Exposition in New Orleans. On this trip, the Bell was greeted as it passed through Biloxi, Mississippi, by none other than the former president of the Confederate States of America, Jefferson Davis. As a U.S. senator, Davis had made sure that the statue of freedom on top of the Capitol Dome in Washington, D.C., did not wear a liberty cap, which he thought might symbolize freedom for slaves. Brushing over the Civil War experience, he reminded the crowd that Southerners had played a key role in winning independence from Great Britain.

Significantly, 1886 marked the installation of the Statue of Liberty in New York Harbor. Donated by France, it was designed to remind Americans of the important role that the French had played in winning the Revolutionary War, as well as in the commitment to liberty that the two nations shared. It remains significant that two of America's choice symbols contain the word *liberty*. Moreover, the pledge to the flag, which was composed shortly after the Statute of Liberty was erected, thereafter denoted a commitment to "liberty and justice for all."

In 1893, the Bell traveled to Chicago for the World's Columbian Exposition, where a 13,000-pound Columbian Liberty Bell replica, composed of thousands of historical objects that had been melted down, was also unveiled. This was the exposition for which John Philip Sousa created one of his most stirring marches, "The Liberty Bell March." Although it now appears that the Columbian Liberty Bell was repossessed and melted down, when the Liberty Bell returned to Philadelphia, it was encased in a new glass display.

In 1895, the Liberty Bell headed back South to the Atlanta Cotton States and International Exposition, where Booker T. Washington urged the audience to employ black people in manual trades rather than hiring immigrants. The following year, the Supreme Court issued its notorious decision in *Plessy v. Ferguson,* officially declaring its policy of "separate but equal." Philadelphia, ever more cognizant of the role of Independence Hall and the Liberty Bell, replaced the ramshackle office buildings that had drowned beside Independence Hall, and restored wings that more closely resembled those from the colonial era.

In 1902, the Liberty Bell headed to Charleston, South Carolina, for the Interstate and West Indian Exposition, where again Booker T. Washington had the nostrum. In 1903, it traveled to the 128th anniversary of the Battle of Bunker Hill. One newspaper, seeking to highlight Boston's own auspicious place in the Revolution, portrayed the Bunker Hill Monument as the male leading the female Liberty Bell in a dance.

In 1904, the Bell traveled again, this time to the Louisiana Purchase Exposition in St. Louis, Missouri. One of the exhibits featured a recreated Philippine native village. It highlighted the increasingly positive reception that social Darwinism was receiving in a nation that had decided, with President William McKinley, that its destiny in the wake of the Spanish-American War was to Christianize and civilize the predominately Roman Catholic population of that newly acquired colony.

In 1908, Philadelphia carried the Bell on a parade commemorating the city's 225th anniversary. In 1913, the city's Emancipation Exposition, which celebrated the 50th anniversary of Lincoln's issuance of the Emancipation Proclamation, brought new attention to the manner in which the Bell and its inscription had been tied to the cause of abolitionism.

In 1915, the Bell made its longest and final trip outside Philadelphia when it went to the San Francisco Panama-Pacific International Exposition. It stopped for three days at the Panama-California Exposition in San Diego on the way back. As it took a circuitous trip through the North to get to California, and then through the South to return to Philadelphia, millions of people came out to see it, often raising their children to kiss or hug the Bell as it made its journeys. In an ugly incident in Arlington, Texas, an African American girl inadvertently triggered a riot when she showed her own affection for the Liberty Bell by kissing it. The aspirations for liberty for all had yet to be fully realized.

The Bell was becoming such a powerful symbol that, in 1915, suffragists in Pennsylvania produced their own replica of the Liberty Bell called the "Justice Bell," and carted the item throughout Pennsylvania to raise support for women's suffrage. Although Pennsylvania rejected its state referendum, women's suffrage was finally adopted nationwide by constitutional amendment with the adoption of the Nineteenth Amendment in 1920.

YEARS OF WAR AND PEACE

Not long after the Bell returned to Philadelphia from California, the nation entered the world war that President Woodrow Wilson had avoided during his first term. People gathered in mutual support at the Liberty Bell as Wilson asked

Congress to declare war, and assembled there again to celebrate when World War I ended. During and after the war, the Liberty Bell was a primary symbol used to raise money for bonds, although it was often used in conjunction with other symbols like the American flag, the Statue of Liberty, and the American bald eagle. A number of patriotic songs from the period followed the same strategy, often decorating the covers of sheet music with powerful images. The image of the Liberty Bell was so powerful that the leaders of Czechoslovakia gathered in Philadelphia to declare their own independence and carried a bell back to their homeland (as did Lithuanians) to express their own desire for liberty.

Although the sesquicentennial celebrations in Philadelphia in 1926 were generally regarded as a failure, they further associated the Liberty Bell with Independence Hall and with the nation's founding. As the failure of the "war to end all wars" became increasingly apparent as Adolf Hitler invaded Europe and Japan ravaged the Far East, enlistees for the coming war took their oaths in front of the Liberty Bell. The college president and banker R. R. Wright soon began laying wreaths there each February 1 in hopes of establishing a National Freedom Day to ensure that the liberty for which Americans were fighting abroad would also be realized at home.

World War II, between the Allies and the Axis powers, had barely ended before the world went into an extended Cold War stance in which the forces of democracy and freedom were aligned against the forces of totalitarian communism. With the advent of nuclear weapons that had ended World War II, the stakes seemed even higher, and the Bell was only one of the symbols that Americans used to vaunt their own values. As the Treasury boosted its bond program by distributing replicas of the Liberty Bell to each of the 50 states and territories, the United States donated a Freedom Bell to West Berlin, and in time, the National Aeronautics and Space Administration (NASA) labeled one of its manned spacecraft after the Liberty Bell.

As African Americans had returned from combat duty to fight against racial injustice abroad, they became increasingly discontent with the discrimination that they still faced at home. They advocated for changes that were brought about by Supreme Court decisions, by civil rights boycotts and demonstrations, and through the power of rhetoric. In 1963, Martin Luther King, Jr. gave a clarion call to "let freedom ring" at the March on Washington, which drew renewed attention to the cause. In the years that followed, civil rights demonstrators, antiwar and prowar demonstrators, and even advocates of lesbian, gay, bisexual, transgender, and queer/questioning (LGBTQ) rights would find that the Liberty Bell was a site where they could attract attention.

In the aftermath of the Vietnam War, the nation was ready to celebrate the bicentennial of its independence, although it chose to do so in towns and cities across the nation rather than concentrating on a single city as it did in 1876. Fearing that Independence Hall might be unable to handle the anticipated crowds of tourists, the National Park Service, which had taken custody of Independence Hall and the Liberty Bell in 1951, decided to move the Bell to a new pavilion. It remained there until 2003, when it again moved to another newly created center. During the bicentennial, Philadelphia continued to play host to a variety of domestic and international leaders, and it continues to do so to this day.

Although it has been the site of numerous demonstrations and the focus of many movements, most tourists who visit Independence Hall and the Liberty Bell perhaps come more to celebrate American greatness than to examine its contradictions. As it became evident that the new Liberty Bell Center would be located yards from the site of the residence where George Washington had kept slaves during his presidency, there were calls for interpretations that highlighted such contradictions. Despite some initial reservations, the National Park Service largely accommodated these concerns. In addition to being presented with more interpretative information to understand the variegated history of the Liberty Bell, tourists might face demonstrators favoring the right to choose or the right to life, or addressing issues of police brutality, poverty, or the death penalty.

THE BELL TODAY

As indicated earlier in this essay, the Liberty Bell continues to be a highly recognizable symbol. Some commentators note that the power of the symbol might be enhanced by the crack, its most obvious flaw. Like the United States, the Bell remains imperfect, and yet its silent plea for liberty continues to ring metaphorically throughout the land. At a time when the nation (if not the world) seems more attuned to popular opinion than ever, there are some who ask whether current notions of populistic democracy should again be leavened by the founding fathers' vision of checks and balances and separation of powers (Rosen, 2018). Even this vision may need to be enlightened by the idea of ordered liberty that subordinates short-term wants to long-term needs and that values genuine dialogue over tweets and invective. This idea was implicit in William Penn's Pennsylvania Charter of Privileges, which the Liberty Bell was designed to commemorate.

The nation will be celebrating the sestercentennial, or semiquincentennial, of its independence in 2026. Although celebrations that are multiples of 50 are generally more tame affairs than those that are multiples of 100, some Americans may perhaps think about the meaning of liberty in a world in which technology is so dominant, the threats to the existence not only of the nation but the world that often seem so grim, and in which governments often seem incapable of meeting the increased demands that are placed upon them.

Will Americans of 2026 still live in a land of liberty? Will today's generation muster the courage that previous generations displayed when they confronted the problems of their times? If liberty survives, will it be the preserve of the white, the rich, the well-connected, and the highly educated, or will it ring throughout all the land, unto all the inhabitants thereof?

For liberty to flourish, Americans must continue to embrace the concept of liberty in both their heads and their hearts. It is my hope that this book will highlight understanding of this concept and one of its most prominent symbols, and that this knowledge will further enhance an emotional attachment, not simply to a cracked icon but to the great principles that it continues to symbolize.

FURTHER READING

Ducibella, Jim. 2017. "The Inside Scoop on Ringing the Wren Bell." College of William
    & Mary, April 27. https://www.wm.edu/news/stories/2017/the-inside-scoop-on
    -ringing-the-wren-bell.php.
"The   Luray   Singing   Tower."   n.d.   https://www.virginia.org/listings/TheArts
    /LuraySingingTower.
"Ring Those Bells: Paul Revere, Bell Maker." n.d. Massachusetts Historical Society. https://
    www.masshist.org/object-of-the-month/objects/ring-those-bells-paul-revere-bell
    -maker-2011-07-01.
Rosen, Jeffrey. 2018. "America Is Living James Madison's Nightmare." *The Atlantic,* Octo-
    ber.   https://www.theatlantic.com/magazine/archive/2018/10/james-madison-mob
    -rule-568351.
Saramago, Jose. 2002. "From Justice to Democracy By Way of the Bells." *Terra Incog-
    nita,* January 22. http://www.terraincognita.50megs.com/saramago.html.
Shalev, Eran. 2014. *American Zion: The Old Testament as a Political Text from the Revo-
    lution to the Civil War.* New Haven, CT: Yale University Press.

Interesting Facts About the Liberty Bell

The Liberty Bell was originally known as "the Old Bell" or the "State House Bell." Abolitionists were largely responsible for designating the bell as the "Liberty Bell."

The word *Pennsylvania* on the Liberty Bell was spelled "Pensylvania," which appears to have been an alternative spelling at the time rather than a mistake.

The original Liberty Bell was cast at the Whitechapel Foundry in London, but it cracked on its first ringing in Philadelphia. The current bell was recast twice, by John Snow and John Pass; the second recasting was done because people complained about the sound of the first recasting.

Despite innumerable stories to the contrary, it does not appear that the Liberty Bell was rung on July 4, 1776, to announce the adoption of the Declaration of Independence. It may have been rung on July 8, when the document was publicly read just outside the State House (today's Independence Hall), but it is not certain that the steeple was in sufficient repair to ring it without the chance of collapsing it.

In 1777, the Liberty Bell was taken from Philadelphia and moved to Allentown, Pennsylvania, to keep it from falling into the hands of the British, who might have sought to melt it down for bullets or other military uses.

The Liberty Bell was ordered 50 years after William Penn gave his Pennsylvania Charter of Privileges to Pennsylvania. This would correspond to the Year of Jubilee, which is referenced in the passage surrounding the quotation from Leviticus 25:10 that is found on the Bell.

From 1885 to 1915, the Liberty Bell took seven trips out of Philadelphia, the last and longest of which was to San Francisco.

The Liberty Bell weighs just over a ton.

The current bell in the steeple of Independence Hall, known as the "Centennial Bell," weighs 13,000 pounds and was donated in 1876.

Scientific analysis indicates that the Liberty Bell may have been more brittle than other bells because it has a greater percentage of tin than comparable bells from the same time period.

The yoke from which the Liberty Bell is suspended is made from American elm.

The "sister" to the Liberty Bell, which was manufactured at Whitechapel Foundry to replace the original, was originally used to strike a clock with a face on the side of the State House, after which it was sold to St. Augustine's Church in

Interesting Facts About the Liberty Bell

Philadelphia, which was burned in a Nativist riot. A recasting of this bell currently resides at Villanova University.

The Columbian Liberty Bell, which was made for the Columbian Exposition in Chicago in 1893 weighed 13,000 pounds and consisted of numerous historic objects that had been melted down. After being displayed, the Bell was apparently melted down by the company that cast it because the company's invoice was never fully paid.

When the Liberty Bell visited San Francisco in 1915, a group of extremists hired a bootblack to place a suitcase bomb near the Bell, but it was thrown into the Bay instead. As the bell proceeded home to Philadelphia, it stopped in Arlington, Texas, where a riot nearly ensued when a young black girl kissed the bell. A woman was crushed to death in Memphis as people swarmed to get a look at the Bell on its return trip to Philadelphia.

One of the most expensive replicas of the Liberty Bell might have been created by a Japanese pearl company; it was displayed at the New York World's Fair in 1939. It included 11,600 pearls, 366 diamonds, and 26½ pounds of silver!

There are replicas of the Liberty Bell in each of the 50 states, as well as in Belgium, Czechoslovakia, France, Germany, Israel, Lithuania, and Japan.

The Liberty Bell is displayed in a Liberty Bell Center near Independence Hall. Near the entrance was the home in which President George Washington was served by slaves during his tenure as the first president of the United States.

The Liberty Bell has been the site of numerous visits by U.S. presidents and foreign dignitaries.

After protestors against the Vietnam War spilled animal blood on the steps of Independence Hall and engaged in similar protests, followers of the Reverend Carl McIntyre, a fundamentalist radio commentator, received permission to carry out a ritual cleansing of the site.

Timeline

1701
William Penn issues his Pennsylvania Charter of Privileges for Pennsylvania.

1731
Construction begins on the Pennsylvania Statehouse.

1732
George Washington is born.

1751
The Pennsylvania Assembly allocates money for a bell to honor the 50th anniversary of Penn's Pennsylvania Charter of Privileges.

1752
The first Liberty Bell is cast by Whitechapel Foundry in England. When the Bell arrives in the United States, it cracks on its first stroke.

1753
John Pass and John Stow, two Philadelphia residents, recast the Bell from England that was cracked.

Construction was finished on a bell tower for the State House, and the Liberty Bell was installed.

An article in *The Gentleman's Magazine* of England from America, dated May 10, declares that the Bell was installed, without mentioning that the original had been cracked and recast.

1754
A second bell arrives from Whitechapel Foundry and is later used to chime the hours of a clock with a face on the side of the State House.

The French and Indian War begins, pitting the French and their Native American allies against the British and the 13 American colonies.

1760
George III becomes king of Great Britain.

1772
Philadelphia residents living near the State House complain that the Bell was being rung too frequently.

1763
The English and their colonial allies emerge victorious in the French and Indian War and acquire Canada.

1765
The Stamp Act Congress meets in New York City in protest against parliamentary taxation.

1769
The Assembly gives permission to the Philosophical Society to construct an astronomical observatory in the State House Yard, from which its members could watch the transit of Venus across the Sun. This platform was later used to read the Declaration of Independence to the public.

1774
The first Continental Congress meets in Carpenter's Hall.

1776
The Second Continental Congress adopts the Declaration of Independence, and bells are rung in Philadelphia on July 8 to celebrate its public reading.

1777
The Liberty Bell and other bells in the city of Philadelphia are moved out of the city in anticipation of British occupation.

The British occupy the State House where the Declaration of Independence had been signed, use the State House as a hospital, and create a pit nearby, where they bury dead horses and other refuse.

1778
The Liberty Bell is returned to the State House. Because the wood steeple that had originally housed it is in disrepair, the Bell is stored in the midlevel of the brick tower above a louvered floor that could be reached by steps.

Members of Congress sign the Articles of Confederation and wait for states to ratify it.

The Liberty Bell of the West rings in Old Kakaskia (in today's Illinois) to mark the town's capture by George Rogers Clark.

1780
On February 28, the Pennsylvania Assembly adopts an act vesting ownership of the Old State House in the Commonwealth.

1781
The old wooden steeple that originally housed the Liberty Bell is removed.

States ratify the Articles of Confederation, which vests primary sovereignty in the states.

1783
After mutinous Revolutionary soldiers surround the State House and demand back pay, the Continental Congress moves to Princeton, New Jersey, and never returns to Philadelphia.

1787

The delegates to the Constitutional Convention meet in the Pennsylvania State House from May through September to draft the U.S. Constitution.

1789

The new Constitution goes into effect, and George Washington becomes the first president of the United States.

1789–1791

The Liberty Bell rings to announce the commencement of classes at the University of Pennsylvania, which are held in nearby Philosophical Hall.

1791

States ratify the first ten constitutional amendments, known today as the Bill of Rights.

1799

The Pennsylvania state capital moves to Lancaster.

1800

The U.S. Congress moves to Washington, D.C.

1802

Charles Willson Peale gets state legislative permission to use the old State House for a museum.

1812

The Pennsylvania state capital moves to Harrisburg.

1814

Francis Scott Key composes "The Star-Spangled Banner" after Americans rebuff an attempt by the British during the War of 1812 to invade Baltimore.

1816

The city of Philadelphia buys the State House and Liberty Bell for $70,000 after the state considers dividing the property in order to sell it.

The Mexican Liberty Bell is rung in conjunction with the reading of a Mexican declaration of independence.

1824

The Marquis de Lafayette visits the United States and rekindles interest in U.S. history. The City Council then names the State House Independence Hall.

1826

The nation celebrates the Jubilee Year of the Declaration of Independence.

Both John Adams and Thomas Jefferson die on July 4.

1827

Charles Wilson Peale's Museum, which had occupied the second floor of Independence Hall, is moved to the newly constructed Philadelphia Arcade.

1828

The city of Philadelphia renovates the State House. It adds a wooden steeple, designed by William Strickland, who specialized in colonial revival architecture, to replace the one that it had removed in 1781. It also orders a new and larger bell from John Wilbank, which was in turn replaced by another with a better tone.

1831

Abolitionist William Lloyd Garrison begins publishing *The Liberator.*

The last line of Samuel Francis Smith's "My Country 'Tis of Thee" exhorts "Let Freedom Ring!"

1833

President Andrew Jackson visits Philadelphia and receives citizens at Independence Hall.

In Philadelphia, 60 abolitionists meet to found the American Anti-Slavery Society.

1835

In what may be the first use of the term *Liberty Bell,* Ranson C. Williams titles an article in the *Anti-Slavery Record* of 1835 as "The Liberty Bell."

1838

A poem is published by abolitionists entitled "The Liberty Bell"; over time, that name replaces references to the State House Bell.

1839

The first of the *Liberty Bell Gift Books* are printed, expressing opposition to slavery.

1844

A mob burns down St. Augustine's Roman Catholic Church in Philadelphia, seriously damaging the "sister" to the Liberty Bell that had been manufactured by the Whitechapel Foundry in England.

Jesse Hutchinson authors the abolitionist song "Get Off the Track! (A Song for Emancipation)," which references the Liberty Bell.

1846

Workmen attempt to repair the crack in the Bell, actually widening it in the process. When the Bell is rung in honor of George Washington's birthday, it cracked further, rendering it mute.

1847

George Lippard publishes "The Fourth of July, 1776," a highly fictionalized account of the ringing of the Liberty Bell after Congress's declaration of liberty.

The first floor of Independence Hall is converted to a museum.

1848

Former president John Quincy Adams, an ardent opponent of slavery, becomes the first person to lie in state in Independence Hall.

The Seneca Falls Convention in New York proposes women's suffrage.

1850

African Americans in Pittsburgh send a Liberty Bell to the citizens of Buxton, Canada, which accepted runaway slaves.

1851

A dog pound, which had been kept in the basement of Independence Hall, is moved.

1852

The Liberty Bell is moved from the tower to the Assembly Room of Independence Hall, where it was displayed on a temporary pedestal.

Delegates from each of the original 13 states meet at a convention in Philadelphia to discuss placing a memorial to the Declaration of Independence and its signers on the grounds outside Independence Hall.

1854

The Liberty Bell is placed on an elaborate octagonal pedestal and topped with a mounted eagle.

1855

The song "Old State House Bell" is published.

1857

The last of the *Liberty Bell Gift Books* are printed.

The U.S. Supreme Court issues the *Dred Scott* decision, declaring that blacks are not, and cannot become, U.S. citizens.

1861

Abraham Lincoln stops by Independence Hall on the way to his presidential inauguration and lauds the Declaration of Independence.

The Civil War, which lasts through 1865, pits Northern and Southern states against each other.

1864

The words "In God We Trust" first appear on American coins.

1865

The Thirteenth Amendment is ratified, eliminating involuntary servitude.

President Lincoln is assassinated on April 15; he lies in state in Independence Hall from April 22–24.

1868

The Fourteenth Amendment overturns the *Dred Scott* decision by extending the rights of citizenship to all persons born or naturalized in the United States.

1870

The Fifteenth Amendment prohibits discrimination in voting on the basis of race or previous condition of servitude.

1871

George S. Hillard publishes *Franklin's Fifth Reader*, which reprints the anonymously published "Independence Bell—July 4, 1776" and further popularizes

George Lippard's story of an aged sexton waiting to ring the Bell when independence was declared.

1873
The framework supporting the Liberty Bell is brought down from the belfry of Independence Hall. It is reattached and displayed under the stairway of the Tower Room, surrounded by a plain iron railing.

1876
The nation celebrates its centennial in Philadelphia, highlighting the Liberty Bell. The Bell was displayed in the vestibule so it would be the first object that most visitors saw when they entered the building.

Independence Hall hosts the original signed Declaration of Independence, which is displayed in a glass-fronted safe.

The Centennial Bell is cast.

1877
The Liberty Bell is removed from its yoke and hung from the ceiling of the tower's first floor room with a chain of 13 links, each representing one of the original colonies.

1885
The Liberty Bell travels to the New Orleans World's Industrial and Cotton Exposition.

1885
Boyle v. New Orleans enjoins New Orleans from using city funds to pay for functionaries to return with the Liberty Bell to Philadelphia.

1885
The Liberty Bell visits the Word's Industrial and Cotton Exposition in New Orleans.

1886
The Statue of Liberty, a gift from France, is dedicated on Ellis Island in New York Harbor.

1893
The Liberty Bell travels to the World's Columbian Exposition in Chicago.

John Philip Sousa composes "The Liberty Bell March."

Katharine Lee Bates pens "America the Beautiful."

The Columbian Liberty Bell is cast.

Charles Keyser publishes *The Liberty Bell, Independence Hall, Philadelphia: A Comprehensive Record of All the Great Events Announced by the Ringing of the Bell.*

1894–1895
After the Liberty Bell returns from the Word's Columbian Exposition in Chicago, it is displayed in a glass case at eye level in Independence Hall.

1895

The Liberty Bell travels to the Atlanta Cotton States and International Exposition.

In *Morton v. City of Philadelphia*, the U.S. Supreme Court upholds Philadelphia's right to send the Liberty Bell out of state.

1896

In *Plessy v. Ferguson*, the U.S. Supreme Court upholds the policy of racial segregation.

1897

The Columbian Liberty Bell was melted down.

1896–1898

The row buildings on either side of Independence Hall are replaced by wings that more closely resemble those of colonial times.

1902

The Liberty Bell travels to the Carolina Interstate and West Indian Exposition in Charleston, South Carolina.

1903

The Liberty Bell travels to Massachusetts for the 128th anniversary of the Battle of Bunker Hill.

1904

The Liberty Bell travels to the Louisiana Purchase Exposition in St. Louis.

1908

The Liberty Bell was paraded on a float in a parade marking the 225th anniversary of the founding of Philadelphia.

1910

Wayne Whipple publishes *The Story of the Liberty Bell*.

1913

J. L. G. Ferris paints *The Bell's First Note*.

Philadelphia hosts the Philadelphia Emancipation Exposition.

1915

The Liberty Bell is displayed on a frame and pedestal, no longer surrounded by glass, and visitors are permitted to touch it.

The first telephone message from Philadelphia to San Francisco records a tapping of the Liberty Bell with small wooden mallets.

Workmen install a "spider" inside the Liberty Bell to stabilize it.

The Liberty Bell travels to the Panama-Pacific International Exposition in San Francisco.

Advocates of women's suffrage commission the Justice Bell, which they transport throughout Pennsylvania.

1917

On March 31, approximately 100,000 people gather at Independence Hall to express support for President Woodrow Wilson's Declaration of War.

On June 14, Flag Day, the Liberty Bell is tapped 13 times to mark the last day of the first Liberty Loan campaign to raise money for World War I.

On October 25, The Liberty Bell takes part in a street parade in Philadelphia for Liberty Loan Day.

1919

In the month of May, the Liberty Bell is moved to the front of Independence Hall to welcome home troops from the 28th Keystone Division, who had served in World War I.

The American Lithuanian Bell is rung for the first time in Chicago.

Czech leaders sign their Declaration of Independence at Independence Hall.

1920

The Liberty Bell was installed on a new base made by the Frederick R. Gerry Company.

States ratify the Nineteenth Amendment, preventing discrimination in voting on the basis of sex.

1921

The citizens of Norfolk, Connecticut, dedicate a replica of the Liberty Bell on Armistice Day.

1923

City officials attempt to restrict picture-taking of the Liberty Bell.

1925

The Order of the Liberty Bell is founded to further patriotism and to honor distinguished service.

1926

The Liberty Bell is rung with a rubber-tipped mallet at midnight of the New Year, and the sound is transmitted throughout the country via radio.

Six other "liberty bells" are gathered from Pennsylvania and displayed around the Liberty Bell as part of the sesquicentennial celebration of American independence.

The U.S. government allows the parchment copy of the Declaration of Independence to return to Independence Hall for the sesquicentennial celebrations.

The U.S. Post Office issues its first postage stamp depicting the Liberty Bell (actually the Luminous Liberty Bell).

Victor Rosewater publishes *The Liberty Bell: Its History and Significance.*

1928

Engineering societies donate a bell to Louvain, Belgium, to commemorate the role of U.S. engineers during World War I.

1929
A stock market crash leads to the Great Depression.

1931
Congress designates "The Star-Spangled Banner" as the nation's official anthem.

1932
Franklin D. Roosevelt is elected as U.S. president and initiates ambitious New Deal programs.

1934
An electronic impulse sent from Rear Admiral Richard E. Byrd's base in Antarctica taps a small hammer against the Liberty Bell for radio transmission throughout the world.

1936
Philadelphia mayor S. Davis Wilson taps the Liberty Bell to commemorate the 18th anniversary of the armistice that ended World War I.

1940
The first Philadelphians drafted under a new law to take enlistment oaths in front of the Liberty Bell.

1941
Japanese planes attack Pearl Harbor, Hawaii, and the United States enters World War II.

1942
R. R. Wright lays a wreath at the Liberty Bell in a successful effort to establish a National Freedom Day. It marks the day that President Abraham Lincoln signed a joint resolution that led to the adoption of the Thirteen Amendment eliminating slavery.

Joseph Shallit, a reporter for the Philadelphia *Record*, is arrested after attempting to take a picture of the Liberty Bell with his Brownie camera.

1944
The Liberty Bell is tapped on D-Day, when Allied forces landed on the shores of Normandy to fight the Nazis.

1945
The United States presents the Philippines with a replica of the Liberty Bell to commemorate their liberation from Japanese occupation.

Pennsylvania authorizes funds to buy three blocks of property to create Independence Park.

1947
A U.S. District Court issues an injunction in *Meyerson v. Samuel,* a decision against a city ordinance banning most political demonstrations in front of Independence Hall.

1950
The United States gives a Freedom Bell to West Berlin, where 400,000 people show up for the ceremony.

1954
Congress adds "under God" to the Pledge of Allegiance to the flag.

1951
Although retaining ownership, Philadelphia transfers custody and operation of Independence Hall to the National Park Service.

1954
The U.S. Supreme Court, in *Brown v. Board of Education,* declares that segregation in public education must end, overturning its earlier decision in *Plessy v. Ferguson* (1896).

1960
Hawaii enters the union and becomes the 50th U.S. state.

1961
The National Aeronautics and Space Administration (NASA) launches the *Liberty Bell 7* spacecraft, which sank shortly after splashdown and was not recovered until 1999.

1962
The Liberty Bell is tapped on first anniversary of the Berlin Wall, which communists had constructed to keep East Germans from fleeing to West Germany.

The National Park Service commissions the Franklin Institute to test that the yoke of the Liberty Bell remains capable of continuing to bear its weight, and it concludes that it can.

Performances of Archibald MacLeish's lunadrama, *The American Bell,* begin in front of Independence Hall.

1963
Dr. Martin Luther King, Jr., gives his famous "I Have a Dream" speech in Washington, D.C., where he urges the nation to "let freedom ring!"

Congress adopts a resolution encouraging the ringing of bells throughout the nation at 2 p.m. EST on July 4.

1965
New York City police discover three members of the Black Liberation Front plotting to blow up the Liberty Bell and other national monuments.

Members of the Young Americans for Freedom seek to protect the Liberty Bell from antiwar demonstrators by forming a circle around it.

1972
The outside face of the Stretch Clock, once powered by the twin to the Liberty Bell, is reinstalled on the west wall of Independence Hall.

1973
The Pennsylvania State Legislature agrees to transfer three blocks of the Independence Mall State Park to the federal government.

The U.S. Supreme Court issues an opinion in *Roe v. Wade* that legalizes most abortions.

1975

The Eastman Kodak Company conducts radiograph tests which showed that, although the Liberty Bell has some small cracks, it could be moved to its new pavilion without major danger of making them worse.

1975

The American Legion Freedom Bell takes a trip on the Freedom Train through the 48 contiguous states.

1976

The Liberty Bell begins its trip from Independence Hall to the new Liberty Bell Pavilion, which was expected to handle the crowds anticipated for the celebration of the bicentennial. It remained there until 2003.

The United States celebrates the bicentennial of its independence.

Members of the American Procrastinators Society show up at Whitechapel Foundry in England to protest the defective Liberty Bell.

James Mann paints a mural depicting the Liberty Bell's move to Allentown, Pennsylvania.

Queen Elizabeth presents the United States with a replica of the Liberty Bell called the "Bicentennial Bell."

The Liberty Bell is moved from Independence Hall to the Liberty Bell Pavilion, where it stays until its move to the Liberty Bell Center in 2003.

1988

John C. Paige publishes *The Liberty Bell of Independence National Historical Park: A Special History Study*, edited by David C. Kimball.

1990

President George H. W. Bush rings the Czech Liberty Bell when he visits Czechoslovakia.

1995

The Justice Liberty Bell is displayed at the Independence Hall Visitor Center to mark the 75th anniversary of the ratification of the Nineteenth Amendment.

1996

On April 1, April Fools' Day, the Taco Bell fast food chain publishes a full-page advertisement falsely claiming to have purchased the Liberty Bell and renamed it the Taco Liberty Bell.

2000

The World Peace Bell is cast.

2001

Mitchell Guilliatt strikes the Bell with a hammer and is arrested.

2002

USA Renaissance commissions Whitechapel Foundry to cast a replica of the Liberty Bell for its 350th anniversary.

Charlene Mires publishes *Independence Hall in American Memory*.

2003

The Liberty Bell is moved to Bohlin Cywinski's Jackson Liberty Bell Center.

The National Constitution Center (NCC) opens near the Liberty Bell.

2004

The Normandy Liberty Bell is cast to commemorate the 60th anniversary of the Allied invasion during World War II.

2005

The Normandy Liberty Bell visits Independence Hall on July 4 for the annual "Let Freedom Ring" celebration.

2010

Gray B. Nash publishes *The Liberty Bell.*

2015

Pope Francis gives a speech praising religious liberty at Independence Hall.

2016

The Spirit of Liberty Bell, a replica of the original, is donated by the Providence Forum to the Museum of the Bible in Washington, D.C.

2017

The Museum of the American Revolution opens near Independence Hall.

2018

The Centennial Bell at Independence Hall is rung as part of a "Bells of Peace" ceremony on November 11 to mark the 100th anniversary of the armistice that ended World War I. The World War I Centennial Commission and the National Park Service designate the Liberty Bell as one of the honorary bells of peace.

2019

The Veterans Stadium Liberty Bell was installed in Citizens Bank Park, where the Philadelphia Phillies baseball team plays.

2026

The nation will celebrate the sestercentennial, or semiquincentennial (i.e., the 250th anniversary), of the Declaration of Independence.

FURTHER READING

Paige, John C. 1988. *The Liberty Bell of Independence National Historical Park: A Special History Study*, ed. David C. Kimball. Denver: Denver Service Center, National Park Service, Department of the Interior.

Sheridan, Phil. FACT SHEET: Liberty Bell Timeline. https://www.nsf.gov/news/special_reports/liberty/press/liberty_bell_timeline.doc.

Stoudt, John Baer. 1930. *The Liberty Bells of Pennsylvania*. Philadelphia: William J. Campbell.

A

Abolitionists and the Liberty Bell

Although the Pennsylvania Assembly ordered a bell for its State House (today's Independence Hall) in 1752, the bell that arrived from England, and was twice recast, was most frequently called the "Old Bell" to distinguish it from its "sister" bell, which also came from England, but in 1754. Today's Liberty Bell was also called the "State House Bell," or, beginning sometime after America declared its independence, the "Independence Bell." Although older usages remained, the Bell became known as the "Liberty Bell," largely as a result of the abolitionists who sought to end chattel slavery.

The Bell was particularly well suited as an image because it was inscribed with a verse from Leviticus 25:10: "Proclaim Liberty throughout all the land unto all the inhabitants thereof." Moreover, this biblical admonition was part of a passage proclaiming that every 50th year would be a Year of Jubilee, during which slaves would be freed and debts forgiven.

In 1833, 60 abolitionists met in Philadelphia to form the American Anti-Slavery Society. The society included Boston abolitionists, led by William Lloyd Garrison, with New York abolitionists, led by Lewis Tappan, as well as residents of Philadelphia. They agreed to a constitution, or Declaration of Sentiments, that called for ending slavery in the United States (Kimball, n.d.).

The first known reference to the bell as the Liberty Bell occurred in an article entitled "The Liberty Bell," probably by Ranson G. Williams, in the 1835 issue of the *Anti-Slavery Record*. He reported visiting the Bell and observed, "Hietherto, the bell has *not* obeyed the inscription; and its peals have been a mockery, while one sixth of 'all the inhabitants' are in abject slavery" (Williams, 1835, 23).

From 1839 to 1857, abolitionists began publishing a series of gift books that they sold, along with handmade crafts, at antislavery fairs (Gustin, 2018). The volumes contained an engraving of a bell with the words, like those on the Bell in the State House, that said "PROCLAIM LIBERTY TO ALL THE INHABITANTS," and placing special emphasis on the word *ALL*. Because some of the subsequent poems in the volumes seem to refer generically to bells rather than to a specific bell, some scholars dispute whether abolitionists planned to associate the bell with a single bell in Philadelphia, or with bells in general.

Justin Kramer thus argues, "It is evident that they [the Friends of Freedom] did not adopt the Philadelphia Liberty Bell as their symbol, something they could easily have done. Rather, they designed their own Liberty Bell" (Kramer, 1975, 88). Similarly, the anthropology professor Robey Callahan has argued that in the early years, "The Friends of Freedom were never referring to the Bell in their literature, but rather to the idea of a bell or bells tolling 'Liberty'" (Callahan, 1999, 66). One difficulty with this view is that the engraving used in Liberty Bell Gift Books was almost identical to that of the Liberty Bell. Moreover, one of the most striking artifacts from the American Anti-Slavery Society was a banner that was taken to antislavery fairs and festivals that featured a picture of a painted image of a Bell surrounded by the words, "**PROCLAIM LIBERTY** THROUGHOUT **ALL** THE LAND, UNTO **ALL** THE INHABITANTS THEREOF" (Sands and Bartlett, 2012, 96; bold for emphasis).

There is no necessary contradiction in thinking that abolitionists were willing to use a specific bell like the Liberty Bell, or bells in general, to further their cause. When Jesse Henderson referred to the "Liberty Bell" in an abolitionist song called "Get Off the Track! (A Song for Emancipation)" that he published in 1844, the Bell seemed to mesh with the sound of the train's whistle, urging wavering ministers and politicians to get off the track or be overtaken by the train of emancipation. The cover of *The Liberty Bell,* published in 1844, had the imprint of a golden bell with various figures surrounding a woman. Two figures are holding a pole with a liberty cap, and to the left, a slave pleads on bended knee for his freedom. At the right, another slave has broken his chains (Gustin, 2018). Although this bell is clearly not a print of the Liberty Bell, it nonetheless clearly shows the words "PROCLAIM LIBERTY" and suggests that it was inspired (at least in part) by the bell at Independence Hall.

Garrison, the author of the *Liberator* and one of the most vocal advocates of abolitionism, favored bringing it about immediately, with little consideration of the consequences. He took a very negative view of the U.S. Constitution, believing that provisions like the three-fifths clause and the Fugitive Slave Clause were egregious compromises with slavery. By contrast, Frederick Douglass, an ex-slave who gave at least two speeches near Independence Hall, believed that the Constitution could be interpreted more positively. Abraham Lincoln, who became president in 1861 and stopped by Independence Hall on the way to his inauguration in Washington, D.C., was among those who believed that, whatever concessions the Constitution might have made to slavery, its ultimate goal had been to bring to fruition the affirmation in the Declaration of Independence that "all men are created equal."

At the end of the Civil War (1861–1865), Americans ratified three amendments to the U.S. Constitution. The Thirteenth Amendment (1865) abolished involuntary servitude. The Fourteenth Amendment (1868) declared that all persons born within the United States were entitled to citizenship with its accompanying privileges and immunities, rights to due process of law, and equal protection of the laws. At least on paper, the Fifteenth Amendment (1865) prohibited discrimination in voting on the basis of race, color, or previous condition of servitude.

Women had played a key role in the abolitionist movement and had been pushing, at least since the Seneca Falls Convention of 1848, for suffrage. Many were disappointed when the Fourteenth Amendment specifically identified this right only for males. Perhaps hoping to play on the success of the earlier movement, women in Pennsylvania commissioned their own "Justice Bell" in 1915, which they used to lobby for suffrage, and finally achieved with the adoption of the Nineteenth Amendment in 1920.

Since then, a variety of groups have sought to use the Liberty Bell either as a symbol or as a place to gather for protests.

See also: African Americans and the Liberty Bell; Declaration of Independence and the Liberty Bell; Inscription on the Liberty Bell; Liberty, Meaning of; *Liberty Bell Gift Books;* Names of the Liberty Bell; Political and Social Movements and the Liberty Bell

Further Reading

Callahan, Robey. 1999. "The Liberty Bell: From Commodity to Sacred Object." *Journal of Material Culture* 4 (1): 57–78.

Gustin, Kelsey. 2018. "The Anti-slavery Fair." August 8. https://www.bpl.org/blogs/post/the-anti-slavery-fair.

Kimball, David A. n.d. "Justice Bell Article." Unpublished document provided by staff of the Independence National Historical Park in Philadelphia.

Kramer, Justin. 1975. *Cast in America: The Historically Accurate, Exciting Story of the Liberty Bell*. Los Angeles: Justin Kramer Incorporated.

Sands, Robert W., Jr., and Alexander B. Bartlett. 2012. *Images of America Independence Hall and the Liberty Bell*. Charleston, SC: Arcadia Publishing.

Williams, R. [Ranson] G. 1835. *Anti-Slavery Record*, vol. I. New York: R.G. Williams for the American Anti-Slavery Society.

Advertising and the Liberty Bell

Like the U.S. flag, the Statue of Liberty, and other patriotic symbols, the name and image of the Liberty Bell are widely used in advertising. This trend was accelerated with the Centennial celebrations in Philadelphia in 1876, during which numerous images and replicas of the Liberty Bell were made and sold as souvenirs. Then, as now, it was common to combine the image of the Bell with images of the U.S. flag and of eagles (Callahan, 1999, 67–68). Banks and insurance companies often used the symbol, with small Liberty Bell–shaped banks used to encourage people to save their coins.

The role of the Bell in advertising was enhanced by the journeys that the Liberty Bell took to various fairs and expositions from 1885 to 1915. By 1886, Landreth's Seed Company, headquartered in Philadelphia, had made the Liberty Bell its graphic logo (Kevles, 2013, 675). Historian Charlene Mires has observed that during its travels, the Bell "became commodified" (Mires, 2002, 161). She observes that on its trip to San Francisco and back in 1915, "it appeared in ads for banks, flour, department stores, rail companies, home furnishings, and movie theatres" (Mires, 2002, 161). In 1916, the Pennzoil Oil Company of Pennsylvania used its name over a picture of the Liberty Bell, with its distinctive crack. Playing off its name, the Bell Telephone Company used a similar logo.

The U.S. government also employed the Liberty Bell, often in conjunction with images of Independence Hall and other icons, to stir interest in its Liberty Bond campaign of World War I, as well as for later fund-raisers during the Cold War. As part of this latter campaign, it distributed replicas of the Liberty Bell to each U.S.

state and territory. Although the trips that the Liberty Bell took to world fairs and expositions obviously generated patriotism, the organizers who requested the visits undoubtedly also had their eye on the financial bottom line.

Callahan has observed that the Bell has become such a ubiquitous symbol that the only two elements that are needed for instant recognition are "the merest outline of a bell and a crack proceeding from its base" (Callahan, 1999, 70). Some logos, however, including that of the Heritage Foundation think tank, use an outline of a bell (with no crack) and a stylized version of its yoke. David Bishop has observed, "Either the yoke, the crack or the inscription, or any combination of them, is sufficient to evoke . . . comfortable feelings" (Bishop, 1975, 35).

Gary Nash observes that the use of the Liberty Bell in advertising has been especially pervasive in the Philadelphia area. To bolster his point, he cites businesses in Philadelphia and the surrounding area, such as the Liberty Bell nightclub, the Liberty Bell Life Insurance Company, Liberty Bell Oil, Liberty Bell Windows, the Liberty Bell Steak Company, Liberty Bell Catering, and the Liberty Bell Alarm Company (Nash, 2010, 184). He notes that it is even possible to buy a Liberty Bell Classic Thong from an undergarment manufacturer (Nash, 2010, 185). It may be small consolation that there are similar products capitalizing on the image and the colors of the U.S. flag.

Nash observes that companies like Anaconda Copper, Doak Aircraft Company, and Western World Champion Ammunition, "splattered the Liberty Bell on their ads," but so did such nondefense-related companies as "Chase and Sanborn coffee, Anheuser-Busch's Budweiser beer, Campbell's soup, Waukesha ginger ale, and Prince Albert tobacco" (Nash, 2010, 185–186). He noted that during the colonial revival period, consumers could buy "a Liberty Bell showerhead, a Liberty Bell teapot (with the crack sealed), or an AM radio with a miniature Liberty Bell mounted on it" (Nash, 2010, 186).

One of the most controversial uses of the Liberty Bell occurred when Taco Bell announced on April 1, 1996, that it had bought the Bell and was renaming it the Taco Liberty Bell. Although the campaign turned out to be an April Fool's hoax, many citizens thought that it denigrated a sacred symbol, whether or not it was meant in fun.

Individuals who enjoy collecting advertising items depicting the Liberty Bell might also consider looking for samplers (especially those tied to significant anniversaries) and postcards, especially those in the early 20th century that were made for Independence Day and other holidays. Posters from the Liberty Loan campaigns also generated interest through the liberal use of images of the Liberty Bell.

See also: Bell Telephone Company and the Liberty Bell; Eagles, Flags, the Statue of Liberty, and Related Symbols; Journeys of the Liberty Bell; Liberty Loans; State Liberty Bell Replicas; Taco Liberty Bell

Further Reading
Bishop, David H. 1975. "Ascent to Significance: The Evolution of the Liberty Bell as a Cultural Symbol." American Studies senior thesis, Temple University, May 2. Located at National Independence Historical Park.

Callahan, Robey. 1999. "The Liberty Bell: From Commodity to Sacred Object." *Journal of Material Culture* 4: 57–78.

Kevles, Daniel J. 2013. "A Primer of A, B, Seeds: Advertising, Branding, and Intellectual Property in an Emerging Industry." *U. C. Davis Law Review* 47: 657–678.

Mires, Charlene. 2002. *Independence Hall in American Memory.* Philadelphia: University of Pennsylvania Press.

Nash, Gary B. 2010. *The Liberty Bell.* New Haven, CT: Yale University Press.

African Americans and the Liberty Bell

Originally designated the "Old Bell" or the "State House Bell," today's Liberty Bell soon became identified with the nation's independence, and accordingly, it was sometimes dubbed the "Independence Bell." In time, abolitionists began referring to the Bell (or at least a bell that they used in their publications) as the "Liberty Bell," and the name stuck. The Bell was a particularly useful symbol during the Cold War, when it helped the United States distinguish itself from communist nations that denied individual rights and liberties.

Many of the leaders of the American Revolution who were calling for liberty from Great Britain, like Patrick Henry, George Washington, and Thomas Jefferson, were still holding fellow human beings in bondage. It was hardly surprising that delegates to the Second Continental Congress deleted a long section in Jefferson's original Declaration of Independence in which he both tried to accuse the British king of bringing slaves to the New World *and* encouraged them to rise up against their owners (Maier, 1997, 239). Still, the Congress left in the words of the introductory paragraphs that announced that "all men are created equal" and affirmed that all were entitled to "life, liberty, and the pursuit of happiness." The colonial quest for liberty certainly led to questions about the continuation of slavery within a government that professed to be republican (Bailyn, 1967, 232–246).

As delegates drafted the U.S. Constitution in 1787, they were embarrassed enough about the anomaly of slavery that they did not mention the institution by name. They did, however, provide that such individuals would count as only three-fifths of a person for the purposes of representation in the U.S. House of Representatives, that Congress would have power to limit the further importation of slaves after 20 years, and that states had the responsibility to return fugitives to the states from which they had fled.

The continuation of slavery provoked a number of flashpoints in U.S. history, most notably when the United States admitted Missouri as a slave state in 1820 but balanced it by admitting Maine as a free state. Similarly, the Compromise of 1850, which was largely engineered by Senator Henry Clay from Kentucky, sought to paper over regional differences. It included the admission of California as a free state; the strengthening of the Fugitive Slave Law; popular sovereignty in Utah and New Mexico concerning the question of slavery; the abolition of the slave trade in Washington, D.C.; and the federal assumption of Texas's debt.

Beginning in the 1830s, however, a strong movement for the abolition of slavery began to form, chiefly in Northern states. These abolitionists designated a liberty bell as one of their most prominent symbols. William Lloyd Garrison vowed in an editorial in the *Liberator* in 1831 to be "as harsh as truth, and as uncompromising as justice" (Vile, 2017, 37). In his view, the time for temporizing was over. In a speech that he gave on Independence Day in 1852, the former slave Frederick Douglass contrasted the freedom that white men were celebrating versus the mourning that members of his own race felt for those who remained in bondage (Vile 2017, 171–176). Douglass, and others, urged the nation to live up to the high ideas that the Declaration of Independence had articulated.

Some Northerners joined together to form an escape route, which became known as the "Underground Railroad," whereby slaves could flee from slave states to free states, and then (to get beyond the reach of the Fugitive Slave Law) to Canada. One of the destinations of slaves was a mission school in Buxton, Canada, just across Lake Erie. After this town expressed willingness to take runaway slaves, an African American church in Pittsburgh raised funds in the early 1850s to send a bell, now designated as one of Canada's liberty bells, that could be rung every time such a fugitive arrived. In correspondence between the two towns, citizens of Pittsburgh reminded those who had arrived in Canada that they were "now in a land of liberty, where the rights and privileges of freemen are secured to you by law," while those from Canada responded, "We are delighted at all times to hear from the friends that we have left in a land of pretend freedom" ("The Liberty Bell," 1850).

In time, Southern states, who feared that Northern states might attempt to outlaw slavery, withdrew from the Union, which the incoming president, Abraham Lincoln, believed it was his responsibility to protect. The bloody Civil War ensued from 1861 to 1865. Over time, the aims of the war ceased being merely about restoration of the Union and came to include the abolition of slavery. Many African Americans enlisted during the war, and a huge majority of them fought on the Union side. On January 1, 1863, Lincoln issued the Emancipation Proclamation, freeing (at least on paper) all slaves behind Southern lines.

At the conclusion of the Civil War, the nation adopted three amendments. The Thirteenth Amendment (1865) abolished slavery throughout the nation, with no compensation to former slaveowners. The Fourteenth Amendment (1868) extended a number of protections, including "privileges and immunities," "due process of law," and "equal protection of the laws," to all persons born or naturalized within the United States (which was meant to include former slaves). The Fifteenth Amendment (1870) further prohibited discrimination in voting of the basis of race or previous condition of servitude.

Although world fairs and expositions often expressed dominant views about the superiority of the Anglo-Saxon race, African Americans joined in celebrations of the journeys of the Bell from 1885 to 1915. An account in the *Philadelphia Press* newspaper of October 9, 1895, which is in the Historic Card File at the Independence National Historical Park in Philadelphia, reports that when the Bell arrived in Atlanta that year, one former slave proclaimed, "Hooray fer de bell what set me free."

Many of the guarantees in the Fourteenth and Fifteenth Amendments would go unenforced until well into the 1960s. In the interim, the nation passed through a period of racial segregation, during which African Americans rarely received equal treatment. Social Darwinism reinforced ideas of racial hierarchy that were often reflected in the fairs and expositions that the Liberty Bell visited from 1885 to 1915.

As soldiers returned from World War II, where the nation had fought Nazi racism, many African American citizens began demanding equal treatment within their own country. Even before the war ended, Richard R. Wright Sr. had begun laying wreaths at the Liberty Bell on February 1 (the day that President Lincoln had signed the joint congressional resolution for the Thirteenth Amendment) to muster support for a National Freedom Day. It was eventually established in 1948, although the adoption of Martin Luther King Day as a national holiday later overshadowed it.

The Liberty Bell became a site for some notable sit-ins and other protests designed to highlight racial inequality. A number of civil rights leaders, including King, tapped on the Liberty Bell to call for freedom and equality for all. In one of Dr. King's most quoted speeches, he used the phrase "Let freedom ring" to emphasize his call for equal rights.

The practice of equal rights often fell far short of the aspirations that America's founders had articulated. When the Bell was moved to its new Liberty Bell Center, it was discovered that it was located not far from the house in which George Washington lived when he was president, in which he kept slaves. In time, these concerns resulted in an exhibit that highlighted this disparity between the nation's ideals and its realities (Nash, 2004).

When the National Museum of African American History and Culture was opened in Washington, D.C., in 2016, a bell from the First Baptist Church in Williamsburg, which was the first such church to be organized by African Americans, was used to ring in the opening.

Philadelphia is the site of a number of museums, churches, and historic homes that honor or commemorate African Americans and their culture, and these have been used to encourage African American tourists to visit (Pope, 2011).

See also: Abolitionists and the Liberty Bell; Canadian Liberty Bells; Declaration of Independence and the Liberty Bell; Independence Hall; Journeys of the Liberty Bell; *Liberty Bell Gift Books;* Names for the Liberty Bell; Oral Tradition and the Liberty Bell; Political and Social Movements and the Liberty Bell; Tapping and Broadcasting the Sound of the Liberty Bell; Virginia Liberty Bell

Further Reading

Bailyn, Bernard. 1967. *The Ideological Origins of the American Revolution.* Cambridge, MA: Belknap Press of Harvard University Press.

Blockson, Charles L. *The Liberty Bell Era: The African American Story.* St. Louis: Regent Publishing.

"The Liberty Bell, 1850"—Buxton Settlement, Raleigh ON—Bells on Waymarking.com. http://www.waymarking.com/waymarks/WMJDN1_The-Liberty_Bell_1850 _Buxton_Settlement_Raleigh_OH.

Maier, Pauline. 1997. *American Scripture: Making the Declaration of Independence.* New York: Alfred A. Knopf.

Nash, Gary B. 2004. "For Whom Will the Liberty Bell Toll? From Controversy to Collaboration." *The George Wright FORUM* 21: 39–52.

Pope, Kitty J. 2011. "Liberty Bell, Originally a Symbol for the Abolishment of Slavery, Also Has Ties to Black History." October 10. https://www.africanamerica.org/topic /liberty-bell-originally-a-symbol-for-the-abolishment-of-slavery-also-has-ties-to -black-history.

Vile, John R. 2017. *The Jacksonian and Antebellum Eras: Documents Decoded.* Santa Barbara, CA: ABC-CLIO.

Allentown

One of the most dramatic adventures of the Liberty Bell took place during the Revolutionary War, as British forces led by General William Howe approached Philadelphia. The Pennsylvania Assembly voted on June 16, 1777, that "the president and council be authorized and empowered to remove as soon as they may think proper, all the bells belonging to the several churches and other buildings and also all the copper and brass in this city, to some place of safety." This order was subsequently reinforced by further instructions from Congress (Stoudt, 1927, 12).

The bells may have left the city on September 16 or 17, but definitely by September 23. Howe arrived in Philadelphia on September 27 (Boland, 1973, 83). The Liberty Bell was among those that were carried by some 700 wagons that left the city under guard. Bells were particularly valued because they could be melted down to make bullets and other military equipment. The wagon in which the Liberty Bell was carried broke down as it passed through the town of Bethlehem, and it had to be moved to another wagon. It appears as though John Jacob Mickley drove the first wagon carrying the Liberty Bell, and Frederick Leaser the second.

When the Bell arrived in Allentown, about 50 to 60 miles northwest of Philadelphia, it is believed to have been hidden below the floor of the Zion Reformed Church. Although the building has been replaced, the church remains and houses a small Liberty Bell Museum that includes a replica of the Bell. The British evacuated Philadelphia on June 18, 1778, the Liberty Bell apparently left Allentown on June 27, and the *Pennsylvania Packet* reported on August 22, "The bells of this City . . . are all returned safe and hung again" (Boland, 1973, 87).

Among the paintings that commemorated this event is one by Edwin Willard Deming (1860–1942), best known for his paintings of Native Americans, entitled "The First Journey of the Liberty Bell," in about 1900. Although the picture disappeared in the 1930s and was being sought in the 1970s by the Independence Hall National Historical Park for display, it appears to have been a large landscape painting that showed the Bell being carried on a wagon led by a black horse down an incline, following a cannon in front, and being carefully guarded by U.S. soldiers (Boland, 1973, 84–85). A flag following the wagon has a picture of a coiled rattlesnake, a common American Revolution symbol later adopted by the U.S. Marines, and often combined with the words "Don't Tread on Me."

See also: Museums of the Liberty Bell; Security for the Liberty Bell; Zion Reformed Church

Further Reading
Boland, Charles Michael. 1973. *Ring in the Jubilee: The Epic of America's Liberty Bell.* Riverside, CT: Chatham Press.

Moore, Ruth Nulton. 1968. *Hiding the Bell*. Philadelphia: Westminster Press.

Stoudt, John Baer. 1927. *The Liberty Bell in Allentown and Allentown's Liberty Bell*. Allentown, PA: Berkemeyer, Kick & Co.

American Freedom Bell

The words "liberty" and "freedom" are often used synonymously, so it is not surprising that there are a number of bells that are designated as "American freedom bells."

One such American Freedom Bell was cast by the Verdin Company on June 6, 2013, with 330 pounds of bronze and 10 pounds of steel from the World Trade Center towers that had been destroyed 12 years before (American Freedom Bell + Spirit of Liberty Collection Exhibits). The bell, which was the brainchild of Richard Rovsek, the founder of the Spirit of Liberty Foundation, has medallions with each of the symbols of U.S. military branches around its waist and 50 stars around its lip.

The American Freedom Bell was first unveiled on Flag Day (June 14) 2013 at Independence Hall before traveling aboard the *U.S.S. Midway* to Honolulu to commemorate Pearl Harbor Remembrance Day (Welch, 2015). It was displayed as part of the "Spirit of Liberty Collection," which included paintings of the Pearl Harbor Monument, Arlington National Cemetery, the World War II Memorial, the Korean War Memorial, and the Vietnam Mall (American Freedom Bell + Spirit of Liberty Collection Exhibits).

The Bell is suspended from the center of a stand. Each of the four legs identifies the bell as "THE FREEDOM BELL." People, often children, are encouraged to ring the bell to honor members of their families who have served or who are deployed in the military.

There is another American Freedom Bell, which the Belk Foundation gave to the people of North Carolina and South Carolina to celebrate the patriotism of the people of Charlotte. It weighs about seven tons and is displayed in a pavilion at the Charlotte Museum of History (Waymarking.com). There is also an American Legion Freedom Bell, which is twice the size of the Liberty Bell; and the Freedom Bell, which the United States gave to West Berlin during the Cold War.

See also: American Legion Freedom Bell; Freedom Bell; Independence Hall; Liberty, Meaning of; Replicas of the Liberty Bell

Further Reading

"American Freedom Bell + Spirit of Liberty Collection Exhibits." USS Midway Museum. https://www.midway.org/calendar-events/american-freedom-bell-spirit-of-liberty -collections-exhibits.

"American Freedom Bell, Charlotte Museum of History—Bells on Waymarking.com." http://www.waymarking.com/waymarks/WM6WKK_American_Freedom_Bell _Charlotte_Museum_Of_History.

USS Bowfin Submarine Museum and Park. December 2, 2015. https://www.facebook.com /bowfinpark/posts/welcome-americas-the-freedom-bell-to-hawaiiwe-are-proud -that-spirit-of-liberty-f/10153766257139839.

Welch, Diane. 2015. "Idea for 'Freedom Bell' Rings Out, Thanks to Rancho Santa Fe Resident." *Rancho Santa Fe Review,* June 14. http://www.ranchosantafereview.com/sdrsf-Freedom-bell-armed-forces-2015jun14-story.html.

American Legion Freedom Bell

The approach of the bicentennial of American independence in 1976 led to renewed attention to the Liberty Bell. One such effort led to the construction of a 16,830-pound replica of the Bell, which is alternately known as the American Legion Freedom Bell, the Freedom Bell (not to be confused with a bell by the same name in Berlin), and the Children's Bell.

The American Legion, which is a long-standing veterans' organization known for promoting patriotism and respect for the U.S. flag, originally had the idea of asking children to donate pennies to be melted down into a replica of the Liberty Bell. Although it abandoned this idea, the bell, which is positioned outside Union Station in Washington, D.C. (the American Legion originally wanted it to be on the National Mall), still has a connection to children. This is evidenced by a plaque in front of it that reads (American Heritage Foundation):

The American Legion Bell is a replica of the Liberty Bell, and can be found at Union Station in Washington, D.C. It was cast by the N. V. Petit and Fristsen Bell Foundry in Holland in 1976 in honor of the bicentennial of the adoption of the U.S. Declaration of Independence. (Brandon A. Gibbs/Dreamstime.com)

THE FREEDOM BELL
DEDICATED TO
THE SPIRIT OF THE
BICENTENNIAL
ON BEHALF OF
THE CHILDREN OF
OUR NATION
GIVEN BY
THE AMERICAN LEGION
AND
AMERICAN LEGION
AUXILIARY 1981

The bell itself has the same inscription as the original Liberty Bell, including the words "Pass" and "Stow," designating John Pass and John Stow, the original American casters.

The bell was designed by the I. T. Verdin Company in Cincinnati, which is now simply the

Verdin Company. However, it was cast by the N. V. Petit and Fristsen Bell Foundry, which is located in Aarle-Rixtel, the Netherlands.

Much as the Liberty Bell took seven trips to various expositions between 1885 and 1915, the American Legion Liberty Bell took a tour of the 48 contiguous states between 1975 and 1976, as part of what was known as the "American Freedom Train." This train was itself patterned after an earlier Freedom Train that traveled the country from 1947–1949 with copies of important documents as a way of highlighting American ideals and promoting good citizenship (Little, 1993).

See also: American Freedom Bell; Children and the Liberty Bell; Replicas of the Liberty Bell

Further Reading
American Heritage Foundation. n.d. "The Story of the 1975–1976 American Freedom Train." http://www.freedomtrain.org/american-freedom-train-consist-041-childrens-bell.htm.
Little, Stuart J. 1993. "The Freedom Train: Citizenship and Postwar Political Culture 1946–1949." *American Studies* 34 (Spring): 35–67.

American Lithuanian Liberty Bell

One of the replicas of the Liberty Bell, known as the American Lithuanian Liberty Bell, illustrates the manner in which various ethnic groups in the United States have sought to spread liberty back in their homelands. The bell was cast in St. Louis, Missouri, and delivered to a preconvention meeting of U.S. Lithuanians in Chicago, whose ancestors had come from the small Baltic region of northeastern Europe, which is so named because it borders the Baltic Sea. Although the American Lithuanian Liberty Bell is shaped like its namesake, at 1,000 pounds, it was just under half its weight.

It was also inscribed differently. One side had a raised image of a Lithuanian mounted knight known as the "Vytis." Below it was a poem, composed by B. K. Balutis, that said (Backaitis, May 12, 2018):

Oh, ring through the ages,
For the children of Lithuania;
For one is not worthy of Liberty,
Who does not defend her!

The opposite side read as follows (Backaitis, May 12, 2018):

The American Lithuanian Convention to Lithuania, June 9, 10 and 11, 1919, Chicago, Illinois. Let this Bell, be a symbol of liberty, a testimonial for future generations of the solicitude and love that American Lithuanians bore for their fatherland Lithuania.

Although the words thus differ from the American Liberty Bell, the sentiments are similar.

About 4,000 people gathered to hear the first ringing of the bell at the Chicago Auditorium Theatre on June 8, 1919. To one side was a woman dressed to represent Columbia (a popular symbol of the day for the United States) and, on the other, a woman representing Lithuania, with girls in native Lithuanian dress in between.

About 500 delegates subsequently met at the American Lithuanian Convention, which was designed to promote support for the freedom of the Lithuanian people, who remained largely under the control of Poland. Perhaps in imitation of the seven trips that the Liberty Bell had made from 1885 to 1915, the bell was marched through Lithuanian-American communities beginning with a parade in Chicago on August 24, 1919, after which individuals who donated $1 were given the opportunity to ring the bell (Backaitis, May 12, 2018). The bell then toured other Lithuanian-American communities until it was returned to Chicago on August 15, 1920, where a mass meeting celebrated the recovery of Vilnius, which was Lithuania's capital. At that time, Lithuanian Americans gave the bell to the Lithuanian government.

The bell reached Lithuania on January 12, 1922, but it was installed in a tower of the War Museum in Kaunas because Poland was again occupying Vilnius. It rang on February 16, 1922, for the fourth anniversary of Lithuanian independence (Backaitis, May 12, 2018). The Soviet Union occupied Lithuania in 1940, then the Nazis captured it, and finally the Soviet Union recaptured it. The bell remained mute until the fall of the Soviet Union in 1989. Since then, it has rung on a regular basis. Today, Lithuania is a member of the European Union.

See also: Replicas of the Liberty Bell

Further Reading

Backaitis, Stan. 2018. "Footprints of Lithuanians in America 1919–1945, Part II—Birth of a Self Reliant Ethnic Community and Watchful Guardians of Their Ancestral Homeland." May 12. https://lithampedia.com/part-2-test-53b9e3a5afea.

Backaitis, Stasys. 2018. "A Gift From the Heart—The American Lithuanian Liberty Bell." *Draugas News,* April 17. https://www.draugas.org/news/a-gift-from-the-heart-the-american-lithuanian-liberty-bell.

"America's Liberty Bells" (Song, 1911)

One of the songs that emerged during World War I was "America's Liberty Bells." It consisted of two stanzas written by Mary E. Glasgow, with music by Luther A. Clark.

As with other music of the time, the first verse associated the bell with the flag (Clark and Glasgow, 1911):

There's a thing that is dear to the hearts of us all,
    Quite close to Old Glory for fame.
It's a thing that once answered our nation's great call;
    Old Liberty Bell, is its name.
And the peace it proclaimed, has been lasting and good,
    But the old bell is shattered and worn.

And so loving hands took it from its great tower,
   Just to shield and to keep it from harm.
Liberty Bell! Brave old Bell!
   full of all our history's charm.

It is difficult to ascertain whether the second verse refers to another specific bell (the Centennial Bell had long been hanging in the tower at Independence Hall), or whether it was purely symbolic (Clark and Glasgow, 1911):

But we're casting another to hang in its place;
   A bell that shall never come down;
That shall peal forth America's freedom and peace
To hill top, and valley, and town.
We shall cast it of metal, so strong and so clear,
That the whole world shall know of its power;
It should ring down through ages, without rent or scar
Our New Liberty Bell in its Tower.

The refrain was quite simple:

Peace! Peace! [Sweet] Freedom and peace!
Bringing new joys every where.

The music was sold by the National Literary and Publishers' Service Bureau in Hannibal, Missouri. The copy on file at the Library of Congress is typed, with handwritten musical notations for the first verse and no illustrative cover.

See also: Centennial Bell; Eagles, Flags, the Statue of Liberty, and Related Symbols; Music and the Liberty Bell

Further Reading

Clark, Luther A., and Mary E. Glasgow. *America's Liberty Bells*. Monographic, 1911. Notated Music. https://www.loc.gov/item/2013564337.

Annecy Liberty Bell Replica

Over time, the Liberty Bell has increasingly been recognized as an international symbol. The symbol was particularly important during the Cold War, when the U.S. government employed it to stress the nation's commitment to freedom and democracy.

During World Wars I and II, the Liberty Bell had been an especially effective way of raising money for Liberty Bonds, with which to finance the conflicts. Then, as World War II transitioned into the Cold War, the government decided to use the Liberty Bell again for fund-raising purposes. To this end, in 1950, the government commissioned the Paccard Bell Foundry in Annecy-le-Vieux (Annecy the Old), in eastern France, to make somewhere between 53 and 57 replicas of the Liberty Bell. The government planned to give them to all of the states and territories that participated in the drive to raise $650 million. The foundry was situated in a town that members of the French resistance had taken back from the Nazis before Allied troops arrived, and the Paccard family had been making bells for generations.

Although flooded with orders from towns across Europe whose bells had been destroyed during World War II, the foundry was able to deliver on this order in time for the pledge drive. In appreciation, the United States gave one of the bells back to the town, which today houses it in the tower of the Basilique Saint Joseph-des-Fins.

Much like the Statue of Liberty, the bell serves not only as a reminder of common ideals, but also of historic friendship between the United States and France. When Treasury Secretary John W. Snyder visited Annecy to present the bell on September 10, 1950, he observed, "It is the hope of the United States that you will look on this bell as a constant reminder of our common faith in democracy. It is intended also to recognize anew a great bond which exists between the peoples of France and the United States—their mutual devotion to the cause of human freedom" (Campbell, 2018, 13).

Annecy created a plaque with similar sentiments (Campbell, 2018, 14–15):

> This bell is one of 57 bells that were made in Annecy during the spring and summer of the year 1950. Each of them is an exact reproduction of the Liberty Bell which resounded to proclaim in 1776 the Independence of America in Philadelphia (State of Pennsylvania), and which the American people have since considered as a symbol of these memorable days.

> These bells have been used since May 15 until July 4, 1950 as an emblem for the campaign of the American Treasury. These bells will be permanently exhibited in each state of the United States and the District of Columbia, Hawaii, Alaska, Puerto Rico and the Virgin Islands. One of these bells was donated to Japan. The inhabitants of Annecy donated a bell to the inhabitants of the city of Independence (State of Missouri), home of the United States President, Mr. Harry S. Truman.

> The Government of America has made the necessary arrangements to give this bell to the city of Annecy in recognition of the technical skill and craftsmanship of its workers and to remind the fact that freedom is a common heritage of France and the United States.

> The American people are hoping, when the inhabitants of Annecy and all over France will look and hear this bell, that they will remember the times when the two nations fought side by side to defend this heritage which made both grand.

The Paccard Bell Foundry has continued to cast reproductions, with the 300th cast in 1989, going to Walt Disney World (Campbell, 2018, 16, which incorrectly says "Disney Land"). It is said to be cast from the original mold, but because it was cast by the Paccard Bell Foundry in France, rather than from the Whitechapel Bell Foundry in England, it seems likely that it was the original mold for the state replicas of the Liberty Bell that were made in the 1950s (Disney Trivia, n.d.). The foundry also cast the 33-ton World Peace Bell, which is now in Lexington, Kentucky, in 1998. The company has an American affiliate in Charleston, South Carolina, which, as of 2018, was selling additional replicas for $75,000 apiece (Campbell, 2018, 16). The town of Sevrier in France, which is close to Annecy, has also opened a museum that tells the long history of bell making.

President Harry S. Truman was on hand to accept a bell from Annecy at his hometown of Independence, Missouri, on November 6, 1950. In the speech that he delivered on this occasion, he tied the bell back to the American Revolution and to "the revolutionary principles of human freedom and political equality." He further linked these ideals to the fight against "Communist imperialism." Citing the biblical verse on the bell, Truman observed, "Our concept of freedom has deep religious roots. We come under a divine command to be concerned about the welfare of our neighbors, and to help one another. For all men are the servants of God, and no one has the right to mistreat his fellow men." At the end of the speech, Truman observed that "the people of Annecy have given this Liberty Bell to us as a symbol of the great fellowship of freedom." He continued on a hopeful note: "The fellowship of freedom is growing. It stands firm against the false prophets of communism, who represent not brotherhood, but dictatorship—not progress, but reaction. The fellowship of freedom will prevail against tyranny, and bring peace and justice to the world. For freedom is the true destiny of man" (Truman, 1950).

See also: Liberty Loans; Replicas of the Liberty Bell; State Liberty Bell Replicas; Statue of Liberty; World Peace Bell

Further Reading

Campbell, Tom. 2018. "The Annecy Liberty Bell Replica." June 19, http://tomlovestheliertybell.com/2018/06/19/the-annecy-liberty-bell-replica.

Disney Trivia. n.d. http://disneytrivia.tumblr.com/post/34501185510/urban-legend-the-liberty-bell-in-liberty-square.

Truman, Harry S. "Address in Independence at the Dedication of the Liberty Bell." Public Papers Harry S. Truman 1945–1953. https://www.trumanlibrary.org/publicpapers/index.php?pid=1440.

Atlanta Cotton States and International Exposition of 1895

The Liberty Bell's third trip to world fairs and expositions took place when it went to the Atlanta Cotton States and International Exposition of 1895, which was held at the city's Piedmont Park. The choice of a Southern site for two of the first three visits demonstrates the manner in which, after the Civil War, the Bell was already being viewed as a symbol of national reconciliation.

The train carrying the Bell left Philadelphia on October 4, 1894, and drove through Pennsylvania, Delaware, Washington, D.C., Virginia, Tennessee, and parts of Georgia before arriving in Atlanta on October 8. As it passed through small towns and cities, it stirred deep emotions. Gary Nash notes that as the train stopped at Ellison, Virginia, Patrick Henry's great-grandson asked permission to touch the Bell, and in Bristol, Tennessee, an 88-year old woman "fell on her knees before the bell and 'invoked a Divine blessing upon the old mass of historic iron'" (Nash, 2010, 99).

The reception in Atlanta was equally ecstatic. Crowds surrounded the train for the last two miles of the trip (Rosewater, 1926, 167). Attendance was further boosted by the declaration of an official "Liberty Bell Day" on October 9, during which public-school children were dismissed from class early, and 12,000 students were provided with free transportation on the city's streetcars (Newman, 1996, 71–72). Undoubtedly due to concerns about the Bell's condition generated on its last trip, it rested on a rubber cushion under a striped canopy (Sands and Bartlett, 2012, 81).

Like the residents of Chicago, Atlanta's leaders, especially Henry W. Grady, the editor of the *Atlanta Constitution*, worked long and hard to attract both the exposition and the Liberty Bell. Atlanta had been largely destroyed during the Civil War, its largest hotel, the Kimball House, had burned in 1883 (although it did get rebuilt), and the nation had experienced a depression in 1893. The exposition was a particularly ambitious endeavor, given that the population of the city was only thought to be about 75,000 in 1895 (Newman, 1996, 75). Labor from chain gangs helped do much of the work of preparing the fairgrounds.

Grady and other Atlanta leaders sought to portray the city as part of the New South, welcoming industrialization and the development of world markets. They also sought to portray Atlanta as a city that had a solution to racial antagonism. To this end, the city sought and received the support of some leading African American leaders, who were given their own pavilion at the fair (which was, however, the only pavilion at which they could purchase refreshments). Like exhibits at the earlier Chicago Exposition, displays here tended to portray Africans and other races as inferior to those of European stock.

On the opening day, Booker T. Washington gave a speech, generally called the "Atlanta Compromise Speech," in which he urged his fellow African Americans to "Cast down your bucket where you are." Specifically, he urged black people to accept the dignity of "common labor." At a time when Northern cities faced strikes and feared the threat of anarchism that immigrants might bring, Washington urged whites "who look to the incoming of those of foreign birth and strange tongue and habits for the prosperity of the South" to put down their own buckets among African Americans, who had already demonstrated themselves to be "the most patient, faithful, law-abiding, and unresentful people that the world has seen." He further stated, "The wisest among my race understand that the agitation of questions of social equality is the extremist folly, and that progress in the enjoyment of all the privileges that will come to us must be the result of severe and constant struggle rather than of artificial forcing." Washington anticipated "a blotting out of sectional differences and racial animosities and suspicions" that would "bring into our beloved South a new heaven and a new earth." Perhaps with the text from Leviticus 25:10 in mind, Washington said the next day, "This is the year of Jubilee for the Negro. It is the beginning of a New Era—the heart of the New South is open today to the Negro as it has never been before—the greatest problem is now with the Negro himself" (Rydell, 1984, 84).

It was almost as though Washington were prophesying the Supreme Court's decision in *Plessy v. Ferguson* the following year, which ensconced Jim Crow laws through its policy known as "separate but equal" and effectively denied the equal liberty for all that the Liberty Bell, emancipation, and the Fourteenth Amendment had promised. An exhibit called the "Old Plantation" at the fair further heightened racial stereotypes, as did an exhibit about African villages.

One of the most fascinating artifacts of the Atlanta Exposition was a stereoview photograph by W. W. Kilburn described as "Bowing to the Old Liberty Bell, Atlanta Exposition." Although its caption would indicate that a group of four African American men are bowing before the guarded bell, closer examination shows that the men appear instead to be searching for something on the ground in front of it (Mires, 2002, 152).

As in Chicago, the exposition featured Buffalo Bill's Wild West Show. John Philip Sousa composed a composition called the "King Cotton March," and evangelist Dwight L. Moody from Chicago build a special tabernacle, where he conducted a weeklong revival (Newman, 1996, 73). Attendance at the exposition received a further boost when President Grover Cleveland visited on October 23, which the city declared to be President's Day.

Although generally hailed as a success—779,560 tickets were sold—the exposition faced many obstacles—including its name, which led some to imagine that it was focusing on a single crop (Newman, 1996, 72). Many exhibits from Europe and Latin America arrived late (most had private rather than governmental sponsors), and the Exposition "Promoted both the [Panama] Canal and Cuban Independence," which would lead the United States into a foreign imperialism that was arguably again at odds with the inscription on the Liberty Bell (Perdue, 2010, 115),

On the return trip, the train somewhat varied its original route. It traveled from Georgia to South Carolina, North Carolina, Virginia, and Washington, D.C., before arriving back in Philadelphia.

See also: African Americans and the Liberty Bell; Journeys of the Liberty Bell; Reconciliation and the Liberty Bell

Further Reading

Mires, Charlene. 2001. *Independence Hall in American Memory.* Philadelphia: University of Pennsylvania Press.

Nash, Gary B. *The Liberty Bell.* New Haven, CT: Yale University Press.

Newman, Harvey K. "Atlanta's Hospitality Businesses in the New South Era, 1880–1900." *Georgia Historical Quarterly* 80 (Spring): 53–76.

Perdue, Theda. 2010. *Race and the Atlanta Cotton States Exposition of 1895.* Athens: University of Georgia Press.

Plessy v. Ferguson, 163 U.S. 537 (1896).

Rosewater, Victor. 1926. *The Liberty Bell: Its History and Significance.* New York: D. Appleton and Company.

Rydell, Robert W. 1984. *All the World's a Fair: Visions of Empire at American International Expositions, 1876–1916.* Chicago: University of Chicago Press.

Sands, Robert W., Jr., and Alexander B. Bartlett. 2012. *Images of America: Independence Hall and the Liberty Bell.* Charleston, SC: Arcadia Publishing.

Washington, Booker T. "Booker T. Washington Delivers the 1895 Atlanta Compromise Speech." *History Matters.* http://historymatters.gmu.edu/d/39.

B

Bayle v. New Orleans (1885)

The first trip that the Liberty Bell took out of the state of Pennsylvania was to the New Orleans World Industrial and Cotton Centennial Exposition in 1885. As the bell was set to return, the mayor and other city functionaries prepared to accompany it on its journey, for which $5,000 was appropriated from city funds.

A city resident (and French citizen) and taxpayer named Joseph Bayle challenged this expenditure. Because of his foreign citizenship (the U.S. Constitution extends jurisdiction to cases involving a foreign citizen and a state), he was able to file his case in the U.S. Fifth Circuit Court of Appeals. It granted an injunction in the case of *Bayle v. New Orleans*, 23 F. 843 (1885). He charged that the expenditure was illegal because it had exceeded its corporate authority.

Judge Don Albert Pardee (1837–1919) accepted this argument and issued an injunction against what he described as "a junketing expedition to go to Philadelphia" (*Bayle v. New Orleans*, 23 F. 843 at 844). Pardee pointed out that in *New London v. Brainard*, 22 Conn. 552, the Connecticut Supreme Court had upheld a similar taxpayer challenge to expenditures by a city corporation for Independence Day celebrations. There had been similar decisions in other states. Pardee observed:

> There being no doubt as to the illegality of the ordinance and the appropriation, and no reasonable doubt as to the appropriateness of the remedy sought, nor as to the jurisdiction of the court, the patriotic phase of the case is not potent enough to affect the action of the Court. If, in Massachusetts, Connecticut, New York, Virginia, and other states, municipal corporations are not permitted to encourage and disseminate patriotism and the love of liberty by celebrations, at municipal expense, of the fourth of July, the surrender of Cornwallis, and other stirring epochs in the history of the country, there would seem to be no reason why this court should hold its hand, and not prevent the city of New Orleans, at the expense of her tax-payers, from advertising the patriotism of her mayor, council, and citizens by appropriate ceremonies and enthusiasm and declaration, in the return of the famous and honored liberty bell to the city of Philadelphia. (*Bayle v. New Orleans*, 23 F. 843 at 845–846)

This case, which was in line with other decisions of the day that sought to use the judiciary to trim the powers of municipalities, was later cited in *Morton v. City of Philadelphia* (1895), in which a Court of Common Pleas in Pennsylvania decided that the city of Philadelphia owned the Liberty Bell and had the right to send it to other cities. The *Morton* decision relied in part on a decision in *Tagg v. City of Philadelphia*, in which a Pennsylvania court allowed the Philadelphia council to host the visiting New Orleans delegation at a special banquet.

See also: Morton v. City of Philadelphia (1895); World's Industrial and Cotton Exhibition in New Orleans (1885)

Further Reading
Bayle v. City of New Orleans, 23 F. 843 (1885).
Morton v. City of Philadelphia, 4 PA. D. 523 (1895).

"Bell and the Glass, The" (Artwork, 2003)

Christian Marclay is a visual artist who was born in 1955. Working with Relache, Inc., and Relache Ensemble, he worked with the Philadelphia Museum of Art to produce a multimedia installation and accompanying music compositions to create "The Bell and the Glass," which was exhibited from May 17 to July 27, 2003. The installation was designed to reflect the artist's twin interests in the Liberty Bell and the enigmatic artwork called "The Bride Stripped Bare by Her Bachelors, Even" by Marcel Duchamp (1887–1968), which is often simply called "The Large Glass."

The installation included "a live music/sound performance by Relache Ensemble, a photo-essay, a video composition, and an installation of objects selected by the artist from his collection, as well as from the holdings of the Philadelphia Museum of Art, Independence National Historical Park, the Atwater Kent Museum, and other institutions" (Philadelphia Museum of Art, 2003). The work was further described as a "double-screen video projection" that "incorporates footage of Marcel Duchamp, clips from Hollywood movies, and shots of the Liberty Bell and of the Duchamp galleries at the Museum" (Philadelphia Museum of Art, 2003). The work stemmed from what is described as "Marclay's longstanding interest in objects that were created to make sound but rendered silent and dysfunctional" (Philadelphia Museum of Art, 2003).

See also: Music and the Liberty Bell; Silence of the Liberty Bell

Further Reading
Philadelphia Museum of Art. May 17, 2003–July 27, 2003. "Museum Studies 7: Christian Marclay, The Bell and the Glass." https://www.philamuseum.org/exhibitions/2003/61.html.

Bell Telephone Company and the Liberty Bell

One of the happiest coincidences in advertising history may well be that the last name of the American inventor of the telephone, Alexander Graham Bell, reminded some of a form of communication that long preceded the telephone.

Bell first demonstrated his invention at the Centennial Exposition in Philadelphia in 1876. In time, the Bell System would become a monolithic communication company. One of its most prominent symbols is that of a Blue Bell. It was apparently the brainchild of Angus Hibbard, the general superintendent for American Telephone and Telegraph Company (AT&T), which was a subsidiary of the American Bell Telephone Company. Hibbard noted in 1888 that blue and white signs

A telephone created by Alexander Graham Bell in 1876. This same year, replicas of the telephone were premiered and demonstrated at the Centennial Exposition in Philadelphia, Pennsylvania. (Hulton Archive/Getty Images)

appeared to stand out better than others, and subsequently he came up with the image of a blue bell (Larned, 2006, 1).

Although they did not have the characteristic crack that so readily distinguishes the Liberty Bell, the signs clearly bore its shape. Moreover, most had an inscription, such as "LONG-DISTANCE TELEPHONE," "BELL SYSTEM," or "LOCAL AND LONG-DISTANCE TELEPHONE" (Larned, 2006). Some were also surrounded by a circle with additional lettering.

Because the bell was a popular symbol that was used, by among others, a Boston fish dealer, it took some time for the company to register the mark (Larned, 2006).

See also: Advertising and the Liberty Bell; Centennial Exposition of 1876

Further Reading

Larned, Larry. 2006. "Birth of the Blue Bell Telephone Sign: The History of the Blue Bell Telephone Sign as Implemented by New England Telephone and Telegraph." https://www.belltelephonesigns.com.

Bells, Belles

There are a number of literary works, some tied to the Liberty Bell, that play off the similarity between the words "bell" and "belle." A belle, of course, is a woman, typically described as young, charming, and beautiful.

A number of pieces of sheet music about the Liberty Bell play on this theme by featuring sketches or photographs of beautiful women on their covers. There is also a Broadway musical, written by Harry B. Smith and others, entitled *The Liberty Belles,* which was performed on Broadway from September 30, 1901, to January 1902, and which described the escapades of a group of schoolgirls who attempt to sneak men in to a midnight supper ("The Liberty Belles," 1901). Apparently, one of its most controversial features was that many of the women in the show were dressed in nightclothes.

During World War II, a number of B-17 Flying Fortresses were designated as "Liberty Belles" and adorned accordingly. World War II also marked the debut of the *Liberty Belle* comic books, whose heroine was also sometimes dubbed "the All-American Girl."

When the Liberty Bell headed to the 128th anniversary of the Battle of Bunker Hill in 1903, a local newspaper published a cartoon portraying the Bunker Hill Monument as a male figure leading the Liberty Bell in a dance (Mires, 2002, 153).

In addition, there have been a number of musical groups, women's sports teams, and social clubs that have dubbed themselves as "Liberty Belles."

See also: Bunker Hill Monument Anniversary in Boston (1903); Liberty Bell as Fighting Inspiration and Symbol; *Liberty Belle* (Comics); Music and the Liberty Bell

Further Reading

"The Liberty Belles." 1901. *The New York Times*, September 29, p. 19.

Mires, Charlene. 2002. *Independence Hall in American Memory*. Philadelphia: University of Pennsylvania Press.

Bell's First Note, The (Painting, 1913)

In 1913, Jean Leon Gerome Ferris (1863–1930) painted a picture titled *The Bell's First Note*. It was designed to represent the testing of the Liberty Bell after its recasting by John Pass and John Stow after the original bell from the Whitechapel Foundry cracked on its first ringing.

The picture portrayed Pass and Stow on the right, the Liberty Bell hanging from a chain in the middle, and a young woman on the left in the company of other well-dressed colonial figures. The woman is posed to hit the bell with a hammer. An explanatory inscription on the frame was as follows:

> The Bell's First Note, 1753: The interior of the Foundry of Pass and Stow at the moment of the testing of the newly cast Liberty Bell. John Pass was a native of Malta, he stands at the right. Isaac Norris in a grey coat was chairman of the committee appointed to superintend the purchase of the State House Bell and Benjamin Franklin is speaking to him. A young woman, a relative of I. Norris, is about to sound the Bell with a hammer. (Rosewater, 1926, 200)

Ferris, a Philadelphia-based artist, was quite prolific, concentrating almost solely on American historical scenes. He is part of the colonial revival movement, which attempted to convey patriotic sentiments through "highly sentimentalized versions of history" (Leminski, 1995, 567), many of which centered on scenes from the

American founding period and the Civil War. One of his more famous paintings, *Writing the Declaration of Independence,* depicts Thomas Jefferson standing at a table where Benjamin Franklin and John Adams are sitting.

When Victor Rosewater wrote *The Liberty Bell: Its History and Significance* in 1926, he reported that a copy of *The Bell's First Note* embellished the drop curtain on the Walnut Street Theater in Philadelphia (1926, 200).

See also: Pass and Stow

Further Reading

Leminski, Karen. 1995. "Picturing American History, 1770–1930." *The Historian* 57 (Spring): 567–572.

Rosewater, Victor. 1926. *The Liberty Bell: Its History and Significance.* New York: D. Appleton and Company.

"Bells of Fate, The" (Song, 1894)

In 1894, W. Witmark & Sons of New York published a piece of sheet music, the words of which were written by Walter H. Ford and the music by John W. Bratton. The song was entitled "The Bells of Fate." The cover, with sketches in blue, portrays a bell with a crack, albeit also with what appear to be (because the words wrap around the bell, not all the words are visible) the words, "Glory to God in the Highest and on Earth Peace Good Will to Men," "A new command I give unto you that you love one another," and "Proclaim Liberty," which were probably borrowed from the Columbian Liberty Bell of the previous year. The title of the song is framed in what appear to be ropes, and the bell itself is topped by several smaller bells and surrounded (from top left to right to bottom left to right, respectively) by pictures of a buoy in the sea, a prison yard, a church steeple with a ringing bell, and an apartment on fire.

The theme of the song is the manner in which bells can signal various life events. The first verse thus portrays church bells bidding people to worship, ringing in joy for a wedding, and tolling for a funeral. These are "The Bells of Fate."

The second verse recounts the story of two shipmates on a sinking ship, both trying to reach a bell buoy, but with only one surviving. The third verse tells of an individual who sacrifices himself while trying to save another from a fire. The fourth verse tells of a mother sadly listening for bells to announce the execution of her son.

The final verse, which comes closest to describing the Liberty Bell, has the following lyrics, which are tied clearly to the American Revolution:

> Round a-bout the ci-ty court-house, stands the crowd with bated breath,
> Each has but one thought, one purpose, "Give me Lib-er-ty or Death,"
> Jus-tice long had been de-nied them, they have been oppressed by might,
> Now the burning question from them, "shall we submit or fight?"
> Hark the ver-y heav-ens trem-ble tyr-an-ny is left be-hind,
> As the old bell loud-ly an-swers, "Lib-er-ty to all man-kind."

Pa-tri-ots from ev-'ry quar-ter, leave their homesteads and their farms,
Wash-ing-ton and other he-roes, heed their coun-try's call "To arms!"

Each verse has a separate chorus, saying "Ding, dong, ding, dong," highlighting
each. The final chorus denotes that this sound "Echoed from State un-to State, Freedom rang out and a nation was born. When proclaimed by the Bells of Fate (Music
Division, the New York Public Library, n.d.).

Like some other songs of the period, "The Bells of Fate" designates today's Liberty Bell as "the old bell."

See also: Columbian Liberty Bell; Music and the Liberty Bell; Names for the Liberty Bell

Further Reading
Music Division, the New York Public Library. n.d. "The Bells of Fate," New York Public
Library Digital Collections. http://digitalcollections.nypl.org/items/510d47de-05d1
-a3d9-e040-e00a18064a99.

Bicentennial and the Liberty Bell

In 1976, the United States celebrated the bicentennial of the American Revolution.
The nation was emerging from the shadow of the Watergate scandal that had led
to the resignation of President Richard M. Nixon, and it was still attempting to rec-
oncile itself to defeat in Vietnam, as well as the domestic turmoil that the war had
brought to college campuses. In the presidential election of that year, the nation
would elect former Georgia governor Jimmy Carter over Gerald R. Ford, who, having been selected by the president and confirmed by majority vote by both houses
of Congress under provisions of the Twenty-fifth Amendment after Vice President
Spiro Agnew resigned, became the nation's first unelected chief executive and
extended a pardon to his predecessor.

Visionary plans to host a world's fair in Philadelphia, similar to that of 1876 and
1926, ultimately failed, and the American Revolution Bicentennial Commission
decided to focus on events throughout the nation rather than concentrating on a single
city (Mires, 2002, 261). One of the symbols that was prominent in the celebration was
an outline of the Liberty Bell, with the crack and the clapper forming the number 76.
The commission organized activities under the headings of "Heritage," "Festival,"
and "Horizons," which were described as follows: "One group of activities would
recall the nation's past; another would stress the purely celebratory note; the third
would address attention to tomorrow's problems and prospects" (Klein, 1977, 258).

Lowenthal (1977) observed that many cities and towns chose to be part of the
celebrations, albeit not always with close attention to historical accuracy. The year
also witnessed scholarly conferences and the publication of a series of bicentennial histories of each of the states, as well as less scholarly cookbooks and essay
contests (Klein, 1977, 259). Television contributed to the celebration by airing a
miniseries called *The Adams Chronicles.*

For its part, Philadelphia prepared for an influx of tourists. Although expecta-
tions of large numbers of tourists may have kept many visitors away, a central

reason for moving the Liberty Bell from Independence Hall to its own pavilion was the concern that Independence Hall would be unable to accommodate the expected number of visitors. For those who could not come to Philadelphia, the American Legion cast a 16,830-pound replica of the Liberty Bell, which it put on a Freedom Train that toured the forty-eight contiguous states.

Although the Centennial Exposition had been a huge success, the Sesquicentennial International Exposition in 1926 had been far less so, in part because Philadelphia considered itself largely to be a manufacturing city, not a tourist locale. By 1976, this mindset had changed, and Philadelphia increasingly came to view itself as a tourist destination (Wilson, 2000).

In addition to witnessing the move of the Liberty Bell from Independence Hall to the Liberty Bell Center, Philadelphia hosted President Ford and Queen Elizabeth II. The queen not only gave a gracious speech but also contributed a Bicentennial Bell to the city.

The Smithsonian Museum of History and Technology (today's National Museum of American History) attempted to recreate the celebration of a century earlier by collecting more than 25,000 objects from the Centennial. It also featured an exhibit entitled "A Nation of Nations," which brought almost 10 million visitors (Gordon, 2013, 117).

Like celebrations before it, the bicentennial was the occasion for the manufacture of numerous souvenirs that either replicated the Liberty Bell or incorporated etchings into glass, or transfers onto ceramics, clothing, and other objects. A writer from *The New York Times* coined the term "Buy-centennial" to describe the more-than-25,000 different products that were created to commemorate the occasion (Gordon, 2013, 123).

The U.S. Post Office also issued a 13-cent stamp that portrayed the words "PROCLAIM LIBERTY THROUGHOUT ALL THE LAND" under a sketch of the Liberty Bell. The U.S. Mint issued a 50-cent coin with a picture of Benjamin Franklin on the front and the Liberty Bell on the back, and a one-dollar coin portraying President Dwight Eisenhower on the front and the Liberty Bell set against the background of the moon in the sky on the back. The year 1976 also marked the release of an album designed to combat tooth decay in children by the heavyweight boxer Muhammad Ali that included a song entitled, "Who Knocked a Crack in the Liberty Bell?"

In 1987, the nation celebrated the bicentennial of the U.S. Constitution, which had also been written in Philadelphia, but one analyst observed, "What planners had envisioned as a six-month celebration of the Constitution had dwindled to a fifteen-hour spectacle on September 17" (Keels, 2017, 334). *Newsweek* commented that "if the people planning Philadelphia's tribute to the Constitution had been in charge in 1776, we'd probably be driving on the left side of the street today" (Keels, 2017, 334). A copy of the Magna Carta, which billionaire Ross Perot had purchased from the relatives of the Earl of Cardigan in 1984, was a highlight of the exhibition in Philadelphia that year ("Perot Purchases a Copy of Magna Carta," 1984). In 2015, the British Museum, in turn, displayed early copies of the Magna Carta, the Declaration of Independence, and the U.S. Constitution to celebrate the Magna Carta's 800th birthday.

In 2003, the state of Ohio celebrated its own bicentennial by commissioning a 230-pound bell for each of its eighty-eight counties. Engineers at the Verdin Company in Cincinnati, which had cast the 66,0000-pound bell for Newport, Kentucky, to celebrate the new millennium, actually built a traveling foundry so the bells could be cast on site in each county. Each bell was etched with both the name of the county and the logo of the state's bicentennial. The total cost of the project was estimated at about $1.9 million. Bells were chosen as emblems of freedom (Emch, 2001).

See also: American Legion Freedom Bell; Bicentennial Bell; Coins, Medals, and Stamps Depicting the Liberty Bell; Sesquicentennial International Exposition; Tourism and the Liberty Bell; "Who Knocked a Crack in the Liberty Bell?" (Song, 1976)

Further Reading

Emch, Dale. 2001. "Ohio Bicentennial: 88 County Bells an Appealing Memorial." *The Blade,* December 16. https://www.toledoblade.com/State/2001/12/16/Ohio -bicentennial-88-county-bells-an-appealing-memorial.html.

Gordon, Tammy S. 2013. *The Spirit of 1976: Commerce, Community, and the Politics of Commemoration.* Amherst: University of Massachusetts Press.

Keels, Thomas H. 2017. *Sesqui! Greed, Graft, and the Forgotten World's Fair of 1926.* Philadelphia: Temple University Press.

Klein, Milton M. 1977. "Commemorating the American Revolution: The Bicentennial and Its Predecessors." *New York History* 58 (July): 257–276.

Lowenthal, David. 1977. "The Bicentennial Landscape: A Mirror Held Up to the Past." *Geographical Review* 67 (July): 253–267.

Mires, Charlene. 2002. *Independence Hall in American Memory.* Philadelphia: University of Pennsylvania Press.

"Perot Purchases a Copy of Magna Carta." 1984. *The New York Times,* September 27. https://www.nytimes.com/1984/09/27/us/perot-purchases-a-copy-of-magna-carta .html.

Wilson, Martin W. 2000. *From the Sesquicentennial to the Bicentennial: Changing Attitudes Toward Tourism in Philadelphia, 1926–1976.* PhD dissertation at Temple University, January.

Bicentennial Bell

In 1976, as the United States was celebrating the bicentennial of its independence, Queen Elizabeth II of Great Britain visited Independence Hall on July 6. Speaking as a descendant of George III, the queen gave a gracious speech in which she indicated "that Independence Day, the Fourth of July, should be celebrated as much in Britain as in America," because Americans had taught its mother nation the valuable lesson that statesmanship consisted of knowing "the right time, and the manner of yielding, what is impossible to keep" (*Men in Blazers,* 2012).

The queen further emphasized that both countries shared the heritage of the Magna Carta, and that British recognition of the rights of people to govern themselves had led to the transformation of "an Empire into a Commonwealth!" (*Men in Blazers,* 2012). The queen's words were considerably more gracious than those of former president Benjamin Harrison. As the Liberty Bell was passing through Indianapolis in 1893, he had observed, "This old bell was made in England, but it

The Belmont County Courthouse in St. Clairsville, Ohio, provides the setting for the Bicentennial Bell. (Jacqueline Nix/Dreamstime.com)

had to be re-cast in America before it was attuned to proclaim the right of self-government and the equal rights of men" (Townsend and Zettle Sterling, 2017). His sentiment was very similar to that of a guidebook prepared in 1875 for centennial celebrations the next year. It said that "the tones learned in Britain could not be repeated in the land prepared for Democracy. The bell on its first trial in this country, was found to have lost its voice" (Paige, 1988, 85).

Queen Elizabeth continued: "This morning I saw the famous Liberty Bell. It came here over 200 years ago when Philadelphia, after London, was the largest English-speaking city in the world. It was cast to commemorate the Pennsylvania Charter of Privileges, but is better known for its association with the Declaration of Independence" (*Men in Blazers*, 2012). That same day, the queen was quoted as saying, "You know this is one of the finest symbols of any country in the world. Everyone knows about the Liberty Bell" (Sands and Bartlett, 2012, 125).

The queen then presented the city with a giant Bicentennial Bell, made at the same Whitechapel Foundry that cast the original Liberty Bell; it weighed 12,446 pounds (Duncan, 2013).

This bell had the following inscription (Duncan, 2013):

> FOR THE PEOPLE OF THE UNITED STATES OF AMERICA
> FROM THE PEOPLE OF BRITAIN
> 4 JULY 1976
> LET FREEDOM RING

The next day, the queen visited the White House, where the Captain and Tennille decided to play "The Way I Want to Touch You" and "Muskrat Love," which provoked considerable controversy (Tauber, 2016).

Originally housed in the brick tower at a visitor's center that was constructed especially for the bicentennial, the Bicentennial Bell was moved in 2013 to create space for the Museum of the American Revolution and has been in storage since that time. There are renewed efforts to feature the bell in the center of a Bicentennial Bell Garden with a plaque commemorating the queen's speech (De Groot, 2018).

See also: Bicentennial and the Liberty Bell; Declaration of Independence and the Liberty Bell; Presidents and Foreign Dignitaries at the Liberty Bell; Whitechapel Foundry

Further Reading

De Groot, Kristen. 2018. "Philly Group Wants the City's Other Liberty Bell Put on Display," March 13. http://www.mcall.com/news/nationworld/pennsylvania/mc-nws-philadelphia-bicentennial-bell-20180331-story.html.

Duncan, Adam. 2013. "NPS Relocates the Bicentennial Bell," January 31. https://www.nps.gov/inde/learn/news/nps-relocates-the-biceteennial-bell.htm.

Paige, John C. 1988. *The Liberty Bell of Independence National Historical Park: A Special History Study*, ed. David C. Kimball. Denver: Denver Service Center, National Park Service, Department of the Interior.

"The Queen's Speech." 2012. *Men in Blazers*, June 13. https://meninblazers.com/2012/06/13/queen-elizabeth-bicentennial.

Sands, Robert W., Jr., and Alexander B. Bartlett. 2002. *Images of America: Independence Hall and the Liberty Bell*. Charleston, SC: Arcadia Publishing.

Tauber, Michelle. 2016. "'Mr. President, It Was Muskrats': Toni Tennille on the Time She Sang 'Muskrat Love' for Queen Elizabeth—in the White House!" *People,* March 19. https://people.com/royals/toni-tennille-on-the-time-she-sang-muskrat-love-for-queen-elizabeth.

Townsend, Jen, and Renee Zettle-Sterling. 2017. "Liberty Cast and Recast." *CAST* (blog). July 4. https://www.castartandobjects.com/blog/2017/7/4/liberty-cast-and-recast.

Bunker Hill Monument Anniversary in Boston (1903)

The shortest out-of-state trip that the Liberty Bell took on its seven journeys from 1885 to 1915, and its only trip to New England, took place in 1903 for the commemoration of the 128th anniversary of the Revolutionary War Battle of Bunker Hill. The cornerstone of the monument, a giant obelisk (initially the largest in the United States) on Breed's Hill, had been laid in 1825 to commemorate the battle that had actually begun before the colonies declared their independence (Clark, 2018, 51). It had been designed to remind city residents and visitors alike of Boston's contribution to the American Revolution.

The Bell left Philadelphia by train on June 15, passing through Trenton, Princeton, New Brunswick, Elizabeth, Newark, Jersey City, Harlem River, Stamford, Bridgeport, New Haven, Willimantic, and Providence before reaching Boston on June 16 (Paige, 1988, 107–108). Princeton, of course, had been the site of a Revolutionary battle; it also was the site of a university, whose president, John Witherspoon, had signed the Declaration of Independence, and whose graduates had included Benjamin Rush, James Madison, and many other statesmen. According to Gary North, "the entire town and gown" showed up for this twenty-minute event (2010, 103). Nash also reports that 20,000 people walked around the Bell when it stopped at New Haven, the home of Yale University (2010, 104).

The Liberty Bell had rung out on June 1, 1774, to mourn the closing of Boston Harbor and other Coercive, or Intolerable, Acts. While Philadelphia had been the site of the Second Continental Congress and the Constitutional Convention of 1787, Boston and the state of Massachusetts (which had elected both John and Samuel Adams to the Continental Congress) had been far ahead of Philadelphia in calling for independence from Great Britain. Charlene Mires thus likened the trip to Boston as "a reunion in which cousins competed for attention, reflecting a rivalry between Philadelphia and Boston as cities that made vital contributions to the American Revolution" (2002, 157). Boston had begun preserving its own landmarks in the 1820s about the same time that Philadelphia had begun to recognize the iconic value of Independence Hall, but Boston had created the Common in front of its Old State House long before Philadelphia did the same (Clark, 2018, 52).

A picture from the time shows the Bell aboard a wagon surrounded by soldiers and dignitaries, with a man dressed as Uncle Sam to the right of the Bell. While the Liberty Bell was in Boston, it was joined by John Brown's Bell, which is sometimes designated as the "second-most important bell in American history," after the Liberty Bell (Lynch, 2008). The John Brown Bell, which ordinarily resides in Marborough, Massachusetts, was the name given to the 700- to 800-pound bell that hung in the armory where abolitionist John Brown carried out a raid in 1859 at Harpers Ferry, Virginia (now West Virginia), before being captured by Robert E. Lee and his marines. When Union forces captured the city in 1861, they removed the bell to keep it from being melted down for weapons—while the bell dropped while being lowered, it did not crack, as the Liberty Bell had (Abshire, 2008, 16). Initially leaving the bell in Maryland in the care of William and Elizabeth Ensminger (later Snyder), who kept it buried for seven years, veterans from Marlborough subsequently brought it to their town in the 1890s, where it hung for many years outside the building of the veterans' organization, the Grand Army of the Republic (GAR). This is the place from which it would have been

The Bunker Hill Monument in Boston, Massachusetts. The monument was built to commemorate the Battle of Bunker Hill, where British and U.S. troops fought during the Revolutionary War in 1775. (Library of Congress)

transported to Boston. Since then, residents of Harpers Ferry have attempted to regain custody of the bell.

Portraying the day the Liberty Bell arrived as the meeting of two relics, Boston's mayor, Patrick Collins, observed in his welcoming speech that the "Liberty Bell kisses the sacred soil of Bunker Hill, making it more sacred than ever" ("Liberty Bell in Boston," 1903). Mires notes that a cartoon in the *Boston Daily Globe* depicted the Bunker Hill Monument and the Liberty Bell engaged in a dance, with the monument playing the role of the leading male partner (2002, 153). In 1968, the John Brown Bell was moved to a stone bell tower, and the GAR building was subsequently razed (Abshire, 2008, 23). A plaque that is attached to the tower says, "The John Brown Bell—Symbol of a nation's efforts to obtain freedom and equality for all people" (Abshire, 2008, 23).

On June 18, the Liberty Bell was back on the tracks. It spent the night at Plymouth, Massachusetts, where the Pilgrims had landed in 1620. It subsequently passed through Middleboro, Taunton, Attleboro, Providence, Stonington, and New London, back through Harlem River, and then through Jersey City before arriving back in Philadelphia on June 18 (Paige, 1988, 109–110).

See also: Journeys of the Liberty Bell; Occasions for Ringing the Liberty Bell

Further Reading

Abshire, Joan. 2008. *The John Brown Bell: The Journey of the Second-Most Important Bell in American History, from Harpers Ferry, West Virginia, to Marlborough Massachusetts.* Marlborough Historical Society. www.historicmarlborough.org/resources/John+Brown+Bell.pdf.

Clark, Justin T. 2018. *City of Second Sight: Nineteenth-Century Boston and the Making of American Visual Culture.* Chapel Hill: University of North Carolina Press.

"Liberty Bell in Boston." 1903. *The Sacred Heart Review* 19 (25), June 20. https://newspapers.bc.edu/?a=d&d=BOSTONSH19030620-01.2.13.

Liberty Bell—at Bunker Hill, Boston, June. 1903. Photograph. Library of Congress. https://www.loc.gov/item/2003653808.

Lynch, Matt. 2008. "For Whom Should John Brown's Bell Toll?" *Wicked Local Marlborough,* July 22. http://marlborough.wickedlocal.com/x1625323222/For-whom-should-John-Browns-bell-toll.

Mires, Charlene. 2002. *Independence Hall in American Memory.* Philadelphia: University of Pennsylvania Press.

Nash, Garb B. *The Liberty Bell.* New Haven, CT: Yale University Press.

Paige, John C. 1988. *The Liberty Bell: A Special History Study.* David C. Kimball, ed. Denver: Denver Service Center and Independence National Historical Park.

C

Campaign Buttons and the Liberty Bell

Philadelphia has been the site of Republican Party presidential nominating conventions in 1856, 1872, 1900, 1940, 1948, and 2000, and of Democratic Party conventions in 1936, 1948, and 2016. Although candidates have in recent years been able to amass the necessary votes through primary elections and other contests that take place prior to these meetings, the sites nonetheless can influence public perceptions of the events. Police responses to demonstrators at the Chicago Democratic Convention of 1968 provide a good example.

Like the U.S. flag, the Statue of Liberty, and similar symbols, the Liberty Bell not only highlights American values, but also taps into deep emotional responses. It is, therefore, hardly surprising that a number of campaign buttons have featured the Liberty Bell. Before it was used in political campaigns, the Bell was portrayed on buttons designed to show support for the Liberty Loan campaign.

Perhaps in anticipation of the sesquicentennial of 1926, all three main presidential candidates used this symbol on buttons in 1924. The Democratic candidate Al Smith's campaign had a button with an outline of the Liberty Bell, on which these words were printed:

American
Liberty
Smith

Meanwhile, the Republican candidate, Calvin Coolidge, had a button with a red, white, and blue stripe with the Liberty Bell in the middle. This may have been a reference to the fact that Coolidge's birthday was July 4. That same year, the Progressive candidate Robert La Follette issued a button with the words "LA FOLLETTE WHEELER" around the side of a depiction of the Liberty Bell, with "'76" and its distinctive crack in the center. The Women's Organization for National Prohibition Reform produced an enamel Liberty Bell pin. Its initials were inscribed in white against the blue yoke of the Bell, the word "REPEAL" on the shoulder, and "18th AMENDMENT" on the waist, against a red background.

In 1936 and 1940, the Republicans Alf Landon and Wendell Willkie used a picture of the Liberty Bell and the words "Ring It Again" on some of their buttons. They were designed to highlight their opposition to what they considered to be the socialistic aspects of Franklin D. Roosevelt's New Deal programs (Gardello, 2014, 72).

In 1948, the Liberty Bell appeared on a button by supporters of Henry Wallace's third-party bid for the presidency, with the words "WIN WITH WALLACE." The

Truman Library has a button for Harry S. Truman's election that same year shaped like the Liberty Bell and the words "IT'S TRUE LIBERTY WITH A TRUMAN" ("Truman Campaign Button," n.d.).

There is also a button for the reelection campaign for President Ronald Reagan with a sketch of the Liberty Bell, complete with its crack, and the words "VOTE REAGAN TO KEEP IT" around the sides. Another button, which says "Reagan Bell Ringer 1984," with a similar bell in the middle, was presumably worn by individuals who rang doorbells for the candidate.

The Liberty Bell undoubtedly has been used to advance causes as well as candidates. The Liberty Bond drives that were conducted during and after World War I sometimes issued buttons that featured pictures of the Liberty Bell. There is a button that was issued in 1915 with the picture of the Liberty Bell in the center, with the dates "1776" and "1915" at the top and bottom and the words "Liberty" and "Justice" on either side, with an attached ribbon with the U.S. flag and another with the words "Votes for Women" ("Liberty Bell Button with Attached American Flag and 'Votes for Women' Ribbon," n.d.). By listing the word "Justice," this button also highlighted the Justice Bell, which was taken on tour throughout Pennsylvania to advocate for the cause of women's suffrage.

See also: Justice Bell; Liberty Loans; Presidents and Foreign Dignitaries at the Liberty Bell

Further Reading

Gardella, Peter. 2014. *American Civil Religion: What Americans Hold Sacred.* New York: Oxford University Press.

"Liberty Bell Button with Attached American Flag and 'Votes for Women' Ribbon." n.d. Ann Lewis Women's Suffrage Collection. https://lewissuffragecollection.omeka.net /items/show/1050.

"Truman Campaign Button." n.d. Truman Library. https://www.trumanlibrary.org /photographs/view.php?id=20596.

Canadian Liberty Bells

American culture has influenced other cultures, especially those of its geographical and ideological neighbors and allies. It is not surprising, therefore, that there are at least three bells in Canada that have been designated as Liberty Bells. At least two of the three have direct ties to the United States.

Canada began as a colony of France, and it was ceded to the British after they defeated the French during the French and Indian War. Even after Canada achieved basic independence in 1867, it remained a member of the British Commonwealth of Nations, and the English monarch remains the head of state of Canada.

During the early phases of the movement to achieve Canadian independence, a bell in St. Denis mustered men to prevent the English from arresting and hanging Louis-Joseph Patineau and others associated with the Members of the Legislative Assembly (MLA). Patineau, however, had the opportunity to flee to the state of Vermont and took advantage of it. In time, Britain decided that it needed to be more responsive to Canadian sentiments for independence. This led to the British North

America Act of 1867, which created the Canadian Confederation, in which the provinces achieved great autonomy.

A ship called *Victoria* transported John A. MacDonald, George Brown, George-Étienne Cartier, and other Canadian representatives from Ontario and Quebec to Charlottestown on August 31, 1865, to negotiate the deal that would lead to the British North America Act. Then, the *Victoria* began to sink off the coast of North Carolina, and its forty-one crew members were saved by sailors on the *Ponvert*, a vessel based in Maine. In appreciation, Paul Pouilot of Quebec City, the captain of the *Victoria,* donated the ship's bell, which had also been rescued, to Rufus Allen, the skipper of the *Ponvert*, who in turn gave it to the Gouldsboro District school board in Maine.

In 2014, the Canadian Museum of History requested the bell for a fifteen-month display, intended to mark the 150th anniversary of the events leading up to the British North America Act. Despite some initial opposition, Roger Bowen, a member of the Gouldsboro village council, persuaded the village to lend the bell to the museum (Bosanac, 2014).

Yet another Canadian Liberty Bell dates back to 1850, when African Americans were still held in bondage in the United States. Many sought to escape to the free soil of Canada through the Underground Railroad. After a mission in Buxton, Canada, just across the border of the United States on the other side of Lake Erie in Ontario, announced that it was willing to accept such fugitives, African Americans in Pittsburgh, when Pennsylvania was a free state (albeit one from which escaped slaves could be recaptured under U.S. Fugitive Slave Laws), sent the town a 550-pound bell to celebrate the arrival of each new former slave. It was inscribed as follows:

CAST BY
A. FULTON,
PITTSBURG PA.
1850
PRESENTED TO THE
REV WM KING BY THE
COLOURED INHABITANTS
OF PITTSBURG, FOR THE
ACADEMY AT RALEIGH
C. WEST

The date of 1850 on the fourth line was flanked by an engraving of an eagle on each side.

Since 1858, the bell has hung in the steeple of St. Andrew's United Church of Canada. A replica, created by sculptor Brett Davis, was dedicated in 2007 and stands outside the Buxton Museum at the Buxton National Historic Site & Museum ("The Liberty Bell, 1850—Buxton Settlement, Raleigh ON—Bells on Waymarking.com," n.d.).

Plaques outside the bell recorded correspondence between the church at Pittsburgh and the Buxton settlement. One such correspondence, dated November 12, 1850, reminds former slaves that "[y]ou are now in a land of liberty, where the rights and privileges of freemen are secured to you by law." Trusting that these individuals would not forget the God of their fathers, it ended with a plea that "when the bell, with all its solemn tones, calls you to the house of God, remember your brethren who are in bonds; and let your prayer ascend to God, that He may, in His own good time, break every yoke and let the oppressed go free; that he may turn both the heart of the Masters and Servants from the bondage of Satan to the service of the one living and true God" ("The Liberty Bell, 1850—Buxton Settlement, Raleigh ON—Bells on Waymarking.com," n.d.).

Members of the Canadian congregation wrote an equally poignant letter in return. It observed, "We are delighted at all times to hear from the friends that we have left in a land of pretend freedom." It further promised to remember those back in the United States in prayer: "[W]e will then remember our brethren who are in less favourable circumstances; and our constant prayer will be that the Bible, the gift of God to man, may no longer be withheld from you by the unrighteous acts of professed Christian legislators; that the power of the oppressors may be broken, and that those who have long been held in bondage may be set free" ("The Liberty Bell, 1850—Buxton Settlement, Raleigh ON—Bells on Waymarking.com," n.d.).

Seventy residents of Buxton are recorded as having fought for the Union during the Civil War, and many of them remained in the United States. In 2007, a delegation from Pittsburgh visited Buxton to renew their earlier friendship and participate in a Labor Day parade (Hayes, 2007).

See also: Abolitionists and the Liberty Bell; Replicas of the Liberty Bell

Further Reading

Bosanac, Alexandra. 2014. "Canada's 'Liberty Bell' Comes Home After 150 Years on U.S. Soil." *Huffington Post,* June 30. https://www.huffingtonpost.ca/2014/06/30/canada -liberty-bell-charlottetown_n_5542988.html.

"The Canadian Liberty Bell." n.d. http://www.riches-lieux.com/wp-content/uploads/2018 /05/The-Canadian-Liberty-Bell.pdf.

Hayes, Monica. 2007. "Local Group to Renew Ties to Canadian City Founded by Ex-slaves." *Pittsburgh Post-Gazette,* August 20. http://www.post-gazette.com/life /lifestyle/2007/08/20/Local-group-to-renew-ties-to-Canadian-city-founded-by-ex -slaves/stories/200708200198.

"The Liberty Bell, 1850—Buxton Settlement, Raleigh ON—Bells on Waymarking.com." n.d. http://www.waymarking.com/waymarks/WMJDN1_The-Liberty_Bell_1850 _Buxton_Settlement_Raleigh_OH.

Cartoons and the Liberty Bell

One evidence of the widespread recognition of the Liberty Bell as a symbol has been its use in cartoons, especially those of a political nature. Jonathan Leigh Tafel observed in his dissertation on the depiction of the Fourth of July holiday in newspaper cartoons from 1890 to the late 1970s that the use of the image of the Liberty Bell skyrocketed over the decades (Tafel, 1979, 145). He noted that although the Bell was a concrete object, it "is abstract in that it has come to represent and stand for the abstract qualities of freedom, liberty, and independence and is seen as a symbol which depicts such meanings" (Tafel, 1979, 145). Consistent with subsequent studies about the fact that many people identify the Bell with its distinctive feature, Tafel further observed that "The cartoonist make use of the crack in the Liberty Bell to accentuate their point" (Tafel, 1979, 147).

In addition, he found that the Bell had been connected to three main themes. One was that of commemoration, emphasizing "liberty, freedom, and individual rights" (Tafel, 1979, 151). Another was that of dissatisfaction, highlighting "discontent with American society" (Tafel, 1969, 151). The third was that of warning, which typically focused on "impending perils" (Tafel, 1969, 152). A striking illustration of the second such usage is found in a posting under American Reform entitled the "Liberty Bell Café" ("Liberty Bell Cafe," n.d.). A cartoon pictures a Native American walking past the Liberty Bell Café. The sign behind him reads, "We're All Americans, Buy War Bonds." (But, note that another sign, in the window of the café, reads, "Indians use back door.")

A number of more recent cartoons have pushed back against having to go through security to see the Bell. One cartoon, published by Pat Martin on September 27, 2015, coincided with the visit of Pope Francis to see the Bell. After an accompanying monk tells the pope that "There's talk you may heal the crack," Francis responds, "That's one miracle only the American people can do."

See also: Independence Day; Security for the Liberty Bell; Symbolism of the Liberty Bell

Further Reading

Callahan, Robey. 1999. "The Liberty Bell: From Commodity to Sacred Object." *Journal of Material Culture* 4 (1): 57–78.

"Liberty Bell Cafe." n.d. *American Reform.* https://sites.google.com/a/nexgenacademy.com /more-than-laissez-faire/african-native-american/african-native-american -political-cartoons-1/liberty-bell-cafe.

Tafel, Jonathan Leigh. 1979. *The Historical Development of Political and Patriotic Images of America: A Visual Analysis of Fourth of July Cartoons in Five Newspapers.* PhD dissertation at Ohio State University.

Casting the Liberty Bell

Although modern processes are more mechanized and sophisticated, bell casting remained much the same for thousands of years.

The process begins when the bell-makers establish the appropriate shape, or profile, for the bell in question. They know that different shapes produce different sounds, which can largely be calculated mathematically before the bells are cast.

Bell-makers first create a mold for the inside of the bell, known as the "core," over which they place a mold for the outside, or "cope," of the bell. The process has been likened to inverting a larger flowerpot over a smaller one and then filling the space between them with metal (Boland, 1973, 31).

For a bell as large as the Liberty Bell, it was common to dig a pit near the spot where the metal (largely a combination of copper and tin) would be melted for pouring. The pit was built over a brick base with a hollow core. It would have a post in the center, to which a spindle would be attached with a wooden board, known as the "strickle board," shaped to mimic the inside of the bell, and rotated. The base would be covered with a mixture of clay, horse manure, cow's hair, and water (Boland, 1973, 31). The Annecy Bell Company of Rance, which made fifty-seven replicas of the Liberty Bell in 1957, apparently also adds egg whites to this mix (Campbell, 2018). Then a fire would be lit inside the brick base and the mixture is shaped by the strickle board to conform to the desired shape of the bell.

Once this core was shaped, it was greased, typically with pig fat, and then covered with layers of straw rope to create a mold for the cope, which was shaped by yet another strickle board. Once the core and the cope were lifted from their clay models, each would have been coated with china clay, with the places on the cope where printing was to be placed filled with soft clay. As one was placed over the other, the cannon loops would be attached to the cope, with one hole left, into which the molten metal could be poured, and another that would allow air to escape. After the metal cooled, the cope would be lifted and the bell tuned. Boland notes that in modern times, cast-iron cores have replaced the mixture of dung and clay, and "mechanically tuned lathes and sensitive electronic tuning instruments are in use" (Boland, 1973, 35).

The Liberty Bell was cast three times. It was created at the Whitechapel Foundry in England in 1752 and then sent by ship to the United States. It cracked on the first ringing, perhaps because it had been damaged in shipping, perhaps because it was overly brittle, or possibly because the individual who rung the Bell did so improperly.

Two local ironworkers, John Pass and John Stow, subsequently offered to recast the bell from the original one, which they would have beaten into small bits, probably with sledgehammers. They also added copper so the bell would not be as brittle. After residents complained about the poor sound of this recasting, Pass and Stow recast the bell again to make the current Liberty Bell.

Whitechapel also sent a "sister" bell to replace the original, which was used to mark time in connection with a clock with faces on the east and west sides of the building. This bell, which was later replaced and sold to a local church, was damaged in a fire and was itself recast. It now resides on the campus of Villanova University.

In 2006, ASM International (the Materials Information Society, previously called the American Society for Metals) recognized the Liberty Bell as a recipient of its ASM Historical Landmark Award, for contributions that it has made to the advancement of understanding of metals and metalworking ("ASM Historical Landmarks," n.d.).

See also: Crack in the Liberty Bell; Pass and Stow; Sister to the Liberty Bell; Whitechapel Foundry

Further Reading

"ASM Historical Landmarks." n.d. https://www.asminternational.org/membership/awards /historical-landmarks.

"Bells and Bell-Founding." 1854. *The Illustrated Magazine of Art.* 3 (15): 167–176.

Boland, Charles Michael. 1973. *Ring in the Jubilee: The Epic of America's Liberty Bell.* Riverside, CT: Chatham Press.

Campbell, Tom. 2018. "The Annecy Liberty Bell Replica." Tom Loves the Liberty Bell .com, June 19. http://tomlovesthelibertybell.com/2018/06/10/the-annecy-liberty-bell -replica.

"Casting the Liberty Bell." National Science Foundation. https://www.nsf.gov/news/special _reports/liberty/01_history_01.jsp.

Kramer, Justin. 1975. *Cast in America: The Historically Accurate, Exciting Story of the Liberty Bell.* Los Angeles: Justin Kramer Incorporated.

Munteanu, Sorin Ion, Ioan Cilbanu, and Viorel Ene. 2011. "The Heaviest Cast Bells Existing in the World—Art of Casting." *Metalurgia International* 16: 56–62.

Celebration 1976 (Print)

Norman Rockwell (1894–1978), born in New York, was a beloved illustrator who celebrated simple American values. His illustrations, which included depictions of Rosie the Riveter and The Four Freedoms, often appeared on the cover of the *Saturday Evening Post*. His last painting and illustrated magazine cover was entitled *Celebration 1976,* or *Liberty Bell* by his museum, which issued a limited-edition lithograph in 1976.

The painting, which measures 45 by 33 inches, features Rockwell himself, with white hair and a cane tucked under his left arm, and smoking a pipe, which was a signature trademark of the artist. He stands with his left side toward the viewer and faces the Liberty Bell, on which he is pictured placing a red ribbon with the words "Happy Birthday," in celebration of the nation's bicentennial. On the floor in front of Rockwell is his open paint box which is, in turn, lying over another red ribbon.

The illustration was commissioned by *American Artist* magazine, and it was Rockwell's second for that magazine. Rockwell signed it in the bottom-right corner.

See also: Bicentennial and the Liberty Bell

Further Reading

Hennessey, Maureen Hart ed. 1999. *Norman Rockwell: Pictures for the American People.* New York: Harry N. Abrams.

"Historic Hand Signed Norman Rockwell Lithograph Entitled 'Celebration' and/or 'Liberty Bell.'" n.d. https://worthingtongalleries.com/shop/art-subject/american -revolutionary-war/historic-hand-signed-norman-rockwell-lithograph-entitled -celebration-andor-liberty-bell.

Centennial Bell

The bell that currently occupies the steeple of Independence Hall is not the Liberty Bell, which has its own exhibition center, but a bell that was donated by Henry Seybert (1801–1883) on the centennial of the Declaration of Independence in 1876. It, in turn, replaced a bell weighing just over two tons that had been crafted by John Wilbank and placed in the tower in 1828.

Born to a wealthy doctor who was later elected to Congress, Seybert studied mineralogy at the École des Mines in Paris and became a leading mineralogist. He became increasingly interested in spiritualism after the death of his father (his mother had died giving birth to him). In the early 1860s, Seybert had attempted to raise subscriptions for a new bell for Independence Hall, but this effort did not succeed. As the centennial approached, however, he decided that he would give the city a 13,000-pound bell (1,000 pounds for each of the original states) and an accompanying clock. In a letter dated April 5, 1876, that he wrote to the Select and Common Councils of the City of Philadelphia, he described the way he hoped to have the bell inscribed as follows (Frazier, 1978, 49):

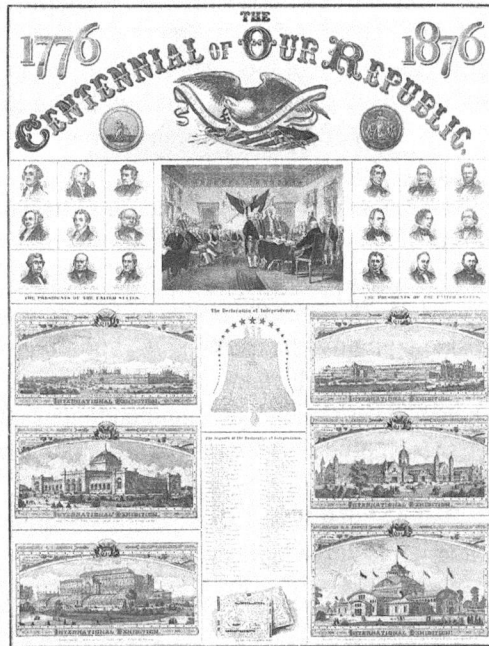

A poster celebrates the centennial, or 100-year anniversary, of U.S. independence. Depicted on the poster are portraits of former presidents, buildings, and what is likely the Liberty Bell in the center, among other patriotic symbols. (Library of Congress)

July the Fourth, 1876
And the arms of the United States of North America, with their motto "E Pluribus Unum," together with the two Scriptural verses: "Glory to God in the highest and on earth, good will toward men," Luke II, 14. "Proclaim liberty throughout all the land unto all the inhabitants thereof," Leviticus XXV, 10. And the following:
"Presented to the City of Philadelphia,
For the Belfry of Independence Hall in the names of
Adam and Maria Sarah Seybert, and Caroline, their daughter
By their son and brother."

Seybert further indicated that he wanted the bell to be rung at noon on July 4, 1876, with the Scriptures passage from Luke to be telegraphed by the U.S. president by Atlantic cable to foreign nations. After prayers, the reading of the Declaration of Independence and the Emancipation Proclamation, and an oration, he further requested that the bell be rung with seventy-six peals, followed at midnight with thirty-seven peals, one for each state in the Union at the time (Frazier, 1978, 50).

After some wrangling over including the family names, and over whether the tower could support a much heavier bell, the city agreed to spend $1,000 to reinforce the building, and Sebert agreed to omit the names.

Seybert purchased the 13,000-pound bell from the Meneely-Kimberly Foundry in Troy, New York. One of the most unique features of the bell was that, in an effort to promote national unity and reconciliation, it included four cannons, including one from each side of the Revolutionary War (in the battle of Sarasota) and the Civil War (in the Battle of Gettysburg). Almost as if to repeat the history of the Liberty Bell, however, it was recast before being brought back to the tower in November 1876, after complaints about the bell's tone.

W. E. Harper of the Seth Thomas Company helped with the clock, which contained weights totaling 4,250 pounds. Apparently, Seybert's plan for the inscription were changed. According to a website of the Friends of Independence National Historical Park, one side of the bell now says, "Presented to the city of Philadelphia, July 4, 1876, for the belfry of Independence Hall, by a citizen," and the opposite side contains "the date '1776' and the great Seal of the United States set in a shield containing thirteen stars." This site further reports that this bell is rung on an hourly basis (Friends of Independence National Historical Park, n.d.).

A speech prepared but apparently not delivered by James Rood Doolittle, a former U.S. senator from Wisconsin, in Chicago on July 4, 1893, referred to the Liberty Bell as "that 'Old Liberty Bell'" (Mowry, 1928, 226). It also called the new Centennial Bell the "GREAT MILLENNIAL BELL" (Mowry, 1928, 232).

See also: Leviticus 25:10; Replicas of the Liberty Bell; Wilbank, John

Further Reading

Bradshaw, Wellesley. 1876. *History and Legends of the Old Liberty Bell in Independence Hall, at Philadelphia. To Which Is Added That of the New Bell.* Philadelphia: C. W. Alexander.

Frazier, Arthur H. 1978. "Henry Seybert and the Centennial Clock and Bell at Independence Hall." *Pennsylvania Magazine of History and Biography* 102 (January): 40–58.

Friends of Independence National Historical Park. n.d. "Other Bells at Independence NHP." http://friendsofindependence.org/other-bells-at-independence-nhp.

Longshore, Jos. S., and Benjamin L. Knowles. 1876. *The Centennial Liberty Bell. Independence Hall; Its tradition and Associations. The Declaration of Independence and Its Signers. With an Appendix Embracing the Opening Ceremonies of the International Exhibition, and of the Centennial Celebration of July 4th, 1876.* Philadelphia: Claxton, Remsen & Haffelfinger.

Mowry, Duane. 1928. "An Address Which Was Not Delivered: Fourth of July Oration of Hon. James R. Doolittle." *Journal of the Illinois State Historical Society* 32 (July): 224–232.

Centennial Exposition of 1876

One way that Philadelphia has highlighted its connection to the Declaration of Independence and the Liberty Bell is through expositions and commemorations. In 1876, the city hosted the nation's first World's Fair, officially designated as the 1876 International Exhibition of Arts, Manufacturers, and Products of the Soil and Mine, but more generally and popularly called the Centennial Exposition. Not everyone would have agreed, but in his annual message of 1876, Philadelphia mayor W. Freeland Kendrick had observed, "All that this country has been, is, or will be has its fountainhead in Philadelphia" (Evensen, 1993, 8).

The exposition was held at Fairmount Park, with the largest building covering twenty-one-and-a-half acres, but the city exerted effort to encourage the 10 million attendees to also stop by Independence Hall to see the Liberty Bell, which had been moved to the vestibule near a life-size statue of George Washington so that the visitors would see it as they first entered the building. The brainchild of Professor John Campbell of Wabash College in Indiana and of General Charles B. Norton, who both had served as the U.S. commissioners of the 1867 Paris Exposition, the Centennial, which was held from May 10 to November 10, 1876, during the period during which Congress was still seeking to reconstruct Southern-state governments, was designed in part to unify the nation and to give it a psychological boost in the aftermath of the panic of 1873.

One of the most prominent displays at the exposition included the arm and torch of the Statue of Liberty, which the French government was giving to the United States as a reminder of the two nations' ties during the Revolutionary War. Henry Seybert also commissioned the Meneely-Kimberly Foundry in New York to cast a 13,000-pound Centennial Bell (he had it recast because the sound of the first version was not considered to be pleasing) that would hang in the steeple at Independence Hall and that rang for half an hour at the beginning of the exposition. Moreover, the federal government sent the original signed Declaration of Independence so that it could be displayed in a glass-fronted safe (Mires, 2002, 126).

One of the highlights of the exposition was a set of 13 centennial chimes that was manufactured by the McShane Bell Foundry of Maryland. Ranging in weight from 300 to 4,000 pounds, they were hung in the main tower, near the main entrance to the exposition. In addition to ringing each morning, noon, and evening, the bells played patriotic music (McShane Bell Foundry, n.d.). The bells were operated by two full rows of manual levers and another row of pedals and were subsequently moved to the Episcopal Cathedral of the Incarnation in Garden City on Long Island, New York (TowerBells.org, n.d.).

Replicas of the Liberty Bell were reproduced in sugar, chocolate, and soap. An exhibit from Kansas featured a twenty-foot model of the U.S. Capitol dome beneath a replica of the Liberty Bell. The done itself was described as being (Horwitz, 1976, 29, 31)

> covered with winter apples of various hues and was supported upon a series of glass columns, filled with barley, oats, corn and other cereals giving them a checkered and pleasing appearance. These, in turn, rested upon a cruciform table, which was literally filled to overflowing with specimens of apples, pears and grains; and at the foot of the latter was a narrow platform filled with vegetables of such gigantic growth as is only known in the west; among them being superb sweet potatoes, colossal ears of corn, beautiful beets, ponderous onions and weighty squashes.

The crowd on the opening day of the fair numbered about 186,000, which was thought to have been the largest gathering on the continent to that point (Nash, 2010, 65). The exhibition churned out thousands of items in the shape of or with the image of the Liberty Bell, while states exhibited replicas of stone, wood, sugar, and even tobacco (Nash, 2010, 66). Much of the fair focused on technological innovations, including Alexander Graham Bell's telephone, a Remington typewriter, a giant Corliss engine, and other inventions (Hingston, 2016). A shantytown, or

"Dinky-Town," sprang up outside the fair, with exhibits more appropriate for a circus midway than for a World's Fair, but it also offered eating and lodging that were significantly cheaper than at the fair and at more established hotels (Randel, 1969, 297–298).

Thousands had gathered at Independence Hall on New Year's Day, which had been heralded with the unfurling of flags, the playing of "The Star-Spangled Banner," and the pealing of bells (Mires, 2002, 132). As in later fairs, the Independence Day holiday was a special highlight. The city suspended regular business for the first five days of the month, the Centennial Bell rang out 13 times at midnight, and a grandson of Richard Henry Lee, one of the founding fathers, read the Declaration of Independence aloud (Randel, 1969, 300). Using the occasion to show that the quest for liberty remained incomplete—for instance, an exhibition hall was dedicated to women's struggle for equality—Susan B. Anthony came to the stage and passed out copies of the Woman's Declaration of Rights, in a quest for women's suffrage that would not ultimately succeed until the ratification of the Nineteenth Amendment in 1920 (Nash, 2010, 73–74).

The centennial celebration was generally regarded as a success. A scholar notes that "the Exhibition fully confirmed the sense, newly born in 1876, that the American nation had a past—a glorious past, one to be proud of and to commemorate" (Randel, 1969, 304). The city hosted a milder, three-day celebration of the centennial of the U.S. Constitution in 1887. In 1926, Philadelphia hosted the Sesquicentennial International Exposition, a far less successful endeavor, in which it made the Liberty Bell a major theme (Wilson, 2000). The city was also a focal point of bicentennial celebrations in 1976.

From May 11, 1976 to August 10, 1996, the Smithsonian Institution devoted the first floor of its Arts and Industries Building in Washington, D.C., to re-creating the Centennial Exposition by filling it with objects that either were displayed or resembled those that were displayed there.

See also: Centennial Liberty Bell; Declaration of Independence and the Liberty Bell; Statue of Liberty

Further Reading

Evensen, Bruce J. 1993. " 'Saving the City's Reputation': Philadelphia's Struggle over Self-Identity, Sabbath-Breaking and Boxing in America's Sesquicentennial Year." *Pennsylvania History: A Journal of Mid-Atlantic Studies* 60 (January): 6–34.

Hingston, Sandy. 2016. "10 Things You Might Not Know About the 1876 Centennial Exhibition." *Philadelphia Magazine,* May 10. https://www.phillymag.com/news/2016/05/10/centennial-exhibition-history.

Horwitz, Elinor Lander. 1976. *The Bird, the Banner, and Uncle Sam: Images of American in Folk and Popular Art.* Philadelphia: J. P. Lippincott Company.

McShane Bell Foundry. n.d. *The McShane Bell Foundry.* Baltimore.

Mires, Charlene. 2002. *Independence Hall in American Memory.* Philadelphia: University of Pennsylvania Press.

Nash, Gary B. 2010. *The Liberty Bell.* New Haven, CT: Yale University Press.

Randel, William Peirce. 1969. *Centennial: American Life in 1876.* Philadelphia: Chilton Book Company.

Rydell, Robert W. 1984. *All the World's a Fair: Visions of Empire at American International Expositions, 1876–1916*. Chicago: University of Chicago Press.

TowerBells.org. n.d. "Garden City: USA—NY." http://www.towerbells.org/data/NYGD NCTY.HTM.

Wilson, Martin W. 2000. *From the Sesquicentennial to the Bicentennial: Changing Attitudes Toward Tourism in Philadelphia, 1926–1976*. PhD dissertation at Temple University, January.

Wolf, Stephanie Grauman. 2013. "Centennial Exhibition (1876)." *Encyclopedia of Greater Philadelphia*. http://philadelphiaencyclopedia.org/archive/centennial.

Chapman, Maria Weston

A sonnet written by Maria Weston Chapman (1806–1885), and published in the first of the *Liberty Bell Gift Books* that she edited, supports the argument that, whether abolitionists conceived of the Liberty Bell as a generic symbol or as a reference to a specific bell, they clearly drew inspiration from the bell that we now call the "Liberty Bell." Chapman, who chose to sign the sonnet only with her initials, specifically noted that her sonnet was "Suggested by the Inscription on the Philadelphia Liberty Bell" (Chapman, 1839, v).

The sonnet is as follows (Chapman, 1839, v–vi):

It is no tocsin of affright we sound,
  Summoning nations to the conflict dire;—
  No fearful peal from cities wrapped in fire
Echoes, at our behest, the land around:—
Yet would we rouse our country's utmost bound
  With joyous clangor from each tower and spire,
  Till yon dark forms of mother and of sire,
Lifting their sullen glances from the ground,
  LIBERTY passes by, with lofty greeting!—
The hills are shaken by the shout of cheer
  From slave made free, and friends long parted meeting.
Join, thou true hearted one,—oppression shaming!
LIBERTY through the land, to all its sons proclaiming.

The sonnet shows that Chapman hoped to accomplish emancipation (perhaps as in the English empire) through moral suasion rather than through force. The last line of the sonnet clearly took its cue from the specific engraving on the Liberty Bell, which is taken from Leviticus 25:10.

See also: Abolitionists and the Liberty Bell; *Liberty Bell Gift Books*

Further Reading
Chapman, Maria Weston. 1839. "Sonnet." *The Liberty Bell*. The Friends of Liberty. Boston: Anti-Slavery Bazaar.

Children and the Liberty Bell

The Liberty Bell, like the U.S. flag, is a symbol that may appeal as much to children as it does to adults. In its early years, the Bell was probably the loudest object in the city of Philadelphia, so it would have caught the attention of both young and old. Over time, children would have come to associate the Bell with meetings, calls to worship, warnings of fire or enemy troops, executions, funerals, and important announcements.

After the Bell cracked sometime in the 1830s or 1840s, it was largely mute, but once lowered from its tower, it became more visual. At over 3 feet tall, with a 12-foot circumference around the lip, the Bell would seem especially formidable to a small child. The raised lettering on the shoulder of the Bell and the crack down its side would provide a further point for little hands to touch and to raise questions in inquiring minds. Children who were not old enough to understand the intricacies of liberty, freedom, or independence could still leave Independence Hall with memories of a giant bell that stood for the United States and American values.

The association between children and the Liberty Bell was enhanced by the seven trips that the Bell took from 1885 to 1915 to various expositions and fairs. Many of the pictures of these road trips show children being lifted to the train car to hug or kiss the Bell. Some 75,000 St. Louis children were recruited to sign petitions to bring the Liberty Bell to the Louisiana Purchase Exhibition in 1904, and another half-million children petitioned Philadelphia to send the Bell to the Panama-Pacific International Exposition in San Francisco in 1915.

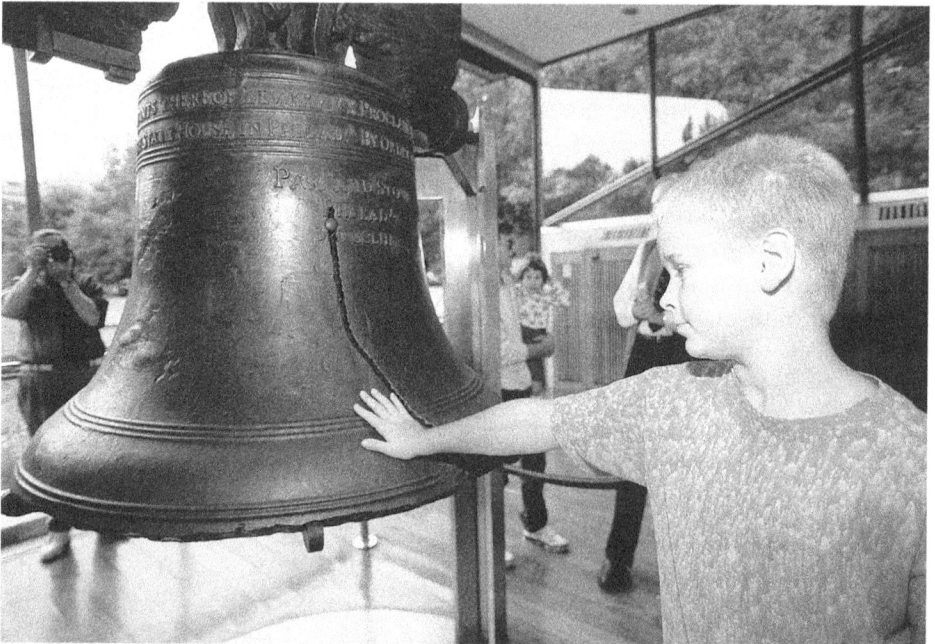

A child touches the Liberty Bell at the Liberty Bell Center in Philadelphia, Pennsylvania. (Joe Sohm/Dreamstime.com)

In describing the trips of the Liberty Bell, Charlene Myers observed that

organizers of Liberty Bell receptions recruited children to join adults in leading roles. Children presented flowers to the bell, sang patriotic songs, and waved American flags. They were given the best places in lines, and Philadelphia's giant policemen often hoisted them onto the bell car to have their pictures taken. Adults saw the Liberty Bell rituals as a way of instilling patriotism in future generations. (Myers, 2002, 154)

A number of children's books explain the Liberty Bell to children. Henry Magaziner's *Our Liberty Bell* (2007) has lots of content, whereas Megan McDonald's *Saving the Liberty Bell* (2005) uses the most colorful illustrations to explain how the Liberty Bell was moved from Philadelphia to Allentown during the Revolutionary War to save it from the British. With the support of the Penn Foundation, the Independence National Historical Park and Eastern National have produced a teacher's guide of over 150 pages with lesson plans for grades K–12 entitled *The Liberty Bell: A Symbol for "We the People,"* which teachers can download from the Internet. It produced another such guide, largely directed to the 150th anniversary of the Civil War, entitled *Bells Across the Land 2015.*

One reason that the Bell probably retains its appeal to children is that it has been frequently reproduced and is easily represented or drawn. In 1976, the American Legion cast a large replica of the Liberty Bell, which was dedicated to children of the United States and is sometimes called the "Children's Freedom Bell."

The appendix of this book contains a list of states and cities that the Liberty Bell visited during the trips that it took. Many children might find it interesting to find the city nearest to them that the Bell visited and the date that it did so. Older children might look for newspaper or magazine articles from that time. Each state has a replica of the Liberty Bell, and students might enjoy discovering where their state's bell is located, and even visiting it.

See also: American Legion Freedom Bell; Journeys of the Liberty Bell; Kissing the Liberty Bell

Further Reading
Bailey, R. J. 2017. *Liberty Bell.* "Hello, America!" series. Minneapolis: Bullfrog Books.
Binns, Tristan Boyer. 2001. *Symbols of Freedom: The Liberty Bell.* Chicago: Heinemann Library.
Douglas, Lloyd G. 2003. *The Liberty Bell (Welcome Books).* Children's Press.
Firestone, Mary. 2007. *The Liberty Bell (American Symbols).* Matthew Skeens, illustrator. Minneapolis: Picture Window Books.
Independence National Historical Park. n.d. *The Liberty Bell: A Symbol for "We the People": A Teacher Guide with Lesson Plans.* http://www.independenceparkinstitute .com/The%20Liberty%20Bell%20Teacher%20Guide%2011-6-07.pdf.
Jango-Cohen, Judith. 2004. *The Liberty Bell.* Pull Ahead Books.
Magaziner, Henry Jonas. 2007. *Our Liberty Bell.* John O'Brien, illustrator. New York: Holiday House.
McDonald, Megan. 2005. *Saving the Liberty Bell.* Marsha Gray Carrington, illustrator. New York: Atheneum Books for Young Readers.
Mires, Charlene. 2002. *Independence Hall in American Memory.* Philadelphia: University of Pennsylvania Press.

National Park Service. 2015. *Bells Across the Land 2015*. Park Resource Packet. https://www.nps.gov/civilwar/upload/PARK-RESOURCE-PACKET-1.pdf.

Rustad, Martha E. H. *Can We Ring the Liberty Bell?* Kyle Poling, illustrator. Minneapolis: Cloverleaf Books.

Steen, Sandra, and Susan Steen. 1994. *Independence Hall*. New York: Dillon Press.

Civil Religion and the Liberty Bell

Although the First Amendment of the U.S. Constitution has long prohibited the United States from establishing a national religion, Americans are often identified as believing certain key tenets, which are thought by some to bind them together in a type of "civil religion." The British writer G. K. Chesterton (1922, 7) thus observed that "America is the only nation in the world that is founded on a creed. That creed is set forth with dogmatic and even theological lucidity in the Declaration of Independence, perhaps the only piece or practical politics that is also theoretical politics and also great literature. It enunciates that all men are equal in their claim to justice, that governments exist to give them that justice, and that their authority is for that reason just."

The Liberty Bell, of course, has been associated with the Declaration of Independence through most of its history. It is one of a much larger number of symbols, such as Plymouth Rock, the U.S. flag, the U.S. Constitution, various monuments and battlefields, songs and anthems, and the sites of the terrorist attacks of September 11, 2001, that bind the nation together.

In a recent book that discusses many of these symbols, Peter Gardella (2014, 3) observed that, taken together, these symbols are "unified by four values—personal freedom (often called liberty), political democracy, world peace, and cultural (including religious, racial, ethnic, and gender) tolerance." Gardella has further tied the Liberty Bell to seven phases of the evolution of this civil religion. He identifies these as the "colonial or primal" phase; the "revolutionary or classical phase"; the national or continental phase (roughly 1824–1846); the "sacrificial phase" (the cracking of the Bell through the Civil War and Reconstruction); the imperial phase; the global phase (the 1930s through Vietnam); and the "multicultural era," which is where he believed the nation was at the time (2014, 4).

Gardella compares the crack in the bell to martyrdom, but he is far from the first to note such religious parallels. In an article that he wrote when he was an advanced doctoral student at the University of Pennsylvania, Robey Callahan likened the Liberty Bell to a "sacred object" or "icon" (Callahan, 1999). Having a scriptural text on the bell undoubtedly enhances its religious dimension; for that matter, bells are probably most frequently associated with churches and places of worship. Tourists are sometimes said to be making pilgrimages to Independence Hall or the Liberty Bell, which is displayed much like relics of the saints and reproduced in numerous copies, much like religious icons (Matero, 2013).

See also: Independence Hall; Liberty, Meaning of; Symbolism of the Liberty Bell

Further Reading

Callahan, Robey. 1999. "The Liberty Bell: From Commodity to Sacred Object." *Journal of Material Culture* 4 (1): 57–78.

Chesterton, G. K. 1922. *What I Saw in America*. New York: Dodd, Mead, and Company.

Gardella, Peter. 2014. *American Civil Religion: What Americans Hold Sacred*. New York: Oxford University Press.

Matero, Frank G. 2013. "Housing the Bell: 150 Years of Exhibiting an American Icon." *Change over Time* 3 (Fall): 188–201.

Coins, Medals, and Stamps Depicting the Liberty Bell

When Victor Rosewater wrote the book *The Liberty Bell: Its History and Significance* in 1926, he noted that, although he anticipated that the Bell might grace one of the sesquicentennial stamps (as it eventually did), it had not yet been portrayed on any official coins or stamps (Rosewater, 1926, 200). However, it had been engraved on a so-called dollar medal for the U.S. Centennial Exposition, which depicted the Bell and the words "PROCLAIM LIBERTY THROUGHOUT THE LAND UNTO ALL THE INHABITANTS THEREOF," as well as an image of Independence Hall on the obverse side. Another version had a Liberty Bell on one side with the same inscription, and George Washington on the other. Still others had the Bell and inscription on one side, and memorials to the Cumberland Street Methodist Episcopal Church or the Union Avenue Baptist Sunday School on the other. The former featured the following words:

> GOD IS OUR REFUGE AND
> STRENGTH, A VERY
> PRESENT HELP IN
> TROUBLE
> PS. LVI I.

By 2010, Gary Nash could report that the Bell in fact had been portrayed on a 2-cent stamp commemorating the Sesquicentennial Exposition (although the portrayal actually appears to be of the 80-foot illuminated replica that was built for the exposition); again on 10- and 13-cent airmail stamps issued in 1960 and 1961 (each including the words "Let Freedom Ring" under an etching of the Bell); and then on a 13-cent stamp with a similar sketch with the words "PROCLAIM LIBERTY THROUGHOUT ALL THE LAND," which was issued for the bicentennial of the Declaration of Independence (Nash, 2010, 178). Similarly, from 1951 to 1956, West Germany issued a

A USA Forever stamp depicts the Liberty Bell, complete with its signature crack. (Alexander Mitr/Dreamstime.com)

number of stamps depicting its Freedom Bell, which hung in Berlin. In 2007, the U.S. Post Office issued its first "Forever" stamp, which could be used no matter how postage rates rose in the future; it featured a computer-generated image of the Bell, complete with its yoke and an obvious crack.

As to official coins, the bicentennial provided the occasion for minting a fifty-cent piece with a picture of Benjamin Franklin on the front and an outline of the Liberty Bell on the back. An earlier fifty-cent coin issued during the sesquicen-tennial had pictured profiles of presidents George Washington and Calvin Coolidge together on the front, and the Liberty Bell and its yoke on the back. Although the crack was visible, the inscription on the Bell was not. A gold $2.50 coin issued the same year portrayed a female Liberty with a scroll representing the Declaration of Independence on the front, and Pennsylvania Hall on the back.

The bicentennial was also the occasion for minting a $1 coin portraying President Dwight D. Eisenhower on the front, and the Liberty Bell, set against the background of the moon, on the back. The lettering on the Bell, as well as the crack, were visible but difficult to see. During the bicentennial, the United States also printed a $2 bill with a picture of Thomas Jefferson on the front and of delegates signing the Declaration of Independence on the back. In addition, the $100 bill, which features an engraving of Benjamin Franklin on the front, contains a small orange image of an inkwell with a picture of the Liberty Bell and its yoke on the back.

The back of the Pennsylvania issue of the popular state quarters portrays a woman against the background of the state's boundaries. Although it does not include the Liberty Bell, it does have the words "Virtue, Liberty, and Independence." The History Channel Club also issued a penny-size coin or token with an eagle and an American shield on one side saying, "THE HISTORY CHANNEL CLUB," and a sketch of the Liberty Bell and "1776" on the other.

In 2018, the Solomon Islands issued 1,776 coins made in 4 ounces of silver in the shape of the Liberty Bell to commemorate the 275th anniversary of the birth of Thomas Jefferson. The inner side of the bell depicts the image of Queen Elizabeth II.

Recipients of the Liberty Bell Award receive a medallion with a picture of the Liberty Bell in the foreground and of globes on the background on either side. In 1973, a brass medal was minted with the Liberty Bell and the words "PROCLAIM LIBERTY THROUGHOUT ALL THE LAND" and "LIBERTY BELL" printed on one side, and on the other was a prayer by evangelist Oral Robert that said, "Heal us in every part of our existence—all that we are and hope to become—our nation, family, ourselves. Heal us and bring us together, O God Amen ORAL ROBERTS. JULY 4, 1973." When Pope Francis visited Philadelphia in 2015, a 1-ounce silver commemorative coin was minted that portrayed his image on one side and the Liberty Bell on the other.

See also: Bicentennial and the Liberty Bell; Freedom Bell; Sesquicentennial and the Liberty Bell

Further Reading

"The Liberty Bell: An Apt Symbol for American Coinage." 2016. *Mint News Blog,* December 28. http://mintnewsblog.com/the-liberty-bell-an-apt-symbol-for-american-coinage.

Nash, Gary B. 2010. *The Liberty Bell.* New Haven, CT: Yale University Press.

Rosewater, Victor. 1926. *The Liberty Bell: Its History and Significance.* New York: D. Appleton and Company.

"So-Called Dollars. U.S. Centennial Exposition 1876 Philadelphia, PA." https://www.so-calleddollars.com/Events?US?Centennial.html.

College and University Campuses with Replicas of the Liberty Bell

Many colleges and universities still have a bell to announce times of day. There are replicas of the Liberty Bell on several U.S. college and university campuses for that purpose.

Two of these are from the 1950 Savings Bond drive, in which the U.S. Treasury Department gave one bell to each state. Both were cast in France. One is found at St. John's College in Annapolis, Maryland. The other is in the Academic Building at Texas A&M University in College Station, Texas. Yet another is found in the New York State Educational Building.

Texas appears to be the favorite spot for campus replicas of the Liberty Bell. Midwestern State University in Wichita Falls, Texas, displays a replica in front of its Hardin Administration Building. The bell was crafted in France and donated to the university in 2008. The Mahler Student Center at Dallas Baptist University also displays a replica of the Liberty Bell, which it allows students to ring once they enroll at the university. Similarly, the Bayou Building at the University of Houston at Clear Lake has a replica of the Liberty Bell, which like the original was cast at the Whitechapel Foundry in England. A professor of legal studies at the university named James Benson spearheaded the effort to get a replica of the Bell to increase interest in civic education on the campus.

In 1996, Fosecco, a manufacturer tied to the global foundry industry, commissioned the West Philadelphia Bronze Company to cast a replica of the Liberty Bell to commemorate the 100th anniversary of the American Foundry Society. Generally designated as the Fosecco Liberty Bell, it is displayed in the Leonhard Building at Penn State University.

In 1976, Lynchburg Baptist College (today's Liberty University) located in Virginia, commissioned a 3,000-pound replica of the Liberty Bell to commemorate both the bicentennial and its renaming to Liberty Baptist College. It moved the replica in 2017 to the bell tower of the seventeen-story Freedom Tower (Menard, 2017). Minnesota State University at Moorhead was recorded as lending its 1,200-pound bell to the Clay County Courthouse in 2013.

The "sister" of the Liberty Bell, which was once connected to the clock in Independence Hall, is located in the Falvey Memorial Library at Villanova University in Pennsylvania. For a time, the Spirit of Liberty Bell, which was ordered by the Providence Forum from the Whitechapel Foundry, was housed at the Williamson College of the Trades in a suburb of Philadelphia. It was transferred from there in early 2016 to the Bible in America Museum in Washington, D.C.

Dickinson College in Carlisle, Pennsylvania, which counts a number of signers of the Declaration of Independence among its founders and early supporters, rings a small replica of the Liberty Bell, cast by the same Whitechapel Foundry, when students move their tassels to indicate that they are no longer undergraduates. The bell is designed to remind students of the college's "revolutionary heritage" and its "commitment to education for democratic leadership" (Durden, 2010).

See also: Replicas of the Liberty Bell; State Liberty Bell Replicas

Further Reading

Araiza, Victor. 2013. "Professor Sparks Project to Bring Liberty Bell Replica to Campus." *UHCL The Signal,* September 16. https://uhclthesignal.com/wordpress/2013/09/16 /professor-sparks-project-to-bring-liberty-bell-replica-to-campus.

Durden, William G. 2010. "Remarks of President William G. Durden." May 23. http://www .dickinson.edu/news/article/252/remarks_of_president_william_g_durden.

Menard, Drew. 2017. "Bells Installed Atop Freedom Tower." April 27. http://www.liberty .edu/news/index.cfm?PID=18495&MID=232358.

Columbian Liberty Bell

There have been numerous replicas of the Liberty Bell, but few are as mysterious as a replica known as the Columbian Liberty Bell. It was designed for the World's Columbian Exposition, which was held in Chicago in 1893.

The bell was apparently the brainchild of William McDowell, a businessman from New Jersey, and Minnie F. Minkley of the Liberty Bell Chapter of the Daughters of the American Revolution in Allentown, Pennsylvania. The idea was to give voice to the original Bell, which could no longer speak because of its crack, and to ring out important events throughout the world (Mires, 2002, 158). It was likely further inspired by a poem by Maud Morris Wagner entitled "The New Liberty Bell," which described people donating heirlooms for a bell to be rung at the births and deaths of kings.

Given that there were 13 original colonies that revolted against Britain, it was likely no coincidence that this bell, like the Centennial Bell in the steeple of Independence Hall, weighs 13,000 pounds. Similarly, like Henry Seybert's original plans for the Centennial Bell, the Columbian Liberty Bell was encircled with the words "GLORY TO GOD IN THE HIGHEST AND ON EARTH PEACE GOOD WILL TOWARD MEN," as well as the words on the Liberty Bell, "PROCLAIM LIBERTY THROUGHOUT ALL THE LAND UNTO ALL THE INHABITANTS THEREOF." The front of the Columbian Liberty Bell also contained the words, quoting Jesus Christ, "A NEW COMMANDMENT I GIVE YOU, THAT YE LOVE ONE ANOTHER," as well as "A.D. 1893" (Mary Baker Eddy Library, n.d.).

Just as the Centennial Liberty Bell had been cast in part from four cannons of the Revolutionary and Civil Wars, the Columbian Liberty Bell was cast from numerous pennies donated by schoolchildren and a variety of other historic artifacts. These included coins from the time of Jesus, the surveying chain of George

Washington, a copper kettle once owned by Thomas Jefferson, a silver spoon belonging to John C. Calhoun, the watch chain of Abraham Lincoln, belt buckles from soldiers, silver thimbles, and other objects whose destruction might otherwise be considered a form of desecration, but whose collective presence was undoubtedly designed to make the bell an instant heirloom.

The Columbian Liberty Bell is sometimes attributed to the Meneely Bell Company—the same company that had cast the Centennial Bell—in Troy, New York (Daughters of the American Revolution, 2014). However, it appears to have actually been cast by the McShane Bell Foundry in Baltimore, which later made some souvenir bells described, in accompanying certificates of authenticity, to have been from metal that was "part of the overflow in casting the great Columbian Liberty Bell" (Mary Baker Eddy Library, n.d.). The replica has a wheel with an attached string by which the bell may be rung. In 1976, the company cast 2,500 replicas weighing 3 ½ pounds and measuring 6 ⅛ inches by 5 ¼ inches by 6 inches to commemorate the bicentennial. Each is marked, "Replica of 1893 Columbian Liberty Bell—J. R. McShane Bicentennial Commemorative."

Although the Daughters of the American Revolution had hoped to ring the bell on July 4, one source says that it did not leave the foundry until August 1893, after which it passed through a number of cities before being installed in front of the exposition's Administration Building (Daughters of the American Revolution, 2014). However, a speech that Hampton L. Carson, a lawyer and scholar, delivered on July 4, 1893, made it seem as though the bell were beside him (Carson, 1974, 499–500):

> And Thou, great Bell! Cast from the chains of liberators and the copper pennies of the children of our public schools, from sacred relics contributed by pious and patriotic hands, baptized by copious libations poured out upon the altar of a common country by grateful heirs, and consecrated by the prayers of the American people, take up the note of prophecy and of jubilee rung out by your older sister in 1776, and in your journey round the globe proclaim from mountain top and valley, across winding river and expansive sea, those tones which shall make thrones topple and despots tremble in their sleep, until all peoples and all nationalities, from turbaned Turks and Slavic peasants to distant islanders and the children of the Sun, shall join in the swelling chorus, and the darkest regions of the earth shall be illumed by the heaven-born light of Civil and Religious Liberty.

Although the Columbian Liberty Bell likely visited Atlanta, at some point either interest or funding lagged, which kept it from being taken on anticipated tours to Mexico City and Runnymeade, England. At this point, stories diverge. Some say that the bell disappeared in Atlanta (Lyon, 1994). Others believe that it may have traveled to Europe and disappeared there. One visitor reported seeing the bell in St. Petersburg, Russia (although there is an even larger Tsar Bell in Moscow, which is cracked and could thus easily be confused with the Liberty Bell), and surmised that it might have later been melted down by Bolsheviks to be used for weapons (HydePark.org, n.d.).

The story likely has a less dramatic ending than any of these reports. An article in *The New York Times* dated November 11, 1896, reports, "The Henry McShane

Manufacturing Company of Baltimore, which cast [the Columbian Liberty Bell], claims that it has never been paid for the work, and yesterday the firm's local agent, with a deputy sheriff, brought the bell from Evanston to Chicago. It will be shipped to Baltimore, where the firm intends to place it on exhibition" (*The New York Times,* 1896). The same article noted, "The bell was attached once before just prior to its final jaunt to the Atlanta Exposition, but a note for $125, the amount of the attachment, was given to secure the debt. The McShane Company claims the bell cost it $1,200" (*The New York Times,* 1896).

Further light has been cast on this bell by Paul Burzanko, a veteran and a machine tool assembler from Cleveland, who became so obsessed with the bell that he spent $7,000 of his own money to reconstruct a personal, fiberglass model of it. As of 1978, he was hoping to raise approximately $120,000 to have a recasting made by 1997, the 100th anniversary of its disappearance. Burzanko said that he had "talked to descendants of the foundry workers" and that "[t]hey confirmed that the bell was melted down for scrap in 1897" (Diggs, 1978).

In another wrinkle to the story, the Daughters of the American Revolution also apparently commissioned a Columbia Peace Plow to be made of leftover metal from the Bell. Marlene Gantt observed that "[t]he wooden part of the plow was designed and put together by Carl Borg of the Moline Furniture Co.," which involved "assembling thousands of pieces of wood into a complicated jigsaw puzzle" that included shapes of "arrowheads, flags, deer, eagles, rosettes, foliage, arabesques and other features of stylized ornament popular in the patriotic art of the 1890's" (Gantt, 1991, 5). The plow, which appears to have been at several exhibitions, including the Paris Exposition of 1900, was displayed by the Chicago Historical Society for the 100th anniversary of the Columbian Exposition; today, it is in the Grand Rapids Public Museum in Michigan ("Deere Helps Create 'Peace Plow' for Chicago World's Fair," 2015).

See also: Atlanta Cotton States and International Exposition of 1895; Centennial Bell; "Liberty's Bell" (Poem); World's Columbian Exposition in Chicago (1893)

Further Reading

Carson, Hampton L. 1894. "Oration Delivered at the Invitation of the City of Chicago and of the World's Fairs Commission, on the Fourth Day of July, 1893, in Jackson Park, Chicago." *Pennsylvania Magazine of History and Biography* 17:49–55.

"Deere Helps Create 'Peace Plow' for Chicago World's Fair." 2015. *John Deere Journal,* November 11. https://johndeerejournal.com/2015/11/deere-helps-create-peace-plow-for-chicago-worlds-fair.

Diggs, Morse. 1978. "He Dreams of Recasting Bell." *Akron Beacon Journal,* July 4.

Gantt, Marlene. 1993. "A Nation Forced This Plow." *The Dispatch* (Moline, Illinois), September 4, 5.

Hydepark.org. n.d. "A Mystery from the Fair." *World's Columbian Exposition of 1893.* http://www.hydepark.org/historicpres/ColumbianExp.htm#mystery.

"A Look Back." 2014. Daughters of the American Revolution, March/April. https://www.dar.org/national-society/celebrate-125/look-back-marchapril-2014.

Lyon, Jeff. 1994. "Humdinger of a Whodunit," *Chicago Tribune,* October 1. http://www.chicagotirbune.com.

Mary Baker Eddy Library. "'A Thrilling Tone': Mary Baker Eddy and the Columbian Liberty Bell." https://www.marybakereddylibrary.org/research/a-thrilling-tone-mary -baker-eddy-and-the-columbian-liberty-bell.

"The McShane Bicentennial Commemorative of the Second Liberty Bell." American Bell Association. https://americanbell.org/aba-forum/topic/columbian-liberty-bell.

Mires, Charlene. 2002. *Independence Hall in American Memory.* Philadelphia: University of Pennsylvania Press.

"Sheriff Has Liberty Bell: It Was Seized on Attachment by the Firm Which Cast It." 1896. *The New York Times*, November 11, 3.

"Who? What? Where?" 1976. *American Legion Magazine*, September, 30.

Composition of the Liberty Bell

Ever since the original Liberty Bell cracked on its first ringing and the existing Bell cracked years after being recast, there has been speculation as to the cause or causes of these events. They range from damage during shipment, to improper ringing, to flaws in the original casting or material.

These questions have led to studies conducted by the Franklin Institute in 1960 on small drillings taken near the area of the current crack in the Bell. The Henry Francis Du Pont Winterthur Museum also conducted tests using X-ray fluorescence analysis.

The Liberty Bell is chiefly made of bronze. Bronze is made mainly from copper and tin but often contains other trace elements. When John Pass and John Stow melted down the first Bell from the Whitechapel Foundry, they concluded that it was too brittle because it contained too much tin. Scholars believe it possible that the Whitechapel Foundry "might have added some bronze or bell metal scrap mistakenly as copper, thus bringing the tin content up to this ultra-brittle range" (Hanson, Carlson, Papouchado, and Nielsen, 1976, 617).

Pass and Stow added more copper when they recast the Bell, in order to get a better tone. The presence of additional elements such as antimony, arsenic, lead, and zinc might indicate that they further added some pewter (which was more accessible in the colonies than tin), which might once again have increased the brittleness. They may also have added one or more silver or gold coins, as at the time that was thought to improve tone quality.

An X-ray analysis of the Bell suggests that there are "wide variations in copper, tin, and lead content in the rim areas on either side of the crack" (Hanson et al., 1976, 616). This further suggests that Pass and Stow, who had never before cast such a large bell on their premises, may have had to melt metal in several batches, which led to a less consistent composition throughout the Bell as a whole.

See also: Casting the Liberty Bell; Pass and Stow; Whitechapel Foundry

Further Reading

Hanson, Victor F., Janice H. Carlson, Karen M. Papouchado, and Norman A. Nielsen. 1976. "The Liberty Bell: Composition of the Famous Failure." *American Scientist* 64 (November–December): 614–619.

"Congratulations, Liberty Bell" (Song, 1933)

The song "Congratulations, Liberty Bell" is attributed to Al Sherman, a composer who lived from 1897 to 1973, although the inside page also lists Joe Goodwin and Al Lewis. The song, which was published in 1933, four years after the stock market crash, appears to have been an attempt to provide encouragement during the Great Depression. It was likely further tied to the election of President Franklin D. Roosevelt and the end of Prohibition. The song's cover features a black sketch of the cracked Liberty Bell above a red, white, and blue image of a flag amid exploding fireworks.

The opening lines notice that "ev'ry one [is] preparing for a celebration . . . Now happy days are ready to begin." The chorus, which was to be repeated, ends with the song's title, "Congratulations, LIBERTY BELL." In what appears to be a coda, the "Butcher, Baker, Candy maker" and the "Farmer in the dell" are urged to "get together" and yell. This could have perhaps symbolized President Roosevelt's New Deal and the resulting coalitions.

See also: Music and the Liberty Bell

Further Reading
"Congratulations, Liberty Bell." 1933. New York: Nattrauss-Schenck Inc.

Congressional Resolution on Ringing Bells on Independence Day (1963)

Although evidence suggests that even if the Liberty Bell were rung after the adoption of the Declaration of Independence, it rang on July 8 rather than on July 4, the earlier date, which marks the day that the Second Continental Congress adopted the Declaration of Independence rather than the one on which it was read to the public in Philadelphia, remains the one on which the nation celebrates Independence Day. Often designated in its early years as the "Independence Bell," much of the reverence for the Liberty Bell was initially generated by its role in announcing this historic event. In later years, its designation as the "Liberty Bell" largely stemmed from its association with abolitionism.

Starting from the premise that the Liberty Bell had originally tolled at two o'clock on July 4, 1776, Congress adopted a joint resolution, initially sponsored by Senator Abraham Ribicoff of Connecticut, on June 26, 1963 (Government Publishing Office, 1963), which

> (1) Declares that the anniversary of the signing of the Declaration of Independence should be observed each year by the ringing of bells throughout the United States at the hour of 2 o'clock, eastern daylight time, in the afternoon of the 4th day of July, or at such other time on that day as may be determined by local authority, and (2) calls upon civic and other community leaders to take appropriate steps to encourage public participation in such observances.

This resolution grew from an article entitled "Make Freedom Ring," which was written by Eric Hatch and Eric Sloan, both of Litchfield, Connecticut, for *This*

Week magazine, which came out on February 17, 1963. It described the bell-ringing as a pre–Civil War custom worthy of being revived (Village of Mt. Morris, n.d.). In urging people to participate, President John F. Kennedy observed (Boland, 1973, 121):

> Bells mark significant events in men's lives. Birth and death, war and peace are tolled. Bells summon the community to take note of things which affect the life and destiny of its people. The Liberty Bell rang to tell the world of the birth of a new country's freedom. Next Thursday, the Fourth of July when the bells ring again, think back on those who lived and died to make our country free. And then resolve with courage and determination to keep it free and make it greater.

Clarence "Sandy" Sandstrom, the chair of the 4 of July Publicity Committee for Mt. Morris, Illinois, encouraged his city to participate. That same April, the city dedicated a small bell (President Ronald Reagan was among the guests at the dedication) and renamed their own Independence Day festival "Let Freedom Ring." It joined participants in 20 states who rang their bell 13 times (one for each of the 13 colonies and original states) on July 4, 1963. Two years later, the owner of the Chicago Cubs agreed to broadcast the ringing of this bell before a baseball game on July 4, and in 1966, Mt. Morris bought a much larger bell, recovered from the bottom of Lake Geneva, and outfitted it with a yoke of slippery elm, designed to replicate that of the Liberty Bell in Philadelphia.

In 1971, the state legislature declared the Mt. Morris Bell to be the official state bell of Illinois. In 1971, a plaque was placed on the site of the bell that proclaimed, "Let Freedom Ring on this occasion of the first official ringing of the Freedom Bell at Mt. Morris, let this message be heard by all Americans: Let us be one nation dedicated as never before to the realization of the promise of freedom for all" (Village of Mt. Morris, n.d.). For 15 years, this bell was connected by phone and rung simultaneously with that of a special bell in Philadelphia.

See also: Independence Day; Names for the Liberty Bell

Further Reading
Boland, Charles Michael. 1973. *Ring in the Jubilee: The Epic of America's Liberty Bell.* Riverside, CT: Chatham Press.

"Freedom Bell." n.d. The Village of Mt. Morris. http://mtmorrisil.net/freedom-bell.

Government Publishing Office. 1963. "Declaration of Independence—Anniversary." June 26. S Con. Res. 25, 77 Stat. p. 944 https://www.govinfo.gov/content/pkg /STATUTE-77/pdf/STATUTE-77-Pg944.pdf.

Conspiracy Theories About the Liberty Bell

In an age when conspiracy theories abound, especially about America's founding fathers and their association with Freemasons, it is probably not surprising that these have been extended to the Liberty Bell. Robert Hieronimus, who has sought to expose such theories, has documented how some groups accuse the founding fathers of having picked the Liberty Bell as a symbol in veneration of "the ancient Babylonian god know as *Bel,* or *Ba'al,* or the derivative name *Beelzebub (Ba'al Zebub)*" (Hieronimus, 1988, 147). Some have apparently relied for proof on a fictional television movie in the 1960s, loosely based on the Skull and Bones society at Yale University, called *The Brotherhood of the Bell,* starring Glenn Ford.

Pointing out that many churches also have bells, Hieronimus observes, "If the fundamentalist-conspiratorial school of semantics were to apply, then the Liberty Bell could just as easily be a coded conspiracy message about Belgians (also abbreviated as 'Bel') trying to take over the world" (Hieronimus, 1988, 149).

See also: Films and the Liberty Bell; Symbolism of the Liberty Bell

Further Reading
Hieronimus, Robert, with Laura Cortner. 2008. *The United Symbolism of America: Deciphering Hidden Meanings in America's Most Familiar Art, Architecture, and Logos.* Franklin Lakes, NJ: New Page Books.

Crack in the Liberty Bell

One of the most distinctive features of the Liberty Bell is its zig-zag crack. Indeed, a contemporary scholar has argued, "Any iconic instance of the [Liberty] Bell requires only to have the merest outline of a bell with a crack proceeding upward from the base" (Callahan, 1999, 71). Although Callahan doesn't say so, depictions of the Bell often also feature the wooden yoke from which it hangs. However, a study of the use of the Liberty Bell in images noted that a majority of them studied did not portray the crack at all (Tafel, 1979, 151).

Although it is known that the original Bell imported from the Whitechapel Foundry in England cracked upon first being struck in Philadelphia, there do not appear to be any contemporary sketches of where the break occurred or what it looked like. After being twice recast by John Pass and John Stow (the second time because of complaints about the quality of sound that it emitted upon striking), the Bell survived for about 75 years or more before again showing obvious damage.

Perhaps because the Bell was initially regarded less as a national symbol than a utilitarian object, a number of stories have originated about how and when it cracked, but most have no contemporary evidence to back them up. Thus, there are stories that it first cracked during the Marquis de Lafayette's visit to Philadelphia in September 1824; that it cracked while clanging to warn of a fire later that winter; that it cracked while announcing Parliament's passage of the Catholic Emancipation Act of 1828; that it broke on February 22, 1832, while pealing for George Washington's birthday; that Emmanuel Joseph Rauch, who, with some other boys, had been invited by the custodian to ring the Bell, cracked it on Washington's birthday in 1835 (this was his recollection in an article in *The New York Times* in 1911); that it cracked on July 8, 1835, while tolling for the funeral procession of Chief Justice John Marshall, who had died in Philadelphia; that it cracked welcoming Henry Clay to the city (possibly in September 1839); that it cracked on Washington's birthday in 1843; and that it was broken in the autumn of 1845 or in 1846 (Paige, 1988, 25–29; Kimball, 1989, 43–47; Voorhis and Heaton, 1976, 17).

Muhammad Ali played on this ambiguity in a song on an album designed to promote children's dental health when he asked, "Who knocked the crack in the Liberty Bell?" and answered "Ali, Ali," as the song reminded children that "Ali's always getting blamed for things he didn't do" (Heller, 2016). Another bit of contemporary folk lore, the "Ballad of Davy Crockett," which was composed for the Walt Disney miniseries that played from 1955–1956, records that:

> But he spoke out strong, so hist'ry books tell
> an' patched up the crack in the Liberty Bell

It is known that as the city prepared to ring bells for Washington's birthday in 1846, William Eckel, who was superintendent of the State House, ordered a crack

A close-up view of the Liberty Bell's famous crack. (Peter West/National Science Foundation)

in the Bell to be drilled out to prevent those parts of the Bell from touching and thus prevent the crack from spreading. This work, which was believed to have been performed by Henry Stone, made the crack more visible and distinctive (Paige, 1988, 29). One souvenir from this project was a small replica cast from the filings, which ended up at the Historical Society of Pennsylvania (Paige, 1088, 29). Apparently, a number of signets were also made from the filings and mounted on gold rings (Springer 1976, 67).

The redrilling proved unsuccessful. In an article entitled "The Old Independence Bell," the *Public Ledger* for February 26, 1846, thus noted (Paige, 1988, 30):

> This venerable relic of the Revolution rang its last clear note on Monday last, in honor of the birth day of Washington, and now hangs in the great city steeple irreparably cracked and forever dumb. It had been cracked long before, but was put in order for that day, by having the edges of the fracture filled so as not to vibrate against each other, as there was a prospect that the church bells would not chime upon that occasion. It gave out clear notes and loud, and appeared to be in excellent condition until noon, when it received a sort of compound fracture in a zig-zag direction through one of its sides, which put it completely out of tune and left it a mere wreck of what it was. We were lucky to get a small fragment of it and shall keep it sacred, in

memory of the good and glory achieved by the old herald of Independence in times long past, and ever to be remembered. It has been suggested that the bell should be recast; and, as it is now entirely useless, but composed of 'good stuff,' the suggestion is entitled to consideration. It can never be replaced but by itself, and although it may not be improved yet, pure as it is, it can be re-formed to much advantage.

Later that year, city officials began thinking of taking the Liberty Bell down and displaying it on a pedestal, but this did not occur until 1852.

One concern over allowing the Liberty Bell to visit other cities was the possibility that the travel would lengthen the crack. There was a report from Chicago that the trip there had resulted in a new crack, which "extends from the old crack nearly 14 inches up and around the crown," although the account was almost immediately questioned (Paige, 1988, 38).

Whereas it is common to think of an item that is cracked as relatively useless (and to identify quirky individuals as crackpots), as Callahan has suggested, the crack in the Liberty Bell has itself become a defining part of the icon. Over time, it has acquired an endearing quality. Like the prints of the nails in the hands of Jesus or the stigmata in the palms of saints, the crack has become a sign of healing and reconciliation, which was particularly evident in the trips that the Liberty Bell took outside Philadelphia, especially to locations in the South that had been part of the rebellion against the Union. Mickey Hart of the Grateful Dead has observed, "Its crack is a reminder that liberty is imperfect, hopefully evolving to include those who have been denied full participation in a democratic society. So vote, or else liberty is meaningless" (Hieronimus 2008, 141).

Canadian-born composer and musician Leonard Cohen (1934–2016) published an album in 1992 with a song entitled "Anthem," which some individuals have associated with the crack in the Liberty Bell. In this song, which evokes a dove, past wars, and signs, Cohen's chorus is as follows (Werber 2016):

> There is a crack, a crack in everything
> That's how the light gets in.

These lyrics see brokenness as a means of resurrection or reconciliation (Fendrick, 2016).

Modern scientific studies of the Liberty Bell suggest that it may have had too high a percentage of tin, which would have made it extra brittle. The process of recasting the bell might have further contributed to this condition (Hanson, 1976).

See also: Civil Religion and the Liberty Bell; Composition of the Liberty Bell; Occasions for Ringing the Liberty Bell; Reconciliation and the Liberty Bell

Further Reading

Callahan, Robey. 1999. "The Liberty Bell: From Commodity to Sacred Object." *Journal of Material Culture* 4 (1): 57–78.

Fendrick, Susan P. 2016. "The Bells That Still Can Ring: On Rest and Action (Parshat Behar, Leviticus 25: 1–26:2). *Huffington Post,* May 24. https://www.huffingtonpost .com/rabbi-susan-p-fendrick/the-bells-that-still-can-ring-on-rest-and-action -parshat-behar-leviticus-251-262_b_10120144.html.

Hanson, Victor F., Janice H. Carlson, Karen M. Papouchado, and Norman A. Nielsen. 1976. "The Liberty Bell: Composition of the Famous Failure." *American Scientist* 64 (November–December): 614–619.

Heller, Jason. 2016. "Remembering Muhammad Ali's Trippy, Anti-Cavity Kids' Record." *Rolling Stone,* June 6. https://www.rollingstone.com/music/music-news/remem bering-muhammad-alis-trippy-anti-cavity-kids-record-64027.

Hieronimus, Robert, with Laura Cortner. 2008. *The United Symbolism of America: Deciphering Hidden Meanings in America's Most Familiar Art, Architecture, and Logos.* Franklin Lakes, NJ: New Page Books.

Kimball, David. 1989. *The Story of the Liberty Bell.* Fort Washington, PA: Eastern National.

Paige, John C. 1988. *The Liberty Bell: A Special History Study.* David C. Kimball, ed. Denver: Denver Service Center and Independence National Historical Park.

Springer, L. Elsinore. 1976. *That Vanishing Sound.* New York: Crown Publishers.

Tafel, Jonathan Leigh. 1979. *The Historical Development of Political and Patriotic Images of America: A Visual Analysis of Fourth of July Cartoons in Five Newspapers.* PhD dissertation at Ohio State University.

Voorhis, Harold V. B. and Ronald E. Heaton. 1976. *Loud and Clear: The Story of Our Liberty Bell.* Revised ed. Norristown, PA: Ronald E. Heaton.

Werber, Cassie. 2016. "'There Is a Crack in Everything, That's How the Light Gets In': The Story of Leonard Cohen's 'Anthem.'" *Quartz,* November 22. https://qz.com /835076/leonard-cohens-anthem-the-story-of-the-line-there-is-a-crack-in -everything-thats-how-the-light-gets-in.

Cuban Liberty Bell

Carlos Manuel de Cespedes was a Cuban slaveowner who regularly called his slaves to work by ringing a bell. On October 10, 1868, three years after the adoption of the Thirteenth Amendment outlawing involuntary servitude in the United States, he promised freedom to his slaves if they would join him in the fight for Cuban independence from Spain. In the process, he launched a 10-year war and became regarded as the father of his country.

On October 6, 1947, Alego Cossio del Pino, who was the Minister of Government for Ramon Grau San Martin, traveled to Manzanillo, Oriente, to persuade members of the city council and the local veterans' association to lend the renowned bell to the government to celebrate the 79th anniversary of Cespedes's call for Cuban independence in 1868. When the groups turned him down, Fidel Castro, who was then a law student at the University of Havana, along with other communist revolutionaries, persuaded the veterans to let them use it instead for a planned demonstration on November 6 against the government of Fulgencio Batista.

As the bell arrived in Havana in 1984, Castro and his fellow revolutionaries were there to be photographed with it. In an odd turn of events, the students failed to guard the bell, and it disappeared overnight, only to reappear a few days later in the custody of a Cuban group believed to be more responsible. The government then returned the bell to its hometown, where it was warmly greeted.

One of the remarkable aspects of this story is that the Cuban Liberty Bell, like that of the United States, is linked not only to national independence, but also to the freedom of former slaves.

See also: Abolitionists and the Liberty Bell

Further Reading
Guerra, Lillian. 2018. *Heroes, Martyrs, and Political Messiahs in Revolutionary Cuba, 1946–1958.* New Haven, CT: Yale University Press, esp. 50–56.

Cumberland County Liberty Bell

In addition to the replicas of the Liberty Bell that the federal government distributed to states and territories in the 1950s, a number of states have other bells that pealed out news of independence in 1776. Indeed, a number of bells throughout Pennsylvania were gathered to be displayed near the Liberty Bell during sesquicentennial celebrations in Philadelphia in 1926.

During that same event, another bell was brought from Bridgeton, in Cumberland County, in the southern part of New Jersey to ring for closing time each day. This bell, which was made in Bridgewater, Massachusetts, rang out for independence on July 7, 1776 (likely a day before bells were rung in Philadelphia) from the county's third courthouse, which was built in 1760–1761. As in Philadelphia, the ringing of the bell was preceded by a reading of the Declaration of Independence and followed by a pulling-down and burning of the King's Arms (Jones, 1998). It was also believed to have rung after a false alarm during the War of 1812 that hostile British troops were approaching.

When a new courthouse was constructed in 1846, the Cumberland County Liberty Bell was used at Fireman's Hall as an alarm bell. In the 1850s, the bell was moved to the West Jersey Academy, where it announced classes. The Bridgeton Board of Education acquired the bell in 1912 and used it for a junior high school. The junior high was then converted to a high school, at which time the Daughters of the American Revolution created a table that proclaimed (Jones, 1998):

> The Bell that Hangs in this Belfry Rang the Tidings of Liberty in 1776 from the Cupola of Cumberland County's First Brick Court House And on Every Independence Day Until the Court House was Razed in 1846. The Bell was Purchased by Subscription And was Cast in Bridgewater, Mass. in 1763. Tablet Placed by Greenwich Tea Burning Chapter Daughters of the American Revolution in 1923.

The town's website says that the Bell was manufactured in Bridgewater, England and that it was made in the key of F (Cumberland County, New Jersey).

The Bell was moved to the Cumberland County Courthouse where it has, with three exceptions, been displayed since 1919. As mentioned previously, in 1926, it went to Philadelphia for the Sesquicentennial Exposition. It was later mounted on a truck and rung to announce the end of World War II. In 1948, it was also put on a float in a parade commemorating Bridgeton's bicentennial.

The bell is now displayed in a glass case at the entrance to the courthouse.

See also: Sesquicentennial International Exposition; State Liberty Bell Replicas

Further Reading

Cumberland County, New Jersey. "Cumberland County Liberty Bell." http://www.co .cumberland.nj.us/libertybell.

Jones, Jean. 1998. "Our Liberty Bell Has No Crack and a More Fascinating History." *Bridgeton Evening News,* June 26. http://www.co.cumberland.nj.us/content/22596 /23487/23597/24194.aspx.

Czech Liberty Bell

Although the metal from which the Liberty Bell was made was originally cast at the Whitechapel Foundry in England, once recast by John Pass and John Stow, the Bell has never left U.S. shores. It has nonetheless become an international symbol for colonial peoples and for those seeking freedom, and was effectively used as a symbol in combating international communism, as demonstrated in part by the Freedom Bell.

This international symbolism of the Liberty Bell was highlighted when, shortly before the armistice that ended World War I, representatives of the Democratic Mid-European Union commissioned the Meneely Bell Company of Troy, New York, which had cast previous replicas of the Liberty Bell, to cast yet another one. This version changed the words from Leviticus 25:10 from "Proclaim liberty through-out all the land" to "Proclaim liberty throughout all the world" (Fried, 2017).

Dr. Thomas G. Masaryk, who was president of the union, signed a declaration of independence on behalf of the Czecko-Slovak republic. He was joined by repre-sentatives described by a Philadelphia newspaper as Poles, Jugo-Slavs, Ukraini-ans, Lithuanians, Rumanians, Italian Irredentists, Unredeemed Greeks, a representative of the Albanian National Council, Jewish people of Palestine, and Armenians ("Slavs Proclaim Independence Shrine," 1918). Among other claims, this declaration affirmed "[t]hat all governments derive their just power from the consent of the governed" and "[t]hat it is the inalienable right of every people to organize their own government on such principles and in such form as they believe will best promote their welfare, safety and happiness" ("Declaration of Common Aims of the Independent Mid-European Nations," 1918). It also called for the estab-lishment of a league of nations.

After this signing took place in Independence Hall, the emissaries proceeded to Independence Square, where children rang the new bell. The bell was subsequently moved to Czechoslovakia, where it rang in 1928 on the 10th anniversary of its inde-pendence (Nash, 2010, 139). Plans to send this bell to the New York World's Fair in 1939 had to be scrapped after the nation became a Nazi protectorate. Czecho-slovakia subsequently fell into the Soviet orbit during the Cold War, but it regained its freedom after the fall of the Berlin Wall in 1989. On January 1, 1993, the nation peacefully split into the Czech Republic and Slovakia.

The bell, initially thought to have been lost during the war, had been hidden in a Prague castle. It was apparently either placed in a tower of St. Anthony's Church in that city in the late 1980s or it was discovered there, covered with special paint that obscured its inscription (Nash, 2010, 139). As many as 14,000 bells from today's Czech Republic were confiscated, and many were destroyed, during World War II (Richter, 2009).

In November 1990, President George H. W. Bush rang the bell when he became the first president to visit Czechoslovakia. On this trip, Bush promised to return a letter previously kept at the Library of Congress that Masaryk had written to President Woodrow Wilson outlining his nation's declaration of independence and constitution ("Bush Rings Liberty Bell in Prague," 1990).

In an address in Prague in 1990, President Bush observed (Bush, 1990):

> In 1776, when our Declaration of Independence was first read in public, a bell tolled to proclaim the defiant thrill of that moment. That bell—we call it, at home, the Liberty Bell—has for 200 years symbolized our nation's deepest dedication to freedom—dedication like your own. Inscribed on this bell are the words: "Proclaim liberty throughout all the land." We want to help you proclaim your new liberty throughout all this proud and beautiful land, and so today we give to you our last replica of the Liberty Bell. You know, one of our patriotic songs proclaims, "Sweet land of liberty—from every mountainside, let freedom ring."

Bush had previously given a small model of the Liberty Bell to President Václav Havel, which he apparently kept on his desk (Rozhlas, 2017).

See also: Freedom Bell; Replicas of the Liberty Bell

Further Reading
Bush, George H. W. 1990. "Remarks in Prague, Czechoslovakia, at a Ceremony Commemorating the End of Communist Rule." November 17. The American Presidency Project. http://www.presidency.ucsb.edu/ws/?pid=19066.

"Bush Rings Liberty Bell in Prague." 1990. *The New York Times,* November 18.

"Declaration of Common Aims of the Independent Mid-European Nations." October 16, 1918. http://www.carpatho-rusyn.org/fame/proc.htm.

Fried, Stephen. 2017. "World War I: 100 Years Later. How the Liberty Bell Won the Great War." Smithsonian.com, April. https://www.smithsonianmag.com/history/how-liberty-bell-won-great-war-180962471.

Nash, Gary B. 2010. *The Liberty Bell*. New Haven, CT: Yale University Press.

Rozhlas, Česky. 2017. "My Prague," January 4. http://www.czech.cz/en/Turistika/My-Prague-%E2%80%93-Zdenek-Lukes.

Richter, Jan. 2009. "The Bells of Prague." Czech Radio, December 26. https://www.radio.cz/en/section/special/the-bells-of-prague.

"Slavs Proclaim Independence Shrine." 1918. *Evening Public Ledger*, October 26, 1.

D

Declaration of Independence and the Liberty Bell

One of the early designations for the Liberty Bell was the "Independence Bell." To this day, one of the events that Americans are most likely to associate with the Liberty Bell is the American Declaration of Independence from Great Britain.

The movement for independence developed as tensions rose between the 13 colonies and Great Britain at the end of the French and Indian War (1764–1763). After this war, during which France ceded Canada to Britain, Britain began seeking new ways of taxing its 13 colonies to help pay for the expenditures it had incurred. For their part, the colonists, who believed they had brought their rights with them from the mother country, believed that such taxation was illegal because they had no representation in the British Parliament, the governing body that enacted tax laws.

Representatives from the Stamp Act Congress met in New York City to protest one of the first of these new taxes. The First Continental Congress subsequently met in Philadelphia in September 1774 after the British adopted a series of Coercive, or Intolerable Acts, against Boston. They had done so to punish the city's residents for their so-called Boston Tea Party, in which Americans dressed as Indians threw tea into the Boston Harbor rather than paying taxes on it. By the time the Second Continental Congress met in Philadelphia in May 1775, fighting had broken out in Lexington and Concord, Massachusetts, between British regular soldiers and colonial Minutemen. Although colonial representatives continued to hope for reconciliation with Britain and were initially unwilling to announce a formal separation, delegates became more adamant after British officials, including King George III, rejected their petitions, and on May 14, 1776, the Congress adopted a resolution encouraging states to adopt new governments.

On June 7, 1776, Richard Henry Lee, a Virginia delegate to the Congress, introduced a resolution for formal independence, and on June 11, the Congress appointed five men to a committee to draft a formal Declaration of Independence, explaining the colonial viewpoint. They were Thomas Jefferson of Virginia, John Adams of Massachusetts, Benjamin Franklin of Pennsylvania, Roger Sherman of Connecticut, and Robert Livingston of New York. Jefferson took the lead role in this task. On July 1, 9 of 13 states meeting as part of a Committee of the Whole agreed to a formal declaration. On the following day, 12 of the states voting in the full Congress agreed to declare independence. (The New York delegates were still unwilling to act until they received instructions from their constituents.)

On July 4, 1776, delegates from these same 12 states voted to adopt the Declaration of Independence to outline the principles for which they stood and to delineate the grievances that had driven them to take this action. They did so in hopes that such a declaration might further encourage foreign aid in their fight against Britain.

The Declaration of Independence was printed either that night or early the following morning, was published in newspapers beginning on July 6, and was then mailed to governors and military leaders throughout the colonies, where the news was announced in open-air meetings. Despite what now appear to be faulty recollections by some of the delegates, the document does not appear to have been read to the public in Philadelphia until July 8, when it seems most likely that the city's bells pealed with the news. Even then, it is not altogether clear whether these bells included the bell in the State House, in part because the steeple in which it was then housed is known to have been in disrepair, and authorities may have feared that vigorous pealing might have led to its collapse.

At a time prior to telegraph, radio, and television, and at a time when most newspapers were published on a weekly rather than a daily basis, bells would have been one of the most efficient ways to spread the news. Numerous reports from the time period indicate that bells rang not only in Philadelphia, but in other towns and cities where the news was announced. On July 15, word arrived in Philadelphia that New York had joined the other colonies by instructing its delegates to vote for independence, and on July 19, Congress ordered that the document be engrossed on the parchment that is now displayed at the National Archives in Washington, D.C., along with the U.S. Constitution and the proposed Bill of Rights. Delegates to the Continental Congress signed the Declaration beginning on August 2 and continuing into the next year.

Even prior to the announcement of the Declaration of Independence, the bell in the State House had rung to announce sessions of the Pennsylvania Assembly and of the Continental Congresses, and it continued to ring to gather citizens to hear news of the Coercive Acts, of new British taxes, and the like. In time, the ringing of bells became a principal way of celebrating Independence Day on subsequent Fourths of July.

The inscription on the Liberty Bell, taken from Leviticus 25:10, said, "Proclaim LIBERTY throughout all the land unto all the inhabitants thereof." The writing of the Declaration of Independence and the subsequent victory of the American Revolution appeared to make this a reality. In explaining the purposes of separation from Britain, the Declaration of Independence had announced that all men (a term that presumably included both sexes) were created equal, that all were equally entitled to "life, liberty, and the pursuit of happiness," and that the people had the right to establish new governments when existing governments did not fulfill these purposes. The liberty that the document envisioned was chiefly political, but it would certainly have included the freedom of conscience and religion that William Penn had envisioned when he founded the colony of Pennsylvania almost a century earlier.

An unattributed poem linked the Liberty Bell to the cause of Revolution (Belisle, 1859, 83–84):

The motto of our father band,
  Circled the world in its embrace—
'Twas "liberty throughout the land,

And good to all their brother race!"
Long here, within, the pilgrim's bell
   Had linger'd—though it often pealed—
Those treasured tones, that erst should tell
   When freedom's proudest scroll was sealed!
Here, the dawn of reason broke
   Upon the trampled rights of man;
And here a moral era woke—
   The brightest since the world began!
And still shall deep and loud acclaim
   Here tremble on its sacred chime—
While e'er the thrilling trump of Fame
   Shall linger on the pulse of Time!

As abolitionists would point out with increasing insistence, although the Constitution (which Americans ratified in 1789) sought to create self-government, and the Fifth Amendment (adopted in 1791) prohibited federal governmental deprivations of "life, liberty, or property" without due process of law, neither set of protections extended to African Americans who were held in slavery. Although the Liberty Bell cracked sometime in the 1830s or 1840s and could no longer announce major events, abolitionists used a bell to indicate this disparity and to call for freedom for all. About the same time, George Lippard and others were circulating popular stories about how expectant crowds gathered outside the Pennsylvania State House on July 4, 1776, awaiting news that would be conveyed by a flaxen-haired boy to an old man in the tower, who would ring the bell announcing their independence.

At the end of the Civil War between North and South in 1865, Congress proposed, and states adopted, the Thirteenth Amendment, which abolished involuntary servitude. In 1868, the Fourteenth Amendment further sought to guarantee "equal protection of the laws" to all citizens, white and black. It further extended the protections of due process against actions by state governments as well as the federal one. The Fifteenth Amendment (adopted in 1870) subsequently prohibited discrimination in voting on the basis of race, color, or previous condition of servitude.

In time, advocates of women's suffrage pointed out that they were not full participants in American liberty. Like earlier advocates of abolition, they sought to identify the Liberty Bell (and their own Justice Bell) with equality for both sexes, and to push for the successful adoption of the Nineteenth Amendment, which prohibited discrimination in voting on the basis of sex. African Americans and other minorities would continue to evoke the image of the Liberty Bell in pushing for even wider liberties.

In 1918, representatives of the Democratic Mid-European Union gathered at Independence Hall to sign a Declaration of Common Aims of the Independent Mid-European Nations. In early 1931, representatives from India, who were seeking their own independence from Great Britain, met at the Liberty Bell to read their own declaration of independence (Independence National Historical Park, Historic Note Card File, Card dated January 26, 1931).

Although his list is thus incomplete, Boland has observed that the Liberty Bell has come to stand for three basic liberties. The rights he identified were "the religious liberty of William Penn's colony; the political liberty of young America; and the liberty of Blacks from slavery" (Boland, 1973, 8).

The Liberty Bell has spent most of its existence either in or near the building that witnessed the writing of the Declaration of Independence. After considerable negotiating, the Declaration of Independence was even brought back to the building during the sesquicentennial celebrations of American independence in 1926 (Stathis, 1978). A bell similar in shape to the Liberty Bell, albeit without its characteristic inscription, was used as the dust jacket of a book published about Thomas Jefferson by Hendrik Willem Van Loon in 1943. The Bell thus remains a palpable symbol of the principles embodied by the Declaration, as well as American aspirations for the extension of such liberties not only at home, but abroad as well.

See also: Abolitionists and the Liberty Bell; Czech Liberty Bell; Independence Day; Inscription on the Liberty Bell; Justice Bell; Liberty, Meaning of; Lippard, George; Occasions for Ringing the Liberty Bell

Further Reading

Becker, Carl. (1922) 1970. *The Declaration of Independence: A Study in the History of Political Ideas.* New York: Vintage Books.

Belisle, D. W. 1959. *History of Independence Hall: From the Earliest Period to the Present Time, Embracing Biographies of the Immortal Signers of the Declaration of Independence, with Historical Sketches of the Sacred Relics Preserved in That Sanctuary of American Freedom.* Philadelphia: John Challen & Sons.

Boland, Charles Michael. 1973. *Ring in the Jubilee: The Epic of America's Liberty Bell.* Riverside, CT: Chatham Press.

Maier, Pauline. 1997. *American Scripture: Making the Declaration of Independence.* New York: Alfred A. Knopf.

Malone, Dumas. 1943. *The Story of the Declaration of Independence.* New York: Oxford University Press.

Stathis, Stephen W. 1978. "Returning the Declaration of Independence to Philadelphia: An Exercise in Centennial Politics." *Pennsylvania Magazine of History and Biography* 102 (April): 167–183.

Van Loon, Hendrik Willem. 1943. *Thomas Jefferson.* New York: Dodd, Mead, and Company.

Vile, John R. 2019. *The Declaration of Independence: America's First Founding Document in U.S. History and Culture.* Santa Barbara, CA: ABC-CLIO.

Democracy and the Liberty Bell

At its inception, the Liberty Bell appears chiefly to have symbolized ideals of religious freedom as incorporated in William Penn's Pennsylvania Charter of Privileges of 1701. Given that this document was also associated with representative government, and that the Pennsylvania Assembly had ordered it, it was also associated with representative democracy, or what came to be known as "republican government."

As relations between the colonies and Great Britain ruptured, chiefly over questions of the authority of the British Parliament, particularly with regard to its power to tax colonists who were not physically represented there, the Bell became associated with the idea of American independence from the mother country. It was a Bell of Independence and accordingly was rung on Independence Day.

Because the Liberty Bell was housed in the State House where delegates assembled in 1787 to write the U.S. Constitution, it was certainly an appropriate symbol for the government they created. In arguing for this new government in "Federalist No. 10," one of the essays advocating adoption of the U.S. Constitution, James Madison distinguished the government under the new Constitution from the pure democracies of antiquity on two grounds. As a continental government, people would not be able to assemble in a single place, as had the men of classical Athens. They would therefore use a system of representative democracy over a large territory that was designed to multiply the number of factions so that no one would gain a majority, and thus refine public opinion through a system of checks and balances. During the presidency of Andrew Jackson, politics took a more populistic direction, as Jackson portrayed himself to be the "tribune" of the people.

Beginning in the 1830s, the Liberty Bell became a key symbol for those who were advocating the abolition of slavery. Even after the slaves were freed, the Bell continued to be a rallying point for individuals seeking equal racial justice. American suffragists would subsequently have a Justice Bell cast to show the disparity of allowing adult males, but not adult females, to vote.

This significant expansion of the franchise, which was finally achieved in 1920 with the ratification of the Nineteenth Amendment, corresponded to a time generally known as the "Progressive Era" in U.S. history. In contrast to the founding fathers, who had sought to divide and balance power, the new emphasis was on more direct democratic mechanisms like the primary system for nominating candidates; the initiative; the referendum; the recall of corrupt officials; greater centralization; and increased emphasis on the role of the president in setting a national agenda.

As the United States entered World War I, President Woodrow Wilson said that it entered the fray because "[t]he world must be made safe for democracy" (Gratz, 2017). A number of the popular songs from the time, such as "Make the 'Old Bell' Ring" (1918) and "Ring Out Ye Bell of Liberty" (1918), emphasized that America's founding fathers fought for "liberty and democracy." A striking cartoon by Herbert Johnson (1878–1946) shows people ringing the bell of world democracy (Johnson, 1912–1941).

This emphasis on the association between democratic forms of government and freedom continued into the Cold War, as the United States faced off against the totalitarian government of the Soviet Union. When John W. Snyder, the U.S. secretary of the treasury, visited France to present a replica of the Liberty Bell to the nation, he thus observed, "It is the hope of the United States that you will look on this bell as a constant reminder of our common faith in democracy. It is intended also to recognize . . . their mutual devotion to the cause of human freedom" (Campbell, 2018).

One indication that the word "democracy" may be associated with a variety of meanings is the fact that the Democracy Bell, designed by Via Lewandowsky and located in Leipzig, Germany, is shaped like an egg. It was commissioned to celebrate the fall of the Berlin Wall and the end of communism. It strikes every Monday night at 6:35 pm to mark the historic fall of the wall on October 9, 1989, and otherwise, the bell strikes when it chooses (Pelling, 2018).

See also: Abolitionists and the Liberty Bell; Independence Day; "Make the 'Old Bell' Ring" (Song, 1918); Names for the Liberty Bell; "Ring Out Ye Bell of Liberty" (Song, 1918)

Further Reading

Campbell, Tom. 2018. "The Annecy Liberty Bell Replica." Tom Loves the Liberty Bell .com, June 19. http://tomlovestheliberty bell.com/2018/06/10/the-annecy-liberty -bell-replica.

Disney Trivia. n.d. http://disneytrivia.tumblr.com/post/34501185510/urban-legend-the -liberty-bell-in-liberty-square.

Gratz, Irwin. 2017. "It Aimed to Make the World 'Safe for Democracy': World War I and Its Aftermath." Maine Public Radio, February 3. https://www.mainepublic.org/post/it -aimed-make-world-safe-democracy-world-war-i-and-its-aftermath.

Hamilton, Alexander, James Madison, and John Jay. 1961. [orig. 1787–1788] *The Federalist Papers*. New York: New American Library.

Johnson, Herbert. Picture of cartoon printed between 1912 and 1941. "Ringing the Bell of World Democracy." Library of Congress. https://www.loc.gov/pictures/item /2016682469.

Pelling, Kirstie. 2018. "The Bell That Tolls for Democracy." May 3. The Family Adventure Project. https://www.familyadventureproject.org/leipzig-bell-democracy-bell.

Dimensions, Weight, and Cost of the Liberty Bell

One of the most concise descriptions of the Liberty Bell, which was apparently gathered with the support of Independence National Historical Park, is provided in a short article compiled by Eileen Miller. Captioned "Measurements of the Bell," it provides the following information:

Circumference around the lip	12 feet
Circumference around the crown	7 ft. 6 in.
Lip to the crown	3 feet
Height over the crown	2 ft. 3 in.
Thickness at lip	3 in.
Thickness at crown	1 ¼ inches
Weight	2,080 pounds
Length of clapper	3 ft. 2 in.

This is similar to information provided by David A. Kimball, who adds that the clapper weighs 44 ½ pounds and the yoke weighs 200 pounds (Kimball, 1989, 46).

Kimball observes that the Whitechapel Foundry in England charged 150 pounds, 13 shillings, and 8 pence sterling (1989, 46). Justin Kramer has said that the circumference around the place of the inscriptions is not 7 feet and 6 inches, but 6 feet, 8¼ inches (1974, 2). There is a bill showing that John Pass and John Stow, the Americans who twice recast the Bell, charged 60 pounds, 13 shillings, 5 pence sterling for their work (Norris Papers, July 3, 1753, Independence National Historical Park, Historic Card File).

The "lip" refers to the rim, the "crown" to the top portion of the bell, and the "clapper" to the metal object that strikes the inside of the Bell. It should be noted that the Bell currently weighs less than when it was cast because of individuals who chipped or chiseled off pieces as souvenirs. The yoke, to which the Bell is attached, is believed to be made of American elm, and it is reinforced with iron and steel.

Many replicas of the Liberty Bell have varied in size and weight. The Centennial Liberty Bell, which is currently housed in the steeple of Independence Hall, weighs 13,000 pounds. Many other replicas have the same shape as the Liberty Bell but are much smaller.

See also: Pass and Stow; Whitechapel Foundry

Further Reading

Baer, John. 1930. *The Liberty Bells of Pennsylvania*. Philadelphia: William J. Campbell.

Kimball, David. 1989. *The Story of the Liberty Bell*. Fort Washington, PA: Eastern National.

Kramer, Justin. 1975. *Cast in America: The Historically Accurate, Exciting Story of the Liberty Bell*. Los Angeles: Justin Kramer Incorporated.

Miller, Eileen. 1976. "The Liberty Bell." *Science and Children* 13 (January): 31–32.

Display of the Liberty Bell in the 1850s

Sometime after 1846, after the Liberty Bell ceased to be functional, it was taken from the tower of Independence Hall where it had hung and moved to the first floor of Independence Hall near the entrance. There, it was placed on an ornate stand. An article in the July 2, 1852, edition of the Philadelphia *Inquirer* thus observed that "The Committee on city property have caused the old Independence Bell to be lowered from its elevation in the State House tower, and placed in the Hall of Independence, on an octagon pedestal, covered with green baize, where it will remain hereafter" (Hall-Quest 1965, 144).

There is a depiction of the bell in a print published in 1856 by Max Rosenthal entitled *Interior View of Independence Hall*; in a "Liberty Bell" sketch by Theo. R. Davis that was published in the July 10, 1869, issue of *Harper's Weekly*; and in an article in the *Public Ledger* of February 21, 1855. The latter describes the bell as being in front of a painting of the Marquis de Lafayette, near a statue of George Washington, and on a pedestal designed by Frederick Graff, the grandson of Jacob Graff, who had rented the rooms in Philadelphia where Thomas Jefferson had written the Declaration of Independence (Kimball, 1989, 65). Rosenthal's print further indicates that there was another large painting in the room (probably of William Penn), as well as dozens of smaller paintings, possibly pictures of the signers of the Declaration of Independence. According to Kramer, the bell was also draped with a U.S. flag (Kramer, 1975, 91).

The white, double-based, wooden pedestal was octagonal and had at each corner fasces (a bundle of rods with an axe dating back to ancient Rome, where it was a symbol of authority for magistrates), which were "surmounted by the Liberty cap [a symbol of freedom worn by freed Roman slaves] and other emblems." These were wound together by "fillets" (ribbons), on which the names of the signers of the Declaration of Independence were engraved. Between the fasces were four shields— "one containing the coat of arms of the United States; a second, the arms of the State of Pennsylvania; a third, the arms of the city of Philadelphia," and the fourth an inscription. This inscription emphasized the connection of the Bell to American independence by proclaiming that "[t]he ringing of this bell first announced to the citizens who were anxiously waiting the result of the deliberations of Congress (which were at that time held with closed doors) that the Declaration of Independence had been decided upon; and then it was that the bell proclaimed liberty throughout all the land to all the inhabitants thereof." The description further observes that "[t]he American flag is gracefully festooned between the fasces, and binds them by its ample folds," that the carving had been executed by "a young man in this city named T. Daily," that the bell was "surmounted by a large gilt eagle," and that "the pedestal is painted with white China gloss; with the coats of arms, names of signers, and inscription by the shields in gilt" (Paige, 1988, 32).

It is enlightening to compare this pedestal with a monument that was proposed for the grounds of Independence Hall by a convention of delegates that met in July 1852 from the original 13 states. A report that it examined said that "the general plan of a monument, contemplates a structure with thirteen sides or faces, united by an entablature, upon which the Declaration of Independence shall be cut into the solid stone, surmounted by a tower or shaft; the thirteen faces to contain such inscriptions and emblazonings as each State shall direct, commemorative of some citizens or citizens of her own, who took part in the responsibility of that Declaration" (*Report of the Proceedings of a Convention*, 1852, 20).

In 1856, the gilded eagle was replaced by a small stuffed eagle, which Charles Willson Peale had previously displayed in his museum at Independence Hall. Charles MacKay, an Englishman who wrote *Life and Liberty in America; or, Sketches of a Tour in the United States and Canada in 1857–58,* opined, "Either the eagle is too small for the bell, or the bell is too large for the eagle." He further noted that a janitor had reported that a visitor had offered a much larger eagle, but it had only one wing, and "as a disabled eagle upon a cracked bell, would have afforded but too many opportunities to the jibers of jibes and the jokers of jokes, the gift was respectfully declined, and the little eagle, strong, compact, and without a flaw, holds his seat upon the relic, until some more ponderous and unexceptional bird shall be permitted to dethrone him" (Paige, 1988, 33). The stuffed bird, once displayed at the Independence National Historical Park Visitor Center, is now displayed in the Second Bank of the United States (Paige, 1988, 32, n.9).

In 1877, the Bell was removed from its stand and suspended by a chain of 13 links (one for each of the original states) in the hallway directly below the clock, where it remained for the next few years (Paige 1988, 35). Although his words were largely metaphorical, in 1876, John Shoemaker, who was the chair of the Centennial Committee, observed that, since slavery had been ended, "Cracked and shattered as the bell may be, the base upon which that motto is cast remains firm and solid, and shaken as has our country been with the din of battle and bloody strife, that principle remains pure and perfect for all time to come, and the whole text, Liberty Jubilee, will be literally carried out in 1876. 'Liberty can now be proclaimed throu all the land to all inhabitants thereof'" (Nash, 2010, 63).

See also: Crack in the Liberty Bell; Display of the Liberty Bell in 1894; Displays of the Liberty Bell; Independence Hall

Further Reading

Byvack, Valentijn. 1998. "Public Portraits and Portrait Publics." *A Journal of Mid-Atlantic Studies* 65: 199–242.

Hall-Quest, Olga W. 1965. *The Bell That Rang for Freedom: The Liberty Bell and Its Place in American History.* New York: E. P. Dutton.

Kimball, David. 1989. *The Story of the Liberty Bell.* Fort Washington, PA: Eastern National.

Kramer, Justin. 1975. *Cast in America: The Historically Accurate, Exciting Story of the Liberty Bell.* Los Angeles: Justin Kramer Incorporated.

Nash, Gary B. 2010. *The Liberty Bell.* New Haven, CT: Yale University Press.

Paige, John C. 1988. *The Liberty Bell: A Special History Study.* David C. Kimball, ed. Denver: Denver Service Center and Independence National Historical Park.

Report of the Proceedings of a Convention composed of Delegates from the Thirteen Original United States Held in Independence Hall on Monday the Fifth, and Tuesday the Sixth of July, 1852, for the Purpose of Considering the Propriety of Erecting One or More Monuments I Independence Square, Philadelphia in Commemoration of the Declaration of Independence, July 4, 1776, and in Honor of the Signers Thereof . . . 1852. Philadelphia: Crissy & Markley, Printers.

Display of the Liberty Bell in 1894

After hanging from a chain of the Liberty Bell tower since 1877, in 1894 the Liberty Bell was lowered and placed in a glass-and-oak case designed by Francis D. Kramer, a noted cabinetmaker whose office was located next to Philadelphia's Christ Church. An article in the *Public Ledger* of June 14, 1894, described it as being (Paige, 1988, 40):

> 5 foot 10 inch square, ten feet high excepting the front which rises to 12 feet; the four sides paneled with American glass four inches wide and 7 feet high in center, at each corner a bronze pillar, over the front a carved eagle, on each corner of the case is a polished bronze torch. Inside the case the bell is supported by the marred yoke which is suspended by bronze columns, all of which fit on a truck four feet square, supported on four rubber-tired wheels. The railing around the case is polished bronze and held by four columns surmounted by bronze torches.

As with the display that was used in the 1850s, the new display was associated with an eagle, this time made of wood and designated "Old Abe" after the mascot of the 8th Wisconsin Regiment, which fought in the Civil War (Paige, 1988, 41).

As the description conveys, the Bell was not simply protected against touching, but, by being placed on a cart, was also provided a means of escape in case of fire. But then, in 1915, the glass was removed so that visitors could touch the Bell (Stoudt, 1930, 125).

See also: Display of the Liberty Bell in the 1850s; Displays of the Liberty Bell; Security for the Liberty Bell

Further Reading

Paige, John C. 1988. *The Liberty Bell of Independence National Historical Park: A Special History Study*, ed. David C. Kimball. Denver: Denver Service Center, National Park Service, Department of the Interior. Accessed through pubs.etic.nps.gov.

Stoudt, John Baer. 1930. *The Liberty Bells of Pennsylvania*. Philadelphia: William J. Campbell.

Displays of the Liberty Bell

As veneration for the Liberty Bell has increased over time, efforts have been made to display it in an appropriate fashion.

The Bell was initially installed in the steeple of the State House, where it is doubtful that anyone other than the bell ringer would have been able to read its famous inscription. Because the Bell could have been melted down into shots or cannon, it was removed from Philadelphia before the British occupation of late 1777 and early 1778, and moved to Allentown, where it was hidden in the basement of the Zion Reformed Church.

When the Bell was returned to the State House in 1778, it was stored at the mid-level of the brick tower over a louvered floor that could be reached by steps. The steeple itself had fallen into disrepair and was finally replaced by a brick tower in 1781. When a new steeple was added in 1828, it housed a larger bell made by John Wilbank, and that remained until it was replaced in 1876 by a still-larger Centennial Bell that stands to this day.

Although interest in the State House increased with the visit of the Marquis de Lafayette in 1824, and Independence Hall, the name originally given to the room where the Declaration of Independence was signed, became applied to the whole building, abolitionist literature appear to have, over time, applied the term "Liberty Bell" to the object that is now so familiar. In 1852, this Bell was accordingly removed to the Assembly Room, where it was first displayed on a temporary pedestal and then moved in two years to a much more elaborate octagonal platform that was mounted by a stuffed bald eagle.

In 1873, the framework that had supported the Liberty Bell was brought down from the belfry, and the Bell was reattached and displayed under the stairway of the Tower Room, surrounded by a plain iron railing. During the Centennial celebrations, the Bell was displayed in the vestibule of Independence Hall, so that visitors would see it as soon as they entered. Perhaps because the framework of the Bell had practically concealed it, in 1877 it was hung from the ceiling of the tower room from a chain of 13 links, representing each of the original colonies (Independence National Historical Park, n.d.).

From 1885 to 1915, the Liberty Bell took seven trips to expositions and fairs throughout the United States. In addition to viewing the Bell at these various venues, many Americans would have seen the Bell on a train that passed through their areas, or in the towns and villages on which it stopped on its tours. After each tour, the Bell would return to Independence Hall. In 1895, it was placed in a large glass case in the Assembly until it was exhibited beginning in 1915 on a simpler frame and pedestal that could be more easily evacuated if there were a fire or other emergency in the building. In its last trip to San Francisco in 1915, the Bell was secured on a train car with special shock absorbers to prevent further cracking.

In anticipation of the large numbers of tourists who would visit the Bell during the nation's bicentennial celebrations in 1976, the National Park Service, which had acquired custody of it in 1951, decided to move it to a nearby pavilion constructed especially for this purpose. In 2003, the Bell was moved to yet another Liberty Bell Center, which provided more panels with interpretative information for visitors. In both the Liberty Bell Pavilion and the Liberty Bell Center, the Bell has been displayed on a simple steel frame in front of a window that looks onto Independence Hall. Although there have been times when the Bell was directly accessible to members of the public who wanted to touch it, it is currently separated from the public by a metal railing.

See also: Allentown; Display of the Liberty Bell in the 1850s; Display of the Liberty Bell in 1894; Independence Hall; Journeys of the Liberty Bell; Liberty Bell Center; Liberty Bell Pavilion; Security for the Liberty Bell

Further Reading

Independence National Historical Park. n.d. "The Story of a Symbol." https://www.nps.gov /parkhistory/online_books/hh/17/hh17h.htm.

Dublin's Freedom and Liberty Bells

At the time America's Liberty Bell was first cast in 1752, 13 English-speaking colonies were still subjects of Great Britain. The Liberty Bell achieved much of its fame based on stories of how it later rang at the signing of the Declaration of Independence, as well as its subsequent association with the movement for African American emancipation.

Like the American colonies, Ireland was long under British colonial rule. Irish Roman Catholics in particular were suspected of disloyalty to the Crown on religious grounds, and they sought religious freedom as the American colonies had. In 1829, when Ireland achieved Catholic emancipation, a bell was rung in a church (once called the Smock Alley Theatre, built in 1622) in celebration. In 1811, Father Michael Blake defied penal laws and rang the bell, for which Daniel O'Connell, known as "the liberator," successfully defended him. One similarity between this bell and its American counterpart is that it was cracked, reputedly when O'Connell rang the bell, an event for which the U.S. Liberty Bell was also rung.

The Dublin Bell was not treasured at first, nor was its U.S. counterpart. As plans proceeded to restore the Dublin Bell in 2014 as part of an initiative designed to increase tourism, the Smock Alley director observed, "This is Dublin's, and Ireland's great freedom bell. In America the Liberty Bell is cased behind eight inches of plate glass, our bell is cased beneath eight inches of pigeon poop" (Kelly, 2014).

St. Patrick's Park in Dublin is also home to another "Liberty Bell." Bearing little resemblance to its American counterpart, the Dublin Liberty Bell is an elongated bell that is hung by a chain to a metal frame that is painted white. A website explains, "It is called the 'Liberty' bell because it is located in one of the 'liberties' [manorial lands that preserved their own jurisdiction] of Dublin" ("Liberty Bell—St Patrick's Park, Dublin, Ireland," n.d.).

See also: Declaration of Independence and the Liberty Bell

Further Reading

Kelly, Olivia. 2014. "Dublin's Freedom Bell to Be Restored." *Irish Times,* March 11. https://www.irishtimes.com/culture/heritage/dublin-s-freedom-bell-to-be-restored-1.1719697.

"Liberty Bell—St. Patrick's Park, Dublin, Ireland." n.d. http://www.waymarking.com/waymarks/WMQZ7D_Liberty_Bell_St_Patricks_Park_Dublin_Ireland.

E

Eagles, Flags, the Statue of Liberty, and Related Symbols

The Liberty Bell is only one of many symbols that stand for the United States and its values. Other prominent symbols include the following: the U.S. flag, which has had numerous iterations; the bald eagle, the national bird that often serves as a symbol of American power; the Great Seal of the United States, which (like the Liberty Bell) is often associated with the American founding; famous statesmen like George Washington, Thomas Jefferson, and Abraham Lincoln; Uncle Sam, who has become far more than a mere cartoon character; famous buildings such as Independence Hall, Monticello, Mount Vernon, the White House, the Supreme Court Building, and the Capitol Building; monuments, like those in Washington, D.C., to honor George Washington and Thomas Jefferson; documents such as the Declaration of Independence; and the Constitution and its words, "life, liberty and the pursuit of happiness," as well as "We the People" and the like.

Although each symbol has its own meaning, together they evoke wider sentiments. It is therefore common to see the symbols displayed together. As described elsewhere in this volume, in the 1850s the Liberty Bell was displayed on an elaborate stand with the names of the signers of the Declaration of Independence, shields, the U.S. flag, and a gilded eagle.

For most of its life, the Liberty Bell has been housed in the Pennsylvania State House, today's Independence Hall. Even after being moved, first to a pavilion in 1976 and then to a designated center in 2003, visitors continue to view the Liberty Bell in front of a window that looks out toward Independence Hall.

Songs that describe the Liberty Bell, especially those written during times of war, tend to identify the Bell with the flag and with the ideals of freedom, democracy, liberty, and justice that it exemplifies. The same is true of posters, like those that were used to encourage investments in Liberty Loans during World War I.

The Liberty Bell is so consistently tied to Independence Day that the otherwise-unverified story persists that it was rung on July 4, 1776, to announce the acceptance of the Declaration of Independence. Accordingly, the Bell is often portrayed against a background of exploding fireworks or along with a depiction of Uncle Sam.

Coins may have a picture of a statesman on one side and the Liberty Bell on the other, while paintings almost always associate the Liberty Bell with the U.S. flag.

See also: Coins, Medals, and Stamps Depicting the Liberty Bell; Display of the Liberty Bell in the 1850s; Display of the Liberty Bell in 1894; Independence Day; Independence Hall; Liberty Bell Center; Liberty Bell Pavilion; Liberty Loans; Music and the Liberty Bell; Statue of Liberty

Further Reading

Horwitz, Elinor Lander. 1976. *The Bird, the Banner, and Uncle Sam: Images of America in Folk and Popular Art*. Philadelphia: J. P. Lippincott Company.

Tippin, Aaron. n.d. "Aaron Tippin Lyrics." https://www.azlyrics.com/lyrics/aarontippin/wherethestarsandstripesandeaglefly.html.

Vile, John R. 2018. *The American Flag: An Encyclopedia of the Stars and Stripes in U.S. History, Culture, and Law*. Santa Barbara, CA: ABC-CLIO.

Vile, John R. 2016. *The Constitutional Convention of 1787: A Comprehensive Encyclopedia of America's Founding*, rev. 2nd ed., 2 vols. Clark, NJ: Talbot Publishing.

Vile, John R. 2019. *The Declaration of Independence: America's First Founding Document in U.S. History and Culture*. Santa, Barbara, CA: ABC-CLIO.

F

Fiction and the Liberty Bell

Many of the most popular myths about the Liberty Bell arose in fiction. The most prominent of these may be that it was rung on July 4, 1776, by an old bellman after receiving word from a young boy that the delegates to the Second Continental Congress had ratified the Declaration of Independence. The works of George Lippard, which were later popularized in poetry, were particularly influential.

Paul Haspel believes that the striking of the clock in Edgar Allan Poe's tale "The Masque of the Red Death" was intended to contrast the ideals of the Liberty Bell against the lingering cancer of American slavery (Haspel, 2012).

Gilbert Morris (1929–2016) was a Christian author who earned a PhD at the University of Arkansas and wrote seven historical fiction books from 1995 to 2000 on the American revolutionary period as part of a "Liberty Bell Series" published by Bethany House. In 2017, Jennifer Froelich wrote a book entitled *Stealing Liberty,* in which teens sent to a detention camp seek to steal the Liberty Bell and inform the public of the ideals for which it originally stood in order to save it from a dictatorial government that is seeking to sell it.

In a very different genre, Henry Turtledove has written an alternative history entitled *In the Presence of Mine Enemies,* in which the United States and Canada abstained from participating in World War II but were later defeated in a third world war. In the book, the Greater German Reich had destroyed Philadelphia with a nuclear weapon but had prisoners dig up the Liberty Bell, after which it was brought to Berlin and, because it was still radioactive, was displayed under leaded glass.

In another twist, Evangelos I. Gegas has published a law review article in which he begins with a hypothetical from the year 2776, at which time he projected that the United States was a "diminished power." In an attempt to illustrate the importance of national symbols, he further hypothesizes that the Liberty Bell was stolen, but that when it was discovered 75 years later in the private collection of a Swiss banker, the United States was unable to repossess it (Gegas, 1997).

There is also a series of comic books entitled *Liberty Belle*, which were published during World War II. They portray a superhero called "The All-American Girl," who obtains her power in part from her association with the Liberty Bell.

See also: Liberty Belle (Comics); Lippard, George

Further Reading

Casey, Janet. G. 2015. *Teaching Tainted Lit: Popular American Fiction in Today's Classroom.* Iowa City: University of Iowa Press.

Gegas, Evangelos I. 1997. "International Arbitration and the Resolution of Cultural Property Disputes: Navigating the Stormy Waters Surrounding Cultural Property." *Ohio State Journal of Dispute Resolution* 13: 129–166.

Haspel, Paul. 2012. "Bells of Freedom and Foreboding: Liberty Bell Ideology and the Clock Motif in Edgar Allan Poe's 'The Masque of the Red Death.'" *Edgar Allan Poe Review* 13 (Spring): 46–70.

Turtledove, Harry. *Liberty Bell: The Liberty Bell In the Presence of Mine Enemies.* Harry Turtledove Wiki. http://turtledove.wikia.com/wiki/Liberty_Bell.

Warren, Charles. 1945. "Fourth of July Myths." *William and Mary Quarterly* 2 (July): 237–272.

Films and the Liberty Bell

The Liberty Bell has appeared not only in song, verse, and other writings, but also in films. One of the sites that was featured in the 2004 movie *National Treasure* was Independence Hall, the site of the Liberty Bell. In actuality, it was a re-creation of Independence Hall at Knott's Berry Farm in Buena Park, California, so as not to chance damaging some of the artifacts at the Bell's real location (Sneff, 2016).

One classic movie, *It's A Wonderful Life,* was produced by Liberty Films in 1946, and it featured the line, "Every time a bell rings, an angel gets its wings." As the movie begins, the title flashes across the screen against the ringing of what appears to be the Liberty Bell. Bells throughout the movie remind viewers that its denouement is set during the Christmas season.

At the end of Cecil B. DeMille's epic *The Ten Commandments,* which was produced in 1956, Moses (Charlton Heston) quotes the inscription from Leviticus 25:10 that is on the Liberty Bell—namely, "Proclaim liberty throughout all the land unto all the inhabitants thereof." Then, he raises a hand in a pose similar to that of the Statue of Liberty (Feiler, 2009).

Another movie, *The Brotherhood of the Bell,* was produced for television in 1970. It starred Glenn Ford and was based on a novel by David Karp, who also wrote the screenplay. In the movie, an elite college society, which seeks wealth and power, is apparently used as proof that the Liberty Bell has Satanic connections. On January 2, 1971, the sitcom *My Three Sons* aired an episode entitled "The Liberty Bell"; while it touched on the themes of freedom and responsibility, it focused more on a character named Jim Bell rather than the object at Independence Hall.

The movie version of the popular play *1776* perpetuated the idea that the Liberty Bell was rung as delegates signed the Declaration of Independence on July 4. It is now believed that if the Bell rang, it would have done so on July 8, when the document was first publicly read in Philadelphia.

In 1983, *Liberty Belle* played on the similarity of the words *bell* and *belle,* as it portrayed student opposition to French colonialism and support for Algerian self-determination. By contrast, the 1981 movie *Blow Out* used the genre of horror to portray a Liberty Bell Stalker, who carves the Liberty Bell into the abdomens of his victims (Nash 2010, 192–193).

The 2007, the satirical movie *Juno* is about an unplanned teen pregnancy. The main character's younger half-sister is named Liberty Bell MacGuff.

An episode of the sitcom *How I Met Your Mother* features the following dialogue, which depicts an unusual way of experiencing the Bell (IMDb):

Ted: And so I licked the Liberty Bell.

Laura: How did it taste?

Ted: Like freedom . . . no, actually it tasted like pennies.

Laura: My God, Did you guys really do that?

Older Ted: We really did. And that was when I realized why I hung out with Barney. I never got where I thought I wanted to go, but I always got a great story.

Another sitcom called *It's Always Sunny in Philadelphia*, which premiered on November 6, 2008, has an episode entitled "The Gang Cracks the Liberty Bell." In it, the gang attempts to have their bar, Paddy's, declared a historical landmark by tying it to the cracking of the Liberty Bell. An episode of another television series, from 1995, entitled *Brotherly Love,* likewise contains an episode called "The Liberty Bell Show," in which one of the characters visits the Liberty Bell and fears that he has accidentally damaged it.

In 2006, Mark Kochanowicz of Philadelphia founded an independent film and video production company called Liberty Bell Films (not to be confused with the earlier Liberty Bell Films). In the television series *The Man in the High Castle,* which features a world governed by Nazis, the Statue of Liberty crumbles, and, in episode 8 of the third season, the authorities melt the Liberty Bell and turn it into a swastika.

See also: Conspiracy Theories About the Liberty Bell; Crack in the Liberty Bell; Declaration of Independence and the Liberty Bell

Further Reading

Feiler, Bruce. 2009. "How Moses Shaped America." *Time*, October 12. http://content.time.com/time/subscriber/article/0,33009,1927303-3,00.html.

How I Met Your Mother (TV Series). "'The Sweet Taste of Liberty.' Quotes (2005)." https://www.imdb.com/title/tt0606117/quotes.

Nash, Gary B. 2010. *The Liberty Bell*. New Haven, CT: Yale University Press.

Sneff, Emily. "Presenting the Facts: National Treasure." Course of Human Events. December 19, 2016. https://declaration.fas.harvard.edu/blog/facts-nationaltreasure.

Freedom Bell

The Liberty Bell was often used as a symbol during the Cold War to represent U.S. support for freedom over totalitarian communism. Much of this effort was directed toward stopping the advance of communism in Europe. To this end, the Central Intelligence Agency (CIA) broadcasted radio reports in Eastern Europe on a channel known as Radio Free Europe (although as might be expected, the public was unaware of the CIA's involvement and were told that the program was privately funded). From an early date, the executive board symbolized the campaign with a bell (Medhurst, 1997, 650).

To emphasize this private tie, a Crusade for Freedom organized beginning in 1948, and it continued until 1965. The crusade was the brainchild of the American diplomat George F. Kennan, who had also authored the doctrine of containment of communism. It was organized by a group called the National Committee for a Free Europe, which was headed by General Lucius Clay, the former military governor of West Berlin, who was also was responsible for organizing the Berlin Airlift in 1948. General Dwight D. Eisenhower, who would later become president of the United States, gave a kickoff address for the campaign to a large audience in Denver on Labor Day, September 4, 1950, which was broadcast not only by major American networks, but also by the Voice of America and Radio Free Europe.

Two days later, an 10-ton bell (some sources give heavier weights), dubbed the Freedom Bell or World Freedom Bell, which was patterned after the Liberty Bell and which the United States had had cast by Gillett & Johnson clock and bell makers in Croydon, England, arrived in New York Harbor. The huge bell was decorated with men representing the five continents that had fought during World War II (namely, Europe, Asia, Africa, Australasia, and North America). They were holding torches. A circle above the figures contained laurels, while the rim contained words paraphrased from Lincoln's Gettysburg Address: "That this world, under God, shall have a new birth of freedom" (Medhurst 1997, 656).

Just as in earlier years the Liberty Bell had toured the country, the Freedom Bell was paraded through New York and to a series of rallies in many other cities. By the end of the year, the Crusade for Freedom had gathered about 16 million signatures on its Freedom Scroll and raised about $1.3 million (Medhurst, 1997, 657).

The bell was subsequently installed in the former city hall in West Berlin, where it was welcomed by more than 400,000 people, some of whom came from what then was communist East Berlin (Nash, 2010, 158). It was rung not only on noon of each day, but also on the occasion of uprisings in Eastern Europe, the construction and later fall of the Berlin Wall, the reunification of Germany, and the 9/11 terrorist attacks as a show of support for the United States.

The bell has been commemorated by several German stamps that were issued from 1951 to 1956, with the clappers shown in different positions on different issues of the stamps (Stamp-Collecting-World, n.d.).

See also: American Legion Freedom Bell; Global Significance of the Liberty Bell; Replicas of the Liberty Bell

Further Reading

Gillett & Johnston (Croydon) Ltd. Our Freedom Bell. https://www.gillettjohnston.com.uk /gillett-johnston-croydon-ltd-our-freedom-bell.

Medhurst, Martin J. 1997. "Eisenhower and the Crusade for Freedom: The Rhetorical Origins of a Cold War Campaign." *Presidential Studies Quarterly* 27 (Fall): 646–661.

Nash, Gary B. 2010. *The Liberty Bell.* New Haven, CT: Yale University Press.

Stamp-Collecting-World. n.d. "West Berlin Stamps Freedom Bell Issues 1951–1956." https://www.stamp-collecting-world.com/westberlin_bells.html.

G

"Get Off the Track! (A Song for Emancipation)" (Song, 1844)

One of the earliest known songs to refer to the Liberty Bell was composed by Jesse Hutchinson, Jr., in 1844 entitled "Get off the Track! (A Song for Emancipation)."

Jesse was a member of the Hutchinson Family Singers, which was established in Milford, New Hampshire, in 1839 (a picture from 1845 shows 10 of the family members). The group is credited with being one of the forbears of modern American pop music (Maxwell, 2017, 3). Initially using costumes from other times and cultures, the Hutchinson Family Singers eventually abandoned such novelties to portray themselves as what Tom Maxell calls "natural-born Americans," and they accordingly made "The Old Granite State" their theme song (Maxell, 2017, 4).

In 1843, while performing in Boston at the Anti-Slavery Society's annual meeting, they added a verse to the song that proclaimed (Maxwell 2017, 5):

Yes, we're friends of Emancipation
   And we'll sing a proclamation
Till it echoes through the nation,
   From the Old Granite State,
   That the Tribe of Jesse
Are the friends of Equal Rights.

About the same time, so-called blackfaced singers composed minstrel songs that mocked African Americans and portrayed them as simple-minded and unworthy.

In time, Jesse Hutchinson composed 11 verses to this tune under the title "Get Off the Track! (A Song for Emancipation)." The opening verse proclaimed (Protest Song Lyrics, n.d.):

Ho! The Car Emancipation,
Rides majestic thro' our nation.
Bearing on its Train, the story,
Liberty, A Nation's Glory.
Roll it along, Roll it along, Roll it along,
Thro' the Nation Freedom's Car, Emancipation.
Roll it along, Roll it along,
Roll it along, thro' the Nation,
Freedom's Car. Emancipation.

Verse four urged ministers and their churches to "Leave behind sectarian lurches" and "Jump on board the Car of Freedom." The next verse urged politicians to "Jump for your lives! Politicians, From your dangerous false positions" (Protest Song Lyrics, n.d.).

As its title suggests, the song analogized emancipation to a railroad car that was gaining momentum and would sweep away all opposition in its wake (the lyrics might also have been associated with the idea of an Underground Railroad, through which slaves could travel to freedom). The ninth stanza evokes the Liberty Bell:

Hear the mighty car wheels humming!
Now look out! The Engine's Coming!
Church and Statesmen! Hear the thunder!
Clear the track, or you'll fall under.
Get off the track! All are singing.
While the Liberty Bell is ringing.

The next stanza continues:

On triumphant, see them bearing,
Through sectarian rubbish tearing;
Th' Bell and Whistle and the Steaming,
Startles thousands from their dreaming.
Look out for the cars! While the Bell rings,
Ere the sound your funeral knell rings.

The final verse thus ends:

See the people run to meet us;
All the Depot's thousands greet us;
All take seats with exultation,
In the Car Emancipation
Soon will bless our happy nation.
Huaaz! . . . Huzza!! . . . Hussa!!! . . . (Protest Song Lyrics, n.d.)

The song was enthusiastically received at the 1844 Anti-Slavery Society annual meeting and stirred popular enthusiasm in a way that was hitherto not associated with the movement. The next year, the Hutchinsons showed their mettle and received a similar positive reception after putting on a performance in Manhattan, where proponents of slavery had threatened them with physical violence.

The Hutchinsons also advocated other reforms as well, including Prohibition and women's suffrage. Although General George McClellan later kicked the group off Union lines, President Abraham Lincoln intervened, saying "It is just the character of song that I desire the soldiers to hear" (Maxwell, 2017, 10).

See also: Abolitionists and the Liberty Bell; Music and the Liberty Bell

Further Reading
Maxwell, Tom. 2017. "A History of American Protest Music: How the Hutchinson Family Singers Achieved Pop Stardom with an Anti-Slavery Anthem." March. https://longreads.com/2017/03/07/a-history-of-american-protest-music-how-the-hutchinson-family-singers-achieved-pop-stardom-with-an-anti-slavery-anthem.
Protest Song Lyrics. n.d. "Get Off the Track! (A Song for Emancipation), Lyrics." http://www.protestsonglyrics.net/Freedom_Songs/Get-Off-The-Track.phtml.

Global Significance of the Liberty Bell

Although the Liberty Bell is a distinct American symbol with a unique American history, it has transcended its national associations and become an internationally recognized icon. Moreover, this development has been long in the making.

Although plans to take the Columbian Liberty Bell abroad appeared to have faltered, Charlene Mires observed that it emphasized "associations between the Liberty Bell and world affairs" (2002, 158). Indeed, she observed that speakers increasingly began to quote the inscription on the Bell as extending liberty throughout "all the world" rather than merely "throughout all the land" (2002, 158). One example of such usage is found in a book by Thomas Rees of 1906, when, in comparing the Mexican Liberty Bell to that of the United States, he observed that both bells spoke the same language—namely, "Proclaim liberty throughout the world and to all the inhabitants thereof" (Rees 1906, 391).

By 1885, Shibo Shiro had written a popular novel entitled *Kajin no Kigu* (Strange encounters of elegant females), which opens at Independence Hall and explicitly refers to the Liberty Bell.

The 1915 work *The Memoirs of Li Hung-chang*, which its author, William Francis Mannix, later revealed to be fictional, also popularized the Liberty Bell in a poem that opined (Mires, 2002, 159):

A student of the philosophy of ages,
Know what this Bell speaks
Is of heaven's wisdom,
Millions of centuries before the earth was born.

The presence of America's first World's Fair in Philadelphia in 1876 and the journey of the Bell to seven expositions and celebrations from 1885 to 1915 furthered its association with global affairs. If the Bell might have appealed in earlier days to nations such as those in Latin America, which relished overthrowing foreign rulers, by the mid-nineteenth century, it was further associated with the movement to abolish slavery. By the end of the nineteenth century, which saw the American acquisition of former Spanish colonies, some Americans believed that the Liberty Bell promoted American values in America's own foreign colonies. During World War I, the Bell was associated with Liberty Loans, which were tied to defeating the forces of repression associated with the German Kaiser. President Woodrow Wilson's "Fourteen Points" speech inspired nations that had not yet attained their sovereignty, and the Czechs, who actually sent representatives to sign a declaration of independence in Philadelphia, had a bell cast that said "Proclaim liberty throughout all the world" (Fried, 2017).

Since then, replicas of the Liberty Bell have appeared in Tokyo, Berlin, Jerusalem, Louvain, Belgium; Albay, in the Philippines; Normandy, France; and Kaunas, Lithuania. Ireland also has two bells designated as "liberty bells," and Cuba and Mexico have their own versions as well. In 1962, Mexican president Adolfo Lopez Mateos presented President John F. Kennedy with a small replica of the Liberty Bell of Mexico. A plaque near the replica of the Liberty Bell in Tokyo observed that in ringing out liberty for Americans in 1776, the Liberty Bell became "thereby a symbol of freedom to not only Americans but to all mankind" ("Hibiya Park Liberty Bell," 2014).

Another indication of the status of the Liberty Bell as an international symbol is the large number of foreign dignitaries who have come to visit it and who have commented on its symbolic significance. During America's 1976 bicentennial celebrations, Britain's Queen Elizabeth II not only gave a speech at the site of the Liberty Bell, but also donated a Bicentennial Bell.

In 2015, the importance of the Bell and related historic sites was further emphasized when Philadelphia became the nation's first World Heritage City. The World Peace Bell, a very large replica of the Liberty Bell, which was cast for the new millennium and is now displayed in Newport, Kentucky, further connected the ideals of freedom and liberty with those of peace. Finally, in 1961, the National Aeronautics and Space Administration (NASA) designated the craft that carried Gus Grissom, the second American in space, as *Liberty Bell 7*.

See also: American Lithuanian Liberty Bell; Bicentennial Bell; Centennial Exposition of 1876; Columbian Liberty Bell; Czech Liberty Bell; Journeys of the Liberty Bell; Liberty Bell of Louvain; *Liberty Bell 7* Spacecraft; Normandy Liberty Bell; Philippine Liberty Bell; Presidents and Foreign Dignitaries at the Liberty Bell; Tokyo, Japan, Replica of the Liberty Bell; World Peace Bell

Further Reading

Fried, Stephen. 2017. "World War I: 100 Years Later. How the Liberty Bell Won the Great War." Smithsonian.com, April. https://www.smithsonianmag.com/history/how-liberty-bell-won-great-war-180962471.

"Hibiya Park Liberty Bell." 2014. *Lost Tokyo* (blog), June 18. http://lost-tokyo.blogspot.com/2014/06/hibiya-park-liberty-bell.html.

Mires, Charlene. 2002. *Independence Hall in American Memory*. Philadelphia: University of Pennsylvania Press.

Rees, Thomas. 1906. *Spain's Lost Jewels: Cuba and Mexico. 1906. Spain's Lost Jewels: Cuban and Mexico*. Springfield: Illinois State Register.

H

Hibernia

The Liberty Bell arrived in Philadelphia from England sometime between August 9 and September 1, 1752. After the Bell was first rung and cracked, the superintendents of the State House who had ordered it attempted to arrange for its return for recasting.

Because the superintendents contacted Captain Richard Budden of the ship *Myrtilla* (meaning "flowering shrub") to take it back to London, many writers have concluded that this must have been the ship that brought it. Records reveal, however, that the only ship that arrived in Philadelphia during the month of August was the *Hibernia*, which is a name for Ireland; or *Snow Hibernia*, *snow* being a designation of a particular type of square-rigged vessel with a trysail mast known as a *snow*. William Child was captain (Paige, 1988, 6). Captain Richard Budden is believed to have delivered the bells and paid the freight for Christ Church on the *Myrtilla* two years later in 1754 (Stoudt, 1930, 130).

The ship took 11 weeks to come from London to Philadelphia. Noting that this was longer than average, scholar Charles Boland assumed that it may have had a rough voyage, and that this could possibly help account for why the Bell cracked on its first ringing (1973, 39).

Because John Pass and John Stow recast the Bell in Philadelphia, the first Bell was never returned, although the Assembly did purchase a second bell from the Whitechapel Foundry in England, which was used in conjunction with a clock on the State House.

See also: Pass and Stow; Sister to the Liberty Bell; Whitechapel Foundry

Further Reading

Boland, Charles Michael. 1973. *Ring in the Jubilee: The Epic of America's Liberty Bell.* Riverside, CT: Chatham Press.

Paige, John C. 1988. *The Liberty Bell of Independence National Historical Park: A Special History Study*, ed. by David Kimball. Denver: Denver Service Center and Independence National Historical Park.

Stoudt, John Baer. 1930. *The Liberty Bells of Pennsylvania*. Philadelphia: William J. Campbell.

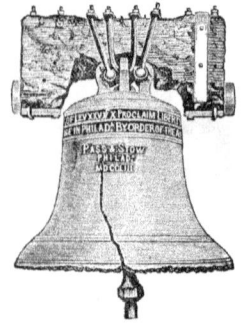

"Independence Bell—July 4, 1776" (Poem, 1871)

Of all the works that has popularized the Liberty Bell, especially among children, none appears to have been more influential than a poem entitled "Independence Bell—July 4, 1776." Although it was anonymously published, it was popularized when it was printed as part of George S. Hillard's *Franklin Fifth Reader*, which was published in 1871.

This poem had a catchy cadence that played on the myth that George Lippard had previously perpetuated in a story called "The Fourth of July, 1776." He described an aged sexton impatiently waiting for word from a flaxen-haired boy as to whether the Second Continental Congress was going to adopt the Declaration of Independence, which proclaimed the 13 North American colonies to be free of Great Britain. Significantly, this poem portrayed the sexton and the boy as being grandfather and grandson, although Lippard's story did not (Nash, 2010, 60).

The poem has nine stanzas. The first portrays people restlessly awaiting news of independence (English Grammar Online, n.d.):

> There was a tumult in the city
> In the quaint old Quaker town,
> And the streets were rife with people
> Pacing restless up and down—.

In the third stanza, readers hear the people trying to get near the door so they can ascertain who is speaking (English Grammar Online, n.d.):

> "Will they do it" "Dare they do it?"
> "Who is speaking?" "What's the news?"
> "What of Adams?" "What of Sherman?"
> "Oh, God grant they won't refuse!"
> "Make some way there!" "Let me nearer!""
> "I am stifling!" "Stifle then!
> When a nation's life's at hazard,
> We've no time to think of Men!"

By contrast, inside the State House, the fourth stanza reports, "Sat the Continental Congress, truth and reason for their guide," as they debated over "a simple scroll" (English Grammar Online, n.d.).

The fifth stanza switches to the "high steeple," where a bellman "weary of the tyrant/ And his iron-sceptered sway" sat "with one hand ready on the clapper of the bell" (English Grammar Online, n.d.).

As the crowd "quivers," in the seventh stanza, a boy emerges from the State House: "Ring!" he shouts, "Ring! Grandpa, Ring! Oh, ring for Liberty!" (English Grammar Online, n.d.).

In the penultimate stanza, the city joins in the ringing of the bell (English Grammar Online, n.d.):

How they shouted! What rejoicing!
How the old bell shook the air,
Tell the clang of freedom ruffled,
The calmly gliding Delaware!
How the bonfires and the torches
Lighted up the night's repose,
And from the flames, like fabled Phoenix,
Our glorious liberty arose!

The final stanza shows that long after the Bell was silenced, the theme of independence continues to resound (English Grammar Online, n.d.):

That old State House bell is silent,
Hushed is now its glamorous tongue;
But the spirit it awakened
Still is living—ever young;
And when we greet the smiling sunlight
On the fourth of each July,
We will never forget the bellman
Who, between the earth and sky,
Rung out, loudly, "independence";
Which, please God, shall never die!

In commenting on its effect in serving to preserve the Liberty Bell as an American icon, Olga Hall-Crest observes, "Perhaps there is no other instance of such distortion of historical facts having so happy an outcome" (Hall-Crest, 1965, 153). The story is not unlike stories that portray George Washington as chopping down a cherry tree in his youth and refusing to lie about it, or the stories falsely attributing the making of the first flag to Betsy Ross. In commenting on the manner in which the American people venerate the Liberty Bell, a publication of the Independence National Historical Park observes, "To understand this unique position of the bell, one must go beyond authenticated history (for the bell is rarely mentioned in early records) and study the folklore which has grown up" (Independence National Historical Park, n.d.).

The Liberty Bell story was further perpetuated by another poem that Henry Clay Work published in 1865 entitled, "Ring the Bell, Watchman!" Although apparently it was written to celebrate the end of the Civil War, Americans later interpreted it as applying to the Liberty Bell in July 1776.

See also: Children and the Liberty Bell; Lippard, George; Names for the Liberty Bell; "Ring the Bell, Watchman!" (Song, 1865); "Song of the Liberty Bell, The" (Song, 1904)

Further Reading

Hall-Quest, Olga W. 1965. *The Bell That Rang for Freedom: The Liberty Bell and Its Place in American History.* New York: E. P. Dutton.

"Independence Bell—July 4, 1776." English Grammar Online. https://www.ego4u.com /en/read-on-literature/poem/independence-bell.

Independence National Historical Park. n.d. "The Story of a Symbol." https://www.nps.gov /parkhistory/online_books/hh/17/hh17h.htm.

Nash, Gary B. 2010. *The Liberty Bell.* New Haven, CT: Yale University Press.

Independence Day

Although the Liberty Bell was installed at the Pennsylvania State House (today's Independence Hall) in 1753, it has long been less associated with the business of this colonial assembly than with the declaration by the 13 English colonies in North America of their independence from Great Britain, which occurred in 1776.

In the popular mind, this event is most closely associated with July 4, which in turn has been most closely associated with the ringing of the Liberty Bell. The actual chronology, however, is somewhat more complicated.

The colonies had been at odds with Britain from the time that the French and Indian War ended in 1763, and Parliament then sought to impose taxes upon them to help defray the expenses. Fighting actually broke out in April 1775 between Patriot Minutemen and British Regulars at Lexington and Concord, Massachusetts. However, there were still many colonists, including representatives to the Second Continental Congress, who sought to avoid full-scale rebellion. To this end, the Congress sent a number of petitions to King George III (to whom they professed allegiance, despite their refusal to accept parliamentary assertions of taxing authority) in hopes that he would intervene on their behalf. It was only after the king refused to heed these petitions and sided with Parliament that the colonies edged toward independence.

Individual colonies had different experiences, but in early 1776, some were in virtual war with their royal governors. On May 10, 1776, John Adams and Richard Henry Lee were among those who supported a resolution that Congress adopted on May 14, which encouraged states to create new governments where royal governments were failing in an effort to prevent anarchy. As states began to create such governments, they began instructing or giving permission to their delegates to the Second Continental Congress to vote for independence.

On June 7, 1776, Virginia's Richard Henry Lee introduced three resolutions to the Continental Congress, the most important of which proposed "that these United Colonies are, and of right ought to be free and independent States," and "that they are absolved of all allegiance to the British Crown" (Vile, 2015, 95). He also introduced resolutions proposing that the colonies seek allies to support their efforts.

Many thought that other nations would not intervene until the colonies had first formally declared their independence and formed a new continental government.

Although the Continental Congress tabled Lee's resolutions for three weeks, it did appoint a committee consisting of Thomas Jefferson (Virginia), John Adams (Massachusetts), Benjamin Franklin (Pennsylvania), Roger Sherman (Connecticut), and Robert Livingston (New York) to draft a Declaration of Independence. The committee submitted its draft to the Continental Congress on June 28, and it began discussions on July 1. After considerable debate, the committee adopted Lee's resolution for independence on July 2. Many, including John Adams, thought that this would be the date on which America would celebrate its independence. He thus wrote a letter to his wife, Abigail, the next day, in which he said (Strauss. 2016):

> The Second day of July 1776, will be the most memorable Epocha, in the History of America. I am apt to believe that it will be celebrated, by succeeding generations, as the great anniversary Festival. It ought to be commemorated, as the Day of Deliverance by solemn Acts of Devotion to God Almighty. It ought to be solemnized with Pomp and Parade, with Shews, Games, Sports, Guns, Bells, Bonfires and Illuminations from one end of this Continent to the other from this Time forward forever more.

In point of fact, July 2 ended up being eclipsed by July 4, the date on which the Continental Congress actually adopted the Declaration of Independence, which explained the reasons for colonial independence to the outside world. That document was printed on the evening of July 4 or the next morning, and copies were sent to each of the states, where it was publicly read. The situation was complicated by the fact that the document was originally printed without the signatures of members of the Continental Congress. The delegates do not appear to have signed an engrossed document until August 2 and the following months, and their names were not publically released until January 1777.

The first public reading of the Declaration of Independence in Philadelphia, done by Colonel James Nixon, the son of an Irish immigrant, took place in front of the State House on July 8. Contemporary accounts indicate that it was accompanied by taking down the king's arms that adorned the courtroom in that building, as well as the lighting of a bonfire, the illumination of houses, and the ringing of bells (Desbler, 1892, 166–167). Because the steeple in which the Liberty Bell was housed was in disrepair, it is not certain whether the Bell was rung, along with other city bells, on this occasion; but George Lippard's highly influential story of 1847, which reported an aged sexton awaiting word from a "flaxen-haired" boy, is known to be a myth (Warren, 1945, 248–254). There were similar readings and celebrations throughout the colonies (Vile, 2019, 217–221).

Although many of the stories surrounding the ringing of the Liberty Bell may be mythical, over time, it became increasingly identified with the cause of independence. In time, the term *independence* was widened to include the fight for slave emancipation, women's suffrage, and other causes.

In the early republic, however, Independence Day often took on partisan dimensions. Charles Warren thus observed that "by 1798, partisan controversies had grown so heated that the two parties could not unite in celebrating the Fourth and they held separate processions, dinners and orations" (1945, 261). This rancor decreased with the demise of the Federalist Party, with the visit of the Marquis de Lafayette to the United States in 1824, and with the simultaneous deaths of John Adams and Thomas Jefferson on July 4, 1826, the 50th anniversary, or Jubilee, of the adoption of the Declaration of Independence (Bernstein 2001).

Although the Declaration of Independence had proclaimed that "all men are created equal," Thomas Jefferson, its primary author, was a slaveholder, and later, freed slaves were largely excluded from the benefits of liberty that the inscription on the Liberty Bell proclaimed. Frederick Douglass, a former slave, was among those who pointed out the disparities between the language of the Declaration and the realities of being black in the United States; he did so most famously in an 1852 speech. By this time, of course, abolitionists had already begun associating the Liberty Bell with the cause of emancipation. President Abraham Lincoln would later say that he had taken his own political principles from the Declaration of Independence, and the end of the Civil War brought an end to slavery with the adoption of the Thirteenth Amendment in 1865.

Although many states had already done so, it was not until 1870 that Congress declared Independence Day to be a national holiday. When the Liberty Bell made trips to celebrations and expositions throughout the United States from 1885 to 1915, it was usually the center of attention at accompanying Independence Day celebrations.

See also: Abolitionists and the Liberty Bell; Declaration of Independence and the Liberty Bell; Independence Hall; Journeys of the Liberty Bell; Lippard, George

Further Reading

Bernstein, Andrew. 2001. *America's Jubilee: How in 1826 a Generation Remembered Fifty Years of Independence.* New York: Alfred A. Knopf.

Desbler, Charles D. 1892. "How the Declaration Was Received in the Old Thirteen." *Harper's New Monthly Magazine* 85 (July): 165–187.

Heintze, James R. 2007. *The Fourth of July Encyclopedia.* Jefferson, NC: McFarland.

Smelser, Marshall. 1970. "The Glorious Fourth—or, Glorious Second? Or Eighth?" *History Teacher* 3 (January): 25–30.

Strauss, Valerie. 2016. "Is July 2 America's True Independence Day? John Adams Thought So." *Washington Post,* July 1. https://www.washingtonpost.com/news/answer-sheet/wp/2016/07/01/is-july-2-the-true-independence-day-john-adams-thought-so/?utm_term=.ebec6b8eef99.

Vile, John R. 2019. *The Declaration of Independence: America's First Founding Document in U.S. History and Culture.* Santa Barbara, CA: ABC-CLIO.

Vile, John R. 2015. *Founding Documents of America: Documents Decoded.* Santa Barbara, CA: ABC-CLIO.

Warren, Charles. 1945. "Fourth of July Myths." *William and Mary Quarterly* 2 (July): 237–272.

Independence Hall

Many artifacts are connected to a physical place, and there has long been a close tie between the Liberty Bell and Independence Hall (which used to be known as the State House) in Philadelphia.

The building was originally planned as a place for the Pennsylvania Assembly to meet. With its gracious Georgian style, inspired by Italian architect Andrea Palladio (who also influenced Thomas Jefferson), it represented British civility and culture in the New World. It is believed to have been designed by Andrew Hamilton, who argued the historic John Peter Zenger libel case in 1734, and supervised by Edmund Woolley.

After the Assembly ordered the Bell, and it was recast after cracking, it was placed in the building's steeple. During British occupation of the city from September 1777 to June 1778 in the midst of the Revolutionary War, the Bell was removed, along with church bells from Philadelphia. It would be reinstalled in the tower and then displayed at various places in the building. The Bell left Philadelphia for seven trips to various world fairs and other expositions between 1885 and 1915, but it always returned to its home at Independence Hall. Although it was held elsewhere in Philadelphia, the World's Fair of 1876 helped bring people to the site, often proclaimed as the most historic building in the nation.

Such a designation might also be given to the U.S. Capitol Building, the White House, or the U.S. Supreme Court, but Independence Hall has the distinction of being the birthplace not only of the nation's two most seminal documents—the Declaration of Independence and the U.S. Constitution—but also of hosting the U.S. Congress from 1790 to 1800. However, the original, engrossed copies of both documents have long been housed at the National Archives in Washington, D.C. Indeed, the only two items that are known to be original to Independence Hall are the chair on which George Washington is believed to have sat while presiding over the Constitutional Convention of 1787, and the ink stand into which delegates who signed both the Declaration of Independence and the Constitution are believed to have dipped their quills.

In 1799, Pennsylvania moved its state capital to Lancaster, and still later to Harrisburg. Within a year, the U.S. Congress had also

Colonel Thomas Crafts reads aloud the Declaration of Independence in Boston, Massachusetts, on July 18, 1776. The first public reading of the Declaration was held in Philadelphia on July 8, 1776. (National Archives)

moved to the newly created District of Columbia. Pennsylvania gave little initial consideration to the building where the Declaration had been signed, allowing the wings and piazzas to be replaced in 1812 by rows of brick office buildings. Pennsylvania initially thought of selling the State House for private development, but the city of Philadelphia stepped in to buy the property. Part of the second floor was used for a museum curated by Charles Willson Peale.

When the Marquis de Lafayette, a hero of the Revolutionary War, visited the city in 1824, the first-floor East Room where the Declaration of Independence and Constitution had been signed was designated as Independence Hall, or the Hall of Independence; in time, the former name became applied to the entire building. The rest of the first floor became a museum, and the second floor became the chambers for the City Council. In 1828, the city decided to renovate the State House, which involved replacing a "sister" bell tied to clocks on the east and west ends of the building with a larger one, which would be replaced with a still-larger one in 1876. Toward the end of the nineteenth century, the building was again renovated, and new archways, similar to the originals, were installed. In 1901, a new building was constructed for City Hall, and Independence Hall was treated solely as a historic site rather than as a working government building from then on (Mires, 1999, 53).

Meanwhile, the Liberty Bell had been moved from its tower to the Assembly Room in 1852 to an octagonal pedestal. In 1876, it was moved to the vestibule; in 1877, it was hung from the ceiling of the tower's first-floor room by a chain of 13 links; in 1894, it was displayed in a glass case; and in 1920, it was installed on a new base made by the Frederick R. Gerry Company. In the 1920s, custodians of the Bell tried to prohibit individuals from taking pictures of it without permission, but there is no such ban at present.

Although Philadelphia retains ownership of the Liberty Bell, the city transferred custody of the Bell and of Independence Hall to the National Park Service. An urban renewal project further opened up the area in front of Independence Hall, where the Liberty Bell Center was eventually located, as well as the outline of the house in which President Washington had lived (and in which he had been served by slaves). In recent years, this area has been further flanked by the National Constitution Center (NCC), an Independence Visitor Center, and a museum of the American Revolution.

One disadvantage of displaying the Liberty Bell within Independence Hall was that the building could accommodate only so many visitors. In anticipation of larger-than-average crowds, the Bell was accordingly moved on the eve of the bicentennial of American independence in 1976 to a new Liberty Bell Pavilion. Sometimes criticized for offering little interpretation, the pavilion was replaced with the current Liberty Center in 2003, in which visitors go past a variety of interpretative panels before viewing the Bell.

For many years, almost everyone who visited Independence Hall would also see the Liberty Bell. Now, many visitors prefer to view the Liberty Bell rather than tour Independence Hall, largely because the latter involves waiting in longer lines and listening to guides. Visitors can instead visit the Liberty Bell at their own pace. In both the previous pavilion and the current center, the Liberty Bell is placed in front of a window with Independence Hall in view, so visitors of the Bell also can look at Independence Hall.

In addition to drawing many tourists, the area surrounding Independence Hall has become a site for commemoration and for numerous protests.

See also: Declaration of Independence and the Liberty Bell; Display of the Liberty Bell in the 1850s; Display of the Liberty Bell in 1894; Journeys of the Liberty Bell; Liberty Bell Center; Liberty Bell Pavilion; Pennsylvania; Photographing the Liberty Bell; Political and Social Movements and the Liberty Bell

Further Reading

Jackson, Joseph. 1943. "Birthplace of a Nation." *Records of the American Catholic Historical Society of Philadelphia* 54 (March): 1–27.

Mires, Charlene. 2002. *Independence Hall in American Memory*. Philadelphia: University of Pennsylvania Press.

Mires, Charlene. 1999. "In the Shadow of Independence Hall: Vernacular Activities and the Meanings of Historic Places." *The Public Historian* 21 (Spring): 49–64.

Riley, Edward M. 1953. "The Independence Hall Group." *Transactions of the American Philosophical Society* 43 (1953): 7–42.

Inscription on the Liberty Bell

When Isaac Norris, Thomas Leech, and Edward Warner, as commissioners for the Pennsylvania Assembly, ordered the making of what is today known as the Liberty Bell, they included instructions for two inscriptions. The first was to say, "By order of the Afsembly of the Povince of Pensylvania, for the State Houfe in the City of Philad[a], 1752" (Kimball, 1989, 4, 19). Below it were to be the words, "Proclaim Liberty through all the land to all the inhabitants thereof—Levit. xxv. 10" (Kimball, 1989, 4, 19). The latter phrase was taken from Leviticus 25:10. The Commissioners requested that the words be "well-shaped in large letters round it," perhaps an indication that they wanted all capital letters (Kimball, 1989, 19).

A comparison with the verses on the current Liberty Bell reveal that the order has been changed, with the verse from Scripture now preceding rather than following the inscription dealing with the order of the Assembly. The current Bell, like its predecessors, also has the name of the manufacturers below both inscriptions.

The bell makers made a number of other changes as well. Consistent with the predominant King James Version of the Bible, they changed the words of Scripture, which Norris was likely quoting from memory, from "thro" to "throughout" and from "to" to "unto." They also changed the citation from "Levit., XXV. 10" to "Lev. XXV X." Rosewater notes that the foundry added a symbol that appears to combine the letters *V* and *S* as an abbreviation for *verse,* albeit without a period (Rosewater, 1926, 144)

The bell makers changed the *fs* (double s) with the more modern *ss* in Assembly (and the *f* in *Houfe* to *s*) and corrected the spelling of the word *Povince* to *Province,* but they left the spelling of *Pensylvania* with one *n*. Although some scholars believe that this was an error in spelling, given that it was in both the

A detailed image of the inscription on the Liberty Bell. The inscription, taken from Leviticus 25:10 of the Old Testament, reads "Proclaim Liberty Throughout All the Land Unto All the Inhabitants Thereof Lev. XXV X." (Jixue Yang/Dreamstime.com)

original request and embossed on the Bell itself, it seems more likely that it was simply an alternative spelling at a time when spellings were not as consistent as they are today. Benjamin Franklin is known to have used alternative spellings for the name of the colony/state, as did contemporary maps of the day. The foundry also shortened the words "for the State house in the City of Philada" to "for the State House in Philada."

By also lengthening two words in the biblical quotation, the Foundry likely intended to even out the lettering on the two lines. Another scholar, Frazier, thus notes that whereas the superintendents had originally called for one phrase of 104 characters and spaces on one line and 83 on the other, the foundry modified the expressions so that there would be 87 on one and 88 on the other (Frazier, 1974, 294). Yet another scholar, Kramer, observes, "The arranging of the texts of the inscriptions was not the work of an amateur" (Kramer, 1975, 49).

At the time when the Whitechapel Foundry cast the original Bell, it typically contained the words, "THOMAS LESTER OF LONDON MADE ME 1752," which thus likely appeared on the original Liberty Bell (Frazier, 1974, 294). The current Bell says, "Pass and Stow, Philada MDCCLIII," to indicate not only that it was recast by a different company, but also that it was cast later than its predecessor. Although some souvenirs in the shape of the Bell use the ampersand symbol, &, the word *and* between *Pass* and *Stow* is spelled out on the Bell itself (Ringone, 1976, 40).

Although all the words on the inscriptions on the Liberty Bell are capitalized, the first letter of most words are larger than the others, as are all the letters in the words LIBERTY, ASSEMBLY, and PENSYLVANIA. The largest letter is the *P* in *Pass* (Kramer, 1975, 19). Justin Kramer notes that although "the practice of placing inscriptions on bells is very ancient," he also thinks that "in eighteenth-century England, inscriptions derived from Sacred Scripture were not ordinarily found on bells: an inscription followed by reference to chapter and verse was unheard of" (Kramer, 1975, 7, 72).

According to the website of the Friends of Independence National Historical Park, the Centennial Bell, which now hangs in the steeple of Independence Hall and which was gifted to the city by Henry Seybert, contains the words, "Presented to the city of Philadelphia, July 4, 1876, for the belfry of Independence Hall, by a citizen." The other side features the date 1776, as well as the Great Seal of the United States within a shield of 13 stars.

A number of bells fashioned to resemble the Liberty Bell have altered the inscription. The famed Justice Bell, which suffragists employed, added the words, "Establish Justice." A replica made by Eastern European countries after World War I proclaimed, "Proclaim liberty throughout all the world" (Fried 2017).

Although the passage on the Bell comes from the part of Scripture designated as the law, rather than that designated as the prophets, it still appears to prophesize both American independence from Britain and the eventual emancipation of American slaves. It is highly doubtful that the Pennsylvania Assembly had independence in mind when it ordered the Bell, and emancipation was likely even further out of mind, at least of those assembly members.

One unattributed poem, which seeks to portray the Bell's historic role, actually ends by calling it God's Bell (Stoudt, 1930):

Bell of the Province once wast thou,
Bell of the State and Nation now,
Bell of the battle when war must be,
Bell of the people that would be free;
Men shall say as thou hang'st alone
God's voice has spoken in thy silvery tone,
Bell in whose keeping all is well,
Speak to us ever, Old Bell, God's Bell.

See also: Justice Bell; Leviticus 25:10; Norris, Isaac, II; Pass and Stow; Whitechapel Foundry

Further Reading

Frazier, Arthur H. 1974. "The Stretch Clock and the Bell at the State House." *Pennsylvania Magazine of History and Biography* 98 (July): 287–313.

Fried, Stephen. 2017. "World War I: 100 Years Later. How the Liberty Bell Won the Great War." Smithsonian.com, April. https://www.smithsonianmag.com/history/how -liberty-bell-won-great-war-180962471.

Friends of Independence National Historical Park. n.d. "Other Bells at Independence NHP." http://friendsofindependence.org/other-bells-at-independence-nhp.

Kimball, David. 1989. *The Story of the Liberty Bell.* Fort Washington, PA: Eastern National.

Kramer, Justin. 1975. *Cast in America: The Historically Accurate, Exciting Story of the Liberty Bell.* Los Angeles: Justin Kramer Incorporated.

Ringone, Louis A. 1976. "Sister to the Liberty Bell." *Records of the American Catholic Historical Society of Philadelphia*, 87 (March–December): 3–32.

Rosewater, Victor. 1926. *The Liberty Bell: Its History and Significance*. New York: D. Appleton.

Stoudt, John Baer. 1930. *The Liberty Bells of Pennsylvania*. Philadelphia: William J. Campbell.

J

John Brown's Bell (see Bunker Hill Monument Anniversary in Boston [1903])

Journeys of the Liberty Bell

Although there are thousands, if not millions, of miniature replicas of the Liberty Bell, at least 300 of which are full-sized, the Bell itself has been a relatively stationary object. Through most of its life, it has been situated somewhere in the Pennsylvania State House, now known as Independence Hall, or somewhere near it in Philadelphia. Although it weighs more than a ton, it is capable of being transported. Indeed, had the Patriots not transported the Bell to Allentown in 1777, the British who occupied the city may well have melted it down to make bullets or cannon.

In 1876, Philadelphia hosted the first World's Fair held in the United States. It commemorated the centennial of American independence and drew many tourists to see the Liberty Bell. Between 1885 and 1915, the Liberty Bell took seven trips, the last of which involved staying at two different sites. All the trips were by train, and most were to expositions or fairs. As the trains stopped or passed through small towns and cities along the way, millions of people, many of whom would never visit Philadelphia, were able to see (and in some cases touch) the Liberty Bell. It was common for individuals to hand their children to the guards surrounding the Bell so they could touch or kiss it. Many also asked the guards to rub pieces of jewelry against the Bell for good luck.

Nations seek unifying symbols. In the United States, citizens have manifested this desire by reproducing and displaying pictures and portraits of George Washington and other founding fathers, by replicas of the bald eagle, and by prints of the Declaration of Independence and the U.S. Constitution. Although it originated much earlier, the Civil War largely marked the emergence of the U.S. flag as such a symbol as well.

The trips of the Liberty Bell, which symbolized both American independence and the later emancipation of slaves, further served as another symbol that embodied American ideals. Philadelphia city fathers used these trips to publicize their city and themselves, but they often turned down requests from others. Eventually, the trips were stopped altogether for fear that traveling would jeopardize the Bell, which already had a large crack.

Cities often hosted fairs and expositions to boost their reputation as progressive places. In general, the themes emphasized American achievements and American

The Liberty Bell, which had been on display at the Louisiana Purchase Exposition of 1904, is loaded onto a train to continue its journey throughout the states. (Library of Congress)

progress, especially in technology. Such progress was often highlighted by anthropological exhibits designed to show Anglo-Saxon superiority to that of other races (Rydell, 1984). Expositions desired to host the Bell in part because it helped increase attendance. Many cities almost ensured this by setting aside a special "Liberty Bell Day," often letting school out for the occasion. Most welcomed the Bell with parades and speeches, giving it further attention if it were present during Independence Day celebrations on July 4.

It is not accidental that the Bell's first trip was to the World's Industrial and Cotton Exposition in New Orleans in 1885, where it served to renew a sense of unity between the Northern and Southern states. Significantly, one of the individuals who greeted the Bell on this trip was Jefferson Davis, the former president of the Confederacy.

The Bell's second tour in 1893 was to the World's Columbian Exposition in Chicago. This Exposition was highlighted by the unveiling of the Columbian Liberty Bell, a 13,000-pound "sister" bell that would itself go to at least one other fair.

In 1895, the Bell took a second trip to the South, this time to the Atlanta Cotton States and International Exposition of 1895. The trip preceded *Plessy v. Ferguson,* the Supreme Court's decision legitimizing the doctrine of "separate but equal," by a year. One of the highlights of this fair was a speech by Booker T. Washington urging African Americans to focus on labor with their hands in order to earn the respect of their white neighbors.

In 1902, the Liberty Bell once again headed South, this time to Charleston, South Carolina, where it was on exhibit at the Interstate and West Indian Exposition. Booker T. Washington was again a featured speaker. This exposition was largely designed to increase American trade with some of the territories that it had acquired during the Spanish-American War of 1898.

The Bell's shortest out-of-state trip was in 1903 to Boston, for the 128th anniversary of the Bunker Hill Monument, which commemorated a Revolutionary War battle that had taken place even before the nation had declared its independence. Although Philadelphia had been the site of the writing of the Declaration of Independence, Massachusetts, Virginia, and other states had preceded Pennsylvania in calling for independence. This trip allowed Boston to claim its part in this heritage.

The Louisiana Purchase Exposition of 1904, which was held in St. Louis, Missouri, was the next place that the Bell visited. Located on the largest site of any such exhibit to date, one of its highlights was the re-creation of Philippine villages by some 1,200 natives.

The Bell's final trip was to the Panama-Pacific International Exposition of 1915 in San Francisco. Although the United States had yet to enter the fray, World War I had already begun in Europe. The Bell undoubtedly stirred American patriotism and enhanced the use that the government would make of it during the next few years in raising money for war bonds. On the way back, the Bell also stopped for a few days at the Panama-California International Exposition of 1915 in San Diego.

Philadelphia officials did reject some plans to send the Bell to Portland, Oregon, to Jamestown, Virginia, and to Paris, among other locales. The travels of the Bell raised special anxiety among residents of Philadelphia who were concerned about its security and feared that jostling the Bell on trips might widen its crack. As she personified the Bell, Adaline May Conway pleaded, "If you really have my welfare at heart, desist, I beg you, from sending me on these long and perilous journeys throughout the land" (Conway, 1914, 62). She continued, "I have been tremblingly conscious of failing strength and an increasing danger of falling to pieces" (Conway, 1914, 63). As no one would think to send the "sacred remains" of American patriots abroad, she ended with, "I pray you let me also rest in peace!" (Conway, 1914, 64).

A poem published by George H. Beans in 1918, entitled "Our Liberty Bell," ended with a stanza that asked:

Shall we jeopardize its safety?
Shall we let the relic go?
Shall we put the bell in danger?
Let the whole world answer no!

That same year, the *New York Tribune* published an article opposing the "periodical hippodroming of the bell around the country" (Independence National Historical Park, Historic Note Card File).

Bells made in the likeness of the Liberty Bell also followed suit. In 1952, the United States sent the 300-pound Old Hickory Liberty Bell, owned by a distilling company, to the World's Fair in Brussels, Belgium. They were motivated by the hope that it would serve as a worthy symbol in combating communism.

Between 1975 and 1976, a Freedom Train carried a newly minted large replica of the Liberty Bell, known as the American Legion Liberty Bell, through all the contiguous 48 states. It was, in turn, patterned in part on an earlier Freedom Train that had toured the country from 1947 to 1949 to promote patriotism and good citizenship. Similarly, the World Peace Bell visited a number of U.S. cities before coming to its permanent home in Newport, Kentucky.

In August 2018, Tom White of Eastland, Texas, brought his Traveling Liberty Bell and Law Memorial to the County Courthouse in Taos, New Mexico. What appears to be a full-sized replica of the Liberty Bell was flanked by Styrofoam tablets with the Ten Commandments. He was protesting a judicial decision. After being requested to do so, White moved his trailer to a nearby church parking lot (Hooks 2018).

David Hall had first driven the Traveling Liberty Bell and copies of the Ten Commandments around the country to funerals honoring soldiers and police officers who had died in the line of duty (Dawdy 2011).

See also: Allentown; American Legion Liberty Bell; Atlanta Cotton States and International Exposition of 1895; Bunker Hill Monument Anniversary in Boston (1903); Children and the Liberty Bell; Columbian Liberty Bell; Louisiana Purchase Exposition, St. Louis (1904); Old Hickory Liberty Bell; Panama-Pacific International Exposition, San Francisco (1915); *Silent Peal from the Liberty Bell, A* (1914); South Carolina Interstate and West Indian Exposition of 1902; World's Columbian Exposition in Chicago (1893); World's Industrial and Cotton Exposition in New Orleans (1885)

Further Reading
Conway, Adaline May. 1914. *A Silent Peal from the Liberty Bell*. Philadelphia: George W. Jacobs.

Dawdy, Shelli. 2011. "On Loss of Belladier David Hall: Bells Must Be Ringing in Heaven." *OKG News,* October 12. http://okgrassroots.com/?p=22253.

Hooks, Cindy. 2018. "Judge's Decision Draws Traveling Protest to Taos." *Taos News,* August 23. http://www.santafenewmexican.com/news/local_news/judge-s-decision -draws-traveling-protest-to-taos/article_41733308-a229-5846-ba68-318fbe0b502f .html.

Nash, Gary B. 2010. *The Liberty Bell*. New Haven, CT: Yale University Press.

Rosewater, Victor. 1926. *The Liberty Bell: Its History and Significance*. New York: D. Appleton.

Rydell, Robert W. 1984. *All the World's a Fair: Visions of Empire at American International Expositions, 1876–1916*. Chicago: University of Chicago Press.

July 4 (see Independence Day)

Justice Bell

Although the Liberty Bell is probably most closely identified as a symbol of the American Revolution, it did not emerge into prominence until leaders of the abolitionist movement utilized it, and advocates of many other causes have subsequently followed their lead. One of the most prominent of such movements was women's suffrage. Although it undoubtedly had other antecedents, this movement is often traced to the Seneca Falls Convention that was held in New York in 1848. This convention drafted a declaration similar to that of the Declaration of Independence, which declared that all men "and women" were created equal. It further issued a call, thought to be quite radical at the time, for women's suffrage.

Advocates of women's suffrage hoped that it might be brought about with other reforms initiated by the Union victory in the Civil War. However, Section 2 of the Fourteenth Amendment (1868) included a provision penalizing states only when they denied the right to vote to male voters. Moreover, the Fifteenth Amendment (1870) prohibited discrimination on the basis of race but made no mention of sex.

After years of pressing for a similar amendment for women, Katharine Wentworth Ruschenberger of Chester County, Pennsylvania, a member of the Pennsylvania Woman Suffrage Association (PWSA), came up with the idea of making a replica of the Liberty Bell to further the cause. In 1915, she personally paid $2,000 to commission a 2,000-pound replica of the Liberty Bell to be cast by the Meneely Bell Company of Troy, New York, which had also cast the much larger Centennial Bell in 1876. In addition to the Scripture passage from Leviticus 25:10 inscribed in

Four advocates of women's right to vote stand beside the Justice Bell. The Justice Bell was cast in 1915 to draw a symbolic parallel between women's suffrage and the freedom for which the Liberty Bell was understood to represent. The Justice Bell was then toured throughout Pennsylvania to draw attention to the women's suffrage movement. (Library of Congress)

the Liberty Bell, the new bell drew from the preamble of the U.S. Constitution to add the words "Establish Justice" ("Philadelphia's 1920 Celebration of the 19th Amendment," n.d.). Although it is thus generally called the "Justice Bell," it is sometimes also called the "Liberty Bell of Suffrage" (Leach, 1984, 207).

Louise Hall and Ethel Harte subsequently organized a Liberty Bell Tour to all 67 counties in Pennsylvania to generate support for a statewide referendum guaranteeing women the right to vote. The Justice Bell was carried on the back of an open truck, from which advocates of women's suffrage spoke. The bell's clapper was chained so that it would not be rung until women achieved this right. Ruschenberger hoped that "the women's Liberty Bell will announce the completion of democracy," just as the original Bell had "announced the creation of democracy" ("Philadelphia's 1920 Celebration of the 19th Amendment," n.d.). Although the women lost Pennsylvania's state vote, in 1920, the Nineteenth Amendment prohibited discrimination in voting on the basis of sex throughout the nation.

On September 25, 1920, the new Justice Bell was finally rung on Independence Square. It rang a total of 48 times, symbolizing each of the states then in the Union" ("Philadelphia's 1920 Celebration of the 19th Amendment," n.d.). Pennsylvania governor William Cameron Sproul announced, "To my opinion, this is one of the four greatest occasions in American history. The first was the declaration of independence; the second, the adoption of our Constitution; the third, the wiping out of slavery, and fourth, the accomplishment of equal rights for women" ("Philadelphia's 1920 Celebration of the 19th Amendment," n.d.).

The Justice Bell could not be kept at Independence Hall, in part because passersby, including soldiers, sometimes apparently mistook it for the original (Mires, 1999, 54). City officials instead drove the bell to a stable in League Island Park (Mires, 2002, 171). Ruschenberger had hoped to build either a "Tower of Justice" or a "Tower of Citizenship" on Independence Square, but she ultimately deeded the bell to the Washington Memorial Chapel at Valley Forge National Park (Mires, 2002, 171). There, it apparently remained in what one article describes as "a chicken-wire cage in the woods, for five decades" before a new rector, Reverend Richard Lyon Stinson solicited the help of the Pennsylvania League of Women Voters and the Daughters of the American Revolution "to help have it installed in the rotunda of the carillon's rotunda" ("Philadelphia's 1920 Celebration of the 19th Amendment," n.d.). In 1995, which marked the 75th anniversary of the ratification of the Nineteenth Amendment, the bell was temporarily displayed at the Independence Historical Park Visitor Center (Mires, 1999, 55).

In December 2014, the Swann Galleries of New York auctioned a gallery of photographs of the Liberty Tour by Louise Hall and Ethel Harte.

See also: Abolitionists and the Liberty Bell; Centennial Bell; Columbian Liberty Bell; Declaration of Independence and the Liberty Bell; Women's Suffrage and the Liberty Bell

Further Reading

"The Hall-Harte Archive of Suffragist Photographs." n.d. https://www.swanngalleries.com /news/2014/12/hall-harte-suffragist-photographs.

Holst, Holly Jean. n.d. "Silent No More: The Justice Bell." http://philadelphiaencyclopedia .org/archive/liberty-bell/justice-bell.

"The Justice Bell Story." n.d. Justice Bell Foundation. http://www.justicebell.org/the-justice -bell-story.

Leach, Roberta J. 1984. "Jennie Bradley Roessing and the Fight for Woman Suffrage in Pennsylvania." *Western Pennsylvania Historical Magazine* 67 (1984): 189–211.

Mires, Charlene. 2002. *Independence Hall in American Memory.* Philadelphia: University of Pennsylvania Press.

Mires, Charlene. 1999. "In the Shadow of Independence Hall: Vernacular Activities and the Meanings of Historic Places." *The Public Historian* 21 (Spring): 49–64.

"Philadelphia's 1920 Celebration of the 19th Amendment." n.d. Justice Bell Foundation. http://www.justicebell.org/philadelphial-celebration.

K

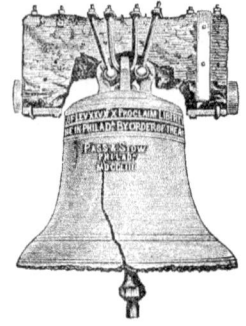

King, Martin Luther, Jr.

Dr. Martin Luther King, Jr. (1929–1968) is probably the best-known civil rights leader of the twentieth century. A Baptist minister, who was born in Atlanta, Georgia, and assassinated in Memphis, Tennessee, was the son of another minister and attended Morehouse College, Crozer Theological Seminary, and Boston University. Influenced by Mahatma Gandhi, who had led the movement for independence in India, King advocated nonviolence resistance in opposing racial segregation. As a pastor, he led the Montgomery bus boycott in 1955 to protest the requirement that African Americans like Rosa Parks must sit in the back of the bus. In 1957, he helped found the Southern Christian Leadership Conference.

While leading a campaign against racial segregation in Birmingham, Alabama, in 1963, King wrote his famous "Letter from a Birmingham Jail," in which he explained why it was sometimes necessary to violate unjust laws. He led a civil rights march on Washington, D.C., in 1963, joined the Student Nonviolent Coordinating Committee, and began the marches in Selma, Alabama, in 1964, as well as in Montgomery in 1965. He was assassinated in 1968 during a "Poor People's Campaign."

King and his March on Washington advocated the Civil Rights Act of 1964, which made discrimination in most places of public accommodation illegal. He also pushed for the Voting Rights Act of 1965. He was a frequent target of the investigations of J. Edgar Hoover, the director of the Federal Bureau of Investigation (FBI), who believed that

Dr. Martin Luther King, Jr. at a speaking podium. (Library of Congress)

he was tied to communist sympathizers, but King remained unintimidated by tapes that Hoover gathered that purportedly revealed scandalous things about him. In 1983, the United States created Martin Luther King Jr. Day, which has somewhat overshadowed National Freedom Day, with its roots related to the Liberty Bell.

King was a gifted orator, and one of his most famous speeches is the "I Have a Dream" speech that he gave at the March on Washington in 1963. Toward the end of his speech, he quoted a line from "My Country 'Tis of Thee," which ends with "let freedom ring." Although songwriter Samuel Francis Smith, a student at Andover Theological Seminary, may well have had church bells rather than the Liberty Bell in mind, many individuals could have associated the words with the Liberty Bell, which abolitionists used as a symbol of their opposition to slavery. Moreover, the Bell had been the site where, beginning in February 1, 1942, Richard R. Wright had begun laying wreaths to engender support for National Freedom Day.

Consistent with the biblical inscription on the Liberty Bell to "Proclaim liberty throughout all the land unto all the inhabitants thereof," as King came to the end of his "Dream" speech, he continually reiterated the words, "Let freedom ring" as he delineated locations from New Hampshire to California to his own native South where he hoped this would happen. He ended with the words of an African American spiritual that proclaimed the words that now adorn his gravesite in Atlanta: "Free at last! Free at last! Thank God Almighty, we are free at last."

In 2013, a group of civil rights leaders from Georgia met atop Stone Mountain, one of the locations often used for gatherings of the Ku Klux Klan that King had mentioned in his speech. The location has been known for its large rock carvings of Confederate president Jefferson Davis, General Robert E. Lee, and General Stonewall Jackson since 1972. The civil rights leaders intended to ring a bell to commemorate King's speech. They subsequently planned to cast a bell inscribed with, "Let freedom ring from Stone Mountain of Georgia," which would be housed on the top of the mountain and rung on important occasions. In 2018, the state senate adopted a resolution supporting a Liberty Bell Monument on the site (Mitchell, 2018). On April 4 of that year, bells rang out 39 times from the base of the mountain in a "Let Freedom Ring" ceremony, one time for each year of King's age at the time he was assassinated (Mannins and Parks, 2018).

See also: Abolitionists and the Liberty Bell; Inscription on the Liberty Bell; National Freedom Day; Oral Tradition and the Liberty Bell

Further Reading

Branham, Robert James. 1996. "'Of Thee I Sing': Contesting America." *American Quarterly* 48 (December): 623–652.

Garet, Ronald R. 2000. "Proclaim Liberty." *Southern California Law Review* 74: 145–168.

King, Martin Luther. 2008. "I Have a Dream Today." *The Guardian,* August 28. https://www.theguardian.com/commentisfree/2008/aug/28/uselections2008.constitution andcivilliberties.

Manins, Rosie, and Tekia L. Parks. 2018. "Freedom Bells Ring at Stone Mountain for MLK." Cross Roads News, April 6. http://www.crossroadsnews.com/news/local /freedom-bells-ring-at-stone-mountain-for-mlk/article_97ae7c02-3864-11e8-b85f -abd90dc39d75.html.

Mitchell, Tia. 2018. "Senators Back Liberty Bell Monument Honoring MLK Atop Stone Mountain." AJC.com, April 4. https://www.ajc.com/news/local-govt—politics /senators-back-liberty-bell-monument-honoring-mlk-atop-stone-mountain /Wk6FuT9oiswR9jrJy8zndJ.

Kissing the Liberty Bell

Few expressions are more intimate than the kiss. Although the act is typically associated with interpersonal contact between family members, close friends, or lovers, individuals sometimes show their reverence for sacred objects by kissing them. One might kiss the coffin of a loved one about to be put to rest, a picture, a Bible (especially upon taking an oath), or a flag. People who have been long at sea might kneel and kiss the ground upon returning home. A devout Roman Catholic might kiss a rosary, the foot of the statue of St. Peter in St. Peter's Basilica in Rome, a statue of Mary, or another holy object. There is a long tradition that a person who kisses the Blarney Stone in Ireland gains the gift of eloquence.

Although today it is not accessible to the public to be touched, it is doubtful that any single object in the United States has been kissed more frequently than the Liberty Bell. As the Bell toured the nation to various World's Fairs, people often lifted up children to kiss it. Therefore, it must have seemed completely appropriate to a young African American girl who kissed the Liberty Bell as it made a stop in Arlington, Texas, in 1915. Unfortunately, because of her race, her act of devotion precipitated a riot, during which she was "jeered, hissed, scolded, and cursed" by a group that a reporter from the African American *Chicago Defender* called "a crowd of fools and idiots" (Fried, 2017).

After the Bell returned to Philadelphia, a visiting French general, Joseph Jacques Cesaire Joffre, bent down and kissed it. Other French troops, as well as U.S. troops headed to Europe to fight in World War I, followed suit (Paige, 1988, 54). When the armistice ending World War I was concluded, thousands of people thronged Independence Hall and kissed the Liberty Bell. This prompted a *Philadelphia Inquirer* reporter to observe, "Most of the throng had become so Americanized that it was difficult to tell the people of one race from those of another" (Fried 2017).

See also: Civil Religion and the Liberty Bell; Journeys of the Liberty Bell

Further Reading
Fried, Stephen. 2017. "World War I: 100 Years Later. How the Liberty Bell Won the Great War." Smithsonian.com, April. https://www.smithsonianmag.com/history/how -liberty-bell-won-great-war-180962471.

Paige, John C. 1988 (date of camera-ready copy). *The Liberty Bell of Independence National Historical Park: A Special History Study.* Denver: Denver Service Center, National Park Service, Department of the Interior. Accessed through pubs.etic.nps.gov.

Koons, Jeff

The Liberty Bell has been the subject of numerous photographs and some works of art. Jeff Koons (b. 1955), who is probably best known for his erotic photographs and his giant sculptures of balloon animals, has created a number of works related to the Liberty Bell. One is the painting *Peg-Leg Liberty Bell,* which features a pirate in front of two pictures of the bell. Another canvas of the Bell features a green Hulk Hogan in the background, an orange geisha, a yellow sketch of Popeye the Sailor Man smoking a pipe, and another female figure, probably Olive Oyl, in the foreground.

Koons has also overseen the construction of what is likely the most accurate facsimile of the Liberty Bell ever made. Koons's replica of the Bell required the work of numerous artists and technicians—he was even granted after-hour access to the Liberty Bell Center in order to research for the piece. Arnold AG, which has been described as "a metal-work mill in Germany," milled the bell, and Dan Terbovich of Horizon Wood milled dried red elm wood to create a similar replica of the Liberty Bell yoke (Lalinde, 2014). The bell, which has been described as "a near-perfect replica of an imperfect object," is displayed on a wishbone stand, like the one once used to display the Liberty Bell, with meticulous efforts to replicate the colors and the patina on both the metal and the wood (Lalinde, 2014).

See also: Replicas of the Liberty Bell

Further Reading

Gopnik, Blake. 2014. "Jeff Koons' Art Rings a Bell." artnet News, September 15. https://news.artnet.com/exhibitions/jeff-koonss-art-rings-a-bell-102236.

Koons, Jeff. Liberty Bell Artworks. http://www.jeffkoons.com/search/node/Liberty%20Bell.

Lalinde, Jaime. 2014. "How to Make a Koons." *Vanity Fair,* June 6. https://www.vanityfair.com/culture/2014/06/how-to-make-akoons-liberty-bell.

Saltz, Jerry. 2015. "Zombies on the Walls: Why Does So Much New Abstraction Look the Same? And Taking in Jeff Koons, Creator and Destroyer of Worlds and Post-Macho God: Matisse's Cut-Outs Are World-Historically Gorgeous." In *The Best American Magazine Writing 2015*, ed. Sid Holt. New York: Columbia University Press, 344–361.

L

Landscapes and Bells

Geographers have long noted that landscaping often reflects the values of civilizations. Ancient Greece and Rome were known for their coliseums, temples, public buildings, and statues, the ruins of many of which remain to this day. In medieval times, cities were often characterized by castles or walls and exemplified by their cathedrals. In the early United States, the skylines of cities were often dominated by churches and tall steeples. The skylines of capital cities are often notable for prominent capitol buildings. Giant office buildings dominate many modern U.S. cities, as do stadiums for sporting events.

Country settings may be known for the sounds of brooks, streams, and animals. Cities are often filled with the sounds of honking car horns, police and ambulance sirens, and the noise of humming factories. Church buildings are often associated with the sound of choirs, congregational singing, and musical instruments. Military bases are punctuated with the sounds of trumpets calling people to rise, march, or sleep.

In early America, one of the most prominent artificial sounds was that of bells, which were often thought to have near-magical powers. *The Golden Legend*, a compilation of the lives of saints written by an Italian friar named Jacobus de Voragine (c.1230–1293), which was later translated into Old English by William Caxton and printed by Wynken de Worde, reports, "It is said the evil spirytes that benm in the region, doubte moche when they here the Bells rongen: and this is the cause why the bells ben rongen, whang rete tempeste and outrages of wether happen, to the end that the fiends and wicked spirytes should be abashed and flee" (quotation on the title page of the *Liberty Bell Gift Books*). Bells played such a prominent role in Russian history, and the history of the Russian Orthodox Church, that communist authorities sought to destroy them (Batuman, 2009).

Because bells may be muffled in sorrow or pealed in joy, and because they may be rung multiple times, they can convey a variety of messages. Almost every city and town, as well as many churches, used bells to call people to meetings, to warn of fires or the advance of enemy troops, to toll for the deaths of monarchs and esteemed leaders, or to inform of the execution of a convict. According to Marcovitz (2003, 16), this was done by ringing a bell nine times. Bells also announced the news of military victories, weddings, and other special events. In addition, they were tied around the necks of farm animals, not only to locate their whereabouts but perhaps as amulets to protect against evil spirits (Lesley, 1853, 306).

Although their primary appeal is to the ear, bells may also take appealing shapes. Just as soldiers or saints may carry marks of their battles or persecutions, so too, the Liberty Bell has a distinctive crack, which some have likened to the marks of martyrdom (Gardella, 2014, 79). Another scholar, Robey Callahan, believes that this crack helped transform the Bell from a mere commodity, or thing, into a sacred object, with its shape and distinctive crack often enough to evoke its memory (Callahan, 1999). Visitors to the Bell might regard their journey as a pilgrimage, rather than just a typical trip to a tourist destination.

At a time when most Americans wear watches or refer to cell phones that provide the time of day, it is important to remember that in earlier times, one of the primary functions of bells was to mark time. The sister bell to the Liberty Bell served precisely this purpose. Bells were often large because they needed to send messages over great distances. The Pennsylvania Assembly appears to have ordered the Liberty Bell not for ornamentation, but because the smaller bell that it replaced was no longer able to announce its messages throughout the whole of Philadelphia.

The tower of Christ Church in Philadelphia had eight bells, which were described as "the wonder of the town" (Eberlein and Hubbard, 1939, 210). They were pealed on Tuesday and Friday evenings (which were market days) until 1871; accordingly, they were sometimes called "butter bells" (Eberlein and Hubbard, 1939, 210).

Bells date back thousands of years, and one of their appeals may be primal, evoking times of joy, sorrow, and fear. Just as the inscription on the Liberty Bell was designed to proclaim liberty "throughout all the land," the power of each method of communication is tied to its ability to announce its respective message.

Bells are often associated with holidays and seasons. Long after few Americans owned horses and even fewer traveled by sled, it is common to speak of "silver bells," "jingle bells," or "sleigh bells" at Christmastime. Volunteers for the Salvation Army still ring bells in front of collection buckets during the season. Similarly, it is common to thinking of "ringing out" the old year and "ringing in" the new year.

During World War II, many European nations were denuded of many of their bells, both by those who wanted to undermine the influence of ancient churches and by armies that melted down bells to make munitions. Just as Americans hid the Liberty Bell from the British when they occupied Philadelphia in 1777, Europeans often hid bells with historic significance.

Today, bells remain in many churches. Perhaps in an effort to hearken back to olden days, bells are still a prominent part of many college and university campuses, usually announcing times, but also sometimes ringing for special events like graduations, or, if they are in chapels, weddings.

In assessing the importance of the Liberty Bell to landscapes, it is important to realize that through most of its history, it was displayed at Independence Hall. Both the Liberty Bell Pavilion and the more recent Liberty Bell Center have displayed the Bell so that a view of Independence Hall remains in the background. Independence Hall is a well-proportioned Georgian building that attempted to display British elegance in a New World setting. Its distinctive steeple, where the Liberty Bell was originally displayed, so resembles that of a church that it, like the Bell itself, sometimes tends to blend the secular and the sacred.

There is a mountain in the North Cascades of the State of Washington that so resembles the Liberty Bell in shape that it is named the Liberty Bell Mountain.

Consistent with this moniker, it features a number of climbing routes, among which include such names as "Freedom or Death," "Serpentine Crack," "Freedom Rider," "Liberty Crack," "Liberty and Injustice for All," the "Independence Route," and "Live Free or Die!" There is an additional Liberty Bell Arch in the Lake Mead area of Arizona. The Marvel Cave in Branson, Missouri, has a large stalagmite formation that is called the Liberty Bell because of its large size and shape. Moving to an artificial structure, the Franklin D. Roosevelt Park in Warm Springs, Georgia, has a Liberty Bell Pool, so named because it is shaped like a giant Liberty Bell.

The image of the Liberty Bell has been printed and painted on many plates and other ceramic objects, embossed or etched in glass, portrayed in photographs, and reproduced in smaller objects that in turn can influence the landscape of American homes. Just as children may wave a flag in delight, so may they display or ring small metal replicas of the Liberty Bell at home or at school.

See also: Children and the Liberty Bell; College and University Campuses with Replicas of the Liberty Bell; Independence Hall; Occasions for Ringing the Liberty Bell; Replicas of the Liberty Bell; Sister to the Liberty Bell; Souvenirs of the Liberty Bell

Further Reading

Batuman, Elif. 2009. "The Bells." *The New Yorker,* April 27. https://www.newyorker.com /magazine/2009/04/27/the-bells-6.

Callahan, Robey. 1999. "The Liberty Bell: From Commodity to Sacred Object." *Journal of Material Culture* 4 (1): 57–78.

Eberlein, Harold Donaldson, and Cortland Van Dyke Hubbard. 1939. *Portrait of a Colonial City, 1670–1838.* Philadelphia: J. B. Lippincott Company.

Gardella, Peter. 2014. *American Civil Religion: What Americans Hold Sacred.* New York: Oxford University Press.

Leslie, J. P. 1853. "The Bell." In *The Liberty Bell.* Boston: National Anti-Slavery Bazaar, 304–315.

Lowenthal, David. 1977. "The Bicentennial Landscape: A Mirror Held Up to the Past." *Geographical Review* 67 (July): 253–267.

Marcovitz, Hal. 2003. *The Liberty Bell.* Part of the *American Symbols and Their Meaning* series. Philadelphia: Mason Crest Publishers.

Leviticus 25:10

The Liberty Bell was commissioned by the Pennsylvania Assembly, which Quakers dominated. Accordingly, it is not surprising that the inscription on the Liberty Bell immortalizes some of the words of Leviticus 25:10, as found in the King James Bible, which was the most prominent Protestant English version of the time. The Bell also contains the specific Scripture reference, which may have been relatively unusual. Justin Kramer thus observes that "in eighteenth-century England, inscriptions derived from Sacred Scripture were not ordinarily found on bells: an inscription followed by a reference to chapter and verse was unheard of" (Kramer, 1975, 52).

The passage from which the Bell quotes is taken from Leviticus, the third book of the Torah (the first five books of the law in Hebrew Scriptures) and of the

Christian Old Testament, which details laws related to priests and Levites. The passage, which quotes words that the prophet Moses received on Mt. Sinai, where he also received the Ten Commandments, is an elaboration upon the Fourth Commandment, which required Jews "To remember the Sabbath day and make it holy" (Ex. 20:8).

Leviticus 25:8–11 thus says:

> And thou shalt number seven sabbaths of years unto thee, seven times seven years; and the space of the seventh Sabbaths of years shall be unto thee forty and nine years. Then shalt thou cause the trumpet of the jubilee to sound on the tenth day of the seventh month, in the day of atonement shall ye make the trumpet sound throughout all your land. And ye shall hallow the fiftieth year, and proclaim liberty throughout all the land unto all the inhabitants thereof: it shall be a jubilee unto you; and ye shall return every man unto his possession, and ye shall return every man unto his family. A jubilee shall that fiftieth year be unto you: ye shall now sow, neither reap that which growth of itself in it, nor gather the grapes in it of thy vine undressed.

In addition to setting aside the Sabbath day for rest and worship, this passage indicated that the people were obligated to set aside every 50th year—some think 49th—as its own Sabbath (Bergsa, 2005). During this year, for which the people were to prepare in advance, they would give the land itself a rest by not sowing or cultivating it. In addition to allowing the land to lie fallow for a year, this year was to be one where tribal lands that had been sold or forfeited to individuals outside the tribe would be returned, debts would be forgiven, and those who had been held in slavery would be freed. Despite this clear command, it is not clear that the year was ever implemented, perhaps foreshadowing the early gap between aspirations for freedom and the continuation of slavery in the United States (Chase, 1990, 134).

An extensive collection of sermons from the American founding period cites two of them that refer to this chapter. The first was from verses 14–17, and the second from verses 44–46 (Sandoz, 1991, 589, 1050). Somewhat ironically, although the first passage references the Year of Jubilee, the latter passage was actually used to justify enslaving foreigners, especially the Gibeonites.

This passage in Leviticus 25 is often tied to a corresponding passage in the opening verses of Isaiah 61. The first two verses of this passage, which Luke [the third of four gospels] 4:16–21 records Jesus, reading in a synagogue at the start of his ministry, saying: "The Spirit of the Lord God is upon me; because the LORD hath anointed me to preach good tidings unto the meek; he hath sent me to bind up the brokenhearted, to proclaim liberty to the captives, and the opening of the prison to them that are bound; To proclaim the accepted year of the LORD, and the day of vengeance of our God; to Comfort all that mourn" (Monshouwer, 1991).

Given the role of the family of Isaac Norris II in the reception of William Penn's Charter Privileges of 1701, a predecessor to subsequent written constitutions, many scholars believe that, in addition to the more practical function of being heard throughout the city, the bell may have been commissioned to mark the 50th anniversary, or Jubilee, of this event. However, the bells ended up being dated 1752 and 1753, their dates of manufacture, rather than the year in which they were commissioned.

This use of the term *Jubilee* may have melded with others over time. The Liberty Bell was thus rung on the 50th anniversary, or Jubilee, of the adoption of the Declaration of Independence (and again upon news of the deaths of John Adams and Thomas Jefferson, on the same day). Just as the Jewish Jubilee was to mark freedom for captives, the Liberty Bell rose to prominence as part of the campaign by abolitionists against American slavery.

Consistent with colonial practice, the Jubilee Year would be announced by a bell rather than by a trumpet or ram's horn—one nineteenth-century source, perhaps trying to bridge this gap, observed that the bell was "the trumpet that told the Britishers a tale of vengeance!" (Watson 1852, 16). Even more consistent with the Christian emphasis on the need for evangelism, liberty would not only be practiced, but "proclaimed" throughout the land. In what would arguably be an exegetical basis for applying the admonition to American slaves, and later to the women's suffrage movement (and even to resident aliens), the proclamation was to be proclaimed not only throughout "all the land," but also to "all the inhabitants thereof," rather than simply to those who would have been recognized as equal citizens.

Malcolm Chase observed that in England, the idea of the Jubilee, especially among Methodists, was "closely associated with ideas of spiritual renewal, religious liberty and the Second Coming" (1990, 137). Within America, Quakers were especially associated with religious liberty, which was a hallmark of the colony of Pennsylvania. In 1857, George B. Cheever authored a book called *God Against Slavery and the Freedom and Duty of the Pulpit to Rebuke it, as a Sin Against God*, in which he based a good amount of his argument on Leviticus 25 (Kramer, 1975, 86).

In 1873, John Shoemaker, who was chair of the Philadelphia Centennial Committee, tied the Liberty Bell to the Jubilee Year. He thus observed (Paige, 1988, 85):

> This is true, there appears to have been no first jubilee to all the inhabitants on our fiftieth anniversary—too many millions of our inhabitants were then in slavery—we then could not fully carry out the text and proclaim liberty to all. But now upon the second fiftieth year we are able to do so. Cracked and shattered as the bell may be[,] the base upon which that motto is cast remains firm and solid, and shaken as has our country been with the din of battle and bloody strife, that principle remains pure and perfect for all time to come and the whole text, Liberty Jubilee, will be literally carried out in 1876. "Liberty can now be proclaimed throu all the land to all inhabitants thereof."

President Gerald R. Ford made remarks at bicentennial celebrations in Philadelphia on July 4, 1976. After observing that he was standing in front of "the great bronze bell that joyously rang out the news of the birth of our Nation from the steeple of the State House," he noted that although "[i]t was never intended to be a church bell," it contained a Bible verse from the book of Leviticus, which "refers to the ancient Jewish year of Jubilee," during which "the land and the equality of persons that prevailed when the children of Israel entered the land of promise" were restored (Ford, 1976). Further observing that "Our Founding Fathers knew their Bibles as well as their Blackstone [referring to Sir William Blackstone, a noted British judge and writer of treatises]," Ford said, "They boldly reversed the age-old political theory that kings derive their powers from God and asserted that both powers and unalienable rights belong to the people as direct endowments from their Creator" (Ford, 1976).

The biblical inscription from Leviticus on the Liberty Bell, like the inscription "In God We Trust" on U.S. coins, the words "one nation, under God" in the pledge of allegiance to the U.S. flag, and such song lyrics as "God bless America," are examples of civil religion that mix secular and sacred symbolism.

In 1926, the Union of Jewish Orthodox Congregations erected a replica of the Liberty Bell in New York City. The biblical inscription was spelled out in Hebrew as "U grathem Dror Ba aretz Lihal Yoshvah" (Paige, 1988, 95).

In 2016, the Museum of the Bible installed what it called "[a]n exact replica of the Liberty Bell" as its first exhibit. Commissioned in 2003 by the Providence Forum to recognize the 300th anniversary of William Penn's Charter of Liberties (which was actually given in 1701) and cast by the same Whitechapel Foundry that cast the original, the replica, which is called "The Spirit of Liberty," weighs 3,200 pounds, which is over 1,000 pounds more than the original (Museum of the Bible, 2016). Guests were permitted the ring the Bell, which peals out an E flat note and is symbolically mounted from wood from what is believed to be the last Liberty Tree, which came from Annapolis, Maryland.

See also: Civil Religion and the Liberty Bell; Inscription on the Liberty Bell; Liberty Trees and Liberty Poles; Norris, Isaac, II; Quakers; Spirit of Liberty Bell

Further Reading

Bergsma, John S. 2005. "Once Again, the Jubilee, Every 49 of 50 years?" *Vetus Testamentum* 55 (January): 121–125.

Caine, Burton. 1997. "'The Liberal Agenda': Biblical Values and the First Amendment." *Touro Law Review* 14: 129–197.

Chase, Malcolm. 1990. "From Millennium to Anniversary: The Concept of Jubilee in Late Eighteenth- and Nineteenth-Century England." *Past & Present* 129 (November): 132–147.

Ford, Gerald R. 1976. "Remarks of Gerald R. Ford in Philadelphia, Pennsylvania (Bicentennial Celebration)," July 4. Gerald R. Ford Presidential Library and Museum. https://www.fordlibrarymuseum.gov/library/speeches/760645.asp.

Freedman, M. Troy. 2018. "Bronze Age and Religious Roots of Modern Debtor-Creditor Law." *Pennsylvania Bar Association Quarterly* 89: 166–177.

Kramer, Justin. 1975. *Cast in America: The Historically Accurate, Exciting Story of the Liberty Bell.* Los Angeles: Justin Kramer Incorporated.

Monshouwer, D. 1991. "The Reading of the Prophet in the Synagogue at Nazareth." *Biblica* 72: 90–99.

Museum of the Bible. 2016. "Museum of the Bible Installs First Exhibit Item: An Exact Replica of the Liberty Bell." Press release, August 16. https://www.museumofthebible .org/press/press-releases/museum-of-the-bible-installs-first-exhibit-item-an-exact -replica-of-the-liberty-bell.

Paige, John C. 1988. *The Liberty Bell of Independence National Historical Park: A Special History Study*, ed. David C. Kimball. Denver: Denver Service Center, National Park Service, Department of the Interior.

Sandoz, Ellis, ed. 1991. *Political Sermons of the American Founding Era, 1730–1805.* Indianapolis: Liberty Fund.

Segal, Rick. 2015. "Fare Well, Liberty Bell." desiringGod, July 4. https://www.desiringgod.org/articles/fare-well-liberty-bell.

Watson, Henry C. 1852. *The Old Bell of Independence; or, Philadelphia in 1776*. Philadelphia: Linsay and Blakiston.

LGBTQ Rights (see Reminder Marches)

Liberty, Meaning of

There are few words dearer in the American lexicon than that of *liberty* and its cousin, *freedom*. A U.S. Census survey indicated that 31 municipalities had the word *liberty* in their names; one of these, Liberty, Texas, has a replica of the Liberty Bell. Moreover, a study of counties within the single state of Iowa showed 20 with a township named Liberty, which ranged in their establishment from 1840 to 1882 (Read 1931, 364).

Another 35 municipalities had the word *eagle,* and another 11 the word *independence* (UPI, 2011). Another 9 included the word *freedom* (Berkes, 2006). A prominent historian has documented the use of the words *liberty* and *freedom* in a book of over 850 pages (Fischer, 2005). One of America's most iconic songs, "My Country 'Tis of Thee," refers to the nation as a "sweet land of liberty." Even before the American Revolution, Patrick Henry reportedly gave a speech in which he proclaimed, "Give me Liberty, or give me death!" Opponents of British policies had gathered under "liberty trees" and around "liberty poles," John Hancock named one of his ships *Liberty,* and one of America's earliest political songs, which John Dickinson authored, was called "Liberty Song."

The inscription on the Liberty Bell, taken from Leviticus 25:10, says: "Proclaim LIBERTY throughout all the land to all the inhabitants thereof." It comes from a Scripture, tied to a 50th Year of Jubilee, in which all lands were to be returned to their ancestral tribes and all slaves freed. Biblical liberty was typically tied to the idea of having the liberty to do what was right. Eskenazi and Wright (2013) believe that biblical liberty had less to do with negative freedom from restraint and more to do with "freedom grounded in a sustainable social order," in which people looked after one another.

When Isaac Norris II ordered the Liberty Bell and decided on its inscription, he knew that it was intended for Pennsylvania, a colony founded and dominated by Quakers, who had their own view of liberty. This is clearly articulated in the Pennsylvania Charter of Privileges that William Penn gave to the colony in 1701, and which the Liberty Bell may have been designed to commemorate. The charter stressed both religious freedom and representative government.

As the conflict between the colonies and Great Britain developed in the years after the French and Indian War, colonies eventually chose independence from the mother country as a way of assuring their own liberties. The Declaration of Independence tied these ideas to the view that "all men are created equal" and that all are entitled to "life, liberty, and the pursuit of happiness." The Fifth Amendment to the U.S. Constitution, later reiterated by the Fourteenth Amendment, which applied to state governments, stressed that government could not deprive individuals of "Life, liberty, or property" without "due process of law," which, it is generally agreed, was similar to the idea of "the law of the land" as this concept was phrased in the English Magna Carta of 1215 (Shattuck, 1891). Documents like the Magna Carta, state constitutions, and the U.S. Constitution were often associated with the idea of "liberty under law." Such a liberty allows government that the people themselves approved through selecting their own representatives, though it is limited when it comes to infringing certain fundamental rights, like those of worship and free speech.

There is deep irony in the fact that many defenders of the liberties of white men also believed that they had the right to own African Americans as property. As abolitionists began to symbolize their own cause with a Liberty Bell, they stressed that such liberty was to extend to "all" people throughout "all" the land, and not simply within the free states. President Abraham Lincoln was among those who believed that the nation could not permanently remain "half slave and half free."

After the Union victory in the Civil War, the Thirteenth Amendment (1865) announced an end to involuntary servitude. When it came to extending "equal protection" of the laws to all persons born or naturalized in the United States, the Fourteenth Amendment (1868) continued to distinguish between the rights of males and females. It thus left the latter without the franchise, even when (at least on paper) the Fifteenth Amendment (1870) prohibited voting discrimination on the basis of race or previous condition of servitude.

This development proved to be a great disappointment to suffragists, many of whom had worked long and hard for black emancipation and enfranchisement. As early as 1848, women had met at Seneca Falls, New York, to issue a new Declaration of Independence that proclaimed that "all men and women" are created equal and levying charges of oppression against their male counterparts.

In 1915, advocates of women's suffrage cast their own Liberty Bell, which was often called the "Justice Bell." They refused to ring the bell until the ratification of the Nineteenth Amendment in 1920 finally prohibited discrimination in voting on the basis of sex.

In the 1960s, the Liberty Bell and Independence Hall became the site of a number of sit-ins and other demonstrations by advocates for expanded rights for African Americans, the pro- and anti–Vietnam War movements, advocates for lesbian, gay, bisexual, transgender, and queer/questioning (LGBTQ) rights, antiabortion protestors, and opponents of capital punishment. Each of these had its own take on the liberty that the Bell proclaims. Dr. Martin Luther King, Jr., used the image of bells when he said "Let freedom ring" in his 1963 "I Have a Dream Speech" in Washington, D.C.

Although it is common to portray American history as a straight line of increasing liberty and progress, such progress has rarely been unilineal, and progress for some groups has sometimes come at the expense of others (Keyssar, 2009; Meachum, 2018). Still the concept of liberty resonates deeply. As Read (1931, 367) observed, "The word has had throughout our history not so much an intellectual significance as an emotional significance. We cheer for liberty. 'Sweet land of liberty' is our favorite national hymn, 'conceived in liberty' in the Gettysburg address, the cracked Liberty Bell as a national totem, Liberty in our coins and currency, the Liberty Loan,—indeed our country does much homage to liberty."

Especially during the Cold War, the Liberty Bell became a symbol for freedom not only within the United States, but throughout the world. One writer has observed, "The bell is undoubtedly our nation's greatest talisman, instantly recognized throughout the world as a symbol of American freedom" (Greiff, 1987, 13). Another has called it "the most powerful symbol of freedom around the world" (Kashatus, 1992, 39). Replicas of the Bell are found not only throughout the United States, but in Belgium, France, Germany, Japan, Israel, and elsewhere.

See also: King, Martin Luther, Jr.; Leviticus 25:10; Liberty, Texas, Replica of the Liberty Bell; Liberty Trees and Liberty Poles; Norris, Isaac, II; Pennsylvania Charter of Privileges (1701); Oral Tradition and the Liberty Bell; Political and Social Movements and the Liberty Bell; *Silent Peal from the Liberty Bell, A* (1914)

Further Reading

Berkes, Howard. 2006. "Happy Fourth, in a Town Named Freedom." NPR, July 4. https://www.npr.org/templates/story/story.php?storyId=5533062.

Eskenazi, Tamara Cohn, and Jacob L. Wright. 2013. "What the Liberty Bell Can Teach Us About America and the Fourth of July." Fox News, July 3. http://www.foxnews.com/opinion/2013/07/03/what-liberty-bell-can-teach-us-about-america-and-fourth-july.html.

Fischer, David Hackett. 2005. *Liberty and Freedom*. New York: Oxford University Press.

Greiff, Constance M. 1987. *Independence: The Creation of a National Park*. Philadelphia: University of Pennsylvania Press.

Kashatus, William C., III. 1992. *Historic Philadelphia: The City, Symbols & Patriots, 1681–1800*. Lanham, MD: University Press of America.

Keyssar, Alexander. 2009. *The Right to Vote: The Contested History of Democracy in America*. New York: Basic Books.

Meacham, Jon. 2018. *The Soul of America: The Battle for Our Better Angels*. New York: Random House.

Read, Allen Walker. 1931. "'Liberty' in Iowa." *American Speech* 6 (June): 360–367.

Shattuck, Charles E. 1891. "The True Meaning of the Term 'Liberty' in Those Clauses in the Federal and State Constitutions Which Protect 'Life, Liberty, and Property.'" *Harvard Law Review* 4 (March 15): 365–392.

UPI. "31 U.S. Towns Have 'Liberty.'" 2011. July 4. https://www.upi.com/31-US-towns-have-liberty/18521309802360.

Liberty, Texas, Replica of the Liberty Bell

In 1960, the Whitechapel Foundry in England, which cast the first Liberty Bell in 1752, cast another for Sallie and Nadine Woods, who were the founders of the Liberty Muscular Dystrophy Research Foundation to research the disease, which affected both of them. They subsequently built a tower in Liberty, Texas, to display the bell, which they rang on April 24, 1976, and then the city earned the designation as a National and State Bicentennial City. The tower was dismantled in 2009 due to structural problems.

The ceremonies welcoming the bell were quite elaborate. It was formally welcomed when it reached Houston aboard the steamship *Letitia Lykes* on August 19, 1960, and formally dedicated on the courthouse square in Liberty on September 13,

1960. The actor John Wayne was on hand to ring the bell, which was flanked by colorful bunting and by two girls in long white dresses and crowns, in apparent representation of Lady Liberty.

As of 2018, the Liberty Rotary Club was selling concrete Liberty Bell replicas for $300 each, including local delivery in order to fund a worldwide project and to construct a new Liberty Bell Tower ("The Liberty Bell Replica," n.d.).

See also: Bicentennial and the Liberty Bell; Replicas of the Liberty Bell; Whitechapel Foundry

Further Reading
"Liberty Bell and Bell Tower." n.d. http://www.cityofliberty.org/About?Liberty_Bell_and _Bell_Tower.aspx.
"The Liberty Bell Replica." n.d. Liberty Municipal Library. https://liberty.ploud.net/about -us/the-liberty-bell-replica.html.

"Liberty Bell" (Song, 1885)

One of the songs that most closely ties the Liberty Bell to the American Revolution was "Liberty Bell," with lyrics by P. Molony and music by Edward Petzsch, and published by A. E. Blackmar & Co., in New Orleans in 1885. Because this date corresponds with the Liberty Bell's visit to the World's Industrial and Cotton Exposition that was held in the city that year, it seems likely that it was written and perhaps set to music for the occasion. At the time, white Southerners, who remained unhappy with the liberties that the Fourteenth and Fifteenth Amendments and congressionally mandated Reconstruction had extended to former slaves, were attempting to emphasize the common bond that Southern states shared with their Northern counterparts in opposing Great Britain during the American Revolution.

The song consisted of two verses and a chorus. The first cited "patriot feelings" evoked by the pealing of the Liberty Bell and its call to rebellion against the British king. The second put a similar focus on opposition to kingly oppression.

The sentiments of both verses are echoed in the chorus (Petzsch, 1885):

And the Liberty Bell calling men to rebel
Rang out the death knell of the king's connoneer.
When the throne-shaking swelled the Liberty Bell
Call'd men to rebel against despotic laws,
Till the Liberty Bell, calling men to rebel
Has toll'd the death knell of the last to be crowned.

See also: Music and the Liberty Bell; World's Industrial and Cotton Exposition in New Orleans (1885)

Further Reading
Petzsch, Edward. 1885. *The Liberty Bell*. Blackmar, A. E. & Co., New Orleans, mono-graphic. Notated Music. https://www.loc.gov/item/sm1885.27891.

"Liberty Bell" (Song, 1952)

In 1952, Louis Maur copyrighted a song entitled "Liberty Bell," which was published in Philadelphia. The cover featured a sketch of the Liberty Bell with a simple depiction of Archibald Willard's famous painting entitled *Yankee Doodle* (but better known as *The Spirit of '76*). The inscription on the Bell and its distinctive crack are both visible.

Noting that individuals come from throughout the county to visit the Liberty Bell, Maur referred to it as "a Pil-lar of to-tal Lib-er-ty" (Maur, 1952). Probably seeking to link the cause of American freedom to that throughout the world, and likely in opposition to communist totalitarianism, Maur's song proclaimed, "A-round the World your cry was heard. Long Live our Free-dom, We want no Serf-dom" (Maur, 1952).

The year 1952 is also when Ted Di Renzo published "Proclaim Liberty," which sought to link the Liberty Bell to the World Freedom Bell, which the United States had recently given to West Berlin.

See also: Freedom Bell; Music and the Liberty Bell

Further Reading
Maur, Louis. 1952. "Liberty Bell." Philadelphia: Grimes Music Publishers.

"Liberty Bell (It's Time to Ring Again)" (Song, 1917)

One indication of the power of a political symbol is the degree to which it is used to rally popular sentiment, especially during times when the nation seems threatened. During World War I, the Liberty Bell was used as a symbol to encourage individuals to invest in Liberty Loans to help finance the war. Popular songs of the day included "The Song of the Liberty Bell," "Liberty Bell Waltz," and "Bell of Bells," but the most popular song was entitled "Liberty Bell (It's Time to Ring Again)" (Nash, 2010, 189–190).

This song was written by Joe Goodwin (1889–1943), with music written by Halsey K. Mohr (1883–1942). It was published in 1917. The song consisted of two verses and a chorus. The cover of the sheet music portrayed three colonial figures. One, probably George Washington, has a sword by his side, and another, probably Betsy Ross, examines the American flag below the Liberty Bell.

The first verse encouraged the Bell to come out of its slumber "to wake 'em up" and "shake 'em up" for "a cause worth ringing for." The chorus likened the nation's current "fix" to that of "sev-en-ty-six," and noted that "Though you're old and there's a crack in you/ Don't for-get Old Glo-ry's back-in' you, / Oh! Lib-er-ty Bell, it's time to ring again" (firstworldwar.com, n.d.).

See also: Liberty Loans; Music and the Liberty Bell

Further Reading
Firstworldwar.com. n.d. "Vintage Audio: Liberty Bell (It's Time to Ring Again)." http://www.firstworldwar.com/audio/libertybell.htm.
"Image 1 of Liberty Bell It's Time to Ring Again." Library of Congress. https://www.loc.gov/resource/ihas.200207770.0/?sp=1.
Nash, Gary B. 2010. *The Liberty Bell*. New Haven, CT: Yale University Press.

"Liberty Bell, Ring On!" (Song, 1918)

One of the songs that emerged toward the end of World War I was a march written by Haven Gillespie, the pen name for James Lamong Gillespie (1888–1971), entitled "Liberty Bell, Ring On!" The accompanying music was composed by Albert Wm. Brown.

The piece consisted of two verses and a chorus. The first verse associated the Liberty Bell with "Justice, Truth, and Freedom" and the principle that "Right ever conquers Wrong" (Hartzell and Feldman, 1918). The second verse further associated the Liberty Bell with a "Destiny . . . Calling all Freemen to the fray" and telling the message of freedom "to the world" (Hartzell and Feldman, 1918).

The chorus begins with the line, "Swing! Ring! Liberty Bell," which is again said to be "Ringing for Freedom" and to be echoing "Where our Flag's unfurled . . . 'round the world" (Hartzell and Feldman, 1918).

The sheet music, which was published by Frank K. Root & Company in Chicago and New York, had a sketch of the Liberty Bell with the crack and lettering visible, on what appears to be a darker image of a shield.

See also: Music and the Liberty Bell

Further Reading

Hartzell, Roy, and Mary A. Feldman. 1918. *The Liberty Bell*. Monographic. Howard Publishing Company, Washington, D.C. Notated Music. https://www.loc.gov/item /2014561560.

"Liberty Bell, Ring On! March Song." 1918. Frank K. Root & Co.: Chicago and New York.

"Liberty Bell, The" (Poem, 1843)

The *Liberty Bell Gift Books* featured writings by numerous foreign contributors, including John Bowring (1769–1856), an English merchant and social reformer. His poem "The Liberty Bell" appeared in the 1843 issue of the book.

Had the Statue of Liberty existed at the time "The Liberty Bell" was written, the poem might have equally applied to it. The first stanza, which evokes "the transatlantic shore," was as follows (Bowring, 1843, 1):

The LIBERTY BELL is hung aloft,
    On the transatlantic shore;
And we hear its echoes, oft and oft,
    Wafted the waters o'er:
And welcomed shall those echoes be!
    Music of Liberty!

The second stanza made it clear that the Bell stood for the liberty not just of white people, but of everyone, especially black people (Bowring, 1843, 2):

Liberty for the white—the few—
    From the oppressor's thrall?
Nay! But Liberty,—Liberty, too,

For the blacks,—for all!
Slavery shall not stamp her ban
   On any men,—or man.

The next two verses liken the people of the earth to "flowers of every shade," and then to stars "Differing, in glory and might: / But glorious every one, star by star" (Bowring, 1843).

The discrimination imposed on black people was not created by God but by man, as the sixth stanza indicates (Bowring, 1843, 3):

Despised there is none—degraded none;
   Each holds its ordered place;
But 'tis man—usurping man, alone,
   Who hath stigmatized his race;
Who hath giv'n his fellow—O shame! O shame!
   A *slave's* ignoble name!

Describing man as "God effigy," the penultimate stanza looks forward to the day when all shall be born free. Similarly, the final verse looks to a time when slavery will be but an outward remnant of the past (Bowring, 1843, 3–4):

Come, then, that bright and benignant time,
   When LIBERTY'S blessed BELL,
And earth re-echoing it, shall shine
   Slavery's final knell;
And Slavery's dreary tales be told
   As a mythic page of old.

See also: Abolitionists and the Liberty Bell; African Americans and the Liberty Bell; *Liberty Bell Gift Books*; Statue of Liberty

Further Reading
Bowring, John. 1843. "The Liberty Bell." *The Liberty Bell*. Boston: Boston-Anti-Slavery Society, 1–4.

"Liberty Bell, The" (Poem, 1893)

Elbridge Streeter Brooks (1846–1902) was an author who specialized in writing patriotic books for children. In his book *Heroic Happenings Told in Verse and Story*, published by G. P. Putnam's Sone, Brooks published a three-part poem in 1893 entitled "The Liberty Bell," which was later republished in *The School Speaker and Reader*, edited by William DeWitt Hyde.

The first part of the work was labeled, "PHILADELPHIA, 1776," and was set in Independence Hall, which was described in the opening two lines as "SQUARELY prim and stoutly built, / Free from glitter and from gilt" (Hyde, 1900, 93). In this section of the poem, Brooks largely repeated the story introduced by George Lippard of a boy who, upon the signing of the Declaration of Independence, tells the man in the belfry that "the deed is done ! / ring! They've signed, and freedom's won!" (Hyde, 1900, 94). The last three lines of this section, like those of the remaining two, announce (Hyde, 1900, 94):

> "Man is man—a slave no longer;
> Truth and Right than Might are stronger.
> Praise to God! We're free; we're free!"

The second stanza is headed "NEW ORLEANS, 1885," and clearly refers to the Liberty Bell's trip to the World's Industrial and Cotton Exposition in New Orleans of that same year. This verse places the Bell among the splendor of the buildings of the exposition, with emphasis on the nearby river, "eternal summer," and the southern flowers among which the Bell sits (Hyde, 1900, 94–95):

> Flower-bedeck'd 'neath sunny skies;
> Old and time-stained, cracked and voiceless, but where
>   All may see it well;
>   Circled by the wealth and power
>   Of the great world's triumph-hour,—
> Sacred to the cause of freedom, on its dais rests the
>   Bell.
>   And the children thronging near,
>   Yet again the story hear
> Of the bell that rang the message, pealing out to land
>   And sea.

This section ends with the same three lines as the previous verse.

The third stanza has no heading other than the Roman numeral III and seeks, like the trip of the Bell itself, to unite both North and South in the message of freedom (Hyde, 1900, 95–96):

> Prize the glorious relic then,
> With its hundred years and ten,
> By the Past a priceless heirloom to the Future handed
>   Down.
>   Still its stirring story tell,
>   Till the children know it well,—
> From the joyous southern city to the Northern Quaker
>   town.
>   Time that heals all wound and scars,
>   Time that ends all strifes and wars,
> Time that turns all pains to pleasures, and can make
>   the cannon dumb,
>   Still shall join in firmer grasp,
>   Still shall knit in friendlier clasp
> North and South-land in the glory of the ages yet to come.
>   And, though voiceless, still the Bell
>   Shall its glorious message tell,

Pealing loud o'er all the Nation, lake to gulf and
    sea to sea:
"Man is man—a slave no longer;
    Truth and Right than Might are stronger.
Praise to God! We're free; we're free!"

See also: Children and the Liberty Bell; Lippard, George; Reconciliation and the Liberty Bell; World's Industrial and Cotton Exposition in New Orleans (1885)

Further Reading
Brooks, Elbridge S. 1900. "The Liberty Bell." In *The School Speaker and Reader*, ed. William DeWitt Hyde. Boston: Ginn and Company, 93–96.

"Liberty Bell, The" (Poem, 1895)

Just as the ringing of bells had sought to unite colonists against Great Britain during the Revolutionary War, the Liberty Bell became a symbol of unity after the Civil War. Three of the journeys that the Liberty Bell took between 1885 and 1915 were to Southern states.

On October 4, 1895, at the time when the Liberty Bell was visiting the Atlanta Cotton States and International Exposition, Florence Earle Coates (1850–1927), who was born and died in Philadelphia, wrote "The Liberty Bell," a poem designed to emphasize such unity. Written from the perspective of the Bell itself, the first two stanzas associated the Bell with other Southern themes and memories:

With pomp attendant, and in garlands drest,
    I journey from my sacred home once more;
Not this time to the new, triumphant West,
    But to a land more dear to me of yore;
A land in memory sweet as the perfume
Of twining jasmine and magnolia bloom.

Though old and broken, for that memory's sake—
    The memory of honored things gone by,
I will forget my length of years, and make
    This pilgrimage unto her Southern sky,
So Georgia's children, too, may face may know,
And wreathe me proudly with their mistletoe.

Recognizing that the North and South had more in common during the Revolutionary period than in later years, Coates sought to emphasize the former over the latter in the next two stanzas:

Their fathers knew me, and in that great hour
    When in the Hall of Freedom, since my home,
They signed the Charter, born of love and power,
    That made them one, I, from the lofty dome

Above them, loudly rang the brave command,
Proclaiming Liberty throughout the land!

Men pass away, but I do not forget;
    And though, alas, I have been silent long,
The echoes of my ringing vibrate yet,
    From pole to pole, in every freeman's song;
And she who share my May, in my December
Shall gaze upon my face, and will remember!

The last two stanzas likely emphasize unity evoking the state of Georgia again by name, and citing citizens from the state who signed the Declaration of Independence (Coates, 1898):

Georgia, to thee I come as to my own,
    Undying laurels for thy heroes bringing,
Who sacrificed themselves to right alone,
    Who signed for Liberty, and set me ringing.
The word they witnessed then, I bear to all,—
We stand, united; we, divided, fall!

O Georgia! And of Wynnnett, Walton, Hall!
    Whose star was one of the sublime Thirteen,—
A pledge of hope and happiness to all,
    A sign of factory, whenever seen,—
That vow the Fathers made, their sons fulfill,
The stars they joined shine on, united still!

See also: Atlanta Cotton State and Industrial Exposition of 1895; Journeys of the Liberty Bell; Reconciliation and the Liberty Bell

Further Reading
Coates, Florence Earle. "The Liberty Bell." *Poems.* Boston: Houghton, Mifflin, and Company, 1898.

Liberty Bell as Fighting Inspiration and Symbol

In addition to being used as an evocative symbol to raise money for Liberty Loans, the Liberty Bell has, like the U.S. flag, symbolized the values for which American soldiers were fighting. Numerous patriotic songs that were written during World War I used images of the Liberty Bell. Americans denigrated the German language, even going so far as to rename sauerkraut, which has a German name, as "Liberty Cabbage" (Kirschbaum, 2015).

During World War II, military training programs ended films with a picture of the Liberty Bell with a superimposed *V,* symbolizing victory (Paige, 1988, 96). Similarly, a set of films entitled "Profiles in Courage" that NBC ran in 1963 were introduced by the ringing of a bell, albeit without a crack. In a play on words, a number of aircraft, including B-17 Flying Fortresses, as well as Consolidated B-24

Liberators that were used during World War II, were designated as "Liberty Belles." They were often decorated by their crews with images of beautiful women.

The Statue of Liberty, in New York Harbor, which was given to the United States by France and installed in 1886, while classically dressed, also epitomizes the way that the peoples of the United States and France have often portrayed the idea of liberty as a woman (Berenson, 2012, 11–12). It has often been associated with welcoming immigrants, many of whom have fled to avoid the devastation of war and persecution.

In World War I, Americans often contrasted their liberty to dictatorial oppression. During the Cold War, Americans further juxtaposed ideals of freedom and liberty against totalitarian communism. One of the American bases in South Korea is known as "Camp Liberty Bell."

See also: Bells, Belles; Liberty Loans; Music and the Liberty Bell; Statue of Liberty

Further Reading

Berenson, Edward. 2012. *The Statue of Liberty: A Transatlantic Story.* New Haven, CT: Yale University Press.

Kirschbaum, Eric. 2014. *Burning Beethoven: The Eradication of German Culture in the United States During World War I.* New York: Berlinica Publishing.

Nash, Gary B. 2010. *The Liberty Bell.* New Haven, CT: Yale University Press.

Paige, John C. 1988. *The Liberty Bell of Independence National Historical Park: A Special History Study,* ed. David C. Kimball. Denver: Denver Service Center, National Park Service, Department of the Interior.

Liberty Bell Awards

Because the Liberty Bell embodies American values, it seems only reasonable that its name would be used to recognize those who embody these ideals.

This was among the purposes of the Order of the Liberty Bell, which was founded and chartered in 1925. The Order listed its purposes as follows (Stoudt, 1930, 126):

> To perpetuate the history of the events connected with the sacred Liberty Bell; to further the spirit of patriotism by proper celebration of these events; to promote a spirit of devotion to the memory of those men and women whose distinguished services aided in securing our liberties; to procure the marking of important historical places and landmarks with proper memorial Tablets, and to confer the Order of the Liberty Bell on distinguished men and women who by their service have advanced the high ideals of liberty and the welfare of mankind.

Beginning in 1989, the philanthropic Philadelphia Foundation began awarding to outstanding public servants the Philadelphia Liberty Medal, which featured an engraving of the Liberty Bell in the foreground and pictures of globes on the back on each side. The first such award was given to Poland's Lech Walesa, a popular labor leader who had helped free his country from communism. Other award winners have been both domestic and foreign leaders, including presidents, Supreme Court justices, civil rights leaders, the Dalai Lama, and Senator John McCain. Since 2006, the nominees and award have been presented by the National Constitution Center (NCC), which is located not far from Independence Hall.

Lawyers have also developed a Liberty Bell Award, which is often given at Law Day events to recognize outstanding nonlawyers who have made contributions to their communities. This award was the brainchild of William P. Daniel of Michigan in 1962, when he was serving as a member of the State Bar Young Lawyers Section (Stockmeyer, 1991, 20).

See also: Coins, Medals, and Stamps Depicting the Liberty Bell

Further Reading

Stockmeyer, Norman Otto, Jr. 1992. "The Liberty Bell Award—Symbol of Law Day." *Michigan Bar Journal* 71 (January): 20–21.
Stoudt, John Baer. 1930. *The Liberty Bells of Pennsylvania.* Philadelphia: William J. Campbell.

Liberty Bell Center

Although the Liberty Bell has spent most of its "life" in Independence Hall, as bicentennial celebrations of American independence approached, the Park Service decided to move it to a pavilion to accommodate the number of anticipated visitors. At midnight on December 31, 1975, the Bell was ceremoniously moved to the Liberty Bell Pavilion, designed by Mitchell/Guiugola. The pavilion was a minimalist structure that provided relatively little commentary and put primary focus on the Bell itself, which could be viewed from both inside and outside (Matero, 2013).

On October 3, 2003, the Bell was transferred to a new Liberty Bell Center, designed by Bohlin Cywinski Jackson and The Olin Partnership, just months after the nearby opening of the National Constitution Center (NCC). Built of red brick, stone, and glass, the Liberty Bell Center consists of "an outdoor interpretive area, an exhibit hall and a tapered cube housing the bell chamber" (Bohlin Cywinski Jackson, n.d.). In contrast to the earlier Liberty Bell Pavilion, the exhibit hall of the Liberty Bell Center provides "Twenty large panels with descriptive text, historical quotations, reproduced images, and original artifacts" (Hyson, 2004, 308).

As the Bell moved, a town crier yelled, "Oye, oye, clear the way for liberty. Let freedom ring. Let freedom ring." The bell was accompanied by actors dressed as historic figures, such as Benjamin Franklin, Thomas Jefferson, Frederick Douglass, and Susan B. Anthony (Morales, 2003).

Not everyone has appreciated the current site. Visiting the Liberty Bell in 2007, conservative commentator Steven Warshawsky complained, "The structure offers no more inspiration than a highway rest stop. It is completely unworthy of the important object found inside" (Warshawsky, 2007). He believed that the Bell was diminished by being displayed in such a large space and the steel cables that cordoned off the Bell from visitors were too harsh. As for the exhibits that he passed, he thought that "the overall thrust of the exhibit is . . . to emphasize the Liberty Bell's ties to various civil rights movements for minorities. In keeping with how history usually is presented these days, the exhibit often seems to be rebuking the nation for its failures in the past to fully live up to the message of the bell's inscription, especially with regard to the treatment of blacks, Indians and women" (Warshawsky, 2007). He also opined that "[t]he Liberty Bell, as presented in the

A visitor reads a panel at the Liberty Bell Center in Philadelphia, Pennsylvania. The Liberty Bell was moved to the center from the Liberty Bell pavilion in 2003. The bell had been located at the pavilion since 1975. (Ritu Jethani/Dreamstime.com)

exhibit, apparently has little relevance to a middle-class white male like myself, except as a tool to scold me and my presumed ancestors for our wrongdoing against others" (Warshawsky, 2007).

As plans were made for the Liberty Bell Center, it was discovered that the entrance was just in front of the house once owned by Robert Morris, which George Washington and John Adams had enlarged and used as the presidential mansion from 1790 to 1800 during their presidencies. Moreover, Washington owned a number of slaves during this time, two of whom—Washington's chef, Hercules, and his wife's slave, Ona Judge—used their sojourn in Philadelphia to escape. The building itself was demolished in 1832.

A number of groups, including one called the Ad Hoc Historians and two African American groups, Avenging the Ancestors Coalition (ATAC) and Generations Unlimited, began exerting pressure on the National Park Service to ensure that the aspect of American history concerning slavery would be incorporated into interpretations of the Liberty Bell (Mires, 2009, 220). Guides had already recognized that the name of the Bell was not its original appellation, but was largely the result of abolitionists who had expropriated the Bell as a symbol for emancipation. The efforts were stimulated by a pathbreaking study of the site by Edward Lawler Jr. (Lawler, 2002; also see Lawler, 2005, and Kurjack, 1953).

In time, an outdoor exhibit that mapped George Washington's house and presented interpretative panels was opened. It delineates various rooms in the original house, including the president's office, the State Dining Room, the Family Dining Room, and the Slave Quarters (Lawler, 2005, 403).

See also: Abolitionists and the Liberty Bell; Liberty Bell Pavilion

Further Reading

Aden, Roger C. 2015. *Upon the Ruins of Liberty: Slavery, the President's House at Independence National Independence Historical Park and Public Memory.* Philadelphia: Temple University Press.

Bohlin Cywinski Jackson. n.d. "Liberty Bell Center." https://bcj.com/projects/liberty-bell-center.

Hyson, Jeffrey. 2004. "Exhibit Review." *Pennsylvania Magazine of History and Biography* 128 (July): 307–310.

El-Khoury, Rololphe, ed. 2006. *Liberty Bell Center: Bohlin Cywinski Jackson.* 2006. New York: ORO Editions.

Kurjack, Dennis C. 1953. "The 'President's House' in Philadelphia." *Pennsylvania History: A Journal of Mid-Atlantic Studies* 20 (October): 380–394.

Lawler, Edward, Jr. 2005. "The President's House Revisited." *Pennsylvania Magazine of History and Biography* 129 (October): 371–420.

Lawler, Edward, Jr. 2002. "The President's House in Philadelphia: The Rediscovery of a Lost Landmark." *Pennsylvania Magazine of History and Biography* 126 (January): 5–95.

Matero, Frank G. 2013. "Housing the Bell: 150 Years of Exhibiting an American Icon." *Change over Time* 3 (Fall): 188–201.

Mires, Charlene. 2009. "Invisible House, Invisible Slavery: Struggles of Public History at Independence National Historical Park." In *Culture and Belonging in Divided Societies: Contestation and Symbolic Landscapes,* Marc Howard Ross, ed. Philadelphia: University of Pennsylvania Press, 216–237.

Morales, Tatiana. 2003. "Liberty Bell on the Move." CBS News, October 9. https://www.cbsnews.com/news/liberty-bell-on-the-move.

Nash, Gary B. 2006. *First City: Philadelphia and the Forging of Historical Memory.* Philadelphia: University of Pennsylvania Press.

Ogline, Jill. 2004. "'Creating Dissonance for the Visitor': The Heart of the Liberty Bell Controversy." *The Public Historian* 26 (Summer): 49–58.

Rybczynski, Witold. 1998. "Moving the Bell." *The Atlantic,* June. https://www.theatlantic.com/magazine/archive/1998/06/moving-the-bell-377128.

Warschawsky, Steven. 2007. "Visiting the Liberty Bell." *Real Clear Politics,* March 18. https://www.realclearpolitics.com/articles/2007/03/visiting_the_liberty_bell.html.

Liberty Bell Classic (1980)

Nations often use the Olympic Games not only to highlight the talent of their athletes, but also to demonstrate the effectiveness of the principles that guide them. Nations consider it a special honor to host such competitions.

In 1980, President Jimmy Carter decided that the United States should not participate in the Summer Olympics because they were being held in Moscow at a time when the Soviet Union had recently invaded Afghanistan. Sixty-five other countries heeded Carter's call to boycott the Games.

Seeking to mitigate the disappointment of the athletes who had prepared for the Olympics, the United States hosted its own games, which twenty-nine other nations attended, in Philadelphia. Undoubtedly seeking to contrast American freedom against Soviet totalitarianism, the United States designated the games as the "Liberty Bell Classic." The games were not nearly as competitive as typical Olympic competitions had been (Neff, 1980).

In retaliation for this boycott, the Soviet Union decided to boycott the 1984 Summer Olympic Games, which were held in Los Angeles, and held its own games. The Soviet Union called its competition the "Friendship Games."

A number of other competitions since then, especially those in and around the Philadelphia area, have been designated as the "Liberty Bell Classic."

See also: Liberty Bell as Fighting Inspiration and Symbol

Further Reading

Ferguson, Kevin. 2012. "History Lesson: If You Don't Like the Olympics, Just Make Your Own." Off-Ramp, July 30. https://www.scpr.org/blogs/offramp/2012/07/30/9216/history-lesson-if-you-dont-olympics-just-make-your.

Neff, Craig. ". . . And Meanwhile in Philadelphia." 1980. SI.com Vault, July 28. https://www.si.com/vault/1980/07/28/824835/and-meanwhile-in-philadelphia-half-a-world-from-lenin-stadium-boycotting-athletes-some-of-whom-gave-olympian-performances-proved-theres-no-alternative-to-the-games.

Liberty Bell Gift Books

The Liberty Bell's current name was popularized by a series of 15 gift books that abolitionists published in Boston most years between 1839 and 1858, which were entitled *The Liberty Bell*. These volumes were sold at a series of fairs that were generally held near Christmas. Although attributed to "Friends of Freedom," they were chiefly edited by Maria Weston Chapman (1806–1885), who was the wife of a wealthy merchant. Many of the contributors were women, who often sought to pitch their appeals in ways that connected with understandings of motherhood that were predominant at that time (Harris, 2009).

The cover of these books pictured a gilded bell and a female figure who symbolized liberty. She held a pole festooned with a liberty cap and faced a kneeling slave, while a slave behind her appeared to have broken his chains. Although the bell is much more ornate than the Liberty Bell, it clearly depicts the words "PROCLAIM LIBERTY," which could also be found on the Liberty Bell.

Page v of the debut publication contains a picture, included in all subsequent volumes, of a ringing bell with the words "PROCLAIM LIBERTY TO ALL THE INHABITANTS," with the largest letters used for the word "ALL." The words are similar to those from Leviticus 25:10, inscribed on the Liberty Bell. Below the image of the bell is a note initialed by Chapman, which says that the words were "SUGGESTED BY THE INSCRIPTION ON THE PHILADELPHIA LIBERTY BELL" (Chapman, 1839). Later in the first volume, Mary Clark authored a poem entitled "Perfect Freedom," which refers to a Liberty Bell, but in terms that would arguably transcend the Bell in Independence Hall. The poem thus ends with the following words (Clark, 1839, 102):

Ring, Liberty Bell! Till that echo thrills
From the ocean rocks to the inland hills!
Till the sound of the scourge and the fetter
  Is o'er,
And wrong and bondage are known no more.

References to a Liberty Bell continued in subsequent volumes. Thus in 1842, a poem "The Liberty Bell," begins with the lines "The Liberty Bell—The Liberty Bell, The tocsin of Freedom and Slavery's knell," and later refers to "Liberty's Jubilee" (Stoudt, 1930, 62–63). Future references to a "liberty bell" are found in a sonnet by Bernard Barton in the 1845 issue, a poem by Irish poet R. R. Marden in the 1847 issue, a sonnet by Anne Warren Weston in the 1852 issue, and a poem by Aureliam F. Raymond in the 1858 issue (Stoudt, 1930, 64–67).

Although the *Liberty Bell* was the most successful, antislavery societies also issued other books during this time. Ralph Thompson identifies these as "the *Oasis, Freedom's Gift*, the *North Star*, the *Star of Emancipation, Liberty Chimes*, [and] *Autographs for Freedom*" (Thompson, 1934, 154). Thompson's study found that the books drew a large number of writers from abroad, chiefly from England and Ireland; included some articles in French and German; and was less jingoistic than similar volumes from the period (Thompson, 1934, 161–162). He notes that the 1844 volume called for secession rather than continuing union with slave states (Thompson, 1934, 162).

Thompson believed that the volumes often sacrificed literary and aesthetic values for advocacy, and that their chief effect was probably that of mobilizing the antislavery faithful than in making new converts (Thompson, 1934, 163). By contrast, scholars Fritz and Fee (2012, 75–76) point to the success of the books in "building and maintaining a sense of community through shared visions and continually reaffirmed ideas," as well as raising money and cultivating relationships among antislavery advocates.

See also: Abolitionists and the Liberty Bell; Chapman, Maria Weston; "Liberty Bells" (Poem, 1851); Madden, R. R.; Moore, R. R. R.; Names for the Liberty Bell; Pierpont, John

Further Reading

Friends of Freedom. 1839. *The Liberty Bell*. Maria Weston Chapman, ed. Boston: Boston-Anti-Slavery Society.

Fritz, Meaghan M., and Frank E. Fee, Jr. 2012. "To Give the Gift of Freedom: Gift Books and the War on Slavery." *American Periodicals: A Journal of History & Criticism* 23: 60–82.

Harris, Leslie J. 2009. "Motherhood, Race, and Gender: The Rhetoric of Women's Anti-slavery Activism in the *Liberty Bell* Giftbooks." *Women's Studies in Communication* 32 (Fall): 293–319.

Stoudt, John Baer. 1930. *The Liberty Bells of Pennsylvania*. Philadelphia: William J. Campbell.

Thompson, Ralph. 1934. "The Liberty Bell and Other Anti-Slavery Gift-Books." *New England Quarterly* 7 (March): 154–168.

"Liberty Bell March, The" (Song, 1893)

One indication of the growing popularity of the Liberty Bell at the end of the nineteenth century and the beginning of the twentieth was the increased number of requests by cities to have the Bell visit for fairs and expositions. Between 1885 and

1915, the Liberty Bell attended seven such events, and as the train carrying the Bell either stopped or passed through the cities, thousands upon thousands of people turned out to see it.

Another indication of the Bell's popularity was an increasing number of references in print and in popular culture, which also popularized other icons like the U.S. flag, the Statute of Liberty, and the bald eagle. Few were more sensitive to popular tastes and knew how to capitalize on them better than John Philip Sousa (1854–1921), the composer and director of the U.S. Marine Band. He became known for his theatrical performances and was nicknamed "The March King" for his martial compositions, which include "The Stars and Stripes Forever" and "The Washington Post March" (Warfield, 2011).

In 1893, Sousa was apparently inspired by seeing the Liberty Bell at the World's Columbian Exposition in Chicago and decided to name one of his marches in its honor (Sands and Bartlett, 2002, 64). It was published by the John Church Company for a variety of instruments and remains a popular tune that is often played at presidential inaugurations and other patriotic events. It also was parodied in the opening titles of the Monty Python troupe's comedy series, *Monty Python's Flying Circus,* which ran from 1969 to 1974.

Unlike some of Sousa's other compositions, "The Liberty Bell March" is not accompanied by lyrics. In 1915, Dick Rabe published a waltz entitled "Bell of Bells," which also appears to have been unaccompanied by lyrics. The cover, probably playing on the word *belle,* which is sometimes used to describe a young woman, pictures the Liberty Bell with its distinctive crack. It is adorned with five roses, which contain the faces of five women in their centers. Although published in Indianapolis, it may well have been inspired by the Bell's 1915 journey to Panama-Pacific International Exposition in San Francisco and the Panama-California Exposition in San Diego, both in California, the home of the annual Rose Parade, which dates back to 1890.

See also: Journeys of the Liberty Bell; Music and the Liberty Bell; World's Columbian Exposition in Chicago (1893)

Further Reading

Sands, Robert W., Jr., and Alexander B. Bartlett. 2002. *Images of America: Independence Hall and the Liberty Bell*. Charleston, SC: Arcadia Publishing.

Warfield, Patrick. 2011. "The March as Musical Drama and the Spectacle of John Philip Sousa." *Journal of the American Musicological Society* 64 (Summer): 289–318.

Liberty Bell Mural

As British troops advanced toward Philadelphia in September 1777, Colonel Thomas Polk of North Carolina and his cavalry transported what today is known as the Liberty Bell from Philadelphia to Allentown, about 60 miles north. This was to prevent the Bell from being melted down for gunshot. While in Allentown, Patriots hid the bell in the basement of the Zion Reformed Church, where it stayed until the Revolution ended.

In 1976, artist James Mann painted an 84 inch–by–240 inch acrylic-on-plaster mural for the Community Federal Saving Bank in Quakertown, Pennsylvania. It depicted the Bell arriving in Quakertown on its way to Allentown.

The mural, which was damaged by a leak in the plaster, was subsequently repaired during the time that the building was owned by *The Intelligencer-Record* newspaper. It currently serves as the office for PhillyBurbs.com, a news community in the suburbs of Philadelphia, and is not open to the public. The mural, which pictures the Bell on a wagon on the road in front of the Red Lion Hotel and the Pennsylvania Liberty Hall, has been depicted in a number of books.

The Smithsonian American Art Museum also has in its possession what it calls a "mural study," which measures 9 3/8 by 23¾ inches, that Gifford Beal (1879–1956) painted in 1938. Consisting of oil on fiberboard, it is entitled "Liberty Bell Brought to Allentown," and depicts men unloading the Bell from a cart drawn by what appear to be four horses. Although no longer on display, it is based on a mural in the Allentown, Pennsylvania, post office ("Liberty Bell Brought to Allentown," n.d.).

See also: Allentown; Zion Reformed Church

Further Reading

"Liberty Bell Brought to Allentown (mural study, Allentown, Pennsylvania Post Office)." n.d. Smithsonian American Art Museum. https://americanart.si.edu/artwork/liberty -bell-brought-allentown-mural-study-allentown-pennsylvania-post-office-1558.

"The Liberty Bell. Col. Thomas Polk's Overnight Bivouac. Quakertown. September 18, 1777." http://www.jamesmannartfarm.com/libbell.html.

Liberty Bell of Louvain

The Central University Library in Louvain, Belgium, is home to a carillon, which includes a Bourdon (a bass bell) of about seven tons that was cast as a memorial to U.S. efforts to save the country in World War I. It was donated by various U.S. and Belgian engineering societies in 1928 ("Liberty Bell of Louvain," n.d.). The shoulder of the bell has the name of these engineering societies, as well as pictures of the Belgium lion and the American bald eagle.

The inscription on the bell, which in found on its waist, reads as follows:

THE LIBERTY BELL OF LOUVAIN
This Carillon in Memory
Of the
Engineers of the United States of America
Who gave their Lives
In the Service of their Country
And its Allies
In
The Great War
1914–1918

The bell strikes on the hour as well as being played with the carillon, which was enlarged to 63 bells in 1983 (Ku Leuven, n.d.). Other Liberty Bell replicas in Europe include the Freedom Bell in Berlin and the Czech Liberty Bell in Prague

See also: Czech Liberty Bell; Freedom Bell; Replicas of the Liberty Bell

Further Reading

Ku Lueven. n.d. "Carillon." Home Erfgoed—En Publiekswerking. https:www.kuleuven .be/junstenerfgoed/expo-events/carillon.

"Liberty Bell of Louvain." n.d. Roads to the Great War. http://roadstothegreatwar-ww1 .blogspot.com/2016/05/liberty-bell-of-louvain.html.

Liberty Bell of the West

The Liberty Bell of the West is found at Old Kaskaskia, on an island that is the only part of Illinois that is west of the Mississippi River. The bell got its name because on July 4, 1778, it was rung to mark Colonel George Rogers Clark's recapture of the town from the British.

King Louis XV had given the bell, weighing about 650 pounds, to a town church, which later became the Immaculate Conception Catholic Church in 1741. It was cast at Rochelle, France, and inscribed with "POUR LEGLISE DES ILLI-NOIS PAR LES SOINS DU ROI D'OUTRE L'EAU" meaning "For the Church of the Illinois by the King across the water." It features the royal lilies of France on one side and a cross and pedestal with a fleur de lis on the other (Heartland Weekend, n.d.).

The town, which was then the capital of Upper Louisiana, and later of Illinois, once had as many as 7,000 residents. It is now almost completely abandoned, largely because it was flooded in 1844 (and many times since). The city became an island, which today can only be reached by car through Missouri. During the flood, the bell, like most of the town's houses, was washed away. It was eventually found in the river. Although Springer (1976, 75) says it was found in 1918, a journal by Mrs. Charles L. French, who visited in the 1890s, claims to have seen it then (French, 1944, 238). In any event, it is currently displayed at Kaskaskia in a brick shrine that is administered by the Illinois Historic Preservation Agency and located near the Immaculate Conception Church (Sznkowski, 2014; Springer, 1976, 75).

The bell is mounted on a yoke that is similar to that of the Liberty Bell. This bell is also cracked. The story of the Liberty Bell of the West resembles that of the Little Liberty Bell of the Old Northwest Territory, which is located in Vincennes, Indiana.

See also: Crack in the Liberty Bell; Little Liberty Bell of the Old Northwest Territory

Further Reading

French, Mrs. Charles L. 1944. "The Last Years of Kaskaskia," *Journal of the Illinois State Historical Society* 37 (September): 229–241.

Heartland Weekend. n.d. "Kaskaskia: Home to the Liberty Bell of the West." http://www .heartlandweekend.com/kaskaskia-home-to-the-liberty-bell-of-the-west.

Lott, Travis. 2017. "Before Becoming a State, Illinois Had Its Own Liberty Bell." *Belleville News-Democrat,* December 3. https://www.bnd.com/news/local/article 187812418.html.

Springer, L. Elsinore. 1976. *That Vanishing Sound.* New York: Crown Publishers.

Szynkowski, Joe. 2004. "Liberty Bell of the West." TheSouthern.com, November 12. https://thesouthern.com/liberty-bell-of-the-west-article_bd64bb58-6a83-11e4 -8c7e-d76b93e7d0a0.html.

Liberty Bell Park

Over time, the Liberty Bell has become not only a national but also an international symbol. One indication of this is the fact that there are replicas of the Liberty Bell not only throughout the United States, but also in Belgium, the Czech Republic, Germany, Lithuania, Japan, and Israel.

The bell in Jerusalem is appropriately displayed in what is known as the Liberty Bell Park, which is also a recreational site. It was designed by the Israeli government to honor the United States, which has been a close ally, during the bicentennial celebrations of American independence in 1976.

The bell hangs from a beam between two concrete pillars. The inscription from the Torah, like that on the U.S. Liberty Bell, is written in English.

A Jewish rabbi observed that the Liberty Bell is more appropriately designated as the "Torah Liberty Bell" rather than the "Taco Liberty Bell," connecting the chain restaurant's use of the Liberty Bell in advertising to the inscription on the Bell from Leviticus (Levine, 2009). He further observed that "liberty is a value that recognizes the worth and dignity of every person. And that certainly is a core Torah precept" (Levine, 2009).

See also: Bicentennial and the Liberty Bell; Inscription on the Liberty Bell; Replicas of the Liberty Bell; Taco Liberty Bell

Further Reading
Levine, Art. 2014. "Behar: The 'Torah'—not 'Taco'—Liberty Bell." *Yerushatenu,* May 9. https://rabbiartlevine.com/Home/tablid/2652/ID/1104/Behar-The-Torah-not-Tac0 -Liberty-Bell.aspx.

Liberty Bell Pavilion

For most of its history, the Liberty Bell has been displayed in Independence Hall. However, as preparations for the 1976 bicentennial approached, there were increased concerns that the building would be unable to accommodate the millions of visitors who were anticipated. The National Park Service accordingly considered moving the Liberty Bell to its own building.

The pavilion, which was built in just over a year, was designed by Aldo Giurgola of Mitchell Giurgola Associates in Philadelphia, located one block away on the mall. It was composed of "American granite, oak, lead-coated copper, glass, and plaster" (Matero, 2013, 198). These were materials that would have been used in the eighteenth century, yet the building was quite modern in design, with "a sloping roof," which "swept up toward Independence Hall, visually linking the new building with the old" (Mires, 2002, 263).

Matero observed that "waiting visitors flanking the structure were first brought through an entry vestibule into a waiting hall and funneled down a nave-like corridor until finally coming to the bell chamber" (Matero, 2013, 198). He further explained, "Didactic information on the site was kept to a minimum, interpretation was largely verbal through official interpreters, and the emotional experience of seeing and touching the bell was visceral" (Matero, 2013, 198). He also believed that the building was not designed to draw attention to itself, but instead to the Bell, which was mounted "on an elegantly simple stainless steel cradle in a low transparent pavilion in a garden with a simultaneous direct view to Independence Hall" (Matero, 2013, 196). For many years prior, the Bell had hung from a wishbone stand. Much as in ancient ostensaria, which contained relics of the saints within transparent shrines of rock crystals, it could be viewed from both inside and outside.

The transfer of the Liberty Bell from Independence Hall to the new pavilion was designed to capture the popular imagination, and, perhaps, stimulate tourism. Charlene Mires observes that although rain washed away plans for fireworks, at midnight on December 31, 1975, the Centennial Bell in the Independence Hall steeple struck 13 times as other bells pealed out in the city. The Bell, which had been mounted on a cart and covered by plastic to shield it from the rain, was moved in a procession led by a fife and drum corps and dignitaries. Hundreds watched as the Liberty Bell was lifted up on its steel supports, and several hundred people stayed to be the first to see and touch the Bell in its new locale (Mires, 2002, 263–264).

Not all were pleased. Matero observes that some visitors compared the starkness of the new pavilion to a transit shelter or public toilet (Matero, 2013, 199). In 2003, the Liberty Bell was moved to the new Liberty Bell Center, which provided greater context for it. Despite fruitless efforts to move the pavilion to the campus of American College in Bryn Mawr, Pennsylvania, which featured other buildings by Romaldo Giurgola, workmen demolished the Mitchell Giurgola Pavilion, saving only the Bell's stainless steel cradle ("American College Wants the Old Liberty Bell Home," 2003).

Matero believes the beauty of the Mitchell Giurgola pavilion was that the display favored "experience over interpretation," much on the order of Maya Lin's celebrated 1982 design for the Vietnam Veterans Memorial in Washington, D.C. (Matero, 2013, 200).

See also: Displays of the Liberty Bell; Liberty Bell Center; National Park Service; Tourism and the Liberty Bell

Further Reading

"American College Wants the Old Liberty Bell Home." 2003. *Philadelphia Business Journal,* October 9. https://www.bizjournals.com/philadelphia/stories/2003/10/06/daily25.html.

Matero, Frank G. 2013. "Housing the Bell: 150 Years of Exhibiting an American Icon." *Change over Time* 3 (Fall): 188–201.

Mires, Charlene. 2002. *Independence Hall in American Memory*. Philadelphia: University of Pennsylvania Press.

Liberty Bell 7 Spacecraft

After World War II, a Cold War ensued between the United States and the Soviet Union, in which the United States attempted to contrast the liberty of its people with the lack of freedom of those who lived under Russian communist rule. The United States thus broadcast a channel called Radio Free Europe in an attempt to spread pro-America sentiment, and also presented a Freedom Bell to the city of West Berlin. In addition, Americans competed with the Soviet Union through technological innovations, which it highlighted through its space program. Although the Soviet Union was the first to launch a satellite and to put a man in space, the United States followed closely behind, and it was the only country ever to land men on the moon and return them safely to Earth.

Virgil "Gus" Grissom poses with the spacecraft known as the Liberty Bell 7. The Liberty Bell 7, piloted by Grissom, was the second U.S. manne spacecraft to be sent into space. (NASA)

The second U.S. flight launching a man into space occurred on July 21, 1961, when Virgil ("Gus") Grissom was sent on a 15-minute flight in a spacecraft known as the *Liberty Bell 7*. The name was especially appropriate, both because the landing capsule was bell shaped and because the United States sought to contrast the liberty of its people against what it saw as the lack of liberty in communist countries. To complete the symbolism, a crack was painted on the capsule. The number 7 was used to evoke the seven astronauts in the original U.S. space program. The previous flight, flown by Alan Shepard, had been designated as the *Freedom 7*.

The flight of the *Liberty Bell 7* went well, and it splashed down not far from where it was supposed to land, but the hatch unexpectedly blew off. The craft dropped to the ocean floor, and Grissom nearly drowned before being picked up by a helicopter. Although there is continuing debate, the consensus appears to be that mechanical errors, rather than Grissom, were to blame. Tragically, Grissom was one of three astronauts killed on the launch pad as they were preparing for the first *Apollo* space flight.

The *Liberty Bell 7* was recovered from the ocean floor in July 1979 with help from an expedition funded by the Discovery Channel. (The malfunctioning hatch has never been found.) It was meticulously cleaned and restored, and today it is displayed at the Kansas Cosmosphere and Space Center in Hutchinson, Kansas (Siebert 2002).

See also: Freedom Bell; Symbolism of the Liberty Bell

Further Reading

French, Francis, and Colin Burgess. 2007. *Into That Silent Sea: Trailblazers of the Space Era, 1961–1965*. Lincoln: University of Nebraska Press.

Leopold, George. 2016. *The Supersonic Life and Times of Gus Grissom*. West Lafayette, IN: Purdue University Press.

"Liberty Bell 7 Capsule Raised from Ocean Floor." 1999. CNN.com, July 20. http://www.cnn.com/TECH/space/9907/20/grissom.capsule.01.

Siebert, Karen. 2003. "Advancing Democracy by Conquering Space, Liberty Bell 7." In *Portrait of Freedom: The 250th Anniversary of the Liberty Bell*. Clearwater, FL: Belmont International, 94–101.

Liberty Belle (Comics)

One sign that a symbol has gained popular resonance is when it becomes so incorporated into popular consciousness that the symbol becomes a superhero. Captain America, with his distinctive red, white, and blue shield, and Wonder Woman, with a similarly colored costume, are examples of this. So, too, was the superhero designated as Liberty Belle, subtitled "The All-American Girl." She wore a blue top with the image of a red bell, and what appears to be a lightning bolt resembling the crack in the Liberty Bell.

Just as the comic character Superman posed as a journalist, Liberty Belle's ordinary persona was "Libby Belle Lawrence, noted woman reporter, radio commentator

Children stand next to a replica of the Liberty Bell at a rally for Liberty Loans. Liberty Loans were sold by the U.S. government in an effort to fund World War I. (Library of Congress)

Average federal expenditures from 1913 to 1916 were less than $750 million, whereas by 1919, they amounted to $18.5 billion (Hilt and Rahn, 2016, 90). Faced with the alternatives of raising taxes, printing money, or borrowing, the government relied chiefly on the latter, ultimately financing only 25 percent with taxes (Kang and Rockof, 2015, 55).

During the war, the government launched four Liberty Loan campaigns, which were followed by a Victory Loan campaign at war's end. In addition to whatever other associations it might have had with the Declaration of Independence, the Constitution, the Fourteenth Amendment, and other famous speeches and documents, the term *Liberty* evoked both the Liberty Bell and the Statue of Liberty. Both were liberally used on posters, along with U.S. flags and other patriotic symbols, in an effort to advertise the loans. Indeed, the trips of the Liberty Bell to various fairs from 1895 to 1915 and the Liberty Loan appeals may have elevated the Liberty Bell into American consciousness, much as the Civil War had elevated the U.S. flag. This positive sentiment appears to have been particularly intense in Rochester, New York, where during both World War I and World War II, individuals who bought a bond were permitted to ring a replica of the Liberty Bell that hung on a Liberty Bell Bridge, which had been constructed over Main Street (Nighan, 2017).

On the last day of the first Liberty Loan campaign, the Liberty Bell was tapped 13 times with a golden hammer. In the second drive and consequent tapping of the Liberty Bell, the hammer was brought from St. John's Church in Richmond,

Virginia, where Patrick Henry had inflamed sentiment for the Revolutionary War with his "Give me liberty or give me death" speech (Fried, 2017). The bell was paraded around Philadelphia for the third and fourth Liberty Loan drives, and struck again for the final drive in August 1918, which triggered the ringing of bells throughout the country. People later thronged around the Liberty Bell, many kissing it, as the Great War, as it had come to be known, came to an end.

The Federal Reserve, which issued a *Liberty Bell Magazine,* and the government's Committee on Public Information enlisted everyone, from prominent movie stars to Boy Scouts and other local groups, to raise money. Although scholars still debate the respective impacts of patriotism and economics (bonds were not subject to taxes) in the drive, there can be little doubt that the former played some role, and that participation was fueled in part by increasing reverence for the Liberty Bell.

See also: Journeys of the Liberty Bell; Symbolism of the Liberty Bell

Further Reading

Fried, Stephen. 2017. "World War I: 100 Years Later. How the Liberty Bell Won the Great War." Smithsonian.com, April. https://www.smithsonianmag.com/history/how-liberty-bell-won-great-war-180962471.

Hilt, Eric, and Wendy M. Rahn. 2016. "Turning Citizens into Investors: Promoting Savings with Liberty Bonds During World War I." *RSF: The Russell Sage Foundation Journal of the Social Sciences* 2 (October): 86–108.

Kang, Sung Won, and Hugh Rockoff. 2015. "Capitalizing Patriotism: The Liberty Loans of World War I." *Financial History Review* 22: 45–78.

Nighan, Michael J. 2017. "Big Bell, Big Bell and School Bells: An Ex-president, the Liberty Bell, and Several Thousand School Teachers Come to Town." *Talker of the Town,* August 7. http://talkerofthetown.com/2017/08/07/big-bill-big-bell-and-school-bells-an-ex-president-the-liberty-bell-and-several-thousand-school-teachers-come-to-town.

Liberty Mosaic

Although it might seem unusual to have a reproduction of the Liberty Bell at a cemetery, the Forest Lawn Memorial Park in Hollywood Hills, California, is far from an ordinary graveyard. Among the many features of this cemetery, which contains the remains of many celebrities, is a replica of the Old North Church of Boston; Plymouth Rock; a statue of a Minuteman; a Court of Liberty with statues of the presidents George Washington, Thomas Jefferson, and Abraham Lincoln; a 162-by-28-foot mosaic entitled "the Birth of Liberty," with more than a million pieces of Venetian glass; and the Hall of Liberty American History Museum, which contains the replica of the Liberty Bell. The cemetery also includes a Plaza of Mesoamerican Heritage.

The massive outdoor mosaic, which is titled, "GOD GAVE US LIBERTY, PEOPLE WHO FORSAKE GOD LOSE THEIR LIBERTY," clearly situates its portrayal of the Liberty Bell within the context of America's colonial forbears and the Revolutionary War. It includes scenes from famous paintings depicting events from the arrival of the *Mayflower* and the signing of the Mayflower Compact, through Revolutionary War battles, the signing of the Declaration of

Independence, the birth of the U.S. flag, and the surrender to General Cornwallis to General Washington at Yorktown.

See also: Landscapes and Bells

Further Reading
Ehrenreich, Ben. 2010. "The End. Death in L.A. Can Be an Odd Undertaking." *LA Magazine,* http://origin-www.lamag.com/features/Story.aspx?id=1362579.

Liberty Trees and Liberty Poles

One reason that the Liberty Bell, which was originally known as the "Old Bell," "the Old State House Bell," or the "Independence Bell," might have its current name is that it resonated with prior names, of which Americans were already familiar.

One tradition that grew out of the American Revolution was that of meeting outdoors, often under trees, to discuss or protest (sometimes by burning tax collectors or others in effigy) various British taxes and other measures. Even before this conflict, Connecticut had celebrated its Charter Oak, Massachusetts identified itself with a Pine Tree, which it later used on its state flag, and Pennsylvania cherished its Treaty Elm (Schlesinger, 1952, 436–437). Although it does not appear to have been designated as a liberty tree, the bell that William Penn had originally used to call people together was hung from a tree, and some early flags either pictured trees or featured the word *Liberty* on them.

Thomas Paine, who rallied colonists to oppose the king in his *Common Sense*, also published a poem, or ballad, in 1774 entitled "Liberty Tree." It told of the Goddess of Liberty planting a Liberty Tree, which flourished and bore fruit that "drew the nations around, To seek out this peaceable shore" (Paine, 1775). As the people contentedly ate their bread "Unvexed with the troubles of silver and gold, The cares of the grand and the great," the "tyrannical powers, Kings, Commons and Lords, are uniting amain To cut down this guardian of ours" (Paine, 1775). The ballad ends with the lines (Paine, 1775):

> From the east to the west blow the trumpet to arms
> Through the land let the sound of it flee,
> Let the far and the near, all united with a cheer
> In defense of our Liberty Tree.

Perhaps borrowing from the tradition of the maypole, in time, liberty trees were often replaced by stripped down liberty poles, from which banners might be waved. This tradition later became popular during the French Revolution, and such poles were accompanied by liberty caps. Liberty caps were symbols dating back to classical times, and used to denote freedom for former slaves (Korshak, 1987). Jefferson Davis, then secretary of war and later president of the Confederacy, was among those who made sure that the Statue of Freedom, which is on the Capitol Dome in Washington, D.C., wore a helmet instead of a liberty cap.

Justin Kramer has argued that the picture of a bell in the *Liberty Bell Gift Book* of 1839, compiled by abolitionists, more closely resembles such a liberty cap than it does the Liberty Bell (1975, 88). A central feature of the new museum of the American Revolution, not far from Independence Hall, is that one room of exhibits is built around a liberty tree.

See also: Liberty Bell Gift Books; Names for the Liberty Bell

Further Reading

Korshak, Yvonne. 1987. "The Liberty Cap as a Revolutionary Symbol in America and France," *Smithsonian Studies in American Art* 1 (Autumn): 52–69.

Kramer, Justin. 1975. *Cast in America: The Historically Accurate, Exciting Story of the Liberty Bell*. Los Angeles: Justin Kramer Incorporated.

Paine, Thomas. 1775. "Liberty Tree—Poem by Thomas Paine." *Poem Hunter*. https://www.poemhunter.com/poem/liberty-tree.

Schlesinger, Arthur M. 1952. "Liberty Tree: A Genealogy," *New England Quarterly* 25 (December): 435–458.

"Liberty's Bell" (Poem)

The Liberty Bell has been the subject of numerous poems, not all of which necessarily appeal to modern literary styles. One of the better known of these compositions is that of Madge Morris Wagner, entitled "Liberty's Bell." Although Gary B. Nash, whose scholarship on the Liberty Bell remains a touchstone, believed that the Bell was composed for the World's Columbian Exposition in 1893, which the Bell visited and the place where the poem was read, it appears to have been written previously because it was published in a collection of her poems, under her maiden name, dated 1885 (Nash, 2010, 90).

The opening stanzas of the poem reference the legend of a bell that the people of a kingdom decided to make out of their most precious possessions, which would only be rung on the birth or death of a king. After the bell was cast, it hung for many years "[o]n its ponderous beams hung high o'er the land," during a time in which a tyrant extended his rule ever tighter over them and the people discovered that (Morris, 1885, 74):

> There was something they found far more cruel than
>   death,
> And something far sweeter than life's fleeting breath.

As the poem continues, the situation suddenly changes (Morris, 1885, 74):

> But, hark! In the midst of the turbulent throng,
> The moans of the weak and the groans of the strong.
> There's a cry of alarm. Some invisible power
> Is moving the long-silent bell in the tower.
> Forward, and backward, and forward it swung,
> And Liberty! Liberty! Liberty! Rung
> From its wide, brazen throat, over mountain and vale,
> Till the seas caught the echo, and monarchs turned
>   pale.

Apparently ringing down through the ages, "Our forefathers heard it—that wild, thrilling tone" (Morris, 1885, 75):

And up from the valley, and down from the hill,
From the flame of the forge, from the field and the
    mill,
They paid with their lives the price of its due,
And left it a legacy, Freemen, to you.

The poem moved from the time of the American Revolution to the time "when the gyves [shackles] were unloosed from our millions of slaves," and it continued through national grief over the deaths of Abraham Lincoln and James Garfield, and recollections of other American patriots (Morris, 1885, 75).

The poem ends with the following lines (Morris 1885, 76):

While dear is the name of child, mother or wife,
Or sweet to a soul is the measure of life,
America's sons will to battle prepare
When its tones of alarm ring aloud on the air;
For Liberty's goddess holds in her white hand
The cord of the bell that swings over our land.

In addition to highlighting the Liberty Bell, the poem appears to have inspired the creation of the Columbian Liberty Bell, which was composed of melted-down items associated with famous people and events in U.S. history.

See also: Columbian Liberty Bell; World's Columbian Exposition in Chicago (1893)

Further Reading
Morris, Madge. 1885. *Poems*. San Francisco: The Golden Era Company.
Nash, Gary B. 2010. *The Liberty Bell*. New Haven, CT: Yale University Press.

Lippard, George

Like other sacred objects such as the American flag, the Liberty Bell is surrounded by myths and legends, not all of which can be tracked to their source. One myth that can be so tracked is a story titled "The Fourth of July, 1776," published by George Lippard (1822–1854), who was a friend of Edgar Allan Poe. The eccentric Philadelphia writer and social reformer, who wrote sensationalistic stories, including his lurid *The Quaker City, or The Monks of Monk Hall* (1845), which exposed the seamy side of Philadelphia life, also wore colorful outfits that often included a cape, a sword-shaped cane, and what Thom Nickels (2014) calls a "brace of loaded pistols around his waist." Lippard also wrote a novel entitled *The Rose of Wissahikon*, which featured a scene of the reading of the Declaration of Independence from the steps of the State House (Kennedy, 2013).

On January 2, 1847, the *Saturday Courier*, a Philadelphia magazine, published "The Fourth of July, 1776." It was reprinted that same year in his book *Washington and His Generals*, which was appropriately subtitled *The Legends of the American*

Revolution. When later printed in June 1854, in *Graham's Magazine* (Vol XLIV, No. 6), it was accompanied by a print on the cover, which was titled "The Bellman informed of the passage of the Declaration of Independence."

Largely set in the steeple of the Pennsylvania State House (today's Independence Hall), the story tells of how an illiterate old man in "humble attire," with "white hair, and sunburnt face," sends a "flaxen-haired boy, with laughing eyes of summer blue," to read the words on the Liberty Bell: "Proclaim Liberty to all the Land and all the inhabitants thereof" (Lippard, 1847). After a long wait, in which the old man fears that the boy has forgotten his task, the boy finally shouts out "RING!" upon news of the signing of the Declaration of Independence, after which the bell-ringer begins fervently ringing the Bell so that all may hear it.

On this day, "the Bell awoke a world, slumbering in tyranny and crime!" Before, there was "terrible poetry in the sound of that State House Bell at dead of night, when striking its sudden and solemn" sound. It had sounded "like a knell of God's judgment" (Lippard, 1847, 393). As Lippard (1847, 393). summarized:

> That sound crossed the Atlantic—pierced the dungeons of Europe—the work shops of England—the vassal-fields of France.
> That Echo spoke to the slave—bade him look from his toil—and know himself a man.
> That Echo was the knell of King-craft, Priest craft and all the other crafts born of the darkness of ages, and baptized in seas of blood.

The scene then flashes back a half-hour earlier to the 56 men gathered in the State House, which is decorated by "a banner, the Banner of the Stars," upon which "sits the Eagle with unfolded wings" (Lippard, 1847, 393). A committee consisting of Thomas Jefferson, John Adams, and Benjamin Franklin approach John Hancock with a parchment, the signing of which "will either make a world free—or stretch these necks upon the gibbet" (Lippard, 1847, 394). As Thomas Jefferson, John Adams, and Richard Henry Lee advocate for the document, a "pale-face man, shrinking in one corner, squeaks out something about axes, scaffolds, and a—Gibbet!" which is followed by an impassioned speech from and otherwise unidentified "tall slender man" in a "dark robe" (Lippard, 1847, 394).

Arguing that the delegates should sign whatever the personal consequences, the speakers foresee the day when kings will face God's judgment. Afterward, delegates rush forward to sign the document. The story ends by returning to the bell (Lippard, 1847, 397):

> "Hark! Hark to the toll of that Bell!
> Is there not a deep poetry in that sound, a poetry more sublime than Shakespeare or Milton?
> Is there not a music in the sound, that reminds you of those awful tones which broke from angel-lips, when the news of the child of [sic] Jesus burst on the Shepherds of Bethlehem?
> For that Bell now speaks out to the world, that—
> GOD HAS GIVEN THE AMERICAN CONTINENT TO THE FREE—THE TOLLING MILLIONS OF THE HUMAN RACE—AS THE LAST ALTAR OF

THE RIGHTS OF MAN ON THE GLOBE—THE HOME OF THE OPPRESSED, FOREVERMORE!"

Lippard ends with the evocation: "Let us search for the origin of the great truth, which that bell proclaimed, let us behold the great Apostle who first proclaimed on our shores. ALL MEN ARE ALIKE THE CHILDREN OF GOD" (1847, 398). As a subsequent story reveals, this apostle is none other than William Penn (Lippard, 1847, 402–403).

An introduction to a book that Henry C. Watson published in 1852 furthered Lippard's story, albeit while focusing on the day that the Declaration was proclaimed rather than when the Continental Congress adopted it: "How the people did crowd around this State-House on the day the Declaration was proclaimed! Bells were ringing all over town, and guns were fired; but above 'em all could be heard the heavy, deep sound of this old bell, that rang as if it meant something! Oh! Them was great times" (Watson, 1852, 16).

Lippard's story has led to widespread misconception that the delegates of the Second Continental Congress signed the Declaration on July 4, 1776, and that the Liberty Bell rang on that day. In truth, although the Congress adopted the Declaration on July 4, it does not appear to have been proclaimed in the city (and accompanied with the ringing of bells, which may or may not have included the Liberty Bell) until July 8. Moreover, it was not until August 2, and the months following, during which delegates signed the document (Vile, 2018).

The man with the sunburned face and the blue-eyed boy with flaxen hair, like the speech given in honor of signing the Declaration, appear to be pure literary inventions.

Charles Warren further traced the influence of Lippard's story to the publication in 1850 of Benson J. Lossing's *Pictorial Field Book of the Revolution*, which reprinted parts of the story almost verbatim. It was further invoked by Joe Tyler Headley in his *Life of Washington* (1854), by D. W. Belisle in his *History of Independence Hall* (1859), and in the form of a poem, "Independence Bell July 4, 1776," in the 1871 *Franklin's Fifth Reader* (Warren, 1945, 252–253). That poem, falsely attributed to Charles Brockden Brown, portrays people waiting with anticipation for the news from the Second Continental Congress (Rosewater, 1926, 130–131). It also features "the bellman, old and gray," who hears a boy, now identified as his grandson, shout "ring, grandfather, Ring! Oh, ring for Liberty!" and ends with the lines (Rosewater, 1926, 127–128):

When we greet the smiling sunlight
    On the Fourth of each July,
We will ne'er forget the bellman
    Who, betwixt the earth and sky,
Rang out loudly, "Independence,"
    Which, please God, shall never die!

See also: Declaration of Independence and the Liberty Bell; Independence Day; Occasions for Ringing the Liberty Bell

Further Reading

Kennedy, Dustin. 2013. "Revising the Public Sphere: George Lippard, Class, and U.S. Nationalism." *ESQ: A Journal of the American Renaissance* 59: 585–617.

Lippard, George. 1847. *George Washington and His Generals: or, Legends of the Revolution*. Philadelphia: G. B. Zieber.

"Missing: Ring, Ring for Liberty!" The Pilgrimage Project. http://oldnorth.georgetown .domains.

Nickels, Thom. 2014. "Philly Writer George Lippard, a Friend of Edgar Allen [sic.] Poe." Huffington Post blog, September 29. https://www.huffingtonpost.com/thom-nickels /philly-wirter-george-lipp_b_5633934.html.

Rosewater, Victor. 1926. *The Liberty Bell: Its History and Significance*. New York: D. Appleton.

Vile, John R. 2018. *The Declaration of Independence: America's First Founding Document in U.S. History and Culture*. Santa, Barbara, CA: ABC-CLIO.

Warren, Charles. 1945. "Fourth of July Myths." *William and Mary Quarterly* 2 (July): 237–272.

Watson, Henry C. 1852. *The Old Bell of Independence; or, Philadelphia in 1776*. Philadelphia: Lindsay and Blakiston.

Lithuanian Liberty Bell (see American Lithuanian Liberty Bell)

Little Liberty Bell of the Old Northwest Territory

The Liberty Bell in Philadelphia was hardly the only bell to witness and proclaim historic events. One such bell that has gained fame is the bell in Vincennes, Indiana, known as the Little Liberty Bell of the Old Northwest Territory. The original bell, imported from Paris, was connected to a small log church and was used to call parishioners to Mass. In December 1778, after the forces of George Rogers Clark had captured the Northwest Territory from the British for the United States, Father Pierre Gibault, who had supported the Patriots' cause, rang the bell for residents to assemble to take an oath of allegiance to the new Congress. The bell was also rung to announce the formal surrender of British troops two months later (Springer, 1976, 73).

The bell now designated as the Little Liberty Bell of the Old Northwest Territory is actually a larger replacement, again cast in France, this time in 1839. It now occupies the steeple of the much more imposing Old Cathedral of Saint Francis Xavier, which is also in Vincennes.

Like the later visits of the Liberty Bell to various fairs and expositions from 1895 to 1915, the Little Liberty Bell demonstrates how the reputation of the Liberty Bell and the values that it symbolized were spread throughout territories that were later admitted to the Union on an equal basis with the original 13 colonies.

See also: Journeys of the Liberty Bell

Further Reading
"The Liberty Bell of the Old Northwest," 1910. *American Catholic Historical Researches*, New Series, 6 (October): 379–380.
Springer, L. Elsinore. 1976. *That Vanishing Sound*. New York: Crown Publishers.

Living Photographs of the Liberty Bell

One indication of an object's ability to stir the public's consciousness is the degree to which such symbols are identifiable and can be used to rally support for specific causes, especially those involving the defense of the nation.

Photographer Arthur Mole (1889–1983), an immigrant from Great Britain who worked in conjunction with John Thomas, was among those who specialized in photographing large groups to portray national symbols. These include the U.S. flag, portraits of the presidents Woodrow Wilson and Franklin D. Roosevelt, military insignia, the Statue of Liberty, and the Liberty Bell.

Mole used 25,000 military personnel from Camp Dix, New Jersey, for his photograph of the Liberty Bell in 1918. The portrayal includes its yoke (where the great majority of the soldiers are concentrated), the word *LIBERTY* spelled out on the shoulder of the Bell, and the characteristic crack, which extended down to the bottom of the clapper.

There is some irony in carefully arranging such large groups (almost as though the individuals were cogs) to portray the concept of liberty (Kaplan, 2001), but one might argue that individual discipline is not inconsistent with the idea of liberty under law.

The Liberty Bell was used to sell Liberty Bonds to support World War I, and again during the Cold War to sell Savings Bonds.

See also: Liberty Loans

Further Reading
Kaplan, Louis. 2001. "A Patriotic Mole: A Living Photograph." *The New Centennial Review* 1 (Spring): 107–139.
Mole, Arthur. 2015. *Arthur Mole—Living Photographs*. Paris; Rvb Books.

Louisiana Purchase Exposition, St. Louis (1904)

Although it came in 1904, a year late, St. Louis, Missouri, which is often identified as the Gateway to the American West, had the honor of hosting the Louisiana Purchase Exposition (Portes and Rossignol, 2009). Among the strategies that the city had used to persuade the leaders of Philadelphia to lend them the Liberty Bell for the event was to recruit 75,000 schoolchildren to sign petitions asking for the favor (Paige 1988, 45). The massive fair, which covered 1,272 acres and was held at Forest Park and the site of today's Washington University, is often known (incorrectly) as the first place that an ice cream cone was sold (a patent had actually been issued to a New Yorker in 1903) and for inspiring the popular song, "Meet Me in

St. Louis." The World's Fair also introduced many people to automobiles for the first time.

As with other fairs, the train, known as the Liberty Bell Special, which brought the Bell, took a circuitous route. It left Philadelphia on June 3, 1904, and it did not arrive until June 8 (the fair had opened on April 30 when President Theodore Roosevelt had thrown a switch from the White House to turn on the electricity for the fair). During this time, it passed through New York, Ohio, Illinois, Wisconsin, Minnesota, Iowa, and back through Illinois before reaching its destination (Paige, 1988, 110–115).

The day that it reached the city was designated as "Liberty Bell Day," and thousands came to greet the Bell. It was displayed at the Pennsylvania State Building, where it was draped by an American flag (Rosewater, 1926, 176); some pictures appear to show the Bell actually resting on a flag (see Nightingale, 2016). Coming only six years after America's acquisition of the Philippines and other territories during the Spanish-American War, the fair featured massive exhibits designed to demonstrate Anglo-Saxon racial superiority, which included 1,200 Filipinos, living in villages designed to show that they were still in need of "civilizing," as well as reconstructed villages from other nations (Rydell, 1984, 167).

A large pond on the premises was also used as a staging ground for model ships to reenact sea battles during the Spanish-American War (O'Neil, 2014). There were also exhibits on the creation of the world and the Galveston Flood (Hylton, 1991, 64). A total of 43 countries and 41 of the 45 U.S. states had pavilions on the grounds, which was also the site of the 1904 Olympics (O'Neil, 2016). Butter art was popular at the fair, and those creations included a replica of the Liberty Bell from New York (Simpson, 2012, 103–104).

The fair was the site of numerous musical performances, many of which were held in the Festival Hall, which could seat up to 3,000 people (Hylton, 1991, 60). The hall was the site of a massive organ, designed by George Audsley and composed of 10,056 pipes. Although the building was demolished, the organ was disassembled and shipped to Wanamaker's department store in Philadelphia, which today is part of Macy's Center City. The instrument is still played each day (Hylton, 1991, 64).

More than 19 million people visited the fair (Nash 2010, 107). The Bell's return trip from November 16–19, 1904, brought it through cities and towns in Illinois, Indiana, and Pennsylvania (Paige, 1988, 114–117).

See also: Children and the Liberty Bell; Journeys of the Liberty Bell

Further Reading

Gilbert, James. 2009. *Whose Fair? Experience, Memory, and the History of the Great St. Louis Exposition.* Chicago: University of Chicago Press.

Hylton, John. 1991. "The Music of the Louisiana Purchase Exposition." *College Music Symposium* 31: 59–66.

Nash, Gary B. 2010. *The Liberty Bell.* New Haven, CT: Yale University Press.

Nightingale, Claudine. 2016. "Sweet Liberty: World's Fairs' Love Affair with the Liberty Bell." Adam Matthew, February 5. https://www.amdigital.co.uk/about/blog/item/sweet-liberty.

O'Neil, Tim. 2014. "Look Back 250. World's Fair of 1904 Was St. Louis's Biggest Show." *STL Today,* August 31. https://www.stltoday.com/news/archives/look-back-world-s -fair-of-was-st-louis-biggest/article_42cfb7bc-121d-5aa3-86a2-6df0b4f70da5 .html#12.

Paige, John C. 1988. *The Liberty Bell of Independence National Historical Park: A Special History Study*, ed. David C. Kimball. Denver: Denver Service Center, National Park Service, Department of the Interior. Accessed through pubs.etic.nps.gov.

Portes, Jacques, and Marie-Jeanne Rossignol, 2009. "Celebration and History: The Case of the Louisiana Purchase." *Empires of the Imagination: Transatlantic Histories of the Louisiana Purchase*, ed. Peter J. Kastor and Francois Weil. Charlottesville: University of Virginia Press, 327–364.

Rosewater, Victor. 1926. *The Liberty Bell: Its History and Significance.* New York: D. Appleton and Company.

Rydell, Robert W. 1984. *All the World's a Fair: Visions of Empire at American International Expositions, 1876–1916.* Chicago: University of Chicago Press.

Simpson, Pamela. H. 2012. *Corn Palaces and Butter Queens: A History of Crop Art and Dairy Sculpture.* Minneapolis: University of Minnesota Press.

Luminous Liberty Bell

The Liberty Bell has been replicated many times, often in small reproductions that can be displayed on a shelf. More than 50 full-size reproductions of the Liberty Bell were given out in the early 1950s to states and territories to recognize their participation in a bond drive. It is still possible to purchase a full-size reproduction of the Liberty Bell for $75,000.

The largest depiction of the Liberty Bell that probably has ever been made was the so-called Luminous Liberty Bell, which was prepared for the 1926 Sesquicentennial Exposition in Philadelphia. Measuring 80 feet tall, the bell spanned Broad Street at Johnson Street in Philadelphia and was built by Frank C. English & Sons from April–May 1926 at a cost of $100,000 (Austin and Hauser, 1929).

Built on an 80-ton skeleton of steel, the bell rested on large wooden pilings with concrete caps. The bell and yoke hung high enough that automobiles could pass under them. At night, 26,000 15-watt bulbs illuminated the bell, and eight 200-watt projectors illuminated the clapper.

There were towers on either side of the bell that displayed the dates 1776 and 1926. They were topped by statues of American bald eagles. Both the original inscription of the Liberty Bell and its distinctive crack were visible. There were concrete shields near the bottoms of the towers.

The Bell, which was depicted on a red-and-white 2-cent stamp, was demolished the year after the exposition closed.

See also: Coins, Medals, and Stamps Depicting the Liberty Bell; Sesquicentennial International Exposition; State Liberty Bell Replicas

Further Reading
Austin, E. L., and Odell Hauser. 1929. "The Sesqui-Centennial International Exposition." Philadelphia: Current Publications.

M

MacLeish, Archibald

Archibald MacLeish (1892–1982) was a Yale-educated poet and playwright who earned a law degree from Harvard University while interrupting his studies to serve in World War I. President Franklin D. Roosevelt appointed him to head the Library of Congress, and later to be assistant secretary of state. MacLeish authored a "Lunadrama" (a play designed to be performed at night) entitled *The American Bell,* in cooperation with the National Park Service and under the sponsorship of the Old Philadelphia Development Corporation and the city of Philadelphia.

The play, which featured actors portraying such historical figures as presidents Thomas Jefferson and John Adams, as well as Thomas Paine and Benjamin Franklin, chiefly focused on the role of the Liberty Bell in proclaiming liberty at the time of the Declaration of Independence and the American Revolution. It also provided historically accurate content about its colonial past. Part of the dialogue contrasted the "clarions," "trumpets," and "drums" of other nations with the American bell and observed that "[a]s long as the bell is ours, we'll be ourselves" (MacLeish, 1962, 11).

MacLeish perpetuated the idea that the Liberty Bell rang at the adoption of the Declaration of Independence rather than, as is now generally believed, on July 8. Thus, the narrator in the play observed that there is a story that when the Declaration of Independence was adopted, "certain cautious Congressmen objected because the steeple was old and weak and the bell might bring it down," a shout arose, "Let it ring!" (MacLeish, 1962, 59). The narrator then responded (MacLeish, 1962, 59):

And so it rang, And Christ Church bells replied. . . .
till all America was ringing with The Bell."

Stage directions further note, "The ringing of the great, strange bell—a wild triumphant rhythm—others answering and answering, farther and farther off but the great bell mastering them all" (MacLeish, 1962, 59).

MacLeish described his intention as that of describing "a positive statement of freedom." Mires notes, however, that "[w]hatever its literary merits, 'The American Bell' flopped as a tourist attraction" (Mires, 2002, 256). Although the drama was inspirational enough to bring some viewers to knell in prayer or to sing "America the Beautiful," many seats remained unfilled. Mires observed, "Neither tourists nor Philadelphians could be persuaded to stay in the historic district after dark, and the spectacle of lights shining on a building was no match for the action of television or the movies, especially for younger viewers" (2002, 256–257).

See also: Declaration of Independence and the Liberty Bell; National Park Service; Tourism and the Liberty Bell

Further Reading

MacLeish, Archibald. 1962. "The American Bell." In *Let Freedom Ring: The Story of Independence Hall and Its Role in the Founding of the United States.* New York: American Heritage Publishing, 49–60.

Mires, Charlene. 2002. *Independence Hall in American Memory.* Philadelphia: University of Pennsylvania Press.

Madden, R. R.

Many of the *Liberty Bell Gift Books* contained an opening poem that referred either to the Liberty Bell or to a generic liberty bell or bells. The books often featured notable poets and essayists not only from the United States but also from abroad.

The opening poem of the 1847 volume, penned by R. R. Madden, was simply entitled "The Liberty Bell." His name was followed by the initials "M.R.I.A.," which might have referred to a medical degree. An article published on February 13, 1886, indicated that Madden had recently died at the age of 88. It was noted in the *British Medical Journal* that he had been a special magistrate in Jamaica, where he had been "a friend of the slaves," and "earned the love and gratitude of the liberated population, and provoked the hatred of the slave-owners, narrowly escaping assassination" (1866, 311). It further noted that he had served as Colonial Secretary of Western Australia.

The opening stanza, printed like similar poems under a sketch of a bell that said "PROCLAIM LIBERTY TO ALL THE INHABITANTS," appeared to refer to a specific bell (Madden, 1847, 1):

> The bell! the bell! the glorious bell
> > Whose merry chimes delight the ear!
> An ever cheering tale they tell,
> > That all true men exult to hear.

The next verse suggests that the Bell's peal crossed the Atlantic, although it is not immediately clear from which side the peals originate (Madden, 1847, 2):

> The glorious bell of Liberty!
> > Another peal comes booming o'er
> The wide Atlantic, charged with glee
> > And tidings glad, to each heart's core.

Two verses later, the author claims to have given "that bell a pull of yore," while two stanzas later, he refers to (Madden 1847, 2–3)

> The peal of THIRTY-FOUR! the peal
> > That made the tropics dance for joy!
> Again I seem to hear and feel,
> > Bliss without bounds, without allow.

The British had abolished slavery in their colonies in 1833, and 1834 would presumably have been the date that the law began to be put into effect when Madden was in Jamaica.

Adding to the international appeal of the poem, Madden referred to the land of William Tell (Switzerland) and associates the Bell with opposition to tyranny, wherever it may be (Madden, 1847, 3):

> The tyrant's knell, in every clime,
>   Where bondage lays its curse on earth,
> The bell of death—is tolled, for crime,
>   Against the land that gave him birth.
>
> Oh for a glorious peal at last
>   Of the true bell of Liberty!
> To rend the air, and strike aghast
>   The monster might of Slavery.
>
> Oh! For a swing of that great tongue,
>   To shake the proud oppressor's throne,
> Where'er it's set: with one ding-dong
>   To bring the potent despot down.

The penultimate stanza is a strong indictment against those, previously identified as under "Mammon's [money's] godless sway," who traffic in human flesh, with specific application to America (Madden, 1847, 4):

> To save the land that holds the graves
>   Of Franklin, Washington, and Penn,
> From laws that make her millions slaves,—
>   And, worse than brutes, of Christian men.

The reference to Penn might be Madden's way of specifically evoking the Liberty Bell in Philadelphia.

See also: Abolitionists and the Liberty Bell; *Liberty Bell Gift Books*

Further Reading
Madden, R. R. 1847. "The Liberty Bell." Friends of Freedom. *The Liberty Bell*. Boston National Anti-Slavery Bazaar.
"Mr. R. R. Madden." February 13, 1886. *British Medical Journal*. 1: 311.

Maintenance of the Liberty Bell

Like other historic objects, the Liberty Bell needs not only to be protected against individuals who might seek to gain notoriety for themselves or their causes by damaging it, but also from natural corrosion. During part of its history, the Bell has been displayed in a glass cabinet, but it is currently displayed on steel poles in the Liberty Bell Center, where it is visible from both inside and outside.

In the 1980s, curators discovered that the Liberty Bell had a white, crystalline formation inside it. It consisted of a type of ammonia that was growing in the Bell as a result of heating because of its exposure to winter sunlight, and apparently also from a plant fertilizer, since discontinued, that the Park Service had been using (Metro, 2014). After washing the Bell with "de-ionized water and ethanol," workers covered it "with coats of arauba wax and microcrystalline wax to protect it from the atmosphere" ("Who Washes the Liberty Bell?" 2014). Curators continue to inspect the Bell for further damage.

See also: Displays of the Liberty Bell; Security for the Liberty Bell

Further Reading
"Who Washes the Liberty Bell?" 2014. *Metro*, April 1. https://www.metro.us/local/who
    -washes-the-liberty-bell/tmWncE—41MI6YEnO7HDs.

"Make the 'Old Bell' Ring" (Song, 1918)

World War I led to the publication of numerous songs that highlighted the Liberty Bell. One was a song written and composed by Rachel C. Hazeltine, and published in 1918, entitled "Make the 'Old Bell' Ring." The cover featured a border of red, white, and blue stripes and a simple sketch of a blue liberty bell (the crack makes it obvious), but the title harkened to an earlier designation of the Bell.

The first verse of the song, with the title printed between two blue bells tied by a string, says that America's fathers fought for "liberty and democracy (Hazeltine, 1918). The second verse stresses, "Our principles will always stand / For right and justice through the land (Hazeltine, 1918). Both verses end with "We'll work and sing and make our 'Old Bell' ring, ding, ding, ding, ding, ding, ding, dong, ding" (Hazeltine, 1918).

Two special "war verses" printed at the bottom of the third page, flanked by two other replicas of the Liberty Bell, direct a specific focus on "Mr. Hun" and the Kaiser, both references to the German foe.

See also: Music and the Liberty Bell; Names for the Liberty Bell

Further Reading
Hazeltine, Rachel C. 1918. *Make the Old Bell Ring*. Monographic. Sam-a-lam, Publisher, Sunnyvale, CA. Notated Music. https://www.loc.gov/item/2013564717.

Mental Health Bell (see Political and Social Movements and the Liberty Bell)

Mexican Liberty Bell

Neighboring nations often borrow customs from one another, so it is not surprising that the nation of Mexico has a bell that it also designates as a Liberty Bell. Father Miguel Hidalgo y Costilla had originally rung this bell, which hung in his

A replica of the Mexican Liberty Bell in Mission Dolores Park in San Francisco, California. The Mexican Liberty Bell was originally located in Dolores, Mexico. (David Edelman/Dreamstime.com)

small church in Dolores, Mexico, on September 16, 1810, to call locals to hear the reading of a Declaration of Independence against the rule of Spain, which was then under the control of Napoleon III of France. Mexicans ring this bell on September 16, which they consider to be their own independence day.

In 1896, this bell was brought to Mexico City. It was accompanied by a cannon that had been inscribed in Spanish with the words, "For the defence of the faith and the purity of Holy Mary" (Rees, 1906, 390).

In 1966, Gustavo Diaz Ordaz, the president of the United Mexican States, presented a replica of this bell to the Mission Delores Park in San Francisco. When President Adolfo Lopez Mateos of Mexico visited the United States in 1962, he gave a replica of the bell, supported on each side by a replica of a child, to President John F. Kennedy.

See also: Replicas of the Liberty Bell

Further Reading

"Mission Dolores Park—The Mexican Liberty Bell Gets a New Home." July 9, 2014. http://sfrecpark.org/mission-dolores-park-the-mexican-liberty-bell-gets-a-new-home.

Rees, Thomas. 1906. *Spain's Lost Jewels: Cuba and Mexico.* Springfield: Illinois State Register.

"Replica of Liberty Bell of Mexico." John F. Kennedy Presidential Library and Museum. https://www.jfklibrary.org/Asset-Viewer/Archives/JFKSG-MO-1963-1179.aspx.

Moore, R. R. R.

One of the poems that tourists see displayed when they approach the Liberty Bell is a poem attributed to H. R. M. Moore, who is listed in the 1844 *Liberty Bell Gift Book* as "R. R. R. Moore." The individual is probably the same person who is identified in an article entitled "Irish Philanthropists" in the 1843 issue of the book, which also identifies him as a member of the Committee of the [Irish] Hibernian

Anti-Slavery Society (*Liberty Bell Gift Book,* 1843, 170). Richard S. Harrison further identifies an "R. R. Moore" as a non-Quaker member of this same society (Harrison, 1991, 116).

Simply entitled "The Liberty Bell," the poem has a universalistic dimension evident in its opening stanza, which equates liberty with freedom (Friends of Freedom, 1844, 1):

> Ring out that hallowed Bell!
>   Ring it long, ring it long;
> Through the wide world let it tell
>   That Freedom's strong.

The second stanza expresses the hope "that the whole world shall be free." The fourth stanza ties the Bell specifically to emancipation (Friends of Freedom, 1844, 2):

> Ring it Southward, till its voice
>   For slavery toll, for slavery toll;
> And Freedom's wakening tough rejoice
>   Both limb and soul.

The next stanza continues (Friends of Freedom, 1844, 2):

> Ring it o'er the negro's grave!
>   Ring it deep, ring it deep;
> Its tones are sacred to the slave,
>   In Freedom's sleep.

The penultimate stanza ties the message of liberty to that of religious nonsectarianism (Friends of Freedom, 1844, 3):

> Ring it, till the bonds of sect
>   Be torn away, be torn away;
> Till every man, as God's elect,
>   Kneel down to pray.

The final stanza further reemphasizes a universalistic message (Friends of Freedom, 1844, 4):

> Ring it, till the world have heard,
>   And felt, at length, and felt, at length;
> Till every living soul be stirred,
>   And clothed with strength.

See also: Abolitionists and the Liberty Bell; *Liberty Bell Gift Books*; Names for the Liberty Bell

Further Reading

Friends of Freedom. 1844. *The Liberty Bell.* Maria Weston Chapman, ed. Boston: Massachusetts Anti-Slavery Fair.

Friends of Freedom. 1843. *The Liberty Bell*. Maria Weston Chapman, ed. Boston: Boston-Anti-Slavery Society.

Harrison, Richard S. 1991. "Irish Quaker Perspectives on the Anti-Slavery Movement." *Journal of the Friends Historical Society* 56 (1) (1991): 106–125.

Morton v. City of Philadelphia (1895)

In *Morton v. City of Philadelphia*, 4 Pa. D. 523 (1895), Judge P. J. Thayer issued an opinion upholding the decision of the Philadelphia City Council to send the Liberty Bell to the Atlanta Cotton States and International Exposition. This decision was challenged by Morton and other city taxpayers.

His opinion was preceded by a series of questions between the Court and one of the lawyers named Carson, in which the latter compared Philadelphia to the Muslim holy city of Mecca, to which pilgrims should come rather than having its accoutrements sent elsewhere. In this discussion, Carson further connected the inscription on the Liberty Bell as a type of prophecy.

In the opinion, Judge Thayer noted that the bell, previously known as the Independence Bell, had become known as the Liberty Bell, and that the city had purchased it along with the state house building and grounds in 1816 for $70,000. Thayer believed that the city's ownership of the Liberty Bell was "as absolute and as untrammeled by conditions as is the title by which any individual holds his personal property" (*Morton v. City of Philadelphia*, 4 Pa. D. 523 at 541). Distinguishing chattels, or movable property, from real property, Thayer observed, "Chattels do not lose their moveable character, nor the essential legal qualities which belong to them because they are the property of a municipality. The city holds the bell by a title as absolute, unconditional and unrestricted as the title by which any private person holds his personal property. It is under its absolute control and dominion" (*Morton v. City of Philadelphia*, 4 Pa. D. 523 at 541).

Noting that the state of Pennsylvania had appropriated $38,000 for its exhibit in Atlanta, and that Georgia was one of the original 13 states that had waged the American Revolution, Thayer addressed concerns that the Bell might be damaged in transit. He observed that "the bell fortunately is not made of fine china, but is a solid mass of over two thousand pounds of metal, and has endured for nearly one hundred and fifty years, although several times sent on such patriotic journeys, the only injury it ever experienced beings when it was cracked while hanging in its accustomed place in the steeple," which the judge believed happened as the bell tolled on the death of Chief Justice John Marshall (*Morton v. City of Philadelphia*, 4 Pa. D. 523 at 542). He further that "it can never be more mute than it is now, even if it should make an annual journey around among the old thirteen, stirring up every where as it goes the memories and the patriotic impulses which are inseparably connected with its history and which themselves can never grow mute" (*Morton v. City of Philadelphia*, 4 Pa. D. 523 at 543). Thayer, therefore, declared that "the city authorities are in the performance of an act both lawful and laudable, and which not only does not deserve legal animadversion, but is in itself entirely proper and praiseworthy" (*Morton v. City of Philadelphia*, 4 Pa. D. 523 at 543).

Moving to the issue of whether the city could appropriate funds to transport the Liberty Bell, Thayer observed that although the decision by the U.S. Fifth Circuit Court judge in *Bayle v. City of New Orleans* (1885) had ruled that the city of New Orleans had no authority to provide expenses for city officials who wanted to travel with the Liberty Bell back to Philadelphia, a Philadelphia judge had permitted that city to pay for the expense of a banquet involving these guests in *Tagg v. City of Philadelphia.* That same judge had concluded "that it is entirely in the discretion and power of councils to appropriate such sums as they may deem expedient for the commemoration of events of public interest, or the entertainment of guests of the city and similar expenditures" (*Morton v. City of Philadelphia*, 4 Pa. D. 523 at 543). Although inclined to rely on a state over a federal judge in cases of conflict, the conflict may be more apparent than real, "for upon such a question much depends upon the several statutes and charters," and "[o]ur Philadelphia charters are very large and confer very extensive powers upon our city council" (*Morton v. City of Philadelphia*, 4 Pa. D. 523 at 544).

Although the City of Philadelphia still retains title to the Liberty Bell, the National Park Service currently has custody of the Bell and displays it in a special pavilion near Independence Hall.

See also: Bayle v. New Orleans (1885); Ownership of the Liberty Bell

Further Reading
Morton v. City of Philadelphia, 4 Pa. D. 523 (1895).

Museums of the Liberty Bell

There is certainly a sense in which the Liberty Bell Center (like the Liberty Bell Pavilion that preceded it) is a museum. Indeed, parts of Independence Hall, where the Liberty Bell has been housed through most of its existence, were used as a museum throughout much of the nineteenth century.

Outside of these locations, there have been at least two buildings that have been designated as Liberty Bell museums. One is the Liberty Bell Museum in Allentown, Pennsylvania, which is located in the basement of the Zion Reformed United Church of Christ Church, where the Patriots hid the Liberty Bell in 1777 and 1778 when British troops occupied Philadelphia. This is the home of the Liberty Bell that was given to the state of Pennsylvania in the 1950s in appreciation of its role in helping to sell bonds. The museum is represented by a blue, stylized bell with a distinctive crack against stripes of red and white and a gold star at the top. The museum also contains Allentown's own Liberty Bell, which is believed to have pealed out independence in 1776, as well as a large hand-painted mural by a local self-taught artist named Wilmer Behler, who died in 1994 at the age of 78. The mural depicts soldiers and wagons bringing the Liberty Bell to the church for safekeeping. From time to time, the museum has had special displays. In 2018, it put on an exhibit entitled "Last One In: American Ideals in Conflict with American Attitudes," in which it provided evidence that concern about immigration is nothing new to the American experience (Howell, 2018).

There was another rather quirky museum that opened in Melbourne, Florida, in 1985 in the city's former water storage tank. A story from RoadsideAmerica, a tourist attraction service, indicates that the museum, first operated by Peter Diaz, an ex-marine, included "a Statue of Liberty made of a store window dummy with a pillow crown, a reproduction of the Declaration of Independence, some old paper money and local Indian artifacts, a merry-go-round horse, and a miniature of the U.S. Capitol covered with glued-on pennies" ("Liberty Bell Memorial Museum (in Transition)," n.d.), although the accompanying picture suggests that it was actually the Lincoln Memorial. An accompanying room, dubbed "Freedom Hall," was said to contain "a wheel from a Viet Cong cart used on the Ho Chi Minh Trail, and another dummy, this one in uniform, who stares at the stump of her missing hand" ("Liberty Bell Memorial Museum," n.d.).

The highlight of the museum was a full-size replica of the Liberty Bell that had been cast by the Whitechapel Foundry in England, which had cast the original. The funds for the bell were apparently raised by a group of children from South Brevard public schools to honor the bicentennial of the Declaration of Independence. The original plans were to house the replica liberty bell in a bicentennial liberty bell memorial tower ("Auction In Melbourne To Help Raise Funds For Replica of Bell," 1976).

See also: Allentown; Independence Hall; Liberty Bell Center; Liberty Bell Pavilion; Pennsylvania; Replicas of the Liberty Bell; Zion Reformed Church

Further Reading

"Auction In Melbourne To Help Raise Funds For Replica of Bell." 1976. *The Orlando Sentinel*, April 30, 14.

Howell, Dave. 2018. "'Give Me Your Tired' . . . or Maybe Not: Allentown Exhibit Reveals Immigration Has Long Been a Thorny Issue." *Morning Call,* March 28. https://www .mcall.com/entertainment/mc-ent-liberty-bell-museum-immigration-exhibit -allentown-20180314-story.html.

"Liberty Bell Memorial Museum." n.d. *Honor America.* http://honoramerica.org/liberty -bell-memorial-museum-2.

"Liberty Bell Memorial Museum (in Transition)." n.d. *RoadsideAmerica.* https://www .roadsideamerica.com/story/13865.

"The Liberty Bell Museum." Libertybellmuseum.org.

Neale, Rick. 2017. "Liberty Bell Museum in Melbourne No Longer Open: Honor America in Limbo." *Florida Today,* December 22. https://www.floridatoday.com/story/news /2017/12/22/liberty-bell-museum-melbourne-no-longer-open-honor-america -limbo/923749001

Music and the Liberty Bell

Bells can be used as musical instruments. In his poem on the Liberty Bell, John Bowring ended his first stanza by referring to the "Music of Liberty" (1853, 1). Music can be used to inform, to soothe, and inspire; it comes in a variety of genres, some with accompanying lyrics and others without them. Just as records often came with colorful covers, sheet music of an earlier generation, often designed for pianos in the home, portrayed striking images. Patriotic music was often accompanied by pictures of eagles, flags, soldiers, and bells.

Bells in general, and the Liberty Bell in particular, appear to have been a fairly popular theme, and in time, the Liberty Bell was transformed into a national icon. Abolitionists appear to have been the first to call the Bell in the Pennsylvania State House the Liberty Bell. An early song by the Hutchinson Family Singers, "Get Off the Track! (A Song for Emancipation)," first published in Boston in 1844, likened emancipation to a train; as if merging the sound of the Bell with the whistle of a train, it announced, "Clear the track! Or you'll fall under. / Get off the track! All are singing. / While the Liberty Bell is ringing."

In 1865, a song entitled "Ring the Bell, Watchman!" although apparently designed to announce the end of the Civil War, also reinforced an earlier mythical account of the ringing of the Liberty Bell by George Lippard by portraying an aging sexton joyfully ringing the Bell. Other early songs, like P. Malony's "Liberty Bell" in 1885, tended to associate the Bell with the proclamation of American independence.

Although it was not accompanied by lyrics, John Philip Sousa dedicated "The Liberty Bell March" at the World's Columbian Exposition in Chicago in 1893 to the Bell. Like other marches, this was particularly suited for stirring military enthusiasm. By contrast, "Bells of Fate," which was published in 1894, celebrated the role that bells played in various phases of life and death, ending with a verse that focused on the role of the "old bell" in proclaiming independence.

As in Sousa's march, both the Liberty Bell and the Statue of Liberty were used to inspire troops during World War I and II and to encourage people to buy bonds, while songs were designed to keep up morale on the home front. Such songs included "Liberty Bell (It's Time to Ring Again)" by Joe Goodwin, which was published in 1917; "The Voice of Liberty" by Ervin Biddle in 1917; "Liberty Bells Are Ringing" by Mark Probasco, which was published in 1917; "Liberty Bell, Ring On!" by Haven Gillespie in 1918; "Make the 'Old Bell' Ring" by Rachel C. Hazeltine; "Ring Out Ye Bell of Liberty" in 1918; "You're a Grand Old Bell" by J. E. Dempsey and Johann C. Schmid in 1919; "Once More the Liberty Bell Shall Chime to All" by Minnie Wilson in 1919; and a more generic "Let the Bells of Freedom Ring" (date uncertain) composed by Raymond A. Browne, which might have also been used during the Spanish-American War, and "America's Liberty Bells," which was composed by Mary E. Glasgow to music by Luther A. Clark during the same time period. Hal Parker wrote "Ring It Again! (The Call of the Liberty Bell)," which was primarily a call to buy Liberty Bonds. The covers of these songs were often bedecked with colorful depictions of the Liberty Bell, often in association with other patriotic symbols like the eagle or flag, which undoubtedly also heightened their patriotic appeal.

The song "My Own Liberty Bell," which also identified the Bell as "grand" and "dear," was written by Fred W. Hager and published in 1926 for the Philadelphia Sesquicentennial Exposition (Nash, 2010, 190). In 1933, "Congratulations, Liberty Bell" was played as Franklin D. Roosevelt assumed the presidency and Prohibition came to an end.

Two pieces of music, both published in 1952, had a Cold War focus. Red Di Renzo's "Proclaim Liberty" tied the Liberty Bell in Philadelphia with the new World

Freedom Bell in Berlin. Louis Maur's "Liberty Bell" proclaimed, "A-round the world your cry was heard" and, in an apparent reference to communism, "We want no Serf-dom."

One of the more amusing musical references to the Liberty Bell is found on a 1976 record designed to combat tooth decay in children and features none other than world champion boxer Mohammad Ali. It asks: "Who Knocked a Crack in the Liberty Bell?" and answers with the words "Ali, Ali." That same year, a group of artists issued "The Ballad of the Liberty Bell," which recorded various events that the Liberty Bell had witnessed during its long history. The alternate side has similar lyrics from "The Flag Speaks." On July 4, 1985, the Beach Boys held a concert believed to have been attended by more than a million people, entitled the "Sea to Shining Sea Concert." The Beach Boys subsequently released an audio CD entitled "Ringing the Liberty Bell!"

In more recent times, Mark O'Connor composed "The Song of the Liberty Bell" for the orchestra that accompanied the Public Broadcasting System (PBS) documentary entitled "Liberty! The American Revolution" in 1997. A description indicates that that the musical is a "replication of the way the voices of liberty in 1776 began with a lonely defiant few—and then swelled to a tremendous national chorus that has resounded through the world for the next two hundred and thirty-three years" ("Mark O'Connor Sheet Music Titles," n.d.).

In a manner similar to the direction that television comedy has taken, modern musical references to the Liberty Bell are often ironic and less reverent (Peterson, 2008). Gary Nash cites Jimmy Bryant's "Liberty Bell Polka" (2003), DJ Clue's "Liberty Bell," and If Hope Dies's "Let Freedom Ring from the Taco Liberty Bell" (2004). He further notes that the *Monty Python's Flying Circus* sketch comedy show for the BBC used Sousa's "Liberty Bell March" as background music for its opening titles (Nash, 2010, 191).

The lyrics to older songs are often difficult to find, and the songs described in this encyclopedia, which are listed under individual song titles, may be more representative than exhaustive and typically feature the visual aspects of the music along with the lyrics. On occasion, music like "The Song of Liberty," which was written by Franklin Grispin, with music by Wassili Leps, uses the Liberty Bell as an illustration on the cover (even though the song itself does not mention the Bell).

The 1876 Centennial and the 1976 Bicentennial were the occasion for the publication of two collections of music, the first entitled "The Liberty Bell" and the second entitled "The New Liberty Bell." Both have a print of the Liberty Bell covered with the text of the Declaration of Independence on the cover (Smith, 1976). In 1941, R. E. Winsett of Dayton, Tennessee (the site of the famed "Scopes Monkey Trial," on teaching the theory of evolution in school), whose family picture is at the front of the book, published a paperback songster of "spiritual songs" entitled "Liberty Bells," which it described as an "Emblem of Religious Freedom." Although the only explicitly patriotic song is "The Star-Spangled Banner" on the inside back cover, song No. 101 is entitled "Prayer Bells of Heaven" and likens prayer to ringing "a prayer-bell at the Lord's right hand." The chorus is of "Prayer-bells of heaven, Oh how sweet-ly they ring (keep ringing), Bearing our message un-to Je-sus the King."

See also: Eagles, Flags, the Statue of Liberty, and Related Symbols; "Liberty Bell, The" (Poem, 1843); Liberty Bell as Fighting Inspiration and Symbol; Liberty Loans; Lippard, George

Further Reading

Bowring, John. 1843. "The Liberty Bell." *The Liberty Bell*. Boston: Boston-Anti-Slavery Society, 1–4.

"Mark O'Connor Sheet Music Titles." n.d. http://www.sitemason.com/site/kGwSPe/liberty .bell.orchestral.html.

Nash, Gary B. *The Liberty Bell*. New Haven, CT: Yale University Press.

Peterson, Russell L. *Strange Bedfellows: How Late-Night Comedy Turns Democracy Into a Joke*. New Brunswick, NJ: Rutgers University Press.

Smith, James G. 1976. "A Report on 'The New Liberty Bell.'" *Choral Journal* 16 (March): 19–25.

Winsett, R. E., ed. 1941. *Liberty Bells*. Dayton, TN: R. E. Winsett.

Myerson v. Samuel (1947)

In *Myerson v. Samuel*, 74 F. Supp. 315 (1947), the U.S. District Court for the Eastern District of Pennsylvania issued a preliminary injunction against Philadelphia mayor Bernard Samuel and Nathan H. Rambo, the chief of the Bureau of City Property in Philadelphia, after they denied members of a left-leaning political group called Progressive Citizens of America the right to hold a protest in the public square in front of Independence Hall, which housed the Liberty Bell. In issuing the denial, Rambo had cited a city ordinance from January 8, 1913, which had limited such demonstrations to public patriotic celebrations that the city had approved.

In deciding that this refusal denied the First and Fourteenth Amendment rights of freedom of speech and peaceable assembly, Judge Guy K. Bard (1895–1953) ruled that there was no evidence that the demonstration was about to lead to the destruction of property. He also pointed out that authorities had previously granted permission for a demonstration against "the British terror," and, drawing from First Amendment precedents, that there was no evidence that the demonstration "will be a clear and present danger to our form of government" (*Myerson v. Samuel*, 74 F. Supp. 315).

A month later, another federal judge issued a similar ruling in *Reilly v. Samuel*, Civil Action 8039, in which he allowed a demonstration by individuals protesting military conscription (Mires, 1999, 50).

The area that borders Independence Hall is now administered by the National Park Service, which allows for a variety of demonstration. In *United States v. Marcavage* (2010), the U.S. Supreme Court ruled that park service officials had provided discriminatory treatment against antiabortion protestors.

See also: Independence Hall; Political and Social Movements and the Liberty Bell; *United States v. Marcavage* (2010)

Further Reading

Mires, Charlene. 1999. "In the Shadow of Independence Hall: Vernacular Activities and the Meanings of Historic Places." *The Public Historian* 21 (Spring): 49–64.

Myerson v. Samuel, 74 F. Supp. 315 (E.D. Pa. 1947).

N

Names for the Liberty Bell

The bell that is displayed in a visitor's center outside Independence Hall, which used to be known as the State House, is almost universally referred to as the Liberty Bell. This was not always the case.

When Isaac Norris first ordered this bell on behalf of the Pennsylvania Assembly, both the colony of Pennsylvania and the 12 other British colonies in North America were closely bound to Great Britain by ties of language, history, law, and consanguinity. If Norris consciously chose the Scripture on the Liberty Bell to emphasize liberty, it was the liberty that the colony believed was guaranteed by the Charter of Liberties that William Penn had given it in 1701, roughly 50 years (a jubilee) before, and implicit in their status as Englishmen protected by common law precedents. The primary purpose of the Bell was to call legislators to the Assembly and to call other important public convocations.

One of the first designations of the bell that was hung in the steeple was the "Old Bell." It was endowed with that name because it was cast (or rather recast) by John Pass and John Stow prior to the time a second bell arrived from the Whitechapel Foundry in England, which was then used in conjunction with a clock. Louis A. Rongione records that "[t]hough scarcely a year older than the Second Bell, the first bell became known as the Old Bell and thus achieved instant antiquity. The second bell was called 'The Other one'" (1976, 5).

An article in *The Gentleman's Magazine* dated July 7, 1753, published in England, said, "Last week was raised and fixed, in the State-House steeple, the great bell, weighing 2080 lb. cast here, with this inscription, 'Proclaim liberty throughout all the land, to the inhabitants thereof." The "great bell" was undoubtedly a reference to its size and weight. The Bell was also sometimes known as the "Province Bell."

Today's Liberty Bell was also often simply called the State House Bell, designating the building that it occupied. Even as other names became more prominent, the name sometimes remained. At a convention planning a monument to the Declaration of Independence in 1852, General Edwin R. V. Wright of New Jersey referred to "that glorious old bell" (Philadelphia. National Convention of The Thirteen Original States, 1852, 47). In 1918, a piece of sheet music by Rachel C. Hazeltine clearly depicted the Liberty Bell on its cover, and it was entitled "Make the 'Old Bell' Ring."

As the Bell became witness to the events leading up to the American Revolution and was associated, at least in the popular mind, with the announcement of independence, it became natural to call it the Province Bell, the Independence Bell, or the Bell of the Revolution (Ditzel, 1968, 52). Henry Watson thus wrote a book in 1852 entitled *The Old Bell of Independence*. This designation, like the Declaration of Independence that was signed in Independence Hall, celebrated the independence of Pennsylvania and its 12 companion colonies, from continuing dependence upon, and subjection to, British rule. A previously published poem, entitled "Independence Bell—July 4, 1776," which appeared in George S. Hillard's Franklin *Fifth Reader* of 1871, indicated that that usage persisted into the second half of the nineteenth century.

Abolitionists are generally credited with designating the bell that was believed to have pealed for independence as the "Liberty Bell." The first use of the term was likely the title of an article in an 1835 issue of the *Anti-Slavery Record*, published by the New York Anti-Slavery Society, in 1835. The author and likely editor, Ranson G. Williams, wrote of visiting Philadelphia and ascending "the tower of the old State House, to take a view of the city" (Williams, 1835, 23). Observing that he had examined "the celebrated Bell" on his descent, he further observed that it weighed 2,300 pounds, and that it was rung when delegates signed the Declaration of Independence and every year since on February 22 and July 4 (suggesting that it may not yet have been cracked prior to his visit). After citing the biblical inscription on the Bell, he commented: "May not the emancipationists in Philadelphia, hope to live to hear the same bell rung, when liberty shall in fact be proclaimed to all the inhabitants of this favored land? Hitherto, the bell has *not* obeyed the inscription; and its peals have been a mockery, while one sixth of 'all the inhabitants' are in abject slavery" (Williams, 1835, 23).

An abolitionist group known as the Friends of Freedom further published a series of annual books, known as the *Liberty Bell Gift Books,* from 1839 to the early 1850s, which were designated as *The Liberty Bell.* Moreover, the illustration of the Bell in the front of the first of these books contained a condensation of the passage from Leviticus 25:10, which reads "PROCLAIM LIBERTY TO ALL THE INHABITANTS" (with the word *ALL* in the largest letters, albeit at the base of the Bell rather than on its shoulder). Moreover, an accompanying sonnet says that it was "SUGGESTED BY THE INSCRIPTION ON THE PHILADELPHIA LIBERTY BELL" (Friends of Freedom, 1839, v).

Despite the similarity, Justin Kramer has argued that the bell that the book depicted was actually patterned, not after the Liberty Bell, but after metals struck on March 12, 1863, to celebrate the first copper coins produced by a steam-powered press on March 23, 1836. This coin featured a liberty cap (a symbol of freedom typically associated with the French Revolution) with the word *LIBERTY* and surrounded by radiating rays. To make this argument, however, Kramer not only ignores the biblical quotation and the description of the sonnet, but also positions the steam-press coin so that the liberty cap is at an angle rather than vertical (1975, 68).

On a more abstract level, but also downplaying the actual words on the abolitionist bell and the description of the accompanying sonnet, Professor Robey Callahan argued that "The Friends of Freedom were never referring to the Bell in their literature, but rather to the idea of a bell or bells tolling 'Liberty'" (Callahan, 1999, 66). Callahan further notes that in the vast majority of histories and tourist guides that were written for the Centennial Exposition of 1876, "the Bell is not referred to as the 'Liberty Bell.' 'Independence Bell' or 'bell of Independence' are its commoner names in 1876," with the term "Independence Bell" being acceptable until at least 1903 (Callahan, 1999, 66).

Prior to the Sesquicentennial in 1926, the Bell typically appeared in conjunction with other American symbols like the eagle, Independence Hall, or the flag, but from that time forward, it often appears by itself (Callahan, 1999, 68). Since then, the Bell, especially as adapted to advertising, has often been highly stylized, relying on "the merest outline of a bell and a crack proceeding from its base" (Callahan, 1999, 70).

In 1828, the bell cast by John Wilbank for the top of the new steeple on Independence Hall became known as "the State House bell" (Kimball, 1989, 39). In 1876, this was replaced by a much larger bell, which is appropriately called the Centennial Bell.

See also: Abolitionists; Centennial Bell; Eagles, Flags, the Statue of Liberty, and Related Symbols; "Independence Bell—July 4, 1776" (Poem, 1871); Independence Hall; Leviticus 25:10; Norris, Isaac, II; Wilbank, John

Further Reading

Callahan, Robey. 1999. "The Liberty Bell: From Commodity to Sacred Object." *Journal of Material Culture* 4 (1): 57–78.

Ditzel, Paul. 1968. "The Story of the Liberty Bell Since 1741," *American Legion Magazine* 85 (December): 24–27; 52–54.

Friends of Freedom. 1839. *The Liberty Bell*. Maria Weston Chapman, ed. Boston: Boston-Anti-Slavery Society.

Kimball, David. 1989. *The Story of the Liberty Bell*. Fort Washington, PA: Eastern National.

Kramer, Justin. 1975. *Cast in America: The Historically Accurate, Exciting Story of the Liberty Bell*. Los Angeles: Justin Kramer Incorporated.

Philadelphia. National Convention Of The Thirteen Original States, 1852. *Report of the proceedings of a convention composed of delegates from the thirteen original United States, held in Independence hall on Monday the fifth and Tuesday the sixth of July, 1852, for the purpose of considering the propriety of erecting one or more monuments in Independence square, Philadelphia, in commemoration of the Declaration of independence, July 4, 1776, and in honor of the signers thereof, in accordance with a preamble and resolutions submitted by A. G. Waterman, esq., of the select council, and adopted by both branches of councils*. Philadelphia, Crissy & Markley Printers, 1852. https://lccn.loc.gov/02004472.

Rongione, Louis A. 1976. "Sister to the Liberty Bell." *Records of the American Catholic Historical Society of Philadelphia* 87 (March–December): 3–32.

Watson, Henry C. 1852. *The Old Bell of Independence; or, Philadelphia in 1776*. Philadelphia: Lindsay and Blakiston.

Williams, R. [Ranson] G. 1835. *Anti-Slavery Record*, vol. I. New York: R. G. Williams for the American Anti-Slavery Society.

National Freedom Day

The Liberty Bell has been linked to many causes, including abolitionism and the establishment of the rights of African Americans. Beginning in 1942, Richard R.

Wright began laying wreaths at the Liberty Bell on February 1 to muster support for the establishment of a National Freedom Day. He chose this day because it marked the date on which President Abraham Lincoln had signed the congressional joint resolution calling for the establishment of the Thirteenth Amendment abolishing slavery.

Wright (1855–1947) was a remarkable man who had been born into slavery and was subsequently educated at a school established by the American Missionary Association (AMA). When General Oliver Otis Howard asked during a visit what message he should take back to the North, Wright said, "Sir, tell them we are rising" (Kachun, 2004, 283). Wright subsequently founded and served as president of the George State Industrial College for Colored Youth, now known as Savannah State University. He was a major in the U.S. army during the Spanish-American War and later moved to Philadelphia, where he founded the Citizens and Southern Bank and Trust Company. Wright's namesake son, who later earned a Ph.D. from the University of Pennsylvania, was also an impressive man, who helped organized the Pennsylvania Emancipation Exposition of 1913 (Mirer, 2004).

Wright was able to tap into the rhetoric of freedom that the nation adopted during World War II in its fight against Nazism and subsequently against communism. He was influential in getting the post office to issue a stamp in 1940 commemorating the Thirteenth Amendment. In a speech that he gave when the stamp was issued, he indicated that he wanted to honor "some central act" that individuals could identify as "the Bill of Rights, or the Magna Charta of the American Negro" (Katchum, 2004, 287). Clearly, Wright intended for his practice of laying a wreath at the Liberty Bell to accentuate this message.

The bill to initiate National Freedom Day was signed in 1942 by Congressman James P. McGranery (D-PA) in the House, and senators Joseph R. Guffey (D-PA) and Harry S. Truman (D-MO) in the Senate. It was adopted by both houses of Congress and signed by Truman, who had assumed the presidency after Franklin D. Roosevelt's death, in 1948.

National Freedom Day appears to be celebrated in Philadelphia more than elsewhere; it has been largely eclipsed by Luther Martin King Day. Some scholars have used this legislation to indicate "that when legislation originates with an individual, there is the danger that implementation may never really be achieved" (Walton et al., 1991, 687).

See also: Abolitionists and the Liberty Bell; African Americans and the Liberty Bell; Pennsylvania Emancipation Exposition of 1913; Wreath-Laying at the Liberty Bell

Further Reading

Katchun, Mitch. 2004. "'A Beacon to Oppressed Peoples Everywhere': Major Richard R. Wright Sr., National Freedom Day, and the Rhetoric of Freedom in the 1940s." *Pennsylvania Magazine of History and Biography* 128 (July): 279–306.

Meakin, Kate. "Wright, Richard R., Sr. (1855–1947)." *BlackPast.* http:www.blackpast.org /aah/wright-richard-r-sr-1855-1947.

Mires, Charlene. 2004. "Race, Place, and the Pennsylvania Exposition of 1913." *Pennsylvania Magazine of History and Biography* 128 (July): 257–278.

Walton, Hanes, Jr., Roosevelt Green, Jr., Willie E. Johnson, Kenneth A. Joran, Leslie Buri McLemore, C. Vernon Gray, and Marion Orr. 1991. "R. R. Wright, Congress,

President Truman and the First National Public African-American Holiday: National Freedom Day." *PS: Political Science and Politics* 24 (December): 685–688.

National Park Service

Although the city of Philadelphia technically owns the Liberty Bell and was responsible for its preservation through the first half of the twentieth century, in 1951 it transferred custody and operation of Independence Hall and the Bell to the National Park Service. This occurred soon after the city bought three blocks north of Independence Hall so that the hodgepodge of warehouses and other disparate buildings could be demolished so that the Hall would be in a more parklike setting appropriate to the years during which the Declaration of Independence and the U.S. Constitution were signed there.

The primary result of this transfer has been a large infusion of federal dollars, which have restored other nearby eighteenth-century buildings (Nash, 2010, 173). Under the direction of the National Park Service, a division of the Interior Department that is responsible for overseeing parks and historic sites throughout the nation, the Bell was removed to the Liberty Bell Pavilion in 1976 to accommodate the crowds that were expected for the bicentennial of the Revolution. In 2003, it was again moved, this time to the Liberty Bell Center, which provided more interpretative information for visitors.

The Park Service faced considerable opposition when it was discovered that the entrance to the Liberty Bell Center was close to the house that served as President George Washington's mansion during his time in office, and in which he had housed some of his slaves. Initially fearful that telling this story might muddle the patriotic message of the site, in due course the Park Service agreed to create an additional historic site outside the center that highlighted the incongruity of slavery within the shadow of Independence Hall.

Although park rangers have generally opened the area outside the Bell to public protests, the Supreme Court ruled in *United States v. Marcavage* (2010) that employees had acted arbitrarily with regard to demonstrations by antiabortion protestors.

The Park Service has issued a number of reports about the Liberty Bell, the most important of which was *The Liberty Bell: A Special History Study* (Paige, 1988). It has also published study guides and lesson plans for elementary and high school students.

See also: Liberty Bell Center; Liberty Bell Pavilion; Ownership of the Liberty Bell; Political and Social Movements and the Liberty Bell; *United States v. Marcavage* (2010)

Further Reading
Greiff, Constance M. 1987. *Independence: The Creation of a National Park*. Philadelphia: University of Pennsylvania Press.

Independence National Historical Park. n.d. *The Liberty Bell: A Symbol for "We the People": A Teacher Guide with Lesson Plans*. http://www.independenceparkinstitute.com/The%20Liberty%20Bell%20Teacher%20Guide%202011-6-07.pdf.

Mires, Charlene. 2002. *Independence Hall in American Memory*. Philadelphia: University of Pennsylvania Press.

Nash, Gary B. 2010. *The Liberty Bell.* New Haven, CT: Yale University Press.

National Park Service. 2015. *Bells Across the Land 2015.* Park Resource Packet. https://www.nps.gov/civilwar/upload/PARK-RESOURCE-PACKET-1.pdf.

Paige, John C. 1988. *The Liberty Bell: A Special History Study.* David C. Kimball, ed. Denver: Denver Service Center and Independence National Historical Park.

New Jersey Liberty Bell (*see* Cumberland County Liberty Bell)

Normandy Liberty Bell

There have been many replicas and reproductions of the Liberty Bell, but one of these, which does as much as any to demonstrate the way that the Bell has become an international symbol, is the bell known as the Normandy Liberty Bell. It was commissioned by Patrick Daudon of France (his name is inscribed on the top of the bell) and cast in 2004 in order to mark the sixtieth anniversary of the Allied invasion of the beaches in northern France in June, 1944. On that day, the Liberty Bell in Philadelphia was tapped seven times to indicate that the fight to regain France from their Nazi occupiers was being made on behalf of liberty.

Often described as an exact replica, it was not only made of the same alloy of copper and tin, but it was cast based on a high-tech scan of the original and tuned, as it is believed the original was, to an E-flat ("Ring the Normandy Liberty Bell at National Constitutional Center," 2005). But it is not identical; it differs from its American cousin in at least five ways. First, it is not cracked. Second, it has an extra inscription saying, "NORMANDY LIBERTY BELL 6 JUIN 2004." Third, although it bears the names of John Pass and John Stow, leading some to believe that it was cast by them, it was actually cast at a Cornille Havard workshop in Normandy at Villedieu-les-Poeles, and specifically indicates, in French, that it was "D'apres [after] PASS AND STOW fondeurs." Fourth, the inscription on the bell from Leviticus 25:10 is in French: "Liberte partout dans le pays pour tour ceux et toutes celles qui y vivent." Fifth, it sits in a cradle.

One advantage of the Normandy Liberty Bell is that, because it is not cracked, it can be rung and transported. In addition to being rung on the sixtieth anniversary of the D-Day Invasion, the Bell subsequently traveled to the National Constitutional Center in Philadelphia, and then in front of Independence Hall, where it was rung on July 4, 2005, for the annual "Let Freedom Ring" celebration. This was part of a two-year trip that included a stay at the National WWII Museum in New Orleans.

The French government is also associated with another American symbol of liberty—the Statue of Liberty, which sits on Ellis Island in New York Harbor. The French gave this statue to the United States in 1886 as a symbol of the mutual American and French alliance against Britain during the American Revolution and of the enduring principles of liberty that both nations have espoused (Berenson, 2012).

See also: Inscription on the Liberty Bell; Pass and Stow; Statue of Liberty; Tapping and Broadcasting the Sound of the Liberty Bell

Further Reading

Berenson. 2012. *The Statue of Liberty: A Translantic Story.* New Haven, CT: Yale University Press.

"Normandy Liberty Bell." The Liberty Bell. http://www.ushistory.org/libertybell/normandybell.html.

"Ring the Normandy Liberty Bell at National Constitutional Center." National Constitution Center, July 22.

Thomas, Lara. 2005. "Liberty Bell Replica Sails to States." Military Sealift Command, August. http://www.msc.navy.mil/sealift/2005/August/libertybell.htm.

Norris, Isaac, II

Isaac Norris II (1701–1766) was a Philadelphia merchant who was educated in England. In 1735, he became a Philadelphia alderman, and he subsequently served for 30 years in the General Assembly, during half of which he was the speaker. He was also a trustee of the Academy and College of Philadelphia.

Norris largely retired from the life of a merchant in 1743, after which he moved to Fairhill, the house his father had built in the Philadelphia suburbs known as Northern Liberties (Reinberger and McLean, 1997). His wife died the following year, leaving him with two children, one of whom would marry John Dickinson, who would later occupy the house. Norris was particularly known for his fine library, which was one of the largest in the region.

Norris's father had helped persuade William Penn to issue the Pennsylvania Charter of Privileges in 1701, which was designed to serve much like a modern constitution in guaranteeing civil rights and liberties. It reflected the Quaker view that God had given people liberty as a gift and that he had given it to everyone, and not just to a small group of the elect. David Hackett Fischer has observed, "Sometimes they spoke of it as the light of liberty" (Fischer, 2005, 53).

Norris, who like his father and William Penn was a devout Quaker, knew Hebrew and was responsible for choosing the verse from Leviticus 25:10—"Proclaim liberty thro' all the land to all the Inhabitants thereof"—that, when tweaked to reflect more exact biblical translation, adorns the Liberty Bell. Some scholars believe that Norris likely ordered the bell to commemorate the 50th anniversary of the Pennsylvania Charter of Privileges. He worked through Robert Charles, the colony's London agent in placing the order.

David Hackett Fischer observed that the bell also served a very practical function, and thus would not have been classified by Quakers, who generally avoided ostentation, as among "needless things." The small Province Bell that Penn had originally donated, and which hung in a tree, was no longer capable of being heard throughout the town. The new bell was designed to do so (Fischer, 2010, 54).

Fischer notes that the bell was an especially appropriate symbol for "[t]he large-minded vision of liberty and freedom" that the Quakers possessed. He observed that "[t]he Quakers were among the few people in the world who extended to others the rights that they claimed for themselves." He further notes, "Their thinking was very different from the Puritan conception of ordered liberty and freedom for the Calvinist elect of New England, and even further from the unruly pluralism of New York" (Fischer, 2005, 54).

Fearing that the change would bring about a diminution of rights, Norris resigned his position as speaker of the Assembly in 1764 after it accepted a change from a propriety to a royal government. By contrast, Norris had refused to join the strict Quaker pacifists who had resigned from the Assembly in 1756 in protest against the French and Indian War (Windhausen, 1967, 347). He is now known for authoring a satire against Andrew Hamilton, the brilliant lawyer who had defended John Peter Zenger against libel charges and was largely responsible for the design of the Pennsylvania State House (today's Independence Hall). In addition to representing different factions within the legislature, Norris believed that Hamilton was unethical and that he had defrauded widows (Carter, 1980).

Although early Quakers were involved both in owning and transporting slaves, they eventually began to believe that slavery was immoral, and they were among the early abolitionists (Frost, 1978). Their opposition, and the eventual elimination of slavery in the United States, seems to imbue the verse on the Liberty Bell with a prophetic quality. Quakers are usually pacifists, and they were sometimes treated harshly by Revolutionary Patriots, who interpreted their religious beliefs as a lack of devotion to their country.

Pennsylvania lawyer Hampton L. Carson, who headed the 1887 Constitutional Centennial had this irony in mind when he delivered an Independence Day speech at the World's Columbian Exposition in Chicago in 1893. He thus observed that God's Providence was revealed in using such "modest men of peace" as "powerful instruments of destruction as they who force the thunderbolts of war" (Rosewater, 1926, 203).

See also: Inscription on the Liberty Bell; Leviticus 25:10; Pennsylvania Charter of Privileges (1701); Quakers

Further Reading

Carter, Katherine D. 1980. "Isaac Norris II's Attack on Andrew Hamilton." *Pennsylvania Magazine of History and Biography.* 104 (April): 139–161.

Fischer, David Hackett. 2005. *Liberty and Freedom.* New York: Oxford University Press.

Frost, J. William. 1978. "The Origins of the Quaker Crusade Against Slavery: A Review of Recent Literature." *Quaker History* 67 (Spring): 42–58.

Norris, George W. 1877. "Isaac Norris." *Pennsylvania Magazine of History and Biography* 1: 449–454.

Reinberger, Mark, and Elizabeth McLean. 1997. "Isaac Norris's Fairhill: Architecture, Landscape, and Quaker Ideals in a Philadelphia Colonial Country Seat." *Winterthur Portfolio* 32 (Winter): 243–274.

Rosewater, Victor. 1926. *The Liberty Bell: Its History and Significance.* New York: D. Appleton.

Windhausen, John D. 1967. "Quaker Pacifism and the Image of Isaac Norris, II." *Pennsylvania History: A Journal of Mid-Atlantic Studies* 34 (October): 346–360.

Occasions for Ringing the Liberty Bell

Bells are often used to summon individuals to meetings, to record the time, and to mark special occasions. Through most of its early years, Independence Hall had a clock connected to a bell that rang to mark the passage of time, leaving the Liberty Bell to fulfill the other functions.

The most complete compilation of times that the Bell rang for other purposes was composed by Charles S. Keyser, who also wrote other books, including at least two delineating travels of the Liberty Bell, in 1893. This compilation lists events beginning with the ringing of the Bell to call together the Pennsylvania Assembly on August 27, 1753, to what he believed to be its last tolling on July 8, 1835, to mark the death of Chief Justice John Marshall. On occasion, however, he seems to list some events, like the introduction of Richard Henry Lee's resolution for independence (which was supposed to have been secret from the general public), which the Bell may or may not have announced.

There are a number of fascinating aspects to Keyser's study. Notably, Keyser associates the first ringing of the Bell after it was recast by John Pass and John Stow with calling the session in which the Assembly decided to continue to issue provincial money "notwithstanding the order of the Lords Justices of the Crown" and "to ordain, make, and enact any laws whatsoever for raising money for the public use, with the assent and approbation of the freemen of the country" (Keyser, 1893, 10). Likewise, he associated the second ringing, on May 17, 1755, with the calling of an assembly that asserted the colonists' rights, as Englishmen, "to judge for ourselves and our constituents of the utility and propriety of laws" (Keyser, 1893, 10).

Keyser sometimes distinguished different rings, sometimes referring to "tolling" or "muffling" the Bell. He noted that the Bell was variously used to call members of the Assembly, merchants, and freemen together.

Moreover, most of the occasions that Keyser associated with the ringing of the bells involved events leading up to the American Revolution. These dates and events included the following:

February 3, 1757, convening the Assembly to send Benjamin Franklin as an envoy to England;

September 12, 1764, to call the Assembly together to inform members of Massachusetts protests against the Sugar Act; and again, 10 days later, requesting their London agent to prevent Parliament from enacting taxes on colonists, who were not physically represented there;

September 9, 1765, to discuss sending a representative to the Stamp Act Congress;

September 21, 1765, to convene the Assembly to consider the Stamp Act;

October 5, 1765, to summon a town meeting as the "Royal Charlotte" arrived with stamps;

September 20, 1766, to convene the Assembly, which voted 4,000 pounds to finance the king's military operations in America;

April 25, 1768, to call a meeting of merchants to oppose British restrictions on colonial manufacturing and related matters;

July 30, 1768, to call a meeting of freemen to give instructions to their legislators to oppose parliamentary taxes;

February 4, 1770, to call Assembly to petition for repeal of tax on tea;

September 27, 1770, to call a meeting of people to oppose parliamentary taxes;

October 18, 1773, to call people to denounce buyers and vendors of tea;

December 17, 1773, to call crowd to prevent unloading of the tea form ship *Polly*;

June 1, 1774, to mourn the closing of the Boston Harbor;

June 18, 1774, to convene people at the State House.

Bells were also rung on February 21, 1761, to proclaim the accession of George III to the British throne, and on January 25, 1763, to proclaim the treaty ending the French and Indian War.

Although there is some doubt as to whether the Liberty Bell Tower was at the time in sufficient repair for the Bell to be rung, Keyser believes that it was rung on July 8, 1776, to accompany the reading of the Declaration of Independence. Keyser says that the Bell also was rung on September 26, 1776, to dissolve the Assembly; on October 24, 1781, to mark the surrender of Lord Cornwallis, on November 27, 1781; to welcome President Washington and his wife; and on April 16, 1783, to mark the Proclamation of Peace.

There is special interest in who would have rung the Bell if it were rung on July 8, 1776. Although a claim has been made for William Hurry, the best candidate appears to be Andrew McNair, who, as doorkeeper to the Pennsylvania Assembly, would have had this responsibility if he were present. It is known that he missed two days between April 30 and November 1, 1776, and it is possible that this would have been one of these days (Alexander, 1925, 660). Apparently of Irish ancestry, McNair was married in November 1746 to Mary Jennings, lived in Philadelphia's South Ward, and was a freemason (Alexander, 1925, 659).

On September 29, 1824, the Bell welcomed Lafayette to the city, on July 4, 1826, to mark the Jubilee of the Declaration of Independence; on July 24, 1826, to mark the deaths of John Adams and Thomas Jefferson, on July 4, 1831, to mark Independence Day; on February 22, 1832, to commemorate Washington's birthday; later that year for the death of Charles Carroll, of Carrollton, the last of the signers of the Declaration of Independence; and on July 21, 1834, for the death of the Marquis de Lafayette.

It is unclear whether Keyser's list is intended to be exhaustive. It seems logical that the Bell may have sounded for the beginning of each legislative session, not simply the ones he singled out for special recognition. Moreover, he said that from 1783 to July 8, 1835, the "bell of Independence, continued for half a century proclaiming its anniversaries and the birth of Washington; tolling also at the death of our great men, and welcoming illustrious men of our own and other nations" (Keyser, 1893, 27).

Rosewater observes that on September 16, 1772, "divers inhabitants . . . living near the state house" petitioned the Assembly to say that they were "much incommoded and distressed by the too frequent Ringing of the great Bell in the Steeple of the State House, the inconvenience of which has often been felt severely when some of the Petitioner's families have been affected with sickness, at which times, from its uncommon size and unusual sound, it is extremely dangerous, and may prove fatal" (Rosewater, 1926, 34).

There is further evidence that the Liberty Bell was rung sometime between June 1789 and through the summer of 1791 to convene classes for the University of Pennsylvania, some of whose students were taking classes in nearby Philosophical Hall (Paige, 1988, 23).

Although the Bell can no long be rung, throughout the last 125 years, it has frequently been tapped, and broadcast via radio and television on special occasions.

See also: Independence Day; Tapping and Broadcasting the Sound of the Liberty Bell

Further Reading

Alexander, Mary D. 1925. "The Ringers of the Liberty Bell." *Journal of the Illinois State Historical Society* 18 (October): 658–667.

Keyser, Charles S. 1893. *The Liberty Bell, Independence Hall, Philadelphia. A Complete Record of All the Great Events Announced by the Ringing of the Bell.* Philadelphia: Allen, Lane & Scott's Printing House.

Paige, John C. 1988. *The Liberty Bell: A Special History Study.* David C. Kimball, ed. Denver: Denver Service Center and Independence National Historical Park.

Rosewater, Victor. 1926. *The Liberty Bell: Its History and Significance.* New York: D. Appleton.

Stoudt, John Baer. 1930. *The Liberty Bells of Pennsylvania.* Philadelphia: William J. Campbell.

Old Hickory Liberty Bell

One of the more elusive replicas of the Liberty Bell is a 110-pound bell, reputedly 90 percent silver, owned by the Old Hickory Distilling Corporation of Philadelphia. The bell was given the nickname of U.S. president Andrew Jackson. The company lent the bell to the city of Philadelphia for display at the Brussels World Fair of 1958. According to an article in the July 14, 1958, issue of the *Observer*, which reported the loan, "the Liberty Bell has been a trademark of Philadelphia Blended whiskey."

In a reflection of Cold War sentiments, the article that described the loan noted, "The Liberty Bell, world renowned representation of freedom and the rights of man, was going to stand in an honored place in the City of Philadelphia exhibit, a symbol no Communist can hope to beat" ("Old Hickory Liberty Bell At Brussels World's Fair," 1958). The article quoted pilot John V. Metzger, who was transporting the bell on a Pan American Clipper, as saying "Well, look at that! The Liberty Bell for the Brussels Fair. We'll show those Russians now . . . !" ("Old Hickory Liberty Bell At Brussels World's Fair," 1958).

The bell apparently was displayed on a wooden base that was "carved from an oak tree more than 200 years old, which was found in the vicinity of Independence Hall" ("Old Hickory Liberty Bell At Brussels World's Fair," 1958). Although the article accurately described the history and inscription on the Liberty Bell in Philadelphia, it did not indicate whether the Old Hickory Liberty Bell had a similar engraving.

The company appears to have stopped production sometime around 1981, and the author of this encyclopedia is unsure whether the bell still exists, and, if so, where it may be found.

See also: Advertising and the Liberty Bell; Replicas of the Liberty Bell

Further Reading

"Old Hickory Liberty Bell At Brussels World's Fair." 1958. *The Observer*, July 14, 13. Located at the Independence National Historical Park in the Historical Note Card File under the Date 14 July 1958.

"Old Liberty Bell" (Poem, 1887)

In 1887, just two years after the Liberty Bell returned from its trip to New Orleans for the World's Industrial and Cotton Exposition in New Orleans, Hattie Howard, an otherwise-elusive poet who appears to have published at least four volumes of verse, published a poem entitled "Old Liberty Bell." The poem is significant both for combining earlier ("the Old Bell") and later ("the Liberty Bell") names for the Bell, for stressing the Bell's role in the American Revolution, for identifying a time when the author believed that the Bell had cracked, and for using the Bell as a symbol of unity.

The first two verses tie the Bell firmly to the American Revolution, but without getting into the controversy as to whether it rang on July 4 or July 8 (Howard, 1887, 62):

O. Liberty herald! Thy echoes I hear,
As down through the century, year after year,
The resonant voice that our forefathers knew,
Triumphant and thrilling, still loyal and true,
In paeans rings out o'er the land that we love,
Proclaiming good-will to the people thereof.

In thy reverberations sonorously mix
With the patriot spirit of Seventy-Six,
The soul, that seems wafted from some distant shore

As if intervening, rough seas passing o'er,
Of 'Old Independence,' obedience to God,
Resistance to tyrants at home and abroad.

The middle verses further tied the Bell to Philadelphia and suggested that it had
been cracked in that city's efforts to greet Henry Clay (Howard, 1887, 62):

From the bosom of Earth wast thou, Liberty Bell,
In crude metal taken, and fashioned so well,
And by skillful artificer given a tongue
In the City of Brotherly Love that first rung,
As Victory's bright, starry pennon unfurled
To the uplifted gaze of a wondering world.

Old Liberty Bell! though corroded with rust,
And choked and half-buried 'neath undisturbed dust,
And haplessly cracked on that memorable day
In overstrained efforts to greet Henry Clay,
Thy clarion notes of the past resound yet,
Recalling the days we would never forget.

As with other poems, the reference to the "starry pennon" ties the Liberty Bell to
the U.S. flag, or pennant. Henry Clay, the U.S. senator from Kentucky who had
been the chief architect of the Compromise of 1850, would be recognized, of course,
as one who had sought reconciliation between North and South, so evoking his
name would ease the transition to the final two verses (Howard, 1887, 73):

Now, Liberty Bell, on thy way to the South,
Thy history travels before; every month
Can the story repeat of the stirring events
That led to the birth-day of Freedom—and hence
To our proud elevation, and paramount worth—
Admired and honored all over the Earth.

May favors auspicious thy wand'rings attend,
And greetings fraternal from Northern hearts blend
With those of our neighbors, tell courtesies kind
Shall "many in one" so harmoniously bind,
That in jubilant tones shall thy aged tongue tell
Of a county united, O Liberty Bell!

One of the most fascinating aspects of the poem is that, presumably as a way of
emphasizing national unity, it avoids any mention of the Bell as a symbol of slave
emancipation. It sought to unite the nation by remembrances of 1776, the year in which
the Declaration of Independence was issued, rather than by evocations of civil war.

See also: Journeys of the Liberty Bell; Names for the Liberty Bell; World's Industrial and
Cotton Exposition in New Orleans (1885)

Further Reading
Howard, Hattie. 1887. *Later Poems*. Hartford: Lockwood & Brainard.

"Old State House Bell" (Song, 1855)

One of the earliest pieces of sheet music known to celebrate the Liberty Bell is entitled, in accordance with usage of the time, as the "Old State House Bell." It was published in 1855 in Philadelphia, New York, and Boston by Stayman & Brothers. The words were written by G. F. Messer, and the music was composed by Francis Weiland, both of whom were from Philadelphia. The cover, which pictured the Bell on an octagonal pedestal with its distinctive crack, was surmounted by an eagle and "Respectfully Dedicated to the American People." The words on the pedestal noted that the picture is "A FAC SIMILE OF THE OLD STATE-HOUSE BELL, WHICH FIRST ANNOUNCED OUR INDEPENDENCE."

The second page of the music contained a shield with a history of the Bell, attributed to Watson's *Annals*. After citing the inscription from Leviticus 25:10 on the Bell, the text observed "[t]hat it was adopted from scripture may to many be still more impressive, as being also the voice of God—that great Arbiter by whose signal providence we afterwards attained to that 'Liberty' and self-government which bids fair to emancipate our whole Continent, and in time, in influence and meliorate the condition of the subjects of arbitrary government throughout the civilized world."

The lyrics observed, "Thy silvery tones were first to tell/ In thunder peals a NA-TION free." Evoking the image of Columbia, the Bell was said to strike "for "Li-ber-ty" (Meeser and Weiland, 1855).

The chorus was, "Then hurrah, hurrah, Boys no land en-joys That which makes our bo-soms swell/ Then hurrah, Boys, hurrah, In peace or war We will fond-ly che-rish that old bell" (Meeser and Weiland, 1855).

The "time hal-lowed Bell" was further associated with sounding "the fu-ne-ral knell" of Britain's "vassal yoke" from its "sa-cred tower." The Bell is identified as "Freedom's Bell," which turns the hearts of its listeners to home" (Meeser and Weiland, 1855).

See also: Music and the Liberty Bell; Names for the Liberty Bell

Further Reading
Meeser, Geo. F., and Francis Weiland. 1855. *The Old State House Bell*. Stayman and Brothers, Philadelphia. Monographic. Notated Music. https://www.loc.gov/item/sm1855.590180.

"Once More the Liberty Bell Shall Chime Liberty to All" (Song, 1919)

A piece of sheet music from 1919 features a cover in soft hues of orange, in which a young man dressed as a doughboy is attempting to console a woman who appears to be staring at his picture and wiping her face with a handkerchief. Entitled "Once

More the Liberty Bell Shall Chime Liberty to All," the words are attributed to Minnie Wilson and the music to Leo Friedman.

Although the song is directed to the soldier's mother, the identical picture is used on another piece of sheet music published by the same company later that year, with words by Leo E. Buehring and music again by Leo Friedman, entitled, "Sweetheart, Don't Forget to Meet Me When I Come." To complicate the situation still further, the picture is also used by another of the company's songs from 1919, this one written by Lovina Warren, entitled "The Bereaved Mother," and yet another written by Irene J. McKiernan entitled, "Since I've Been a Soldier."

"Once More the Liberty Bell Shall Chime Liberty to All" has two verses and a chorus. The first verse attempts to console the soldier's mother by indicating that he's going to fight for his country. The second looks ahead to returning to the land where "the dear old Liberty Bell—Shall chime its wond'rous call—Liberty, Liberty to all" (Friedman and Wilson, 1919).

The chorus refers to the United States as "that sweet land of liberty," and as "the home of the brave and free." Evoking another song of the period, and another from the Civil War, the song ends with "Tramp, tramp, tramp, the boys are marching; the boys are marching on" (Friedman and Wilson, 1919).

See also: Music and the Liberty Bell

Further Reading

Friedman, Leo, and Minnie Wilson. 1919. *Once More the Liberty Bell Shall Chime Liberty to All.* Monographic. North American Music Company, Chicago. Notated Music. https://www.loc.gov/item/2013565446.

Oral Tradition and the Liberty Bell

One of the fascinating aspects of the Liberty Bell is that it is a symbol that evokes both oral and visual images. From the beginning, the bell was known for its prescription, taken from Leviticus 25:10, to "Proclaim LIBERTY Throughout All the Land to All the Inhabitants Thereof." As a bell, it was, of course, originally designed to ring out important occasions, many of which were initially connected to the events leading up to the American Revolution. As a crack largely silenced the aural aspect of the Bell, the image of the Bell itself, with its large, zigzag crack, became an emblem in its own right.

Although scholars, especially those who study constitutional law, largely focus on written texts, some of the most memorable texts in the popular mind are those associated with the national anthem, "The Star-Spangled Banner," and songs like "America the Beautiful" and "My Country 'Tis of Thee." The last line of the first verse of the latter song, written by Samuel Francis Smith (1808–1895) in 1831, when he was a student at Andover Theological Seminary, and which was first performed by a school group at Boston's Park Street Church on July 4, 1831, exhorts "Let Freedom ring!" (Branham, 1996, 625–626).

Smith may well have envisioned church bells, rather than the Liberty Bell, which was only just beginning to be used as an abolitionist symbol. Whatever image he had in mind, though, as a student of theology, he would almost certainly have been familiar with the passage from Leviticus on the Bell. Moreover, popular associations with the Bell undoubtedly give a particular resonance to the idea of letting freedom "ring."

Ronald R. Garet (2000) has noted that many of America's famous speeches, most notably Frederick Douglass's 1852 speech "What to the Slave Is the Fourth of July" and Martin Luther King, Jr.'s. "I Have a Dream" speech (1963), have appealed to the oral tradition associated with preaching and the ringing of bells. This was especially appropriate in light of the role that the Liberty Bell had played as a symbol of abolitionism.

In his speech, Douglass evoked the exiled Jews in Babylon, who hung their harps on willow trees because they found it difficult to sing songs of mirth in a strange land. In addition to evoking the ringing of the bells of freedom, in his speech, King cited an old African American spiritual, who proclaimed "Free at last, free at last, thank God Almighty, I'm free at last."

See also: Inscription on the Liberty Bell; King, Martin Luther, Jr.; Leviticus 25:10

Further Reading

Branham, Robert James. 1996. "'Of Thee I Sing': Contesting America." *American Quarterly* 48 (December): 623–652.

Garet, Ronald R. 2000. "Proclaim Liberty." *Southern California Law Review* 74: 145–168.

"Our Liberty Bell" (Song, 1918)

World War I was a particularly fertile time for songs about the Liberty Bell. One such song, entitled "Our Liberty Bell," was both written and arranged by Olive M. Skelton. She also designed the cover, which featured the sketch of a man in colonial clothes pulling a rope to ring the Liberty Bell, which appears attached to a beam. A statement just above the title of the song on the first inside page observes that the song was "Respectfully Dedicated to our President of U.S.A.," a reference to Woodrow Wilson.

The song, which has three regular verses and an encore verse, consistently refers to the Bell as the "dear Liberty Bell." The first verse ties the song to World War I by indicating that the Bell was designed to ring out for those (Skelton, 1918):

Who fought a bitter fight
To save the day for Liberty
And teach the Teutons [a name for Germans] right.

The second verse expresses the hope that the Bell will "in future years . . . Let peace and plenty here abound" (Skelton, 1918).

Moving from sound to sight, and perhaps hoping to evoke the Statue of Liberty, the third verse refers to lives inspired by the bell as "a beacon."

The encore verse further associates the "dear Liberty Bell" with "our noble President" who "paved Liberty's way." This verse ends as follows (Skelton, 1918):

Ring out your mission well
Ring out ring out for Liberty

Ring out dear Liberty Bell
Ring out Liberty.

One indication of the power of the Liberty Bell during this time period was its widespread use in the Liberty Loan campaign to raise money to help pay for the war.

See also: Liberty Loans; Music and the Liberty Bell

Further Reading
Skelton, Olive M. 1918. *Our Liberty Bell.* Monographic. Olive M. Skelton, Exeter, Canada. Notated Music. https://www.loc.gov/item/2009371952.

Ownership of the Liberty Bell

If one were to follow a contemporary commercial and delineate those things that can be purchased with money and those that are "priceless," the Liberty Bell would undoubtedly fit into the second category. Its value stems not from the minimal value of the bronze of which it is composed or the wooden yoke from which it hangs, but from its long association with important events and movements in U.S. history, and from the emotional significance that it has for both American adults and their children.

As an object, however, the Bell was sometimes dickered over for its commercial value. It was originally purchased by the Pennsylvania Assembly from the Whitechapel Foundry in England and recast by John Pass and John Stow. When the state capital moved from Philadelphia to Lancaster, and later to Harrisburg, the state, which had adopted a law claiming ownership of the State House in 1780, decided to sell the State House and its contents. It made an offer to the city of Philadelphia for $70,000, which was accepted in 1816. When the city replaced the "sister" to the Liberty Bell that drove the clock in the building, it offered it for scrap value, but the individual to whom the offer was made left it there instead, and the city later sold it to a church.

In 1893, the Pennsylvania Supreme Court issued a decision *In re Washington Monument Fund*, which affirmed that the city owned the Bell "in fee simple," which essentially meant with no restrictions. Throughout the twentieth century, Philadelphia began to recognize the value of Independence Hall, the Liberty Bell, and other attractions to lure tourists who could add to the city's economy. In 1951, the city, while retaining ownership of the Liberty Bell, transferred custody and operation of Independence Hall to the National Park Service.

Concerned that Independence Hall might be unable to accommodate the large number of visitors anticipated for the bicentennial, in 1976, the Park Service moved the Bell to a Liberty Bell Pavilion. It stayed there until 2003, when it was moved to a new Liberty Bell Center, also in sight of Independence Hall, with greater interpretative information to guide visitors.

The priceless quality of the Liberty Bell was demonstrated on April 1, 1986, when Taco Bell sparked national outrage when it ran full-page newspaper advertisements announcing that it had purchased the Liberty Bell and that the Bell would spend half of each year at the company's California headquarters. (It was an April Fool's Day joke, of course, but the affront was quite real.)

See also: Dimensions, Weight, and Cost of the Liberty Bell; Independence Hall; Liberty Bell Center; Liberty Bell Pavilion; National Park Service; Sister to the Liberty Bell; Taco Liberty Bell; Tourism and the Liberty Bell; *Washington Monument Fund, In re* (1893)

Further Reading
In re Washington Monument Fund, 154 Pa. 621 (1893).

P

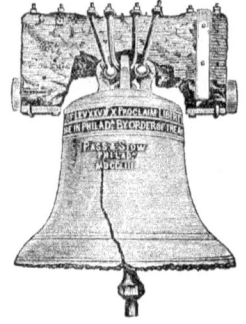

Panama-Pacific International Exposition, San Francisco (1915)

Between 1885 and 1915, the Liberty Bell left Philadelphia on seven occasions, for fairs, expositions, and commemorations. The last and longest of these trips was the one that the Bell took by train to the Panama-Pacific International Exposition in San Francisco in 1915. Interest in the Bell had undoubtedly been heightened when earlier that year, a tapping of the Bell had been transmitted by the Bell Telephone Company from Philadelphia to the city that was to host the Panama-Pacific International Exposition.

Each trip the Liberty Bell had taken had increased concerns over its safety, so special lobbying efforts were needed to lure it from its home city. One of the most effective of these techniques (used previously to entice the Bell to the Louisiana Purchase Exposition in St. Louis, Missouri) was a petition signed by a half-million California children who had been encouraged to do so on October 11, 1912, which San Francisco had designated as Liberty Bell Day (Nash, 2010, 110). The petition was presented to Philadelphia mayor Rudolph Blankenburg on a reel of more than 10 feet in diameter (see Sands and Bartlett, 2012, 87). The trip had initially been opposed by Pennsylvania's U.S. senator Boies Penrose, sometimes known as "the Big Grissly" (Fried, 2017). One writer, pointing out that this was the Liberty Bell's first trip beyond the Mississippi River observed that by going to the West, the Bell was literally fulfilling the prophetic mandate of Leviticus 25:10: "Proclaim Liberty throughout all the land" (Stewart, 1915, 48).

At the time of the trip, Europe was already engulfed in World War I, and German U-Boats had sunk the *Lusitania* on May 7. San Francisco and San Diego both had plans for a World's Fair celebrating the Panama Canal, and the Bell spent a few days in the latter city after leaving San Francisco on its way back to Philadelphia. Both fairs, aided by the Smithsonian Institution, were premised on the idea of progress, which its directors saw embodied in the triumph of Anglo-Saxon ideals over those of the Spanish and other civilizations. Herbert Hoover, then an engineer, observed, "In these days of stifling struggle our people need something to bring back to them the heritage, not only of the combat of immediate fathers in the upbuilding of the West, but also to bring to the people that they have a heritage of race" (Rydell, 1984, 208).

As the Prospectus of the San Diego Exposition further explained, "California has treasured the missions long. Those who have seen them have carried their inspiration away, yet left it strong to inspire others. It is an inspiration and an appeal that can never die. The soldiers and the adventurers are remembered. The priest-civilizer still lives" (Rydell, 1984, 208). Reconstructions of villages from Africa, Samoa, and the American West prior to European settlement further conveyed the point.

For safety reasons, the train carrying the Bell was to go no faster than 35 miles per hour, and sometimes no more than 18 (Stewart, 1915, 48). Moreover, it was carried on a train that included "the best-cushioned rail car in history, with the biggest springs ever used" (Fried, 2017). Philadelphia had provided literature about the Bell for distribution along the trip, including a 32-page booklet entitled "The Liberty Bell, San Francisco to Philadelphia, November, 1915" (Sands and Bartlett, 2012, 94).

The itinerary of the Bell demonstrates that it did not take the shortest route. Instead, from July 5 through July 16, 1915, it wound its way through Pennsylvania, Ohio, Indiana, Illinois, Iowa, Kansas, Missouri, Nebraska, Colorado, Wyoming, Utah, Idaho, Oregon, and Washington before traveling through Red Bluff, Chico, Marysville, and Sacramento before finally reaching San Francisco (Paige, 1988, 117–126). Crowds reacted with great enthusiasm to the Bell. A reporter from the Denver *Times* observed (Fried, 2017):

> Women drew gold and diamond bracelets from their arms without fear of pickpockets from the vast mob. Little children drew rings from their fingers and took gold lockets and chains from their necks. Prosperous businessmen, who looked as if sentiment played a small part in their everyday dealings with the world, handed up heavy gold watches and chains. Negroes, who showed a solid and dazzling expanse of white teeth, and even men ragged and unshaven, hobos apparently, dug down into their pockets and pulled out dilapidated pocket knives with the same simple but fervid words: "Please touch the bell with that."

As the Bell stopped briefly in the small town of Grinnell, Iowa, almost 3,000 people showed up. Showing that the symbol could be used for multiple purposes, a local group followed the visit with a Liberty and Peace Pageant designed to keep the United States from entering World War I (Kaiser, 2017, 4).

It is estimated that 5 million Americans viewed the Bell on its trip West (Nash, 2010, 123). It was greeted by a parade and a crowd of about 114,000 that carried it to the so-called City of Ivory—the buildings of the exposition (Nash, 2010, 124). More than 19 million people attended the exposition, and one 10th of them are estimated to have kissed the Liberty Bell (Nash, 2010, 127).

As its name suggested, the exposition that the Liberty Bell attended was designed to commemorate the completion of the building of the Panama Canal the previous year, an act that had been effectuated when the United States supported a revolution that had helped Panama break away from Columbia, as well as the 400th anniversary of the European discovery of the Pacific Ocean. Hailed as one of the most important engineering accomplishments in world history, the canal offered the promise of increasing and facilitating trade, as vessels would no longer have to go around the tip of South America to reach the West Coast of North America.

Prominent exhibits, including one on Race Betterment, reinforced the need for racial purity and the perceived dangers of interracial marriage. Other displays, like the African Dip, which portrayed a huge image of a "savage African," and a Sperry Flour booth in the Palace of Food Products, in which women dressed as mammies served pancakes, promoted racial stereotypes. A planned "Negro Day" was cancelled after interest in it waned (Hudson, 2018, 38–39). Although African American Buffalo Soldiers of the 24th Infantry had escorted the Bell to the depot on its way home, many blacks had skipped the Panama-Pacific Exposition in favor of attending the Lincoln Jubilee in Chicago, which celebrated 50 years of African American emancipation (Bruno, 1916, 6).

One of the more iconic photographs from the exposition was a picture of a man identified as Chief Little Bear, complete in a Native American headdress composed of feathers, a beaded vest with a portrayal of a horse and a tomahawk in his left hand, gently touching the Bell with his right hand (Sands and Bartlett, 2002, 93).

The path of the Bell on its way home to Philadelphia was about as circuitous as its trip there. The Bell spent November 12–14 at the Panama-California Exposition in San Diego (there had been a major effort on the part of both cities to solicit its presence) before heading to Arizona, New Mexico, Texas, Louisiana, Mississippi, Tennessee, Kentucky, Illinois, Indiana, Kentucky, Ohio, New York, Pennsylvania, and New Jersey, and then arriving back in Philadelphia on November 25, 1915 (Paige, 1988, 127–141). Although he had initially opposed transport of the Bell, Senator Penrose accompanied the Bell on its return trip, likely with the hope that it might help him in a contemplated presidential run the following year (Fried, 2017).

One of the most shocking incidents of the trip occurred as the train stopped in Arlington, Texas. A riot broke out when an African American girl, following the example of children throughout the trip, kissed the Bell. Similarly, a woman apparently was crushed to death by the crowd that gathered around the Bell in Memphis (Fried, 2017). On a more positive note, an estimated 30,000 people greeted the Bell when it arrived for a 40-minute stop at Rochester, New York, where the mayor had requested all factory whistles, gongs, and bells in the city to sound at 11 a.m., the anticipated time of the stop (Nighan, 2017).

As many as one in four American people at the time viewed the Liberty Bell on its trip (Rossen, 2017). The enthusiasm that the Bell had generated on this and other trips, and its use as an emblem, undoubtedly contributed to the success of the Liberty Loan initiative carried out during World War I to raise money for the conflict (Fried, 2017).

See also: Children and the Liberty Bell; Inscription on the Liberty Bell; Journeys of the Liberty Bell; Kissing the Liberty Bell; Liberty Loans

Further Reading

Bruno, Lee. 2016. "Let Freedom Ring: Buffalo Soldiers and the Liberty Bell." *Argonaut— Journal of the San Francisco Museum and Historical Society* (Winter): 6–15.

Fried, Stephen. 2017. "World War I: 100 Years Later. How the Liberty Bell Won the Great War." Smithsonian.com, April. https://www.smithsonianmag.com/history/how -liberty-bell-won-great-war-180962471.

Hudson, Lynn M. 2010. "'This Is Our Fair and Our State': African Americans and the Panama-Pacific International Exposition." *California History* 87: 26–45; 66–68.

Independence National Historic Park Collection. 1915. Bell Scrapbook Image Guide.

Kaiser, Daniel. 2017. "When the Liberty Bell Visited Grinnell." Grinnell Stories, May 6. http://grinnellstories.blogspot.com/2017/05/when-liberty-bell-visited-grinnell .html.

Nash, Gary B. 2010. *The Liberty Bell*. New Haven, CT: Yale University Press.

Nighan, Michael J. 2017. "Big Bell, Big Bell and School Bells: An Ex-president, the Liberty Bell, and Several Thousand School Teachers Come to Town." *Talker of the Town,* August 7. http://talkerofthetown.com/2017/08/07/big-bill-big-bell-and-school-bells-an-ex-president-the-liberty-bell-and-several-thousand-school-teachers-come-to-town.

Paige, John C. 1988. *The Liberty Bell of Independence National Historical Park: A Special History Study*, ed. David C. Kimball. Denver: Denver Service Center, National Park Service, Department of the Interior. Accessed through pubs.etic.nps.gov.

Rossen, Jake. 2017. "When the Liberty Bell Went on a National Tour." Mental Floss, May 8. http://mentalfloss.com/articles/500549/when-liberty-bell-went-natiuona-tour.

Rydell, Robert W. 1984. *All the World's a Fair: Visions of Empire at American International Expositions, 1876–1916*. Chicago: University of Chicago Press.

Sands, Robert W., Jr., and Alexander B. Bartlett. 2002. *Images of America: Independence Hall and the Liberty Bell*. Charleston, SC: Arcadia Publishing.

Stewart, J. A. 1915. "The Liberty Bell's Great Trip." *Journal of Education* 82 (June 15): 48–49.

Pass and Stow

Under the biblical inscription of the current Liberty Bell are the names "PASS AND STOW" and on the two subsequent lines, "PHILADELA and MDCCLIII." These would have replaced the words "THOMAS LESTER OF LONDON MADE ME 1752" that were likely on the original bell cast by the Whitechapel Foundry in London (Frazier, 1974, 294).

There is relatively little information on John Pass and John Stow, the American brass makers who offered to recast the Bell after the first one cracked upon its first ringing. Pass, whose name was first and who is believed to have been the elder of the two, was a native of Malta, which had a history of bell casting. He had also previously owned the Mount Holly Iron Furnace in Burlington County, New Jersey (Nash, 2010, 8–9). A notice in the Pennsylvania *Gazette* of March 17, 1752, said that "John Pass brass Founder, is removed from Third Street, to the sign of the Three Bells, in Second Street, opposite to Mr. John Lawrena's, and next door but two [sic] Mr. William Whitebeard's, at the sign of the King's Arms, Philadelphia: Where may be had all sorts of brasses" (Giannini, 1997). Because Pass is known to have signed for money with an "X" mark, it is possible that he was illiterate (Paige, 1988, 8). It appears as though Pass's original name may have been Giovianni Pace, that he may have been an apprentice to the bell founder Joachin Vella, in Medina Malta, and that he may have gone from there to Canada, and then to Pennsylvania, because of its religious liberty (Kramer, 1975, 19). A number of Maltese citizens volunteered to serve in the French navy and also served in the American Revolution (Lubig, 2011, 8).

John Stow (1727–1754) was born in Philadelphia to Charles and Rebecca Snow. He is known to have been a charter member of the Union Library Company, and he owned a foundry on Second Street at the "Sign of the Three Bells," which were used to symbolize such a shop. It was there that the Bell was pulverized into small pieces that could be melted down (Nash, 2010, 9). Histories of the Liberty Bell sometimes call John Stow "Charles," apparently confusing him with his father, the doorkeeper of Pennsylvania's executive council, who may have suggested that he could do the job rather than send the original Bell back to England (Kramer, 1975, 15).

Bronze is composed chiefly of copper and tin. Although tin generally enhances the ringing sound, too much tin makes bronze extra brittle. Pass and Stow accordingly added 1 ½ ounces of copper for each pound of the original Bell, which may account for the fact that the new version did not have a pleasant sound. After being teased about the sound, they decided to recast the Bell once more, presumably altering its medal composition once again. It is possible that this was when they may have added some pewter, which would help account for the presence of other elements that have been detected in scientific studies of the current Bell (Hanson, Carlson, Papouchado, and Nielsen, 1976). The Assembly paid Pass and Stow 60 pounds, 13 shillings, and 5 pence for their work (Paige, 1988, 11).

Although the Bell rang successfully for close to 75 years, the recasting might itself have made the new rendition even more vulnerable to the crack that eventually developed (Nash, 2010, 11).

See also: Composition of the Liberty Bell; Crack in the Liberty Bell; Inscription on the Liberty Bell; Whitechapel Foundry

Further Reading

Frazier, Arthur H. 1974. "The Stretch Clock and the Bell at the State House." *Pennsylvania Magazine of History and Biography.* 98 (July): 287–313.

Giannini, Robert L., III. 1997. "A New Way to Look at 'Pass and Stow.' Independence National Historical Park, May 1.

Hanson, Victor F., Janice H. Carlson, Karen M. Papouchado, and Norman A. Nielsen. 1976. "The Liberty Bell: Composition of the Famous Failure." *American Scientist* 64 (November–December): 614–619.

Kramer, Justin. 1975. *Cast in America: The Historically Accurate, Exciting Story of the Liberty Bell.* Los Angeles: Justin Kramer Incorporated.

Lubig, Joseph M. 2011. *Maltese in Michigan.* East Lansing: Michigan State University Press.

Paige, John C. 1988. *The Liberty Bell of Independence National Historical Park: A Special History Study*, ed. by David Kimball. Denver: Denver Service Center and Independence National Historical Park.

Penn, William (see Pennsylvania Charter of Privileges [1701])

Pennsylvania

With the exception of seven trips that the Liberty Bell made outside Pennsylvania from 1885 to 1915, the Liberty Bell has remained within the state from 1952 until the present. Contemporary understanding of the Liberty Bell, particularly in the early years, was largely shaped by this venue, as well as by the city of Philadelphia. Whereas the original embossed copies of the Declaration of Independence and the Constitution are now displayed at the National Archives in Washington, D.C., the Liberty Bell remains in Philadelphia, not far from the building where it originally hung.

Pennsylvania began as a proprietary colony that was formed from a parcel of land (that became today's Pennsylvania and Delaware) that King Charles II of England gave to William Penn in compensation for debts that the king owed to Penn's father, who had been an admiral. Penn, who was a member of the Society of Friends, or Quakers, had suffered persecution for his faith in England and viewed Pennsylvania (meaning "Penn's forest") as a haven for individuals of all faiths who were willing to practice their beliefs peacefully.

Taking its place as the most important of the so-called middle colonies, Pennsylvania served as a good meeting place for colonies as a whole to air their grievances against England because it was fairly well geographically centered. Moreover, Philadelphia, its largest city, was not only the most populous in the colonies, but also the second most populous in the English-speaking world. As the American Revolution approached, colonies like Massachusetts and Virginia were at the vanguard of those that wanted to declare independence, while Pennsylvania played a more reluctant role. This partly resulted from the continuing influence of Quakers, who were generally pacifists and whose patriotism was sometimes questioned for that reason.

Carpenter's Hall in Philadelphia (the city's name means "brotherly love" in Greek) was the site of the First Continental Congress. The Pennsylvania State House (today's Independence Hall) was the site of the Second Continental Congress that proposed the Declaration of Independence and the Articles of Confederation and the Convention of 1787 that proposed the U.S. Constitution. It was also the site of the U.S. Congress from 1790 to 1800, while Washington, D.C. was being built.

William Penn, whose heirs continued to lead the state long after his death, is believed to have brought a bell with him from England to Philadelphia to announce important meetings and events. As the Assembly Speaker, Isaac Norris II and the Pennsylvania Assembly began looking for a bell, the sound of which would be loud enough to summon legislators who were not in its immediate vicinity. They may have intended to commemorate the 50th anniversary, or Jubilee, of Penn's Pennsylvania Charter of Privileges of 1701 as well. This document had both affirmed principles of religious liberty and created the unicameral Pennsylvania Assembly, which continued up to the time of the American Revolution. Given Penn's own religious convictions, and that of the Quakers who followed him, the verse from Leviticus 25:10 was especially appropriate: "Proclaim liberty throughout all the land unto all the inhabitants thereof."

Pennsylvanians were seeking a change in their own government. Some sought to become a royal colony instead of a propriety colony, but the colonies as a whole were seeking their independence from Great Britain. A Whig party called for establishing a more democratic government. To this end, its members boycotted the colonial assembly, creating a provincial constitutional convention and appointing a Council of Safety to govern until the creation of a new government (Doutrich, 1988, 39).

The state appears to have added its assent to the Declaration of Independence only after Robert Morris and John Dickinson either absented themselves on July 4, or else they were present but did not cast their votes within the state's delegation. It is not altogether certain that the Liberty Bell, which was then in a decaying steeple, was rung to announce the Declaration of Independence, but it is known that many bells throughout the city rang on July 8 upon the reading of the document from the State House, and that similar celebrations were held in other towns and cities in Pennsylvania and other states as the Declaration was read there too.

Philadelphia remained a city with divided loyalties during the Revolutionary War. As British general William Howe approached the city that he would occupy through part of 1777 and 1778, Patriots removed the Liberty Bell and other church bells to Allentown, Pennsylvania, so they would not fall into enemy hands and be melted down for bullets or cannon.

In time, the Liberty Bell would become known not simply as a symbol for independence from Great Britain, but also as an antislavery symbol. Quakers were among those who had led the opposition to slavery, and on March 1, 1780, Pennsylvania became the first state to adopt an Act for the Gradual Abolition of Slavery.

When the nation decided in 1787 that the existing government under the Articles of Confederation was inadequate, Pennsylvanians had also decided that the constitution that they had adopted shortly after Congress had declared independence was too democratic. Early ratification of the new U.S. Constitution by Pennsylvania was a sign that the state was itself on the verge of changing its own constitution to reflect the same kind of checks and balances that the new federal system embodied. Among other changes, the new constitution brought it more in line with that of other states by changing the state assembly from a unicameral to a bicameral body, as well as strengthening the hand of the governor.

Philadelphia was the site of the first World's Fair in the United States in 1876, and it has served as a subsequent site for other celebrations of the Declaration of Independence and the U.S. Constitution, including sesquicentennial celebrations in 1926 and 1937. In 1913, the state hosted the Pennsylvania Emancipation Exposition. In 2015, Philadelphia was designated as a World Heritage City. By then, the Liberty Bell had been removed from Independence Hall and taken first to a Liberty Bell Pavilion and then to a Liberty Bell Center, both of which set it in front of large windows that faced Independence Hall.

In recent years, urban renewal has created a parklike area in front of Independence Hall, and a new Constitution Center and a Museum of the American Revolution have been built on sites near the hall. Both the city and state have become increasingly cognizant of the role of the Liberty Bell and other historic sites to draw tourists from throughout the United States and around the world. Presidents and world leaders often come to Philadelphia to see the Liberty Bell and sometimes to give speeches there. Pennsylvania sports teams and businesses often use the Liberty Bell as emblems. Sometimes residents get indignant that tourists come not to visit traditional sites, but to see the city in which the *Rocky* movies were filmed (Mendte, 2013).

See also: Allentown; Centennial Exposition of 1876; Declaration of Independence and the Liberty Bell; Independence Hall; Inscription on the Liberty Bell; Journeys of the Liberty Bell; Liberty Bell Center; Liberty Bell Pavilion; Pennsylvania Emancipation Exposition of 1913; Presidents and Foreign Dignitaries at the Liberty Bell; Quakers; Sesquicentennial International Exposition; Tourism and the Liberty Bell; Year of Jubilee

Further Reading

Doutrich, Paul. 1988. "From Revolution to Constitution: Pennsylvania's Path to Federalism." In *The Constitution and the States: The Role of the Original Thirteen in the Framing and Adoption of the Federal Constitution,* ed. Patrick T. Conley and John P. Kaminski. Madison, WI: Madison House, 37–54.

Mendte, Larry. 2013. "It's Time to Ditch Rocky Philadelphia." *The Philly Post,* July 7. https://www.phillymag.com/news/2013/07/05/time-ditch-rocky-philadelphia.

Mires, Charlene. 2002. *Independence Hall in American Memory.* Philadelphia: University of Pennsylvania Press.

Stille, Charles J. 1889. "Pennsylvania and the Declaration of Independence." *Pennsylvania Magazine of History and Biography* 13 (January): 385–429.

Tiedemann, Joseph S. 2010. "A Tumultuous People: The Rage for Liberty and the Ambiance of Violence in the Middle Colonies in the Years Preceding the American Revolution." *Pennsylvania History: A Journal of Mid-Atlantic Studies* 77 (Autumn): 387–431.

Vile, John R. 2019. *The Declaration of Independence: America's First Founding Document in U.S. History and Culture.* Santa Barbara, CA: ABC-CLIO.

Vile, John R. 2016. *The Constitutional Convention of 1787: A Comprehensive Encyclopedia of America's Founding,* rev. 2nd ed., 2 vols. Clark, NJ: Talbot Publishing.

Pennsylvania Charter of Privileges (1701)

Scholars continue to disagree as to whether the Liberty Bell was intended to mark a 50th anniversary, which would correspond to a biblical Jubilee Year, as outlined in the verses that surround Leviticus 25:10, inscribed on the Bell. However, there is a clear consensus that, if the leaders of the Pennsylvania Assembly intended to mark such a jubilee, the event they would have been celebrating was the Pennsylvania Charter of Privileges, which William Penn (1644–1718) gave to the colony in 1701.

Penn was a Quaker who came to the American colonies largely to escape religious persecution and establish a refuge for other dissenters (see Peck 1992, 85–87, for an account of his trial for preaching in England). Serving as a proprietor for lands that the British king had given him, Penn undoubtedly sought to encourage immigration to his "holy experiment" by drafting a frame of government that would make his protections for individual liberties explicit. The result was that Pennsylvania became "the most religiously diverse colony, along with New York" (Green, 2015, 42). The first charter, of Frame of Government, which Penn drafted in 1682–1683, may be best known not only for providing for such liberties, but also for recognizing that future exigencies would call for some alterations. It thus permitted amendments with the consent of the governor and six-sevenths of the assembly, while guaranteeing that such revisions would not impinge on civil liberties (Vile, 2015, vol. II, 347).

The charter that Penn issued on October 28, 1701, likely would give an indication of the kinds of liberty that Isaac Norris II would have thought he was celebrating by inscribing the biblical admonition, "Proclaim liberty throughout all the land to all the inhabitants thereof." The very first section contains the following words (Penn, 1701):

> BECAUSE no People can be truly happy, though under the greatest Enjoyment of Civil Liberties, if abridged of the Freedom of their Consciences, as to their Religious Profession and Worship: And Almighty God being the only Lord of Conscience, Father of Lights and Spirits; and the Author as well as Object of all divine Knowledge, Faith and Worship, who only doth enlighten the Minds, and persuade and convince the Understandings of People, I do hereby grant and declare, That no Person or Persons, inhabiting this Province or Territories, who shall confess and acknowledge One almighty God, the Creator, Upholder and Ruler of the World; and profess him or themselves obliges to live quietly under the Civil Government, shall be in any Case molested or prejudiced, in his or their Person or Estate, because of his or their conscientious Persuasion or Practice, nor be compelled to frequent or maintain any religious Worship, Place or Ministry, contrary to his or their Mind, or to do or suffer any other Act or thing, contrary to their religious Persuasion.

This document also delineated the creation of a legislative assembly, which would become one of the most powerful in the colonies.

Section 5 of the charter allowed criminal defendants to have the same privilege "of Witnesses and Council as the Prosecutors," and Section 6 guaranteed that all would have access to the "ordinary Course of Justice."

Section 8 showed respect for private property by providing that lands would not be forfeited if their owner committed suicide. This final section further reiterated that: "because the Happiness of Mankind depends so much upon the Enjoying of Liberty of their Consciences as aforesaid, I do hereby solemnly declare, promise and grant, for me, my Heirs and Assigns, That the First Article of the Charter relating to Liberty of Conscience, and every part and Clause therein, according to the true Intent and Meaning thereof, shall be kept and remain, without any Alteration, inviolably for ever" (Penn, 1701).

Thomas Jefferson and James Madison were among the American statesmen who later worked to secure freedom of conscience, as well as other First Amendment rights like freedom of speech, press, peaceable assembly, and petition, at both the state and national levels in the United States.

See also: Leviticus 25:10; Liberty, Meaning of; Norris, Isaac, II; Pennsylvania; Quakers; Year of Jubilee

Further Reading
Green, Steven K. 2015. *Investing a Christian America: The Myth of the Religious Founding.* New York: Oxford University Press.

Peck, Robert S. 1992. *The Bill of Rights and the Politics of Interpretation.* St. Paul, MN: West Publishing Company.

Penn, William. 1701. "Pennsylvania Charter of Privileges." UShistory.org. http:www.ushistory.org/documents/charter.htm.

Vile, John R. 2015. *Encyclopedia of Constitutional Amendments, Proposed Amendments, and Amending Issues, 1789–2015,* 4th ed., 2 vols. Santa Barbara, CA: ABC-CLIO.

Pennsylvania Emancipation Exposition of 1913

Among the events that Americans would commemorate similar to the biblical Year of Jubilee, in which debts would be forgiven and slaves would be freed, none probably come closer than the 50-year celebrations of the Emancipation Proclamation that Abraham Lincoln issued in 1863.

In 1913, leading African Americans sought to mark the 50th anniversary of the Emancipation Proclamation by holding celebrations in New York and Philadelphia. The event in Philadelphia, to which the state contributed $95,000, began on September 13 and lasted for three weeks. It was held on the south side of the city in what then was known as the "City Plaza" (later named "Marconi Plaza"), which had stronger ties to the Italian-American community than to African Americans (Mires, 2004, 265).

The buildings that were constructed were temporary, so they did not leave a permanent mark. Charlene Mires notes, however, that a replica of the Liberty Bell was created for the occasion, thus serving to reunite the Bell "with the idea of emancipation recalling its use as a symbol by abolitionists of the 1830s and 1840s" (Mires, 2004, 276). She further notes that this was important "because the antislavery symbolism of the Liberty Bell had fallen from public memory during the later nineteenth century, when the bell was consistently celebrated as a survival of the American Revolution" (Mires, 2004, 276).

The sesquicentennial celebrations of independence that were held at the same plaza in Philadelphia in 1926 further highlighted the Liberty Bell, with a massive, 80-foot Luminous Liberty Bell, with 26,000 electric lights. In 1937, the year of the sesquicentennial of the U.S. Constitution, a small plaque was erected on the square commemorating American adherence to the rule of law (Mires, 2004, 276).

Major Richard R. Wright began laying wreaths at the Liberty Bell on February 1 of each year to commemorate President Lincoln's signing of the congressional joint resolution proposing the Fifteenth Amendment. In time, his efforts led to the establishment of National Freedom Day, but that has been somewhat eclipsed by Martin Luther King, Jr., Day.

See also: Abolitionists and the Liberty Bell; Luminous Liberty Bell; National Freedom Day; Sesquicentennial International Exposition; Year of Jubilee

Further Reading
Mires, Charlene. 2004. "Race, Place, and the Pennsylvania Exposition of 1913." *Pennsylvania Magazine of History and Biography* 128 (July): 257–278.

Phil Tovrea's Liberty Bell Replica

One indication of the appeal of the Liberty Bell is that private individuals remain interested in purchasing replicas. A Phoenix cattle baron named Phil Tovrea purchased one such replica in 1950. He was visiting France in May 1950 when the Paccard Bell foundry of Annecy was casting replicas that the U.S. Treasury Department had commissioned to give to U.S. states and territories that were participating in a bond drive.

Tovrea made friends with Alfred Paccard of the foundry and decided to order a bell for himself to display in front of the Tovrea Land and Cattle Company administrative offices in Phoenix, which was near the Stockyards restaurant. The bell had the original lettering, but not the distinctive crack of the Liberty Bell.

In time, the company and restaurant fell on hard times, and the Bell disappeared. In 2004, the Jokake Company purchased the property and renovated the Stockyards Restaurant. During the restoration, company owners happily found that the bell had simply been covered by brush, and they reinstalled it on a new mount, which is now on display (Campbell 2017).

See also: State Liberty Bell Replicas

Further Reading

Campbell, Tom. 2017. "Phil Tovrea's Liberty Bell Replica: Phoenix Arizona." Tom Loves the Liberty Bell.com, November 30. http://tomlovestheliberty bell.com/2017/11/30/phil-tovreas-liberty-bell-replica-phoenix-arizona.

Philippine Liberty Bell

One of the legacies that Americans have left in the Philippines, which the Spanish ceded to the United States after the Spanish during the Spanish-American War, and to which they finally granted independence on July 4, 1946 (it had previously given the colony commonwealth status in 1935), was a replica of the Liberty Bell. Americans gave the bell to the provincial government of Albay on April 1, 1945. Not long after the U.S. entry into World War II, the Japanese drove American forces from the islands, and General Douglas MacArthur had famously vowed to return.

The bell that Americans gave to the Philippines was inscribed as follows (Legazpi City Albay, April 1, 2017):

> To the People of Albay
> We present this
> Symbol of your Liberation
> April 1, 1945
> Individually or collectively
> If oppression ever knocks at your door.
> Feel free to ring this bell.

Originally placed under a dome in Penaranda Park, the bell is now displayed at the Legazpi City Museum.

For many years, controversy has centered on another set of bells that U.S. soldiers took from the Catholic Church in Balangiga, which apparently were used by insurgents to signal a surprise attack on September 28, 1901, that resulted in the deaths of 48 soldiers. The bells, which were long kept at an air force base in Cheyenne, Wyoming, and on a U.S. base in South Korea, were a continuing source of U.S.-Filipino friction. The Pentagon announced plans to return the bells in August 2018, after Congress lifted a ban on their return (Browne, 2018). The bells were returned on December 11, 2018 (Gutierrez, 2018).

See also: Global Significance of the Liberty Bell

Further Reading

Browne, Ryan. 2018. "Pentagon to Return Bells Captured in the Philippines over 100 Years Ago." *CNN Politics,* August 14. https://www.cnn.com/2018/08/14/politics/pentagon-philippines-balangiga-bells/index.html.

Gutierrez, Jason. 2018. "U.S. Returns Bells Taken as War Booty from Philippines in 1901." *The New York Times,* December 11. https://www.nytimes.com/2018/12/11/world/asia/balangiga-bells-united-states-philippines.html.

"Legazpi City Albay." 2017. Facebook, April 1. https://www.facebook.com/510888042351492/posts/the-72-year-old-liberty-bell-the-gift-given-by-the-americans-to-the-people-of-al/1301442873296001.

Photographing the Liberty Bell

The Liberty Bell has become such an iconic image that it can be symbolized by almost any bell-shaped object with a crack in it (Callahan, 1999). Yet beginning sometime in the 1920s, custodian Harry Baxter began prohibiting anyone from taking a picture of the Liberty Bell without his permission. In justification, he observed that he was "getting tired of seeing pictures of chorus girls, chewing-gum promoters and the like standing beside the bell" (Quoted from an undated press clipping by Paige, 1988, 57).

Although Baxter undoubtedly hoped to enhance the dignity of the Liberty Bell, the action appeared highly arbitrary, especially since there was no law prohibiting such pictures. Moreover, he apparently routinely granted permits to commercial photographers to take such pictures. Seeking to test this constitutionality of this practice, Joseph Shallit, a reporter for the *Philadelphia Record*, decided on July 3, 1942, to attempt to take a photograph with a Brownie camera, only to be arrested and carried off to jail. In an engaging story, he recounted that he lived only three blocks away from Independence Hall, often visited, and frequently witnessed the disappointment of visitors who were prohibited from taking pictures.

When he got his camera out, a guard pointed to a sign that said "No Photographing Allowed Inside of Building" (Shallit, 1942, 1). When he protested, "There's no law against it," the chief of the Bureau of City Property responded, "We make the laws here." After his arrest, Shallit was also asked "Are you a Communist?" which seemed a bit ironic given that the nation was at the time allied with Russia against Nazi Germany, but that reflected the heighted fear of terrorism that the war raised (Shallit, 1942). He pointed out that if someone had nefarious designs on the Bell, there was no prohibition on photographing the outside of the building, which would be a more likely target.

Shallit was arrested, despite the fact that he brought with him Edgar Scott, the president of the Philadelphia Stock Exchange, and Norman J. Griffin, a U.S. commissioner and former president of the Catholic Historical Society, but he received widespread support. He was found innocent of breaching the peace, but the guards continued to require permits until late in the decade (Paige, 1988, 57).

Absent any evidence that such photographs inflicted any damage to the Liberty Bell, such regulations would almost surely be considered to be violations of First Amendment rights of speech, press, and expression.

See also: Advertising and the Liberty Bell; Pennsylvania; Security for the Liberty Bell

Further Reading

Callahan, Robey. 1999. "The Liberty Bell: From Commodity to Sacred Object." *Journal of Material Culture* 4 (1): 57–78.

Shallit, Joseph. 1942. "Reporter Taking Snapshot of Liberty Bell Arrested; You Can Buy One for 5c." *Philadelphia Record*, July 4, 1.

Pierpont, John

One of the poems published in the *Liberty Bell Gift Books* was a poem that John Pierpont (1785–1866), a Unitarian minister, published in 1842. He was also a Unitarian minister.

It is unclear whether the first stanza refers to the fact that it has been a year since the last issue of the *Liberty Bell Gift Books,* or whether it refers to another contemporary event (one possibility might have been the repeal of the gag rule in Congress, but that did not occur until two years later). It goes as follows (Pierpont, 1842, 1):

> THE LIBERTY BELL—the Liberty Bell—
> The Tocsin of Freedom and Slavery's knell
> That a whole long year has idle hung
> Again is wagging its clamorous tongue!
>   As it merrily swings,
>   Its notes it flings.

A tocsin is an alarm bell, while a knell is a ring of death. The bell is thus ringing in anticipation of the death of slavery.

Just as the Liberty Bell was thought to have sounded for the Declaration of Independence and was also used as a symbol of slave emancipation, the second stanza says that the bells resound "[o]n the dreamy ears of planters and kings," and tells of "manacles [chains] broken." Pierpont tied such freedom to the proclamations by "prophets of Freedom" and to the "tongues of flame," which descended on the early disciples at Pentecost (1842, 2).

The next verse imagines the sounds of the bell being carried "on the wings of the North-East wind" to "the Western Ind [ies]" (Pierpont, 1842, 3). As the poem proceeds, Pierpont imagines the work of emancipation beginning in "the North" and in "New England's hills" and then continuing to "the beauty of Southern plains" (1842, 3).

While slaveholders continue to gloat over the "helpless bond-slave's bust," the year of Jubilee will come because "Jehovah is just" (Pierpont, 1842, 4). The last lines suggest, however, that abolitionists can help in this divine work:

> Of the friends of the bondman urge it along.
>   Let the same chime fall
>   On the ears of all,

Who tread on the neck of the negro thrall,
   Till they start from the ground,
   As they will at the sound
When the trumpets of angels are pealing around.
   And the murdered slave
   Comes forth from his grave,
And smiles at the flash of th' Avenger's glaive [sword],
   And the world shall accord
   In the righteous award
To both tyrant and slave, in that day of the
   Lord.

Although it omits the image of grapes being squeezed, the imagery of this song is otherwise suggestive of some of the imagery that will later appear in Julia Ward Howe's "The Battle Hymn of the Republic," which was used to rally troops during the Civil War.

See also: Abolitionists and the Liberty Bell; *Liberty Bell Gift Books*; Year of Jubilee

Further Reading
Pierpont, John. 1842. "The Liberty Bell." Friends of Freedom, *The Liberty Bell*. Boston: Massachusetts Anti-Slavery Fair.

Political and Social Movements and the Liberty Bell

Just as a variety of movements have sought to identify themselves with the U.S. flag, many have sought to link their causes to the symbolism of the Liberty Bell.

Given that the Bell is generally believed to have marked the 50th anniversary of the Pennsylvania Charter of Privileges that William Penn had granted to Pennsylvania in 1751, it is logical to associate the Bell both with the religious liberty that this Charter guaranteed and with representative government, which it sanctioned.

The concept with which the Liberty Bell is probably most closely associated is American independence. Whether or not the Bell itself was rung when John Nixon read the Declaration of Independence from a platform outside the State House on July 8, it is known that other bells did ring in the city to call the people to witness this event. Such bells subsequently became a regular part of Independence Day celebrations. The fact that Patriots removed the Bell from Philadelphia during British occupation was another sign that it was clearly aligned in the public mind with their cause, although any bells might have been melted down into bullets or cannon.

Often known in the early years as the "Old Bell," the "State House Bell," or the "Independence Bell," the movement that appears most responsible for the Bell's current designation was the abolitionist movement. Its yearly *Liberty Bell Gift Books* used a liberty bell (scholars still debate whether they actually intended to represent *the* Liberty Bell) to symbolize their cause, sometimes with pictures of broken chains below it. The cause of abolitionism seemed to tie logically to the biblical

Year of Jubilee, the 50th year when slaves would be freed and debts would be forgiven.

Perhaps in part because of the perceived effectiveness of this campaign that eventually led to the adoption of the Thirteenth Amendment, which abolished involuntary servitude in 1865, advocates of women's suffrage, who met at Seneca Falls, New York, in 1848 and rewrote the Declaration of Independence to include equal rights for women, also evoked the Liberty Bell. They eventually made a replica, with its clapper disabled, which they drove around Pennsylvania calling not simply for liberty, but also justice for all. This movement ultimately succeeded with the adoption of the Nineteenth Amendment in 1920.

Faced with a potential demonstration by the Industrial Workers of the World, in 1913, Philadelphia passed an ordinance banning all gatherings at Independence Square other than "patriotic meetings to celebrate some event in the history of the Nation, State, or City" (Mires 1999, 50). However, when the city tried to use the ordinance in 1947 to prohibit Joseph Myerson of the Progressive Citizens of America from protesting, a federal judge declared the action unconstitutional, as did a judge a month later when reacting to a demonstration against military conscription (Mires, 1999, 50). The city subsequently tried to evade these rulings by limiting demonstrations to certain specific days, most of which were tied either to patriotic or ethnic holidays (Mires, 1999, 55–56). When the National Park Service assumed control of the park in 1951, it attempted to honor the First Amendment rights of protestors.

It was logical to associate the symbol of abolitionism with further movements for equal rights for African Americans. Beginning in 1942, Major Richard R. Wright began laying wreaths at the Liberty Bell to secure recognition of February 1—the day that President Abraham Lincoln signed the congressional joint resolution proposing the Thirteenth Amendment—as National Freedom Day. Although this specific objective was accomplished in 1948, the Liberty Bell continued to be the site for demonstrations by students and others who pushed for more substantive civil rights legislation. One such sit-in by students from the University of Pennsylvania took place on March 12, 1965. The writer of a letter to local newspapers was quite unhappy, observing, "If our cradle of liberty is to be periodically used as a flophouse to further the cause of liberty, please close it. Too many men have bled and died in forthright demonstrations of defense of freedom, and this defense did not include the license of disobedient juveniles to make their own rules" (Mires, 1999, 60).

It doesn't exactly qualify as a social protest, but in the 1950s, the Mental Health Association, which had long worked against the practice of shackling mentally ill patients with chains, made a statement by calling upon asylums to donate such shackles. The McShane Bell Foundry of Baltimore subsequently melted these into a 300-pound bell, typically called the Mental Health Bell, on April 13, 1953. The bell reads, "Cast from shackles which bound them, this bell shall ring out hope for the mentally ill and victory over mental illness" ("The Mental Health Bell," n.d.). This symbolism was reminiscent of that used by abolitionists in fighting slavery in the early nineteenth century.

A picture from 1966 shows advocates of gay rights participating in one of the "Annual Reminder Day Pickets" outside Independence Hall (Sands and Bartlett, 2012, 112). Apparently, they were met with incredulity. A columnist from the *Philadelphia Inquirer*, reporting on a gay rights demonstration in 1967, observed that after visitors look at the signs (Mires 1999, 61):

> They look like they can't believe what they are reading. They inch across the street. Yep, that's what those signs say, all right. The bolder ones stand around and stare. And you can hear the mumbling. "Are those people all . . . I mean, they look okay . . . do you think they are really . . . that is, both the men and women too?" A couple of the marchers walk through the crowd giving out mimeographed handbills explaining the protest. The handbills are accepted . . . but not with anything resembling a friendly smile.

In 1970, thousands of people, including consumer advocate Ralph Nader, showed up to Independence Hall for Earth Day and signed a "Declaration of Interdependence" (Gardella, 2014, 74).

A picture taken in 1971 shows two protestors carrying a replica of the Liberty Bell in front on Independence Hall during an antiwar rally on December 19, 1971 (Sands and Bartlett, 2012, 111). The year 1966 witnessed both pro–Vietnam War and anti–Vietnam War protestors outside Independence Hall, where the Bell was then housed (Mires, 2002, 252).

A picture from 1970 shows labor activist Cesar Chavez, with labor official George Meany, holding a grape box beside one of the Whitechapel replicas of the Liberty Bell (probably the one in California), which they chained until the strike by grape workers ended that July (Boland, 1973, 112). In 1999, demonstrators supporting Mumia Abu Jamal, who had been convicted of murdering a police officer in Philadelphia, occupied the building (Gardella, 2014, 74). In 2001, the Liberty Bell was the site of one of many vigils by "Women-and-Men-in-Black," who protested the continuing Israeli occupation of the West Bank, Gaza, and East Jerusalem ("Liberty Bell Vigil of Women & Men in Black," 2001).

As the Independence National Historical Park began plans for the current pavilion for the Liberty Bell in the early 2000s, the site itself became not simply the location, but the catalyst for demonstrations by those who pointed out that the entrance was close to the site of the house where George Washington and his family had stayed while he was president, and where he had kept some of his own slaves. Protests against ignoring this ironic juxtaposition eventually resulted in exhibits that pointed to this incongruity (Olgine, 2004).

In *United States v. Marcavage* (2010), the U.S. Supreme Court decided that the sidewalk outside the entrance to the Liberty Bell Center was a traditional public forum, and that authorities could not treat antiabortion protestors differently than those advocating other causes. In recent years, demonstrators have gathered in front of the Liberty Bell to smoke joints as part of the Smokedown Prohibition event (Lipp, 2013).

On February 20, 2018, a group of 11 undocumented youths and supporters held a vigil at the Liberty Bell as part of a 15-day walk from New York City to Washington, D.C., to show their support for the DREAM Act, which was designed to provide security against deportation for individuals who were brought to the United States in their youth as undocumented aliens (Cosecha, 2018).

See also: Abolitionists and the Liberty Bell; Justice Bell; *Liberty Bell Gift Books*; National Freedom Day; Reminder Marches; *United States v. Marcavage* (2010)

Further Reading

Boland, Charles Michael. 1973. *Ring in the Jubilee: The Epic of America's Liberty Bell.* Riverside, CT: Chatham Press.

Cosecha. 2018. "Immigrant Youth Walking for DACA Rally at Philadelphia Liberty Bell." Popular Resistance.org, February 20. https://popularresistance.org/immigrant-youth -walking-for-daca-rally-at-philadelphia-liberty-bell.

Gardella, Peter. 2014. *American Civil Religion: What Americans Hold Sacred.* New York: Oxford University Press.

"Liberty Bell Vigil of Women & Men in Black." 2001. The Shalom Center, September 8. https://theshalomcenter.org/content/liberty-bell-vigil-women-men-black.

Lipp, Kenneth. 2013. "Watch About 200 People Smoke a Joint at the Liberty Bell." *The Philly Declaration,* March 17. https://phillydeclaration.org/2013/03/17/watch-about -200-people-smoke-a-joint-at-the-liberty-bell.

"The Mental Health Bell." n.d. Mental Health America. http://www.mentalhealthamerica .net/bell.

Mires, Charlene. 2002. *Independence Hall in American Memory.* Philadelphia: University of Pennsylvania Press.

Mires, Charlene. 1999. "In the Shadow of Independence Hall: Vernacular Activities and the Meanings of Historic Places." *The Public Historian* 21 (Spring): 49–64.

Ogline, Jill. 2004. "'Creating Dissonance for the Visitor': The Heart of the Liberty Bell Controversy." *The Public Historian* 26 (Summer): 49–57.

Sands, Robert W., Jr., and Alexander B. Bartlett. 2002. *Images of America: Independence Hall and the Liberty Bell.* Charleston, SC: Arcadia Publishing.

Presidents and Foreign Dignitaries at the Liberty Bell

Philadelphia was the home of the First and Second Continental Congresses, and Independence Hall was the site of the writing of the Declaration of Independence, the Articles of Confederation, and the U.S. Constitution. Philadelphia served as the capital under presidents George Washington and John Adams, whose quarters, which have since been demolished, were literally feet away from the current Liberty Bell Center. As the birthplace of the nation, Philadelphia has hosted many presidential visits, especially on Independence Day, and almost all the modern presidents have been photographed by the Liberty Bell. Those who have spoken in or near Independence Hall, however, typically concentrate more on explicating the Declaration of Independence than on musings on the Bell. Independence Hall and the Liberty Bell have also been visited by many foreign dignitaries.

After both the Pennsylvania Assembly and the U.S. Congress moved out of Independence Hall, it was sometimes used as a levee room, or reception area, for important visitors to the city. Thus, in 1833, U.S. president Andrew Jackson and Henry Clay were both given use of the Hall for that purpose. Later visitors included presidents Martin Van Buren, William Henry Harrison (during his brief, one-month tenure), John Tyler, James K, Polk, Millard Fillmore, Franklin Pierce, and James Buchanan (Riley, 1953, 35).

As he headed toward his first presidential inauguration, Abraham Lincoln visited Independence Hall, where he raised an American flag and referenced the Declaration of Independence. He said that its principles had been the source of his own political ideals. He would later lie in state at Independence Hall, as John Quincy Adams, Henry Clay, and Arctic explorer Kent Kane had done before him (Riley, 1953, 37–38). U.S. president Ulysses S. Grant appeared with Brazilian emperor Don Pedro II during the Centennial Exposition in Philadelphia in 1876.

Former Confederate president Jefferson Davis greeted the Liberty Bell on its journey to New Orleans in 1885 for the World's Industrial and Cotton Exposition. As the Bell came through Biloxi, Mississippi, he chose to

An image of the Liberty Bell (center) is surrounded by portraits of twenty-four U.S. Presidents. (Library of Congress)

emphasize its association with the American Revolution rather than the cause of emancipation, which he opposed. He thus observed: "Yon sacred organ that gave voice to the proudest declaration that a handful of men ever made when they faced the greatest military power on the globe; when a handful of men declared to all the world their inalienable right, and staked life, liberty and property in defense of their declaration. It was with your clear tones you sent notice to all who were willing to live or die for liberty and felt that the day was at hand when every patriot must do a patriot's duty" (Liberty Bell: Journey to New Orleans, *Daily Picayune,* 1885). President Grover Cleveland gave the opening address at the World's Columbian Exposition in Chicago in 1893, where the Liberty Bell appeared. President Woodrow Wilson delivered a speech on Independence Day in 1914 at Independence Hall, but he focused on the meaning of the Declaration of Independence rather than the Liberty Bell.

In 1918, Thomas G. Masaryk, president of the Democratic Mid-European Union, who was from Czechoslovakia, signed his nation's Declaration of Independence at Independence Hall. Afterward, children rang a replica of the Liberty Bell, which was subsequently transported to Masaryk's home country.

Calvin Coolidge, the only U.S. president ever to be born on July 4, gave his speech on July 5, 1926, the year of the nation's sesquicentennial celebrations of independence. Like Wilson, he concentrated on the Declaration of Independence (Coolidge, 1926). He observed

> that people at home and abroad consider Independence Hall as hallowed ground and revere the Liberty Bell as a sacred relic. That pile of bricks and mortar, that mass of metal, might appear to the uninstructed as only the outgrown meeting place and the shattered bell of a former time, useless now because of more modern conveniences, but to those who know they have become consecrated by the use which men have made of them. They have long been identified with a great cause. They are the framework of a spiritual event. The world looks upon them, because of their associations of one hundred and fifty years ago, as it looks upon the Holy Land because of what took place there nineteen hundred years ago. Through use for a righteous purpose they have become sanctified.

That same year, Queen Marie of Romania also attended the sesquicentennial celebrations. Ken Finkel (2016) observed that when Herbert Hoover visited Philadelphia during his 1932 presidential campaign, he reportedly praised "William Penn, the Liberty Bell, and 'the greatness of this city and of this Commonwealth'— anything to avoid acknowledging the fact that the Great Depression had left at least one in four Philadelphians unemployed."

Although President John F. Kennedy spoke at Independence Hall on July 4, 1962, he also focused on the Declaration of Independence rather than the Liberty Bell. In 1962, Mexican president Adolfo Lopez Mateos presented Kennedy with an 11 ¾-inch replica of the Liberty Bell of Mexico; the original hangs above the entrance to the National Palace and is rung every September 16 to commemorate Mexican independence from Spain ("Replica of the Liberty Bell of Mexico," n.d.). Ethiopia's emperor, Haile Selassie, visited the Bell in 1963, as did Jordan's King Hussein the following year (Horning, 2010). President Lyndon Johnson visited the Liberty Bell soon after giving a speech on the challenge of civil rights, while President Richard Nixon used Independence Hall as the backdrop for signing the Revenue Sharing Act of 1972 (Sands and Bartlett, 2012, 122).

Gary Nash observes that numerous foreign leaders visited the Liberty Bell when it was viewed as "an international symbol of anti-Communism" (2010, 162). Visitors included the mayor of West Berlin, the premier of Iran, Israel's prime minister David Ben-Gurion and ambassador Abba Eban, Nelson Mandela of South Africa, and many others (Nash, 2010, 162–163).

The bicentennial of the nation's independence brought none other than Queen Elizabeth II to Independence Hall. In a speech, the queen observed, "This morning I saw the famous Liberty Bell. It came here over 200 years ago when Philadelphia, after London, was the largest English-speaking city in the world. It was cast to commemorate the Pennsylvania Charter of Privileges, but is better known for its association with the Declaration of Independence" ("The Queen's Speech," 2015). She later stated, "You know this is one of the finest symbols of any country in the world. Everyone knows about the Liberty Bell" (Sands and Bartlett, 2012, 125). Months earlier, King Carl XVI Gustaf of Sweden visited the Bell as well (Horning, 2010).

In his own remarks on July 4, 1976, President Gerald R. Ford observed that he was speaking in front of "the great bronze bell that joyously rang out the news of the birth of our Nation from the steeple of the State House" (Ford, 1976). Citing the Bible verse that was inscribed on the Bell, Ford said that America's founding fathers "boldly reversed the age-old political theory that kings derive their powers from God and asserted that both powers and unalienable rights belong to the people as direct endowments from their Creator" (Ford, 1976). Later that month, West German chancellor Helmut Schmidt visited the Liberty Bell and tapped it with his knuckles (Sands and Bartlett, 2012, 126).

Poland's Lech Walesa, who had led the opposition to communist rule in his home country, visited Independence Hall on July 4, 1989, when he was awarded the Liberty Medal. The Dalai Lama visited the next year (Morgan, 1990). Giving the sign of peace at the Bell, he said, "I believe this is a reminder to American people—who enjoy so much freedom in this country—that in other parts of the world . . . there is no freedom. You cannot be truly free if not everybody is free" (Sands and Bartlett, 2012, 118). The Bell has also been visited by numerous icons of civil rights, including Martin Luther King, Jr. and Rosa Parks, as well as by movie stars and other celebrities.

The Ronald Reagan Presidential Library and Museum features a replica of the Liberty Bell, complete with its signature crack. In November 1990, President George H. W. Bush visited Prague (the first U.S. president to do so) and rang the Czech Liberty Bell. When President Bill Clinton was inaugurated in 1992, he asked Americans to bring "bells of hope" on January 17, the first of five days of celebration tied to the event. Encouraging people throughout the nation to ring bells of any kind, after visiting Thomas Jefferson's Monticello, Clinton took a bus to Washington, D.C., where he led a procession across the George Washington Bridge to ring one of the replicas of the Liberty Bell that was made during the bicentennial (Eaton, 1992). On July 4, 1993, Clinton visited the Bell, after which he awarded the Liberty Medal to former political foes Nelson Mandela and Frederik W. de Klerk of South Africa for their part in bringing about racial reconciliation in their nation (Broder, 1993).

Speaking at the Independence Day celebration in Philadelphia on July 4, 2001, President George W. Bush observed that "to see the Liberty Bell is a moving experience. In America, we set aside certain places and treasures like this to protect them from the passing of the years. We grant them special care to mark a moment in time" (Bush, 2001). Repeating the idea that "[t]he Liberty Bell was originally cast to mark the 50th anniversary of William Penn's Charter of Privileges," Bush associated this with "the first guarantee of religious freedom in this Commonwealth" (Bush, 2001). He observed that "the Founders would be pleased to see that we have respected this right of the people and the limitation of the Government. They knew what dangers can follow when Government either dictates or frustrates the exercise of religion" (Bush, 2001).

In 2002, in a published letter to designate the 250th anniversary of the Liberty Bell, the future U.S. president Donald J. Trump associated the Liberty Bell with "freedom," especially "the liberty to think big." He also associated it with "free enterprise," explaining that "America has flourished because we have been allowed to flourish. We have the ability and conditions required for success, and we've had the faith to persevere and the tenacity to keep moving forward. There is nothing this country and her citizens cannot attain" ("Portrait of Freedom," 2002, 21).

Philadelphia has been the site of numerous national nominating conventions. In 2015, Pope Francis visited the Liberty Bell and delivered a speech on religious freedom that acknowledged the contributions of William Penn ("For Pope Francis, It's Imperative: Religious Liberty Is a Gift from God. Defend It," 2015). The Liberty Bell was incorporated into the logo of the World Meeting of Families that the Pope attended while in Philadelphia (Stoddard, 2015). The image of the Liberty Bell was also incorporated onto the reverse of a 1-ounce silver coin issued to commemorate the occasion.

Some visits to the Liberty Bell have been controversial. In 2013, after Mariela Castro, the daughter of President Raul Castro of Cuba and a noted sexologist, visited the Liberty Bell, U.S. representative Ileana Ros-Lehtinen of Florida commented, "It's insulting that the Cuban dictator's daughter and standard-bearer of the Castro dictatorship would visit a symbol of America's successful struggle for freedom from its colonial masters" (Robles, 2013). Malcolm Lazin, the executive director of the Equality Forum, which was honoring Castro for her advocacy of gay rights, responded, "The Liberty Bell is a symbol of freedom not only for America, but a symbol around the globe" (Robles, 2013). Ironically, in 1987, Cuba's Hector Morales had stowed away on a ship, jumped off with a life ring, which he lost, and was saved by swimming to a lighted bell buoy, the ringing of which drove him to distraction before he was rescued (Liberty Bell: Journey to New Orleans, *The Orlando Sentinel*, 1987).

See also: Bicentennial Bell; Czech Liberty Bell; Declaration of Independence and the Liberty Bell; Global Significance of the Liberty Bell; Mexican Liberty Bell

Further Reading

Broder, John M. 1993. "Clinton Honors S. Africa Ex-Foes at Liberty Bell." *Los Angeles Times,* July 5. http://articles.latimes.com/1993-07-05/news/mn-10250_1_south -africa.

Bush, George W. 2001. "Remarks at an Independence Day Celebration in Philadelphia." The American Presidency Project, July 4. http://www.presidency.ucsb.edu/ws/?pid =73536.

Coolidge, Calvin. 1926. "Speech on the 150th Anniversary of the Declaration of Independence." Teaching AmericanHistory.org, July 5. http://teachingamericanhistory .org/library/document/speech-on-the-occasion-of-the-one-hundred-and-fiftieth -anniversary-of-the-declaration-of-independence.

"Cuban Stowaway Clings To His Own Liberty Bell." 1987. KNT News Service, January 9. http://articles.orlandosentinel.com/1987-01-09/news/0100100009_1_hector -morales-clang-cuba.

Eaton, William J. 1992. "Clinton Asks Americans to Ring in His Inaugural." *Los Angeles Times,* December 19. http://articles.latimes.com/1992-12-19/news/mn-2132_1 _inaugural-event.

Finkel, Ken. 2016. "Philadelphia Politics and the Presidential Campaign of 1932." Phillyhistory.org, October 10. https://www.phillyhistory.org/blog/index.php/2016/10 /philadelphia-politics-and-the-presidential-campaign-of-1932.

"For Pope Francis, It's Imperative: Religious Liberty Is a Gift from God. Defend It." 2015. Catholic News Agency, September 26. https://www.catholicnewsagency.com/news /for-pope-francis-its-imperative-religious-liberty-is-a-gift-from-god-defend-it -39467.

Ford, Gerald R. 1976. "Remarks of Gerald R. Ford in Philadelphia, Pennsylvania (Bicentennial Celebration)," July 4. Gerald R. Ford Presidential Library and Museum. https://www.fordlibrarymuseum.gov/library/speeches/760645.asp.

Horning, Timothy. 2010. "Touching Liberty (Literally)." *Discoveries from the City Archives,* August 23. https://www.phillyhistory.org/blog/index.php/2010/08/touching-liberty -literally.

"Liberty Bell: Journey to New Orleans." *Independence Hall in American Memory* [Contains reports from major newspapers of the day]. http://www.independencehall -americanmemory.com/the-liberty-bell/liberty-bell-journey-to-new-orleans.

Morgan, Sue. 1990. "Dalai Lama Visits Liberty Bell." UPI, September 22. https://www .upi.com/Archives/1990/09/22/Dalai-lama-visits-Liberty-Bell/7587653976000.

Nash, Gary B. 2010. *The Liberty Bell.* New Haven, CT: Yale University Press.

"The Queen's Speech." 2012. *Men in Blazers*, June 13. https://meninblazers.com/2012/06 /13/queen-elizabeth-bicentennial.

"Replica of the Liberty Bell of Mexico." n.d. John F. Kennedy Presidential Library and Museum. https://www.jfklibrary.org/asset-viewer/archives/JFKSG/JFKSG-MO -1963-1179/JFKSG-MO-1963-1179.

Riley, Edward M. 1953. "The Independence Hall Group." *Transactions of the American Philosophical Society* 43 (1953): 7–42.

Robles, Frances. 2013. "A Daughter of the Cuban Revolution Visits the Liberty Bell." *The New York Times,* May 3. https://thelede.blogs.nytimes.com/2013/05/03/liberty-bell -visit-by-fidel-castrtos-sexologist-niece-angers-cuban-americans.

Sands, Robert W., Jr., and Alexander B. Bartlett. 2002. *Images of America: Independence Hall and the Liberty Bell.* Charleston, SC: Arcadia Publishing.

Stoddard, Christine. 2015. "The Liberty Bell in Papal Visit Graphics." *Arlington Catholic Herald,* September 24. https://www.catholicherald.com/news/the_liberty-bell_in _papal_visit-graphics.

Tremel, Andrew. "Presidents of the United States (Presence in the Region)." *Encyclopedia of Greater Philadelphia.* http://philadelphiaencyclopedia.org/archive/presidents -of-the-united-states.

Trump, Donald J. 2002. "Portrait of Freedom." In *Portrait of Freedom: the 250th Anniversary of the Liberty Bell.* Clearwater, FL: Belmont International.

Q

Quakers

The Liberty Bell was originally ordered by the Pennsylvania Assembly in 1751. The Assembly had been created by the colony's first proprietor, William Penn, who was a member of the Religious Society of Friends, or Quakers. He and has fellow Quakers, who emphasized the importance of the "inner light" of the Holy Spirit in interpreting the Bible and often punctuated their services with periods of silence and reflection, had not only sought religious freedom for themselves, but also were willing to give it to others. Because Penn had granted his revised Charter of Privileges to Pennsylvania in 1701, it seems reasonable to believe that the Pennsylvania Assembly may in part have intended the Bell to commemorate the 50th anniversary, or Year of Jubilee, of this document, which was designed to see that the colony would be a "holy experiment" within the New World, not unlike the "city on the hill" that the Puritans had attempted to found, albeit with greater freedom.

Isaac Norris II, who headed the assembly, chose the words of the Bell from Leviticus 25:10. It came from a passage describing a Year of Jubilee, in which debts would be repaid and slaves would be freed.

In 1671, George Fox, one of the founders of the Quaker movement, suggested a modified form of the Year of Jubilee, in which slaves would become free after serving for a set number of years (Frost, 2014, 32). Some Quakers continued to hold slaves, but, in part because of the influence of Quakers, Pennsylvania became the first state to provide for gradual emancipation for slaves. Many Quakers (such as Lucretia Mott) became leading abolitionists, and, in time, the Quakers disowned members who continued to hold slaves. Many members of the group were also ardent advocates of women's rights.

Quakers were pacifists, who opposed slavery in part because they thought (presciently) that maintaining the practice could require the use of military force (Frost, 2014, 34). Quakers also pointed to what they believed would be the adverse consequences of slavery on family life (Frost, 2014, 34–35).

Despite their opposition to slavery, Quakers often parted company with those who sought to eliminate slavery through violence. William Frost observed, "Because of their religious beliefs, the normal response of Friends to extreme evil they cannot stop is to offer help to the victims," such as through "supporting the Underground Railroad" and "aiding the freedman in the Civil War" (Frost, 2014, 40).

See also: Abolitionists and the Liberty Bell; Norris, Isaac, II; Pennsylvania; Pennsylvania Charter of Privileges (1701); Year of Jubilee

Further Reading

"Delaware Freedom Ways: The Quaker Idea of Reciprocal Liberty." n.d. *Erenow.* https:// erenow.com/common/fourbritishfolkwaysinamerica1989/102.html.

Frost, J. William. 2014. "Why Quakers and Slavery? Why Not More Quakers?" In *Quakers and Abolition*, ed. Brycchan Carey and Geoffrey Plank. Champaign, IL: University of Illinois Press, 29–42.

May, Isaac Barnes. "Religious Society of Friends (Quakers)." *Encyclopedia of Greater Philadelphia.* http://philadelphiaencyclopedia.org/archive/religious-society-of-friends -quakers.

R

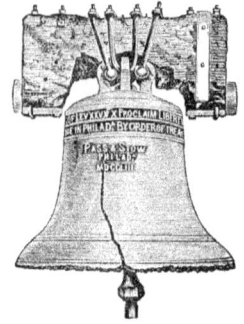

Reconciliation and the Liberty Bell

Throughout much of its history, the Liberty Bell has been a living symbol. Although it has a central core of meaning, the emphasis has varied from celebrating religious freedom, to serving as a symbol of colonial independence from the mother country (as well as unity against a common foe), to serving as a beacon for the enslaved, to being a symbol of freedom and democracy in opposition to foreign autocracy or totalitarianism, to being a symbol for civil rights, gay rights, and other contemporary issues.

Although the abolitionists appear to have given the Bell its primary designation as a "Liberty" Bell, once emancipation was achieved, it was used as a symbol of reconciliation. A banner from the Centennial Exposition that was held in Philadelphia in 1876 portrayed an eagle surrounded by flags, over the Liberty Bell surrounded by 13 red stars and a blue border with 38 white stars. The top of the banner read (Jeffbridgeman.com, n.d.):

CENTENNIAL UNION
IT PROCLAIMED LIBERTY IN
1776

The bottom of the banner said:

LET IT PROCLAIM
PEACE UNITY
1876.

Nowhere was the effort to use the Liberty Bell as a symbol of reconciliation clearer than in the trips that it took from 1885 to 1915. Of the seven trips that the Bell took out of state, three were to Southern states—namely, to the World's Industrial and Cotton Exposition in New Orleans in 1885, the Atlanta Cotton States and International Exposition of 1895, and the South Carolina Interstate and West Indian Exposition of 1902, in Charleston.

Requests for the Bell, and speakers at these events, typically highlighted the manner in which all U.S. territories, North and South, East and West, were now united by it. This was also reflected in Hattie Howard's poem, "Old Liberty Bell," by Florence Earle Coates's poem "The Liberty-Bell," and in numerous songs of the period.

In 1799, the German poet Friedrich Schiller completed a poem entitled "The Song of the Bell," in which he noted the role of the Bell in events from births, to weddings, to deaths. He emphasized the importance of republican values by stressing the ingredients needed to cast a bell. Cognizant that revolutionaries sometimes spawned events that they could no longer control, which is what he thought he witnessed in the French Revolution, Schiller hoped that the bell he described could be a unifying symbol:

Near the end of the poem, he thus wrote (Wertz, 2005, 45):

COME IN! Come in!
Ye workmen all, do come ye close in,
That we commence the Bell to christen,
Concordia its name be given,
To concord, in an intimate communion,
The loving commons gathers she in union.

See also: Atlanta Cotton States and International Exposition of 1895; Journeys of the Liberty Bell; "Liberty Bell, The" (Poem, 1895); Music and the Liberty Bell; Political and Social Movements and the Liberty Bell; South Carolina Interstate and West Indian Exposition of 1902; Symbolism of the Liberty Bell; Union "Liberty Bell" Polka (Song, 1860); World's Industrial and Cotton Exposition in New Orleans (1885)

Further Reading

Bridgeman, Jeff R. n.d. "Antique Flags and Painted Furniture." Jeffbridgeman.com.
Wertz, Marianna. 2005. "Friedrich Schiller's 'The Song of the Bell.'" *Fidelio* 14 (Spring–Summer): 36–45.

Reminder Marches

In addition to being a symbol of U.S. independence from Great Britain, in the late 1830s and thereafter, the Liberty Bell became a symbol for the abolitionist movement. In the twentieth century, it became the site for individuals who used sit-ins and other demonstrations to protest against racial segregation.

Seeing the effectiveness of these movements, and counting on the power of the inscription of the Liberty Bell to proclaim liberty "throughout all the land unto all the inhabitants thereof," Frank Kameny, Barbara Gitting, and other advocates of rights for lesbian, gay, bisexual, transgender, and queer/questioning (LGBTQ) people launched the first of four annual Reminder Marches on Sunday, July 4, 1965. Described as "One of the first organized [LGBTQ] protests in our nation's history," the demonstrators dressed professionally and held signs saying "SUPPORT HOMO-SEXUAL CIVIL RIGHTS" and "HOMOSEXUALS SHOULD BE JUDGED AS INDIVIDUALS" (Spikol, 2015). The marches preceded the Stonewall Riots of June 18, 1969, in Greenwich Village, New York, which were precipitated by a police raid on a gay bar. The riots are often credited for initiating the gay rights movement.

The Philadelphia marches had followed a sit-in on April 25, 1965, after a nearby restaurant, Dewey's Diner, refused to serve individuals who appeared to be gay or lesbian. It was followed in turn by a second demonstration on May 2, after which the restaurant began serving everyone (Royles, 2016). Although the demonstrations appear to have brought attention to the cause, many onlookers were initially incredulous that individuals would openly identify with a cause that many of them associated with deviant behavior (Mires, 1999, 61).

In 2015, an event was held commemorating the 50th anniversary of the first Reminder protests. The occasion was accompanied by what one participant described as "LGBT themed exhibits at the National Constitution Center, National Museum of American Jewish History, the African-American Museum of Philadelphia and the Liberty Bell Center" (Wilson, 2015).

See also: Political and Social Movements and the Liberty Bell

Further Reading

Mires, Charlene. 1999. "In the Shadow of Independence Hall: Vernacular Activities and the Meanings of Historic Places." *The Public Historian* 21 (Spring): 49–64.

Royles, Dan. 2016. "Civil Rights (LGBT)." *Encyclopedia of Greater Philadelphia.* http://philadelphiaencyclopedia.org/archive/civil-rights-lgbt.

Spikol, Liz. 2015. "How Philadelphia Helped Give Birth to the LGBT Rights Movement." *Philadelphia Magazine,* June 28. https://www.phillymag.com/g-philly-2015/06/28/annual-reminder-lgbt-philadelphia.

Wilson, Ryan. 2015. "Celebrating the Founders of the LGBT Movement in Philadelphia." Human Rights Campaign, July 9. https://www.hrc.org/blog/celebrating-the-founders-of-the-lgbt-movement-in-philadelphia.

Replicas of the Liberty Bell

Because the Liberty Bell weighs more than a ton and there is fear that its current crack could widen if it were exposed to further stress, it seems unlikely that it will ever again make out-of-state tours, as it did to various expositions and fairs between 1885 and 1915. Like the Statue of Liberty, however, it is relatively easy to make small replicas of the Bell that tourists can buy. The World's Fair and other expositions have often featured exhibits of the Liberty Bell made from butter, nuts, fruits, or chocolate. A highlight of the sesquicentennial of American independence in Philadelphia in 1926 was a massive, 80-foot replica of the Liberty Bell that was lit at night by 26,000 bulbs, under which cars could drive. It seems likely that no bell has been replicated in life-size more than the Liberty Bell.

Today's Liberty Bell is actually the third casting. The original bell, made by the Whitechapel Foundry in England, cracked on its first pealing. John Pass and John Stow of Philadelphia pulverized the Bell and recast it, and then recast it again to obtain a better sound. In the meantime, the city had ordered a "sister" bell, which was connected to clock faces on the east and west sides of the State House—this bell was later moved to St. Augustine's Church, where it was damaged in a fire in 1844 and later recast (Rongione, 1976). It is now displayed at the Falvey Memorial Library at Villanova University.

In 1876, long after the Liberty Bell had been cracked and could no longer be rung, Henry Seybert donated a 13,000-pound bell that was cast by the Meneely-Kimberly Foundry in Troy, New York, called the Centennial Bell (like the Liberty Bell, it was recast to get a better sound). It remains in the tower at Independence

Hall to toll the hours (Frazier, 1978). Another bell, which came to be known as the Columbian Liberty Bell, was cast by the same factory for the Columbian Exposition, which was held in Chicago in 1893. This bell, of similar weight, appears to have been melted down in 1897 after being repossessed by the McShane Bell Foundry, the company that cast it, for failure to pay (Diggs, 1787). Paul Barzanko, a Cleveland veteran who became obsessed with the Columbian Liberty Bell, subsequently spent $7,000 on a fiberglass reproduction of that bell, but it is uncertain whether it still exists or whether it is currently displayed. Barzanko's plans to have the bell recast by 1997 apparently faltered.

In 1913, a replica of the Liberty Bell was apparently made for the Pennsylvania Emancipation Exposition of that year, but little else is known about it. In 1915, advocates of women's suf-

The World Peace Bell, located in Newport, Kentucky, is one of the largest replicas of the Liberty Bell in the world. (Oblongbard/ Dreamstime.com)

frage cast a replica of the Liberty Bell known as the Justice Bell, which toured Pennsylvania trying to drum up support for the cause. That bell is now part of the carillon of the Washington Memorial Chapel at Valley Forge National Park in Pennsylvania.

As World War I was coming to an end, representatives of the Democratic Mid-European Union commissioned the Meneely Bell Company of Troy, New York, to cast another replica of the Liberty Bell, which now proclaimed "liberty throughout all the world." After being hidden from the Nazis during World War II, that bell now sits in the tower of St. Anthony's Church in Prague. The American Lithuanian Liberty Bell, a 1,000-pound replica of the Liberty Bell that Americans of Lithuanian descent gave to the Lithuanian government in the early 1920s, is located in a tower of the War Museum in Kaunas. Beginning in 1940, it remained silent during years of occupation, first by Nazis and then by Soviet forces. The Bell has been rung regularly since the fall of the Soviet Union in 1989.

In 1928, engineering societies in the United States and Belgium commissioned a bell of about seven tons to commemorate engineers of the United States who had given their lives on Belgium soil during World War I. It is known as the "Liberty

Bell of Louvain." In similar fashion, Patrick Daudon of France had a bell cast in 2004 to commemorate the 60th anniversary of the Allied invasion of the beaches in northern France in June 1944 to defeat Hitler. This Normandy Liberty Bell was transported to the United States and rung in front of Independence Hall for the "Let Freedom Ring" celebration of July 4, 2005, before being transported back to France.

In 1950, the U.S. Treasury Department commissioned the Paccard Bell Foundry in Annecy, France, to manufacture one full-size replica of the Liberty Bell for each of the U.S. states and territories in conjunction with a bond drive. The foundry donated one of the bells to be displayed at Independence, Missouri, the home of President Harry S. Truman. Most others are on display at or near state capitals. One is displayed at the Liberty Bell Museum in Allentown, Pennsylvania, and at least one is on display in Tokyo.

The U.S. government gave one of the bells that were cast for the states back to Annecy in 1950, and it is housed in the tower of the Baslique Saint Joseph-de-Fins in that town. That same year, the United States commissioned a 10-ton bell, known as the Freedom Bell or World Freedom Bell; it was manufactured by Cast & Johnson, clock and bell makers based in Croydon, England. It then went on tour in New York and other cities before going to West Berlin, where it was installed in the former city hall. In 1960, Sallie and Nadine Woods, who founded the Liberty Muscular Dystrophy Research Foundation, purchased a reproduction of the Liberty Bell from the Whitechapel Foundry, which they subsequently installed in a tower in Liberty, Texas.

In 1968, the Whitechapel Foundry began casting 2,400, 20-pound, 15-inch, numbered replicas of the Liberty Bell, probably in anticipation of the forthcoming bicentennial celebrations of U.S. independence. They were sold for $756 each. They were underwritten by the Liberty Bell Foundation, formed by the barrister Donald Crawford and the former journalist Anthony Gibbey. The bells were not cracked, just as the Whitechapel Foundry continued to insist that the original was not cracked when it was sent from England (Darling, 1968).

In 1975, Edward Piszek (1918–2004), the president of a frozen fish company named Mrs. Paul's Kitchen, commissioned the casting of the Liberty Bell from the original mold retained by the Whitechapel Foundry in England. He later donated the house in Philadelphia where Tadeusz Kosciuszko had briefly lived to the Independence National Historical Park and sent this new version of the Bell on a tour of states that constituted the original 13 colonies.

In 1976, Queen Elizabeth II visited Independence Hall, where she gave a speech and donated a bell, designated as the Bicentennial Bell, weighing 12,446 pounds and cast at the Whitechapel Foundry that had cast the original. First housed in a tower that was demolished in 2013 to make room for the Museum of the American Revolution, as of March 2018, this Bell remained in storage.

In 1976, Lynchburg Baptist College unveiled a replica of the Liberty Bell, weighing about 3,000 pounds, to celebrate the bicentennial and to mark its renaming to Liberty Baptist College, which is now Liberty University. In 2017, the university moved the Bell, previously exhibited in a pavilion, to its 17-story Freedom Tower, where it is now part of a carillon of 25 bells (Meynard, 2017).

In 1976, a local businessman named Jim Grimm raised money to purchase a replica of the Liberty Bell for his hometown of Hamilton, Ohio. Richard Jones (2013) believes that it was 1 of 15 full-size replicas that the Whitechapel Foundry cast that year. After the wooden yoke began to decay, the bell was stored in a city garage, but it was restored to its place outside the city municipal building in 2014 (Machi, 2014).

The American Legion loaded a 16,000-pound replica of the Liberty Bell on a Freedom Train, which toured the 48 lower contiguous states. President Gerald Ford rang the bell 13 times when he visited Independence Hall on July 4, 1976, and Chief Justice Warren Burger later rang it for the bicentennial of the U.S. Constitution in 1987. This Bell was sold at auction in 2007 for $54,970.

In 1976, Israel decided to honor the U.S. bicentennial by constructing the Koret Liberty Bell Park in Jerusalem. It includes a replica of the Liberty Bell. Children from South Brevard public schools raised money during the bicentennial for a replica of the Liberty Bell, to be cast by the Whitechapel Foundry. It was one of the highlights of the Liberty Bell Memorial Museum in Melbourne, Florida, before it closed. Similarly, the Jaycees of Marietta, Georgia, presented a replica of the Liberty Bell, that was rung 13 times on July 4, 1976, and in successive years each Independence Day, in honor of the 13 original colonies. This bell is now displayed in the Glover Park in Marietta ("Liberty Bell-Glover Park—Marietta, GA.—Exact Replicas on Waymarking.com," n.d.).

That same year, the Liberty Bell Education Foundation, established by businessmen in Minnesota, had a replica of the Liberty Bell cast in France and took it to schools in 36 states, where more than a million children saw it ("Liberty Bell," n.d.). The foundation subsequently put the bell in a timber frame building at the Highground Veterans Memorial Park near Neillsville, Wisconsin, where it remains on display. In 1976, the city of Hamilton, Ohio, also purchased a replica of the Liberty Bell. It is currently displayed in front of the municipal building, known as the Mueller Building, on High Street, after having been in storage for a number of years after its original yoke decayed (Jones, 2014).

In 1996, Fosecco, which provides products to the foundry industry, commissioned the West Philadelphia Bronze Company to cast a rendition of the Liberty Bell, without its crack, to mark the 100th anniversary of the American Foundry Society. That bell, generally designated as the Fosecco Liberty Bell, is displayed at the Leonhard Building, which houses the Harold and Inge Marcus Department of Industrial and Manufacturing Engineering at Penn State University ("The Liberty Bell at Penn State," n.d.).

The largest replica of the Liberty Bell is the 66,000-pound World Peace Bell, which was cast in 1998 for the advent of the new millennium in 2000. Cast by the Paccard Bell Foundry in France, it is located in front of the courthouse in Newport, Kentucky. In 2002, Renaissance USA commissioned the Whitechapel Foundry to cast a replica of the Liberty Bell to mark the 250th anniversary of the original. That bell is now displayed in Green Bay, Wisconsin.

The Providence Forum also asked the Whitechapel Foundry to make a replica of the Liberty Bell, which it dubbed the "Spirit of Liberty Bell," to mark the 300th anniversary of Penn's Charter of Privileges. In 2016, it donated this bell to the Museum of the Bible in Washington, D.C., where it was to be the centerpiece for the "Bible in America" exhibit. Two years earlier, Jeff Koons, a noted contemporary artist, crafted a laser-scanned version of the Liberty Bell.

The Paccard Bell Foundry, which made replica bells for each of the states, is known to have made at least 300 replicas of the Liberty Bell, which as of 2018 could be purchased for $75,000 each. Smith's Bell and Clock Service in Camby, Indiana, advertises that it offers full-scale, half-scale, and one-third-scale replicas, but its website does not appear to post any prices.

Given its long history and the values that it symbolizes, there are probably other replicas as well. Moreover, a number of states, like Virginia and Pennsylvania, have designated other historic bells, especially those who are believed to have rung on the occasion of American independence, as "liberty bells."

The Liberty Bell has become a symbol for freedom, and related ideals, not only throughout the United States, but also throughout much of the rest of the world.

See also: American Legion Freedom Bell; American Lithuanian Liberty Bell; Annecy Liberty Bell Replica; Centennial Bell; College and University Campuses with Replicas of the Liberty Bell; Columbian Liberty Bell; Czech Liberty Bell; Freedom Bell; Justice Bell; Koons, Jeff; Liberty, Texas, Replica of the Liberty Bell; Liberty Bell of Louvain; Liberty Bell Park; Normandy Liberty Bell; Pass and Stow; Robinson's Liberty Bells; Sister to the Liberty Bell; Spirit of Liberty Bell; State Liberty Bell Replicas; Two-Hundred-and-Fiftieth Anniversary Liberty Bell; Virginia Liberty Bell; Whitechapel Foundry; World Peace Bell

Further Reading

Boland, Charles Michael. 1973. *Ring in the Jubilee: The Epic of America's Liberty Bell.* Riverside, CT: Chatham Press.

Darling, Henry R. 1968. "Crackless Liberty Bell That Rings Coming Here from London in June." *Philadelphia Sunday Bulletin*, February 25, Section 1, 32.

Diggs, Morse. 1978. "He Dreams of Recasting Bell." *Akron Beacon Journal*, July 4.

Frazier, Arthur H. 1978. "Henry Seybert and the Centennial Clock and Bell at Independence Hall." *Pennsylvania Magazine of History and Biography* 102 (January): 40–58.

Gantt, Marlene. 1993. "A Nation Forced This Plow." *The Dispatch* (Moline, Illinois), September 4, 5.

Jones, Richard. 2013. "Residents Start Fund to Save Hamilton's Liberty Bell." *Journal-News,* October 13. https://www.journal-news.com/news/residents-start-fund-save -hamilton-liberty-bell/sMtzGJL8uNCFYXLONXBclJ.

Jones, Richard O. 2014. "Piece of Local History Restored; The Liberty Bell Rings Again!!!" Butler County Historical Society, April 23. http://bchistoricalsociety.com/main /2014/04/piece-local-history-restored-liberty-bell-rings.

"Koret Helps Renovate Jerusalem's Liberty Bell Park." n.d. *Jewish News of Northern California.* https://www.jweekly.com/1999/09/03/koret-helpsprenovatepjerusalem-s -liberty-bell-park.

"The Liberty Bell at Penn State." n.d. Penn State College of Engineering. https://www.ime .psu.edu/department/liberty-bell.aspx.

"Liberty Bell." n.d. The Highground. https://www.thehighground.us/tributes_and_facilities /liberty-bell.

"Liberty Bell—Glover Park—Marietta, GA.—Exact Replicas on Waymarking.com." n.d. http://;www.waymarking.com/waymakrs/WM42V1_Liberty_Bell_Glover_Park _marietta_GA.

"Liberty Bell Replica." n.d. Smith's Bell and Clock Service. http://www.smithsbellandclock
.com/bells-indianapolis/liberty-bell-replica.

Machi, Vivienne. 2004. "Hamilton Celebrates Return of Liberty Bell." *Journal News,*
April 27. https://www.journal-news.com/news/hamilton-celebrates-return-liberty
-bell/v9VVU3axPdAFeWrmRkS0VO.

Menard, Drew. 2017. "Bells Installed Atop Freedom Tower." April 27. http://www.liberty
.edu/news/index.cfm?PID=18495&MID=232358.

Richter, Jan. 2009. "The Bells of Prague." Czech Radio, December 26. https://www.radio
.cz/en/section/special/the-bells-of-prague.

Rongione, Louis A. 1976. "Sister to the Liberty Bell." *Records of the American Catholic
Historical Society of Philadelphia* 87 (March–December): 3:32.

"Ring It Again! (The Call of the Liberty Bell)" (Song)

Sometime during or shortly after World War I, Hal Parker composed words and music to a song called "Ring It Again! (The Call of the Liberty Bell)" (Parker, 1911).

One significant aspect of the song, the copy of which is in the Library of Congress, written by hand, is that it clearly designates the bell as the Liberty Bell.

The song begins, "Ring it again! Ding Dong! Freedom's Refrain! Ding Dong! Rung by the Liberty Bell. Ding Dong! Come one—come all! Ding Dong! Answer the Call. Ding Dong! It has a message to tell!"

The message is to "Buy a Bond! Buy a Bond! Buy a Liberty Bond!" The song further urges listeners to "Be the man behind the man behind the gun! Let your dollars fight for every mother's son!" Anticipating the day when the soldiers will be marching into Berlin, it ends with "Ring it as before you rang it. Give five billion more! And we'll go marching to Berlin!"

A handwritten note on the Library of Congress copy, which is undated, says it is "to be published later."

See also: Liberty Loans; Music and the Liberty Bell; Names for the Liberty Bell

Further Reading
Parker, H. 1911. *Ring It Again! The Call of the Liberty Bell*. Monographic. Notated Music. https://www.loc.gov/item/2014563357.

"Ring Out Liberty Bell" (Song, 1918)

Among the tunes composed to rally the troops during World War I was a patriotic march entitled "Ring Out Liberty Bell." It was composed by Fred W. Hager (1874–1958) and copyrighted in 1918.

Referring in the opening lines to the "Old Bell," one of its prior designations, the song proclaims that "It's time to ring Old Bell . . . for Freedom's Cause." As in other songs of the period, this objective is also tied to that of ringing "for Democracy."

The chorus is simple and direct (Hager, 1911):

Ring Out Liberty Bell
Swing out Liberty Bell
Ring for Democracy
O'er Land and Sea
Ring Liberty Ring—
From hills Liberty Bell—
From dells Liberty Bell—
Call our Minute Men to form a-gain
Oh! Liberty Ring Out.

See also: Music and the Liberty Bell

Further Reading
Hager, Frederick W. 1911. *Ring Out Liberty Bell Patriotic March Song.* Monographic. Notated Music. https://www.loc.gov/item/2013564757.

"Ring Out Ye Bell of Liberty" (Song, 1918)

Among the songs that were composed during World War I was a piece entitled "Ring Out Ye Bell of Liberty," which was published in Philadelphia by the Song-writers Bureau in 1918. Both words and music were by Thomas Williams. The fairly plain cover featured a sketch of the Liberty Bell below the title of the song. The crack is visible on the Bell, but its inscription is not. The words indicate that the song was dedicated to D. Earle Williams of the 312 Field Artillery unit and Charles C. Williams of the U.S. Navy (presumably sons, brothers, or other relatives of the song's author).

The first of three verses indicates that the nation celebrates its freedom every Independence Day, but the Bell that once shouted out this freedom is now silent. The second verse praises the founding fathers and their gift of the Constitution, "That dem-o-cra-cy might live / For-ev-er and for-ev-er In-de-pen-dence it did give" (Williams, 1918). The third verse indicates that the nation will fight to preserve its freedom. "We ded-i-cate our-selves a-new/To keep our coun-try free./From ty-rants and from trai-tors/A real dem-o-cra-cy" (Williams, 1918).

The chorus furthered the association between the Bell and American values (Williams, 1918):

Ring out, ring out, Ye Bell of Lib-er-ty;
Your voice is free-dom's might-y shout for all e-ter-ni-ty.
Hail, hail, hail, hail, ye friends—a-cross the sea,
Hail, hail, hail, hail, ye sons of lib-er-ty.
To arms, to arms, to arms, and fight for vic-to-ry.
Ring out, ring out, ring out, ring out for lib-er-ty.

See also: Democracy and the Liberty Bell; Independence Day; Music and the Liberty Bell

Further Reading
Williams, Thomas. 1918. *Ring Out Ye Bell of Liberty*. Monographic. The Songwriters Bureau, Philadelphia. Notated Music. https://www.loc.gov/item/2014564543.

"Ring the Bell, Watchman!" (Song, 1865)

One of the most lyrical songs about bells that has become associated with the Liberty Bell is the song "Ring the Bell, Watchman!" which was written by Henry Clay Work (1832–1894) and published by Rott & Cady and S. Brainar's Sons in 1865.

The song seems to follow closely the legend of the Liberty Bell that was generated by George Lippard in his story "The Fourth of July, 1776," which was first published in the *Saturday Courier* in 1847 and has been said to have had a particular impact on children's love for the Liberty Bell (Nash, 2010, 57). However, the song never actually uses the term *Liberty Bell,* or any of the other names by which that bell had been called. Moreover, research suggests that the song was actually written to commemorate the ringing of church bells to announce the end of the Civil War.

It would appear that the joy evoked by ringing the Liberty Bell for independence in 1776 was so close to the joy that would have been evoked by the end of the nation's bloodiest war that it would be easy to conflate the two events, especially because the latter resulted in the freedom for African American slaves.

Work's poem has no mention of the "flaxen-haired boy" of the Lippard story, focusing instead on the "silver locks" of the sexton, who, as in Lippard's story, awaits news in the belfry. The first verse sets the stage (Work, 1865):

High in the belfry the old sexton stands,
Grasping the rope with his thin bony hands
Fix'd is his gaze as by some magic spell
Till he hears the distant murmur,
Ring, ring the bell.

Each successive stanza ends with the same refrain, "Ring, ring the bell."
The chorus indicates that the bells will peal a message of joy (Work, 1865):

"Ring the bell, watchman! Ring! ring, ring!
"Yes, yes! The good news is now on the wing.
"Yes, yes! They come and with tidings to tell.
"Glorious and blessed tidings, Ring, ring the bell!"

The second verse paints a picture of the sexton first dropping to his knees (presumably in thanksgiving to God) before rising with vigor to ring the bell. The third verse refers to "the first signal gun" that sounds "from the hilltop" to be echoed back in the valley.

The final verse seems to confirm that Henry Clay Work was referring not to the beginning of the uncertain struggle of 1776, but to the glorious news of the end of the conflict in 1865, although the words would apply almost equally well to Independence Day celebrations (Work, 1865):

> Bonfires are blazing and rockets ascend
> No meagre triumph such tokens portend
> Shout! Shout! My brothers for "all, all is well!"
> 'Tis the universal chorus
> Ring, ring the bell.

The cover of the sheet music consists mostly of lettering, but there is a small image in the top of the *R* in the word *Ring,* with a picture of a fairly sedate man with a receding hairline and a suit and bow tie gently pulling on a rope with only his right hand. Although the bell, which is situated to his left in the sketch, has the shape of the Liberty Bell, it has neither the lettering nor the crack of the Liberty Bell (Work, 1865).

See also: Independence Day; Lippard, George; Music and the Liberty Bell; Names for the Liberty Bell

Further Reading

Hill, Richard S. 1953. "The Mysterious Chord of Henry Clay Work" *Notes* 10 (March): 211–225 and 10 (June): 367–390.

Nash, Gary B. 2010. *The Liberty Bell*. New Haven, CT: Yale University Press.

Work, Henry C. 1865. *Ring the Bell, Watchman!* Root & Cady, Chicago. Notated Music. https://www.loc.gov/item/ihas.200002355.

Ringing of the Liberty Bell

Whereas the twin to the Liberty Bell, which was connected to the Stretch Clock, was struck by a large hammer connected to the clock mechanism, the Liberty Bell was rung by hand. Justin Kramer, who has examined the headstock, or yoke, of the Bell believes that the yoke indicates "that the bell was originally equipped with a wheel and a stay," and that the headstock has been turned "in a position that is 180 degrees different (front to back) from the way the bell had formerly been mounted" (Kramer, 1975, 56). Kramer further argues that "[t]he original wheel was most likely made of oak and securely fastened to the wooden headstock, whose gudgeons [socket-like cylindrical fittings] were supported on a massive wooden framework in a manner that permitted the bell to swing freely. A rope was attached to the large wooden wheel and run over a pulley to a room beneath the bell deck" (1975, 56).

Kramer further noted, "Each tug on the bell rope produced a single note on the bell. To tug properly on the bell rope did not require a great deal of physical strength but it did require considerable know-how on the part of the bell ringer" (1975, 57).

Mary Alexander has written two studies indicating that the doorkeepers of the Pennsylvania Assembly were designated as official ringers of the Liberty Bell. The doorkeeper at the time of the writing of the Declaration of Independence was Andrew McNair, although had he been absent on July 8, 1776, the day the Bell would have been rung to announce independence, someone else (possibly William Hurry who was so credited in a history of a Philadelphia church) might have taken his place (Alexander, 1929, 4). Even though the Pennsylvania Assembly was not in session on July 8, 1776, it was apparently customary for the bell ringer for the Assembly to continue such work for the Congress (Alexander, 1929, 4).

Relatively little is known about McNair, who was likely of Scottish or Scotch-Irish descent. However, he is known to have married Mary Jennings in 1746, to have died on February 18, 1777, and to have been a freemason (Alexander, 1929, 3).

See also: Occasions for Ringing the Liberty Bell; Sister to the Liberty Bell

Further Reading

Alexander, Mary D. 1929. *Andrew McNair and the Liberty Bell 1776*. Chicago: University of Chicago Press.

Alexander, Mary D. 1925. "The Ringers of the Liberty Bell." *Journal of the Illinois State Historical Society*, 18 (October): 658–667.

Kramer, Justin. 1975. *Cast in America: The Historically Accurate, Exciting Story of the Liberty Bell*. Los Angeles: Justin Kramer Incorporated.

RINGING OUT LIBERTY (Painting, 1930)

In 1930, the Pennsylvania Railroad commissioned the American artist-illustrator Newell Convers (N. C.) Wyeth (1882–1945) to do a series of four patriotic portraits. One of these, 40 inches tall and 27 inches wide, was entitled *RINGING OUT LIBERTY*.

This painting, later made into posters, featured a man in a tricornered hat vigorously ringing the Liberty Bell in the tower of the State House, as well as three other figures. A young girl looks toward the viewer with her hands over her ears, while a man in colonial garb and a boy waving his hat look out from the tower, into which light is streaming. The bottom of the painting has the words, "July 8, 1776, PHILADELPHIA, HOME CITY of the PENNSYLVANIA RAILROAD." Wyeth, who was known for researching the subjects of his paintings, recognized that if the Bell were rung for the Declaration of Independence, it would have been rung the day the Declaration was read to a crowd outside the State House rather than on July 4, the evening during which it was printed.

The painting was sold by Swann Auction Galleries of New York in 2013.

See also: Declaration of Independence and the Liberty Bell

Further Reading

"N. C. Wyeth Biography." Brandywine Conservancy, Museum of Art. https://www.brandywine.org/museum/nc-wyeth-catalogue-raisonne/biography.

Lot 161: Newell Convers Wyeth (1882–1924). *Ringing Out Liberty*. 1930. 40 × 27 inches (102 × 69 cm.). The Pennsylvania Railroad Company. https://www.invaluable.com/auction/lot-newell-convers/wyeth-1882-1945-.-ringing-out-lib-74 caf424a5.

Roadside Exhibits of the Liberty Bell

When people cannot visit symbols, they often look for substitutes. There is at least one replica of the Liberty Bell in each of the 50 states and in a number of foreign territories and nations. There have been at least two Liberty Bell Museums, one in Allentown, Pennsylvania, which remains open, and another in Melbourne, Florida.

World fairs and expositions have often highlighted agricultural abundance by featuring replicas of the Liberty Bell made of diverse materials, including butter, sugar, and corn (Simpson, 2010). For many years, a Robinson's (later Macy's) Department Store in Los Angeles contained 42 replicas of the Liberty Bell as part of its outside façade, designed by Phil Tovrea.

A war memorial, which was dedicated on Armistice Day in 1921, in Norfolk, Connecticut, features a replica of the Liberty Bell in a stone exhibit. Dave Pelland has described the monument as featuring "three archways rising from a triangular base with long branches" with the bell hanging "below the intersection of the archways" and the monument topped with "a stone design that appears to resemble an eternal flame" (Pelland, 2010). A plaque reads ("World War I Memorial—Norfolk, CT—U.S. National Register of Historic Places on Waymarking.com," n.d.):

> 1917 THE WORLD WAR 1918
> IN HONOR OF THOSE WHO GAVE AND THOSE
> WHO OFFERED THEIR LIVES FOR LIBERTY
> THE PEOPLE OF NORFOLK HAVE BUILT
> THIS MONUMENT AND CROWNED IT WITH
> THE LIBERTY BELL
> IN THE FAITH THAT IT WILL RING THE
> KNELL OF WAR
> AND PROCLAIM THE BROTHERHOOD OF MAN.

In smaller lettering, the plaque adds;

> THE BELL WAS DONATED BY MARY ELDRIDGW
> IT IS A CAREFUL REPRODUCTION OF THE
> ORIGINAL LIBERTY BELL IN INDEPENDENCE HALL.

It has not been decisively determined whether the bell is identical in size to the Liberty Bell or a somewhat smaller-scale model. A letter dated July 18, 1921, which is found in the note card files at the Independence National Historical Park indicates that the bell was made by the Old Meenley Bell Foundry of Watervliet, New York, and that it included a 1/8th-inch, chiseled crack, filled in with black so that the bell could be rung "on all Patriotic Occasions."

Goessel, Kansas, boasts a "Life-size" and "exact replica of the Liberty Bell" that is made "of turkey red wheat straw" ("Liberty Bell Made of Wheat," n.d.). Local Mennonites apparently created this bell to be displayed at the Smithsonian during bicentennial celebrations in 1976.

After a replica of the Liberty Bell made of wire mesh, plywood, and concrete that Vern Kleven created for Milan, Minnesota, in 1976, began to deteriorate, local citizens raised $5,000 to replace it in 2016. The town was especially delighted that the celebrations were joined by immigrants from Micronesia (Cherveny, 2016).

Rapid City, North Dakota, recently built a replica of Independence Hall with 47 life-size figures patterned after John Trumbull's painting of the signing of the Declaration of Independence. The exhibit features a newly minted replica of the Liberty Bell, albeit with a false crack that enables individuals to ring it (Associated Press, 2014).

See also: Museums of the Liberty Bell; Phil Tovrea's Liberty Bell Replica; Replicas of the Liberty Bell; Robinson's Liberty Bells

Further Reading

Cherveny, Tom. 2016. "Milan Dedicates New Liberty Bell." *West Central Tribune,* August 26. http://www.wctrib.com/news/4102857-milan-dedicates-new-liberty-bell.

"Liberty Bell Made of Wheat." n.d. RoadsideAmerica. https://www.roadsideamerica.com /story/16559.

"Liberty Bell Replica Goes on Display in Rapid City." 2014. Associated Press, June 1. https://www.panhandlepost.com/liberty-bell-replica-goes-on-display-in-rapid -city.

Pelland, Dave. 2010. "World War Memorial, Norfolk." CTMonuments.net, October 11. http://ctmonuments.net/20-10/10/world-war-memorial-norfolk.

Simpson, Pamela H. 2010. "A Vernacular Recipe for Sculpture—Butter, Sugar, and Corn." *American Art* 24 (Spring): 23–26.

Wiggins, Michael. 2015. "Independence Hall and Liberty Bell Exhibit." Indegogo, May 12. https://www.indiegogo.com/projects/independence-hall-and-the-liberty-bell -exhibit#.

"World War I Memorial—Norfolk, CT—U.S. National Register of Historic Places on Way-marking.com." n.d. http://www.waymarking.com/waymarks/WMGM97_Norfolk _World_War_I_Memorial_Norfolk_CT.

Robinson's Liberty Bells

In what may well have been the grandest display of Liberty Bell replicas anywhere, a Robinson's department store in Los Angeles that was built between 1972 and 1973 featured a white façade with three strings, each containing 14 scale replicas of the Liberty Bell. Each was hand-lettered and had an imitation of the crack. A description further suggests that the architect may have substituted wind chimes for clappers, thus presenting "an aural intrigue" ("Robinson's Liberty Bells," n.d.).

The display is known to have been created by Welton Becket and Associates, which was founded by Welton Becket (1902–1969). Once the largest such firm in the world, it was responsible for such iconic buildings as the Pan Pacific Auditorium, the General Electric Pavilion, the Capital Records Building, and the Cinerama Dome.

Although William Pereira, an associate of Becket's, sometimes incorporated bells in other department stores that he built, the idea of replicating the Liberty Bell is apparently unique to the Los Angeles store. California is, of course, known for its Spanish-style missions, many of which contain bells and are surrounded by legends, but the reason for choosing Liberty Bells in unknown ("California Bell

Legends: A Survey," 1945). It seems possible that they were chosen either in remembrance of the visit of the Liberty Bell to the Panama-Pacific International Exposition of 1915, or in anticipation of the bicentennial celebrations in 1976.

The store closed in 2014, and the bells were dispersed. At least two are known to have gone to the San Fernando Valley Relics Museum in Chatsworth, California, which has subsequently moved to the Van Nuys Airport

See also: Bicentennial and the Liberty Bell; Panama-Pacific International Exposition, San Francisco (1915); Replicas of the Liberty Bell

Further Reading

"The Architecture of Welton Becket & Associates." n.d. *The Frillo Gazette.* http://thegrillogazette.blogspot.com/2011/03/architecture-of-welton-tecket-html.

"California Bell Legends: A Survey." 1945. Written by The Editors. *California Folklore Quarterly* 4 (January): 18–28.

"Robinson's Liberty Bells." n.d. Atlas Obscura. https://www.atlasobscura.com/places/robinson-s-liberty-bells.

"Welton Becket." n.d. Los Angeles Conservatory. https://www.laconservancy.org/architects/welton-becket.

S

Security for the Liberty Bell

For many of the years that the Liberty Bell has been exhibited, individuals have sought to touch it, kiss it, or both. Indeed, when the Liberty Bell went to the Atlanta Exposition in 1895, boys were allowed to run coins over its surface for good luck (Rosewater, 1926, 167). The Liberty Bell was accompanied by guards when it was taken to Allentown in 1777 to be hidden from the British in the Zion Reformed Church. It was also guarded when it made subsequent trips to world fairs and other out-of-state expositions, but the jagged rim of the Bell is testimony to the fact that many individuals have sought to chip off pieces as souvenirs, and there are even stories of boys who try to knock pieces off with paving stones (Nash, 2010, 27). Moreover, according to an article in the *Public Ledger* of October 24, 1893, it was alleged that private watchmen guarding the bell had actually been chipping off pieces as souvenirs to give to visitors (Paige, 1988, 40). In 1914, a curator at the Liberty Bell named Wilfred Jordan claimed that about 25 pounds of the Bell "has been maliciously cold-chiseled off the lip of the bell," and that people called him at least three times a year claiming to have small bell, rings, crosses, or other objects made from it (Paige, 1988, 91).

One of the concerns over displaying the Liberty Bell in Independence Hall centered on fears that if the building were engulfed in flames, rescuing it would be impossible. In 1894, the Bell was accordingly removed from the ceiling and replaced in an oak case constructed by Francis D. Kramer. The *Public Ledger* of June 14, 1894, described the case as follows (Paige 1988, 40):

> 5 foot 10 inch square, ten feet high excepting the front which rises to 12 feet; the four sides paneled with American glass four inches wide and 7 feet high in center, at each corner a bronze pillar, over the front is a carved eagle, on each corner of the case is a polished bronze torch. Inside the case the bell is supported by the marred yoke which is suspended by bronze columns, all of which fit on a truck four feet square, supported on four rubber-tired wheels. The railing around the case is polished bronze and held by four columns surrounded by bronze torches.

In 1914, after renewed fears about the safety of the Bell in the event of a fire, workers placed collapsible skids on the truck holding it and attaching ropes. A test conducted in January 1915 established that the Bell could be removed in a mere 55 seconds (Paige, 1988, 50).

As the Liberty Bell took its longest trip to the Panama-Pacific International Exposition in San Francisco in 1915, the train carrying it was scheduled to go no more than 35 miles per hour, and sometimes much slower (Steward, 1915, 48). Prior to the trip, workers had already installed a metal "spider" contraption within the

Bell to distribute its weight and prevent further lengthening of its crack. During its stay in San Francisco, the Bell was put into a fireproof vault each night (Rosewater, 1926, 187).

As San Francisco was planning a parade to send the Liberty Bell back to Philadelphia from the Panama-Pacific International Exposition of 1915, a group of what Stephen Fried describes as "preparedness extremists" paid a bootblack $500 to drop off a suitcase bomb near the Liberty Bell, but instead he threw the bomb into the bay. No one probably would ever have known of the plot had it not been revealed in a subsequent investigation of a bombing by the same group at a subsequent parade that killed 10 people (Fried, 2017). As the Bell was transported back to Philadelphia, the train car carrying it had to be moved to protect it from a fire that threatened to ignite oil tanks that were nearby (Paige, 1988, 52).

During the sesquicentennial celebrations in 1926, the U.S. Marine Corps provided an honor guard of nine men who stood watch over the Liberty Bell from 9 a.m. until 8 p.m. They insisted that men take off their hats and prohibited taking photographs without official permission (Paige, 1985, 59). On June 21, 1937, at an annual convention of the National Association of Insurance Commissioners, firefighters demonstrated to delegates how they could pour two heavy streams of water over Pennsylvania Hall within less than three minutes after an alarm (Sands and Bartlett, 2012, 15).

The Japanese attack on Pearl Harbor, Hawaii, on December 7, 1941, created additional concerns about security for the Liberty Bell. More guards were assigned to protect it, and there was even discussion of sending it to Fort Knox, Kentucky, for safekeeping along with the nation's gold (Paige, 1985, 64). In 1942, the Insurance Company of North America offered to build an underground shelter to protect the Bell in case of attack, but the project was first delayed due to lack of governmental authorization to use needed steel for this project, and then abandoned after a study indication that constructing a vault under Independence Hall might weaken the understructure of the building (Paige, 1985, 65). In 1944, Charles A. White was taken to the hospital for mental observation after he threw what Paige describes as "a baseball-size rock at the Liberty Bell as a protest gesture against a transportation strike" (1985, 67).

In 1916, the Black Tom explosion, set off by German agents, destroyed a munitions plant in Jersey City and sent debris into the Statue of Liberty ("Take a Tour of Lady Liberty's Torch (Right This Second)," 2018). In 1965, the New York City police arrested three communists associated with the Black Liberation Front for plotting to dynamite the Liberty Bell, the Statue of Liberty, and the Washington Monument. Fortunately, police were able to arrest the suspects before they did any harm (Greiff, 1987, 186). A U.S. Circuit Court upheld their conviction, against a number of challenges, in *United States of America v. Walter Augustus Bowe, Robert Steele Collier, and Khaleel Sultarn Sayyed* (360 F.2d 1 2d Cir. 1966). A poet identified as "Caconrad," and whose other information about the Liberty Bell appears correct, reports that in the 1970s, police, claiming to be concerned about the possibility of a concealed weapon, shot a hippie who "ran through Independence Hall and right past the Liberty Bell" (Caconrad, 2015). In 1976, someone attacked the Bell with an automobile exhaust pipe (Fischer, 2005, 50).

As a relic, the Liberty Bell can arouse strong emotions, both among those who cherish the ideals it represents and for those who might loathe them. Moreover, while there are thousands of flags that individuals may burn in protest, there is only one original Liberty Bell. There is the further potential that individuals seeking notoriety might attack the Bell simply for publicity. In 1997, Stud Bykofsky, of the *Philadelphia Daily News,* to demonstrate the need for greater security, managed to carry a Smith & Wesson .357 Magnum through nine of the ten top tourist spots in Philadelphia, including the Liberty Bell, without having to go through a metal detector—the exception was the U.S. Mint (Bykofsky, 1997).

On April 6, 2001, Mitchell Guilliatt, a 26-year old white man from Nebraska, wearing military fatigues and carrying a guitar and a bamboo pole, pulled a sledgehammer out from under his raincoat at the end of a tour and struck the Liberty Bell a number of times on the side opposite its famous crack. He apparently shouted, "God lives" while doing so. Asked 12 years after the incident about his intentions, Guilliatt said "The scripture on the bell was an inspiration to me. Liberty is something God gives and men receive" (Maule, 2013). Apprehended by park rangers, he was sentenced to nine months in prison and ordered to repay the $7,093 that it cost to repair the gouge he had made in the Bell.

Early on the morning of November 21, 1970, a dynamite bomb destroyed a replica of the Liberty Bell in the city hall rotunda in Portland, Oregon, but the incident did not kill or injure anyone. Decades later, the perpetrator still remains unknown (KGF Staff, 2016).

In January 2013, Carlos Balsas, an immigrant from Portugal who lived in Tempe, Arizona, was accused of threatening to blow up the Liberty Bell. However, after a bomb squad examined two black backpacks that he left in front of a nearby business, no explosives were found ("Police Charge Man over Liberty Bell Threat," 2013). Balsas was subsequently acquitted after testimony seemed to indicate that the controversy may have arisen, at least in part, from a misunderstanding of language ("Portuguese Man Acquitted in Liberty Bell Threat," 2013).

Two men from Philadelphia were eventually sentenced to 20 years in prison and ordered to pay $5.2 million in restitution after being convicted for breaking into a Wilmington, Delaware, jeweler and taking, among other objects, a five-inch, four-pound sculpture of the Liberty Bell guarded by a bald eagle. It had been made from one of the world's largest rubies and was bedecked with 50 diamonds. Despite a reward of $10,000, the item was never recovered (Reyes, 2016).

The terrorist attack on the World Trade Center on September 11, 2001, raised further concerns over the Liberty Bell and other sacred objects, which remain constantly guarded to this day. Today, visitors have to pass through metal detectors before they view the Bell.

See also: Civil Religion and the Liberty Bell; Zion Reformed Church

Further Reading
Bykofsky, Stu. 1997. "Pistol-Packing Tourist." *Philadelphia Daily News*, February 28, 9.

Caconrad. 2015. "Poet in the Crack of Liberty: My Life with Christopher, 1988." Poetry Foundation. https://www.poetryfoundation.org/harriet/2015/06/poet-in-the-crack-of-liberty-my-life-with-christopher-1988.

Fischer, David Hackett. 2005. *Liberty and Freedom*. New York: Oxford University Press.

Fried, Stephen. 2017. "World War I: 100 Years Later. How the Liberty Bell Won the Great War." Smithsonian.com, April. https://www.smithsonianmag.com/history/how-liberty-bell-won-great-war-180962471.

Greiff, Constance M. 1987. *Independence: The Creation of a National Park*. Philadelphia: University of Pennsylvania Press.

KGF Staff. 2016. "Bombing at Portland City Hall Still Unsolved 45 Years Later." KGW.com, January 12. https://www.kgw.com/article/news/investigations/bombing-at-portland-city-hall-still-unsolved-45-years-later/283-839117.

"Liberty Bell Attack Earns Prison Term." 2002. *Los Angeles Times*. April 24. http://articles.latimes.com/2002/apr/24/news/nm-39656.

"Man Seized After Attacking Liberty Bell." 2001. *Los Angeles Times*. April 7. http://articles.latimes.com/2001/apr/07/news/mn-48188.

Maule, Bradley. 2013. "Striking a Chord For Liberty." Hidden City Philadelphia, April 5. https://hiddencityphila.org/2013/04/striking-a-chord-for-liberty.

Nash, Gary B. 2010. *The Liberty Bell*. New Haven, CT: Yale University Press.

Paige, John C. 1988. *The Liberty Bell: A Special History Study*. David C. Kimball, ed. Denver: Denver Service Center and Independence National Historical Park.

"Police Charge Man over Liberty Bell Threat." 2013. CNN, January 27. https://www.cnn.com/2013/01/27/justice/pennsylvania-liberty-bell-threat/index.html.

"Portuguese Man Acquitted in Liberty Bell Threat." 2013. AP, October 22. https://www.apnews.com/42ae1b07528146d1bcc9e0203585c442.

Reyes, Jessica. 2016 "Robbers Who Stole Millions in Jewelry Sentenced." *The News Journal,* April 25. https://www.delawareonline.com/story/news/crime/2016/04/25/smash-and-grab-jewelry-robbers-get-20-years-prison/83494108.

Rosewater, Victor. 1926. *The Liberty Bell: Its History and Significance*. New York: D. Appleton.

Sands, Robert W., Jr., and Alexander B. Bartlett. 2002. *Images of America: Independence Hall and the Liberty Bell*. Charleston, SC: Arcadia Publishing.

Stewart, J. A. 1915. "The Liberty Bell's Great Trip." *Journal of Education* 82 (June 15): 48–49.

"Take a Tour of Lady Liberty's Torch (Right This Second)." 2018. *The New York Times,* November 13. https://www.nytimes.com/interactive/2018/11/13/nyregion/statue-of-liberty-torch-ar-ul.html?action=click&module=Top%20Stories&pgtype=Homepage.

Teunissen, John J., and Evelyn J. Hinz. 1974. "The Attack on the Pieta: An Archetypal Analysis." *Journal of Aesthetics and Art Criticism* 33 (Autumn): 43–50.

United States of America, Appellee, v. Walter Augustus Bowe, Robert Steele Collier, and Khaleel Sultarn Sayyed, Defendants, 360 F.2d 1 (2d Cir. 1966).

Sesquicentennial International Exposition

The Sesquicentennial International Exposition of the Declaration of Independence, held in Philadelphia in 1926, was among the least successful anniversaries celebrated in the city. In contrast to the centennial celebrations of 1876, the 1926 exposition was poorly attended and ended up in debt. The year had begun on a much more hopeful note, with a radio broadcast of a rubber mallet hitting the Liberty

Bell (Rosewater, 1926, 193), but those responsible for constructing the event got behind, which affected the preparations. Further, the weather during the exposition was among the rainiest in Philadelphia's history.

Although the celebration prominently highlighted the Liberty Bell and Independence Hall in its literature, as well as in numerous souvenirs that were produced for the occasion, the initial grandiose plans for the exposition—including delaying it until 1927 and calling it "The Liberty Fair for World Peace and Progress"—were scaled back, as many city residents questioned the wisdom of spending money on an exposition rather than on city infrastructure and housing (Wilson, 2000, 68). The exhibition became further involved in political infighting within the city leadership. Controversies included whether it should be opened on Sundays (in time, it was), and over whether it should feature a prize fight between Jack Dempsey and Gene Tunney, as it eventually did (Evensen, 1993). At a time when most city jobs were based on manufacturing, many city leaders did not appreciate the value of tourism, and many opposed using Fairmount Park, which had been used for the centennial celebrations. Eventually, the buildings were situated near the League Island Naval Yard, a swampy area that required extensive draining and filling (Wilson, 2000, 88).

Charlene Mires credits the celebration with demonstrating "that Philadelphians along with the rest of the nation had developed a regard for the Liberty Bell that was both different and separate from Independence Hall" (2002, 166). One of the most visible sites at the exposition was an 80-foot replica of the Liberty Bell constructed of 80 tons of steel, lit at night by 26,000 15-watt bulbs, and large enough for automobiles to drive under. A proposed Tower of Light, which was to send a beam 70 miles away, reached 75 feet in height but was never completed (Wilson, 2000, 91). On a more positive note, six other bells from Pennsylvania, which were believed to have joined the Liberty Bell in announcing the Declaration of Independence in 1776, were gathered in a display around the Bell.

Only about 6.5 million of the projected 30 million visitors attended, with the day of the controversial Dempsey-Tunney fight bringing in the most, 140,268 (Williams, 2000, 94). Queen Marie of Romania was among the event's most important visitors (Keels, 2017, 258–281).

The work on the site resulted in today's Franklin Delano Roosevelt Park and the Philadelphia Sports Complex. The stadium became known as the Municipal Stadium (and later J.F.K. Stadium) before being destroyed in 1992 ("Philadelphia, United States 1926, Sesqui-Centennial International Exposition," n.d.).

See also: Centennial Exposition of 1876; Luminous Liberty Bell; Tapping and Broadcasting the Sound of the Liberty Bell; Tourism and the Liberty Bell

Further Reading

Evensen, Bruce J. 1993. "'Saving the City's Reputation': Philadelphia's Struggle over Self-Identity, Sabbath-Breaking and Boxing in America's Sesquicentennial Year." *Pennsylvania History: A Journal of Mid-Atlantic Studies* 60 (January): 6–34.

Keels, Thomas H. 2017. *Sesqui! Greed, Graft, and the Forgotten World's Fair of 1926*. Philadelphia: Temple University Press.

Mires, Charlene. 2002. *Independence Hall in American Memory*. Philadelphia: University of Pennsylvania Press.

"Philadelphia, United States 1926, Sesqui-Centennial International Exposition." n.d. America's Best History. https://americasbesthistory.com/wfphiladelphia1926.html.

Rosewater, Victor. 1926. *The Liberty Bell: Its History and Significance*. New York: D. Appleton.

Wilson, Martin W. 2000. *From the Sesquicentennial to the Bicentennial: Changing Attitudes Toward Tourism in Philadelphia, 1926–1976*. PhD dissertation at Temple University, January.

Seybert, Henry (see Centennial Bell)

Shape of the Liberty Bell

Bells are shaped so as to provide melodious sounds. The shape of the Liberty Bell, which curves continually from a smaller top to a wider lip, was and remains fairly standard for bronze bells. There is an alternative Germanic shape, which Neil Goeppinger describes as having "a ridge around the outside of the sound bow with a straight surface running from that ridge to the lip of the bell" (2016, 26). Robert Hieronimus further notes that "Asian bells tend to be barrel-shaped, whereas Western bells tend to resemble an upside-down tulip, flared at the bottom (1988, 144). One example of an Asian bell is the Korean Bell of Friendship, a 17-ton bell that South Korea gave to the United States during its 1976 bicentennial celebrations. It is displayed at the Angels Gate Park in San Pedro, California, underneath a pagoda. Goeppinger observes that foundries have "their own unique bell shape," which in turn makes each of their sounds unique (2016, 26).

Whereas bronze bells are generally cast from a mold that is only used once, those for iron and steel bells are usually reused. Goeppinger observes, "They are shorter from the lip to the top as a percentage of the diameter of their mouth" and typically have a rougher finish (2016, 26).

The shapes of bells, also known as their profiles, are designed to enhance their tone or "timbre" (Kramer, 1975, 21). A 1976 study indicates that "[t]he diameter of the bell's mouth was to be fifteen times the thickness of the soundbow, which is the lower lip of the bell struck by the clapper. The diameter of the shoulder (usually the inscribed upper portion of the bell) was to be seven and a half times the thickness of the soundbow. Bell makers learned by trial and error the proper size and weight for the clapper" (Hanson, Carlson, Papouchado, and Nielsen, 1976, 614).

See also: Casting the Liberty Bell; Dimensions, Weight, and Cost of the Liberty Bell

Further Reading

Goeppinger, Neil. 2016. *Large Bells of America: History of Church Bells, Fire Bells, School Bells, Dinner Bells and Their Foundries*. Sarasota, FL: Suncoast Digital Press.

Hanson, Victor F., Janice H. Carlson, Karen M. Papouchado, and Norman A. Nielsen. 1976. "The Liberty Bell: Composition of the Famous Failure." *American Scientist* 64 (November–December): 614–619.

Hieronimus, Robert, with Laura Cortner. 2008. *The United Symbolism of America: Deciphering Hidden Meanings in America's Most Familiar Art, Architecture, and Logos*. Franklin Lakes, NJ: New Page Books.

"Korean Bell of Friendship." SanPedro.com—San Pedro, California. https://sanpedro.com
    /san-pedro-area-points-interest/korean-bell-friendship.

Kramer, Justin. 1975. *Cast in America: The Historically Accurate, Exciting Story of the
    Liberty Bell*. Los Angeles: Justin Kramer Incorporated.

Silence of the Liberty Bell

One of the most recognizable features of the Liberty Bell is its crack, which makes
ringing impossible without the threat of further damage. The crack is actually larger
than it was originally because William Eckel, who superintended the State House
in the 1840s, commissioned Henry Stone to drill out the existing crack so that the
Bell could be rung again. From time to time, various individuals have suggested
that it should be recast (as it was after its original crack) so that it might ring again
(Fosmoe, 2015), but the general consensus appears to be that its silence makes the
Bell more powerful than if it were to be physically restored so that it might ring
again.

The crack has contributed to making the Bell more visually distinctive (Callahan, 1999), even as it has silenced its voice or tongue, the name that some have
given to its clapper. When advocates of women's suffrage cast their own Justice
Bell, they taped the clapper so that it would not ring until the nation gave women
the right to vote. Labor activist Cesar Chavez later used a similar strategy, chain-
ing a replica of the Liberty Bell until a strike by grape workers was ended.

The Bell's inability to produce its intended audible sound has certainly not pre-
vented it from being used as a voice for numerous causes. These have included
American independence, the abolition of slavery, women's suffrage, civil rights,
lesbian, gay, bisexual, transgender, and queer/questioning (LGBTQ) rights, and
other issues.

A poem entitled "Independence Bell—July 4, 1776," which was printed in *Hillard's Fifth Reader* in 1871, observed ("Independence Bell—July 4, 1776." n.d.):

> That old State House bell is silent,
> Hushed is now its glamorous tongue;
> But the spirit it awakened
> Still is living—ever young

"The Liberty Bell," a poem written by Florence Earle Coates on the occasion of
the Bell's visit to the Atlanta Cotton State and International Exposition, observed
that (Coates, 1898):

> Men pass away, but I do not forget;
>   And though, alas, I have been silent long,
> The echoes of my ringing vibrate yet,
>   From pole to pole, in every freeman's song;
> And she who shared my May, in my December
> Shall gaze upon my face, and will remember!

Poets seem particularly adept at playing on the silence of the Liberty Bell. One of the most creative is found in the lyrics to Leonard Cohen's "Anthem," in which he contrasts sound and light by observing (Werber, 2016):

Ring the bells that still can ring
Forget your perfect offering
There is a crack, a crack in everything
That's how the light gets in.

See also: Crack in the Liberty Bell; "Independence Bell—July 4, 1776" (Poem, 1871); Justice Bell

Further Reading

Callahan, Robey. 1999. "The Liberty Bell: From Commodity to Sacred Object." *Journal of Material Culture* 4 (1): 57–78.

Coates, Florence Earle. "The Liberty Bell." *Poems.* Boston: Houghton, Mifflin, and Company, 1898.

Fosmoe, Margaret. 2015. "Notre Dame Grad Student Seeks Liberty Bell Fix." South Bend Tribune.com, February 20. https://www.southbendtribune.com/news/local/notre-dame-grad-student-seeks-liberty-bell-fix/article_d4fd733f-89f3-5aff-b780-25f1a14e0c74.html.

"Independence Bell—July 4, 1776." n.d. https://www.ego4u.com/en/read-on-ligerature/poem-independence-bell.

Werber, Cassie. 2016. "'There Is a Crack in Everything, That's How the Light Gets In': The Story of Leonard Cohen's 'Anthem.'" *Quartz,* November 22. https://qz.com/835076/leonard-cohens-anthem-the-story-of-the-line-there-is-a-crack-in-everything-thats-how-the-light-gets-in.

Silent Peal from the Liberty Bell, A (1914)

In 1914, Adaline May Conway (b. 1882) published a short book entitled *A Silent Peal from the Liberty Bell.* In the book, she personified the Bell as a being that embodied the spirit of liberty. She accordingly shared the "memories" of the Liberty Bell from its birth in England, through its painful recasting, to the historic events it had witnessed, and its recent journeys throughout the United States.

One of the highlights of the book was a poem that began with the words "the Spirit of Liberty," which was presumably its title. The Bell explained that it first heard the words of the spirit it was to embody aboard ship on its journey from England to America. The opening lines proclaim (Conway 1914, 16):

I am the Spirit of Liberty
And I speak
Through the voices
Of all free things
In earth and sky and sea.

As the poem continued, Conway further identified the Spirit of Liberty with that of Justice in opposition to tyranny (Conway, 1914, 16–17):

Where Justice dwells
I hover near:
Where oppressors rule
I enter there
To kindle in hearts of men
The fire of protest, that burns unquenched.
Until they rise in wrath
To wrench themselves free
And overthrow the Tyrant's power.

As the poem progressed, the Spirit of Liberty within the Bell perceived that "War-clouds are gathering / Over the Sea!" It ended with the following words (Conway, 1914, 17):

But I, the Spirit of Liberty,
Shall so inflame the hearts of men
That when the storm breaks
The world shall see
The miracle of Weakness conquering
   Strength!

Most of Conway's book concentrates on the role of the Liberty Bell as a witness to events surrounding the American Revolution against Britain. It ends with a plea to allow the Bell to remain at peace in Philadelphia, rather than taking further trips around the country.

See also: Journeys of the Liberty Bell; Liberty, Meaning of

Further Reading
Conway, Adaline May. 1914. *A Silent Peal from the Liberty Bell*. Philadelphia: George W. Jacobs.

Sister to the Liberty Bell

The bell that is today displayed as the Liberty Bell Is the third casting of the bell that was originally ordered from the Whitechapel Foundry in England. That bell, which had been ordered by Isaac Norris II on behalf of the Pennsylvania Assembly in 1751, arrived sometime on or before September 1, 1752, at which time Norris observed, "The bell is come on shore and in good order and we hope it will prove a good one" (Rosewater, 1926, 9). On March 10, 1753, Norris noted that although "our bell was generally liked and approved of . . . in a few days after my writing I had the mortification to hear that it was cracked by a stroke of the clapper without any other violence, as it was hung up to try the sound" (1926, 9–10).

Although the Assembly decided to send it back to England, a Captain Budden, who was in charge of the next ship headed back to England, was unable to take it back, and two local workmen, John Pass and John Stow, offered to melt the old Bell down and recast it. Believing that the original Bell had been too brittle, they added an ounce and a half of copper to each pound of the original Bell. On March 10, 1753, Norris reported that "the letters, I am told, are better than in the old one" and that "they made the mould in a masterly manner and ran the metal well" (Rosewater, 1926, 10). On April 14, 1753, however, Norris further recorded that "upon trial, it seems they have added too much copper in the present bell which is now hung up in its place, but they were so tiezed [teased] with the witticisms of the town, that they had a new mould . . . and will be very soon ready to make a second essay" (Rosewater, 1926, 10–11).

By November 8, 1753, Norris reported that the new Bell (the third) was being used, but that "though some are of the opinion it will do, I own I do not like it" (Rosewater, 1926, 11), presumably because he did not like its tone. Some members of the assembly were considering sending the Bell back to Whitechapel in partial payment for the new one. After the new Bell arrived, however, on August 13, 1754, the Assembly resolved that "the said Superintendants do pay for the new Bell and keep the Old One for such Uses as this house may hereafter appoint" (Rosewater, 1926, 12). Louis Rongione thus observes, "Though scarcely a year older than the Second Bell, the first bell became known as the Old Bell and thus achieved instant antiquity. The second bell, which presumably could be distinguished only by the names of an English rather than an American maker, was called 'The Other One'" (Rongione, 1976, 5).

The Old Bell was installed in the wooden steeple in the center of the State House (as today's Independence Hall was then called), which would later be replaced due to decay. The new "sister" bell was installed in a cupula on the side of the building and attached to a clock that resembled a giant grandfather clock made by a Philadelphia clockmaker by the name of Thomas Stretch. In 1759, Stretch received 494 pounds, 5 shillings, and 5½ pence, but this included not only the cost of the clock, but also its maintenance for six years (Rongione, 1976, 6).

In 1828, after the city decided to renovate the State House, it decided to order a new bell to be placed in the steeple, to be tied to a four-faced clock placed in the cupula and illuminated at night (Nash, 2010, 26). It accordingly sold the "sister" bell and the Thomas Stretch Clock to St. Augustine's Church. After it was unable to pay for the bell, the city remitted the payment with the understanding that the clock would benefit not simply the church, but members of the surrounding community as well (Frazier, 1974, 309). That church, in turn, was burned in a riot led by the Native American Party on May 8, 1844. Although the clock appears to have been beyond repair, the bell was salvaged and recast by Joseph Bernhard, who now owned the Wilbank Factory, in 1847. It says "CAST BY J. BERNHARD PHILA 1847" (Eckhardt, 1943).

According to Arthur H. Frazier, the bell "was suspended from a tree at St. Thomas of Villanova's College (now Villanova University), where it served as the 'College Bell' for about fifty years" (1974, 311). It was then moved to the Church of St. Nicholas of Tolentine on Jamaica, Long Island, but was returned to Villanova in 1941.

It has its own cradle and is now located in the Falvey Memorial Library (Frazier, 1974, 311). In 1976, the bell was displayed on the mezzanine floor of the Penn Mutual Building behind Independence Hall as part of a display entitled "Area Universities Bicentennial Exhibit" (Rongione 1976, 31).

In 1973, workmen installed a replica of the Thomas Stretch Clock at Independence Hall, which remains to this day.

See also: Names for the Liberty Bell; Norris, Isaac, II; Whitechapel Foundry; Wilbank, John

Further Reading

Eckhardt, George H. 1955. *Pennsylvania Clocks and Clockmakers: An Epic of Early American Science, Industry, and Craftsmanship.* New York: Devin-Adair Company.

Eckhardt, George H. 1943. "Sister of the Liberty Bell Now Clans in Belfry of Villanova College." *New York Sun*, April 30.

Frazier, Arthur H. 1974. "The Stretch Clock and Its Bell at the State House." *Pennsylvania Magazine of History and Biography* 98 (July): 287–313.

Kramer, Justin. 1975. *Cast in America: The Historically Accurate, Exciting Story of the Liberty Bell.* Los Angeles: Justin Kramer Incorporated.

Nash, Gary B. *The Liberty Bell.* New Haven, CT: Yale University Press.

Rongione, Louis A. 1976. "Sister to the Liberty Bell." *Records of the American Catholic Historical Society of Philadelphia* 87 (March–December): 3:32.

Rosewater, Victor. 1926. *The Liberty Bell: Its History and Significance.* New York: D. Appleton.

Slot Machines

On trips that the Liberty Bell took to various fairs and expositions from 1885 to 1915, individuals often raised pieces of jewelry and other objects for the guards to rub against the Liberty Bell that they could then carry for good luck. Combined with the fact that the ringing of bells may generate the kind of excitement that enhances the gambling experience, it may not be surprising that a slot machine known as the "Liberty Bell" became particularly popular in California in the 1890s.

Originally invented by Charles Fey, who had been born in Bavaria, his three-reel machine displayed only three symbols at a time that, when matched, resulted in a jackpot. The machine has been described as "a counter-model three-reel machine with one coin slot, an actuating lever on its right side, and a pay-off cup under its footed front. In addition to playing card symbols on its 20-symbol reels, there are liberty bells, stars, and horseshoes" (Tamony, 1968, 120). Stars and horseshoes, like bells, were all associated with good luck.

Fey distributed the machines throughout saloons, gaming locations, and brothels in San Francisco and surrounding areas. Rather than patenting the device or copyrighting the name, he refused to sell or lease the machines, instead operating them on a percentage basis (Fey, 1975, 57). This proved such a good strategy that he was able to open his own factory in San Francisco. He encountered his own bit of bad luck, however, when one of this machines was stolen from a saloon; it landed in the hands of the Mills Novelty Company in Chicago. Its owners took the machine apart and began manufacturing its own Mills Liberty Bell slots. Before long, Caille

Brothers Manufacturing Company in Detroit and the Watling Manufacturing Company in Chicago began manufacturing their own Liberty Bell models. Fey's own business was destroyed by the San Francisco earthquake of 1906 and the subsequent fires.

Today, a marker at the corner of Market, Bush, and Battery Streets in San Francisco notes Fey's achievements: "Charles August Fey began inventing and manufacturing slot machines in 1894. Fey pioneered many innovations of coin-operated gaming devices in his San Francisco workshop at 406 Market Street, including the original three-reel bell slot machine in 1898. The international popularity of the bell slot machines attests to Fey's ingenuity as an enterprising inventor whose basic design of the three reel slot machine continue to be used in mechanical gaming devices today" (Noe Hill, n.d.).

In 1977, William Electronics manufactured a "Liberty Bell" pinball machine. It prominently featured a picture of a ringing Liberty Bell against the blue canton of an American flag, with a circle of stars in the top-right corner of the backboard.

See also: Advertising and the Liberty Bell; Journeys of the Liberty Bell

Further Reading

Fey, Marshall A. 1975. "Charles Fey and San Francisco's Liberty Bell Slot Machine." *California Historical Quarterly* 54 (Spring): 57–62.

Noe Hill. n.d. "Liberty Bell Slot Machine." https://noehill.com/sf/landmarks/cal0937.asp.

Tamony, Peter. 1968. "The One-Armed Bandit." *Western Folklore* 27 (April): 117–124.

"Song of the Liberty Bell, The" (Song, 1904)

On August 14, 1904, the *Boston Sunday Herald* published a "Music Supplement," resembling a piece of sheet music, entitled "The Song of the Liberty Bell." The words were attributed to Jack Allison, and the music to William H. Penn. The copyright (1898) belonged to Sol Bloom, who had helped supervise construction at the World's Columbian Exposition in Chicago in 1893 and who would later serve in the U.S. House of Representatives and lead the nation's sesquicentennial of the U.S. Constitution in 1937 ("The Song of the Liberty Bell," 1904).

The cover featured the title with a picture of an orange bell and an oval photo of a woman against the backdrop of what appeared to be a branch. The song, with two verses, closely followed the words of the poem "Independence Bell—July 4, 1776," which portrayed a fictitious sexton waiting to hear word from his grandson that the delegates to the Second Continental Congress had declared liberty.

The chorus was as follows (Music Division, the New York Public Library, n.d.):

Ding, Dong, rang out the lib-er-ty song, Ding, dong,
Ding, dong, thrill-ing each heart in that throng: Ding, dong
Ding, dong, rang the old man, let glo-ri-ous mu-sic swell

Ring out the sto-ry of Free-dom and Glo-ry, The song of the Lib-er-ty Bell.

Mark O'Connor would later compose another orchestral arrangement of "The Song of the Liberty Bell" to accompany the Public Broadcasting System (PBS) documentary entitled *Liberty! The American Revolution*.

See also: "Independence Bell—July 4, 1776" (Poem, 1871); Music and the Liberty Bell

Further Reading

Music Division, the New York Public Library. n.d. "The Song of the Liberty Bell" New York Public Library Digital Collections. http://digitalcollections.nypl.org/items /510d47df-f216-a3d9-e040-e00a18064a99.

"The Song of the Liberty Bell." 1904. Music Supplement to the *Boston Sunday Herald*, August 14.

South Carolina Interstate and West Indian Exposition of 1902

By the beginning of the twentieth century, the Liberty Bell had traveled to the World's Industrial and Cotton Exposition in New Orleans in 1885, the World's Columbian Exposition of 1893 in Chicago, and the Atlanta Cotton States and International Exposition of 1895. On January 6, 1902, the Bell took its fourth ambassadorial journey, once again to the South. This time it went to the South Carolina Interstate and West Indian Exposition.

As on past trips, the city of Philadelphia prepared a rousing send-off, complete with a twenty-one-gun salute, and the Bell received an enthusiastic welcome on its journey. It passed through Mechanicsburg, Carlisle, Shippensburg, Chambersburg, and Greencastle, Pennsylvania; through Hagerstown, Maryland; through Shepherdstown and Charlestown, West Virginia; through Berryville, Luray, and Roanoke, Virginia; through Bristol, Johnson City, Greeneville, and Morristown, Tennessee; through Ashville, North Carolina; and through Columbia and Savannah, Georgia; before arriving at Charleston (Paige, 1988, 106).

Schoolchildren were often on hand to see the Bell, and they were often lifted up to it to touch or kiss it. In Carlisle, Pennsylvania, students at a Native American school played the national anthem as others sang patriotic songs (Cress, 2016).

January 9, the day of the Bell's arrival, was designated as "Liberty Bell Day," and schools and city businesses were closed. A large crowd accompanied the Bell to the exposition grounds before it was moved to the Pennsylvania building (Rosewater, 1926, 170).

As with earlier trips, the mayor of Charleston had argued that the Bell's visit would foster patriotism and promote Northern and Southern unity (Paige, 1988, 44). As for the city itself, its leaders were trying to recover from the devastation of the Civil War, a destructive hurricane in 1885, and an earthquake in 1886 (Harvery, 1997, 115). They were interested in restoring the prominence of the city's port in interstate and international trade, particularly in the aftermath of the Spanish-American War, and the opportunities it opened up for trade with Cuba, Puerto Rico, and the Spanish West Indies. The fair featured monumental buildings influenced chiefly by Italian and Spanish designs.

As with the Atlanta Exposition, this event featured a separate "Negro building," visited by relatively few whites, which sought to highlight the usefulness of black labor in both agriculture and industry. January 1, which was the anniversary of the Emancipation Proclamation, was proclaimed as "Negro Day," and a later visit by Booker T. Washington reaffirmed the position he had taken in Atlanta, when he said, "We cannot lift ourselves up by mere complaint, adverse criticism and con-demnation. We must exhibit to the world more and more each day tangible, visible, indisputable evidences of our progress and worth to the country" (Smyth, 1987, 214). Women also highlighted their achievements in a separate building (Bland, 1993).

The exposition was not a complete success. Harvey observes, "By 1905, Charles-ton had slipped further in its percentage of America's import trade, falling behind most of the other southern ports" (1997, 127). He believes that the members of the Charleston elite still held onto a "noncommercial, sentimental image" that remained at odds with "the message of progress" that the exposition had sought to convey (Harvey, 1997, 127).

The Liberty Bell returned to Philadelphia on Tuesday, June 10. On a prior stop in Washington, D.C., William H. Brown gave a speech in which he attempted to explain the Bell's appeal (Rosewater, 1926, 170):

> This Bell should be, and has been, an inspiration of patriotism in all the towns through which we have passed on our journey from the Charleston fair. Thousands of people, have flocked to see it throughout the South, not in Charleston alone, but at every point where we have stopped for even the smallest length of time. That the significance of this relic is appreciated through the South and the love of liberty throughout the South is as strong today as it was in the stirring times when this piece of brazen metal pro-claimed freedom to the world, has been evidenced by the reception it has had wher-ever we have been.

While the Bell was in Washington, D.C., the marine band played "The Liberty Bell March," which John Philip Sousa had composed for the 1893 Columbian Exposition.

See also: Children and the Liberty Bell; Journeys of the Liberty Bell; "Liberty Bell March, The" (Song, 1893)

Further Reading

Bland, Sidney R. 1993. "Women and World's Fairs: The Charleston Story." *South Caro-lina Historical Magazine* 94 (July): 166–184.

Cress, Joseph. 2016. "Ringing in 1902: Local Residents Rang in 1902 by Admiring the Liberty Bell." *The Sentinel.* https://cumberlink.com/news/local/history/ringing-in -local-residents-rang-in-by-admiring-the-liberty/article_863b36c5-7879-557f -831b-a73de94c80ff.html.

Harvey, Bruce. 1997. "Architecture for the Future at the Charleston Exposition, 1901–1902." *Perspectives in Vernacular Architecture* 7: 115–130.

Paige, John C. 1988. *The Liberty Bell of Independence National Historical Park: A Spe-cial History Study*, ed. David C. Kimball. Denver: Denver Service Center, National Park Service, Department of the Interior. Accessed through pubs.etic.nps.gov.

Rosewater, Victor. 1926. *The Liberty Bell: Its History and Significance.* New York: D. Appleton.

Smyth, William D. 1987. "Blacks and the South Carolina Interstate and West Indian Expo-sition." *The South Carolina Historical Magazine* 88 (October): 211–219.

Souvenirs of the Liberty Bell

Those who are seeking to collect materials related to the Liberty Bell have many options. During the bicentennial celebrations in 1976 alone, it is estimated that as many as 25,000 items were produced to commemorate the occasion. Indeed, a reporter even coined the term "Buy-centennial" (Gordon, 2013, 123). Many souvenirs were tacky or garish, but it was also possible to find higher-end items from this commemoration and others.

The Philadelphia Museum of Art has an antique, brown-glazed stoneware replica of the Liberty Bell, just over 10 inches in height, which may have been made by L. B. Beerbower of Elizabeth, New Jersey, sometime between 1880 and 1904. The McCoy Pottery factory produced a number of striking pieces early in the twentieth century. One is a large umbrella stand that portrays an outline of Independence Hall on one side and the Liberty Bell on the other (the original is signed "Ferrell," but there are also reproductions). Another is a Liberty Bell planter with a bell (sometimes gilded) hanging over what appears to be a wishing well. One such version has the words "4th JULY 1776" on the front, whereas another (sometimes described as a mistake) has the words "8th JULY 1776" (Hanson, Nissen, and Hanson, 1997, 188). In point of fact, although it is not known for certain whether the Liberty Bell rang for the Declaration of Independence, if it did, it rang, with other bells, on July 8 rather than on July 4.

Numerous platters, goblets, and other pressed glass objects were manufactured by the Gillinder Glass Company to commemorate the nation's centennial. They feature a Liberty Bell with a distinctive crack and the words, "DECLARATION OF INDEPENDENCE" around it, as well as "100 YEARS AGO." This pattern was reproduced with the dates 1776 and 1976 for the bicentennial. Fostoria Glass has produced numerous clear glass items, from bowls to candlesticks to punch bowls, that have frosted, coin-shaped decorations that feature the Liberty Bell and a colonial figure. Baccarat has produced a blue paperweight with a frosted Liberty Bell.

One of the more attractive set of drinking glasses that was manufactured for the bicentennial has a gold rim, with the translucent outline of the Liberty Bell surrounded by stars; they have the dates "1776" and "1976" on one side, and the text of the Declaration of Independence on the other. As one looks through the Liberty Bell to the inside of the cup, one can see a picture of George Washington and his troops crossing the Delaware River, thus reinforcing the association of the Liberty Bell with the American Revolution.

Numerous plates and bowls from a variety of manufacturers commemorate the Liberty Bell, often in conjunction with other patriotic symbols, especially Independence Hall, the American flag, the bald eagle, and other symbols. The author has a beautiful, clear glass bell shaped like the Liberty Bell and its yoke, which was probably produced for the bicentennial of the U.S. Constitution as it is inscribed with the words of the preamble to the U.S. Constitution rather than the opening words of the Declaration of Independence.

The Liberty Bell highlighted numerous prints and programs that were printed in connection with the centennial, the sesquicentennial, and the bicentennial. Sheet music related to the Bell is often quite colorful. The image of the Liberty Bell may also be found on hand towels. The Bell was a particularly prominent symbol for the sesquicentennial celebrations. This was also the first year that a stamp was issued with a picture of the Liberty Bell (in this case, the Luminous Liberty Bell that had been built specifically for the Sesquicentennial Exposition). There are numerous postcards that bear the image of the Liberty Bell. In addition to some so-called dollars from 1876 that depict the Liberty Bell, it has also been depicted on a 50-cent coin, on a dollar coin, and on some medals.

Brass replicas may range from one or two inches in size to full-scale replicas, which can still be purchased for $75.000. Ironically, some are manufactured overseas. It is common to find small glass savings banks in the shape of the Liberty Bell, as well as a number of posters for Liberty Loans that were made during World War I and soon thereafter incorporated the Liberty Bell in their depictions.

The Liberty Bell is often depicted on jewelry, T-shirts, neckties, scarves, and other clothing and ornaments. There is a busy, but beautiful, "Let Freedom Ring" cross-stitch pattern from the bicentennial. Some of the most striking images of the Liberty Bell are found on sheet music from the late nineteenth and early twentieth centuries, some of which are described in this book. There are also a variety of souvenir spoons and charms that depict the Liberty Bell.

Those who enjoy collecting books might seek to collect the *Liberty Bell Gift Books,* which were published by antislavery societies in the nineteenth century. There are a variety of bookends that depict the Bell, as well as paperweights and decks of cards. Higher-end collectors might look for Liberty Bell slot machines. Also, a number of advertising logos have included the Bell as part of their design. Buttons from the Liberty Loan campaigns, as well as political buttons, especially from the presidential election of 1924, depict the Bell as well.

Those who associate the Liberty Bell with Second Amendment rights might purchase one of Remington's .45-caliber custom Liberty Bell pistols. The gun has a picture of the Liberty Bell with a ribbon saying "PROCLAIM LIBERTY" on the handle, and another picture of the Liberty Bell and the words "LET FREEDOM RING" on one side and "NOW AND FOREVER" on the other.

See also: Bicentennial and the Liberty Bell; Campaign Buttons and the Liberty Bell; Centennial Exposition of 1876; Coins, Medals, and Stamps Depicting the Liberty Bell; *Liberty Bell Gift Books*; Music and the Liberty Bell; Replicas of the Liberty Bell; Slot Machines; Statue of Liberty

Further Reading

Gordon, Tammy S. 2013. *The Spirit of 1976: Commerce, Community, and the Politics of Commemoration.* Amherst: University of Massachusetts Press.

Hanson, Bob, Craig Nissen, and Margaret Hanson. 1997. *McCoy Pottery: Collectors Reference & Value Guides.* Padukah, KY: Collector Books.

Spirit of Liberty Bell

In 2001, the Providence Forum, which is dedicated to preserving, defending, and advancing "the faith and values consistent with those of our nation's founding" ("Spirit of Liberty Bell," n.d.) commissioned the Whitechapel Foundry in England, which had cast the first Liberty Bell, to make a replica (substituting an etched rather than an actual crack) to commemorate the 300th anniversary of William Penn's Charter of Privileges ("Spirit of Liberty Bell," n.d.). Although described as "an Exact Replica," it was about 1,000 pounds heavier (Museum of the Bible, 2016). To further enhance the connection to America's past, the yoke was further constructed from wood from the last of the original liberty trees.

On January 12, 2016, the forum transferred the Bell, which it had previously housed at the Williamson College of the Trades, to the Museum of the Bible in Washington, D.C., where it was to be a highlight of the "Bible in America" exhibit.

See also: Eagles, Flags, the Statue of Liberty, and Related Symbols; Inscription on the Liberty Bell; Leviticus 25:10; Liberty Trees and Liberty Poles; Pennsylvania Charter of Privileges (1701); Replicas of the Liberty Bell

Further Reading

"Liberty Bell." Philadelphia Museum of Art. http://www.philamuseum.org/collections/permanent/302817.html.

Museum of the Bible. 2016. "Museum of the Bible Installs First Exhibit Item: An Exact Replica of the Liberty Bell." Press release, August 16. https://www.museumofthebible.org/press/press-releases/museum-of-the-bible-installs-first-exhibit-item-an-exact-replica-of-the-liberty-bell.

"Spirit of Liberty Bell." n.d. Providence Forum. https://providenceforum.org/project/spirit-liberty-bell

State Liberty Bell Replicas

In 1950, the U.S. Treasury Department commissioned the Paccard Bell Foundry in Annecy, France, to manufacture a replica of the Liberty Bell for each of the U.S. states and territories. The bells were designed to stimulate interest in a drive to sell $650 million in bonds.

States could display the bells in any public, noncommercial setting, and most did so in the state capital, often near the capitol building. Apparently, there were two bells in Washington, D.C., one of which may have been an extra that was kept by the Treasury Department and that has since disappeared (Campbell, 2018). The United States donated one such bell to the city of Annecy, where it continues to be displayed in a tower. That city, in turn, gave one to the city of Independence, Missouri, the hometown of then-president Harry S Truman. Another such bell was given to Tokyo. In 1976, the bicentennial of American independence, the national government made an effort to ring all the bells simultaneously on July 4.

According to Tom Campbell, six American copper companies paid for the bells, and American steel companies paid for their mounts (2018, 18). Perhaps not surprisingly, the state liberty bells do not appear to have generated nearly the same interest as the original. Tennessee's is tucked away on the grounds of the State Capitol. Tom Campbell and Robert English, who have set out to visit each of the Liberty Bell replicas, reported that some of the bells are located in odd places, including the one in Kansas that English says "is stored in the basement of the Capitol in a parking garage," where "[i]t is disassembled and just wasting away" (Levy, 2017).

In 2015, Ed Martinez, Jr. was fishing on Sand Island, which is part of Hawaii, and discovered the bronze slab for Hawaii's replica, which he returned ("Piece of Historic Liberty Bell Recovered on Sand Island," 2015).

Many states have additional replicas that were apparently individually commissioned. In addition to its replica that is displayed in the Department of Archives and History in Montgomery, Alabama boasts replicas in both its Constitutional Village in Huntsville and in its American Village in Montevallo (Kazek, 2015).

Paccard has made numerous smaller-scale replicas of the Liberty Bell. In 2018, full-size replicas could be purchased for $75,000 each. As of 2017, a spokesperson indicated that "[w]e've done probably five or six or eight in the last seven or eight years. We did one at Fort Huachuca Army Base in Arizona. There's one at Midwestern State University in Wichita, Texas. So we've done a few" (Levy, 2017). John C. Paige published a list sent by Flora Ranney and compiled by Elizabeth Stevens specifying the location of 53 of the bells as of November 1957 (Paige, 1988, 142–143). However, it did not include the bells in Annecy or Tokyo, it listed only one for the District of Columbia, and the only bell it lists for Missouri is the one in Independence. In 1970, a dynamite bomb destroyed Oregon's replica of the Liberty Bell in the city hall rotunda in Portland, and the perpetrators have never been identified. Curiously, that bell is included on a more recent list of Liberty Bell replicas by state.

See also: Annecy Liberty Bell Replica; Tokyo, Japan, Replica of the Liberty Bell

Further Reading

Campbell, Tom. 2018. "National Treasury: The Case of DC's Missing Liberty Bell." Tom Loves the Liberty Bell.com, April 21. http://tomlovesthelibertybell.com/2018/04/21/national-treasury-the-case-of-dcs-missing-liberty-bell.

Kazek, Kelly. 2015. "Replicas of 12 World-Famous Things You Can See Right Here in Alabama." AL.com, February 24. https://www.al.com/living/index.ssf/2015/02/12_replicas_of_world-famous_si.html.

Levy, Dan. 2017. "Philly Export: The United States Actually Has More Than 50 Liberty Bells." Billy Penn.com, May 29. https://billypenn.com/2017/05/29/philly-export-the-united-states-actually-has-more-than-50-liberty-bells.

"Liberty Bell Replica Locations." n.d. Tom Loves the Liberty Bell.com. http://tomlovesthelibertybell.com/liberty-bell-replica-locations.

Paige, John C. 1988. *The Liberty Bell of Independence National Historical Park: A Special History Study*, ed. David C. Kimball. Denver: Denver Service Center, National Park Service, Department of the Interior. Accessed through pubs.etic.nps.gov.

"Piece of Historic Liberty Bell Recovered on Sand Island." 2015. KNON2 Staff, November 20. https://www.khon2.com/news/local-news/piece-of-historic-liberty-bell-recovered-on-sand-island_2018030911415441/1025654071.

Warnock, Kae. 2016. "That Rings a Bell!" National Conference of State Legislatures Blog, July 1. http://www.ncsl.org/blog/2016/07/01/that-rings-a-bell-.aspx.

Statue of Liberty

It is probably no coincidence that two of America's most iconic symbols, the bell that is the subject of this book, and a statue that France gave to the United States, are both preceded by the word *Liberty*. Moreover, both are tied to American

independence, and to the document by which the Second Continental Congress declared it.
Ironically, both were also made
abroad and are associated with
famous verses—one from the
Bible and the other from a
nineteenth-century poet.

The Liberty Bell, cast in 1753,
is the older symbol. It was cast
by the Whitechapel Foundry in
England and may have been
designed to mark the 50th anniversary of William Penn's Charter of Liberties. Often originally
called the "Old Bell" or the
"State House Bell" (after the
building in which it was housed),
it became increasingly associated with individual liberty as
abolitionists used the verse that
is embossed on it to argue for
African American emancipation.
This verse, taken from Leviticus
25:10 says, "Proclaim Liberty
throughout all the land to all the
inhabitants thereof." The Bell
originally gained much of its
popularity because it was believed to have pealed out independence upon the signing of the Declaration of Independence. The Liberty Bell was completed and dedicated in 1886.

The Statue of Liberty in New York, New York.
(PhotoDisc)

Whereas the Pennsylvania Assembly commissioned and paid for the Liberty
Bell, the Statue of Liberty, or "Liberty Enlightening the World," was a gift to the
United States from the nation of France, with which the 13 colonies had been
allied during the Revolutionary War. Located on Ellis Island in New York Harbor, the statue that personifies liberty as a woman in classical dress holding a
torch in her right hand was designed by Frederic Auguste Bartholdi and built by
Gustave Eiffel, best known for the tower that he designed in Paris. Her left hand
holds a tablet that says, "JULY IV MDCCLXXVI" (July 4, 1776 in Roman
numerals), thus commemorating the day the Second Continental Congress adopted
the Declaration of Independence.

Whereas the Liberty Bell was chiefly associated with the movement for the
emancipation of slaves, the Statue of Liberty has been primarily used as a symbol of American acceptance of immigrants. Its base contains a poem penned by
Emma Lazarus (1849–1887) entitled "The New Colossus," which compares Lady

Liberty to the Colossus of Rhodes, which stood for military victory. It says (Lazarus, 1883):

> Give me your tired, your poor,
> Your huddled masses yearning to breathe free.
> The wretched refuse of your teeming shore.
> Send these, the homeless, tempest-tost to me,
> I lift my lamp beside the golden door!

Like the Liberty Bell, the Statue of Liberty is a major tourist site, albeit more visible because it is outside. Whereas the Liberty Bell is associated with sound, the Statue of Liberty is associated with light. Like the Liberty Bell, it is a nearly universal symbol that is often reproduced on pins, buttons, and replicas. Although the parts of the Statue of Liberty were constructed abroad, once in place, it could never travel the nation as the Liberty Bell did from 1885 to 1915. The Liberty Bell Plaza and Ellis Island have been regarded both as sacred spots and as convocation places for political demonstrations.

In 1965, a group of African Americans and a Canadian plotted to blow up the Statute of Liberty, the Liberty Bell, and the Washington Monument, but they were discovered before they had a chance to act (Grieff, 1987, 186). One advantage that the Statue of Liberty may have over the Liberty Bell is that it may be easier to personify the former because it is in the shape of a woman. It is also much larger. In a tongue-in-cheek article, Ben Mathis-Lilley (2016) suggested commissioning a bell that would dwarf Independence Hall.

See also: Declaration of Independence and the Liberty Bell; Inscription on the Liberty Bell; Liberty, Meaning of; Security for the Liberty Bell

Further Reading

Berenson, Edward. 2012. *The Statue of Liberty: A Transatlantic Story.* New Haven, CT: Yale University Press.

Greiff, Constance M. 1987. *Independence: The Creation of a National Park.* Philadelphia: University of Pennsylvania Press.

Lazarus, Emma. 1883. "The New Colossus." NPS.gov, November 2. https://www.nps.gov/stli/learn/historyculture/colossus.htm.

Mathis-Lilley, Ben. 2016. "We Need to Make the Liberty Bell Way Bigger." *The Slatest,* July 26. http://www.slate.com/blogs/the_slatest/2016/07/26/the_liberty_bell_is_too_small.html.

Moreno, Barry. 2000. *The Statue of Liberty Encyclopedia.* New York: Simon & Schuster.

Statue of Liberty—Ellis Island Foundation, Inc. n.d. "Statue History." https://www.libertyellisfoundation.org/statue-history.

Surface of the Liberty Bell

In comparison to most other bells, the Liberty Bell has a relatively rough surface. This probably stems from at least two factors. First, tests show that ratios among metals in the bell vary from one spot to another, which likely indicates that when

John Pass and John Stow recast the bell from the original, which cracked on its first ringing, they probably used a series a small crucibles, rather than a single one, when they poured the metal into the bell mold (Hanson et al., 1976, 617). Second, since their primary work did not involve casting bells, they may not have had the sophisticated machinery to polish their bells once they were cast. Most reproductions and souvenirs of the Liberty Bell are more polished than the original.

The lettering on the Liberty Bell is raised, and a number of stories from the past recount blind visitors to the Bell being allowed to run their fingers not only over the letters, but also on the crack. The current Liberty Bell Center allows visitors to touch reproduced lettering on the Bell in one of the displays leading up to it.

See also: Composition of the Liberty Bell; Maintenance of the Liberty Bell

Further Reading
Hanson, Victor F., Janice H. Carlson, Karen M. Papouchado, and Norman A. Nielsen. 1976. "The Liberty Bell: Composition of the Famous Failure." *American Scientist* 64 (November–December): 614–619.

Symbolism of the Liberty Bell

Like the Statue of Liberty, the Liberty Bell is not valued for the materials of which it is composed but because of what it symbolizes, which is enhanced by its long history and associations with key events. In the case of the Liberty Bell, these include its ties to the American Revolution and the Declaration of Independence, to abolitionism, to women's suffrage, to civil rights, to the fight against totalitarianism during World War II and the subsequent Cold War, and to other expansions of liberty throughout U.S. history. Jonathan Tafel thus observed, "Although representing a concrete entity, the Liberty Bell is abstract in that it has come to represent and stand for the abstract qualities of freedom, liberty, and independence and is seen as a symbol which depicts such meanings" (1979, 145).

These associations have been enhanced by the number of visitors who have seen and touched the Bell, as well as by trips that the Liberty Bell took to other states and cities between 1885 and 1915. Its symbolism has been further enhanced by its association with other sacred places, like Independence Hall and the city of Philadelphia, and other sacred objects, like the flag, the bald eagle, and other symbols of American ideals.

The words on the bell, "Proclaim liberty throughout all the land unto all the inhabitants thereof," which are taken from Leviticus 25:10, give some grounding to the meaning that the Bell was intended to convey. Gary B. Nash says that the Bell has been "a stand-in for the nation's vaunted values: independence, freedom, unalienable rights, and equality" (Nash, 2010). He further says that "Americans have adopted it, along with the flag, as a symbol of justice, the rule of law, and the guardian of sovereign rights" (Nash, 2010). When visiting the Bell on September 22, 1990, the Dalai Lama, who was photographed showing the sign of peace in front of the Bell, observed, "I believe this is a reminder to American people—who enjoy so much freedom in this country—that in other parts of the world . . . there is no freedom. You cannot be truly free if not everybody is free" (Sands and Bartlett, 2012, 118).

As a speech by onetime Philadelphia mayor Charles F. Warwick demonstrates, however, these ideals are subject to considerable interpretation and expansion. He used the Bell to argue that the United States was responsible for civilizing natives of colonies that it had taken from Spain during the Spanish-American War (Warwick, 1903).

Robey Callahan has observed that, partly as a result of its wide use in advertising, "[f]or all practical purposes the Bell's image has become an iconic legisign. Any iconic instance of the Bell requires only to have the merest outline of a bell with a crack proceeding upward from the base" (1999, 71). Even the crack may not be necessary. The Heritage Foundation, a conservative think tank, thus uses a simple image that incorporates a bell shape (with no crack) underneath a yoke like that of the Liberty Bell. David Bishop has observed, "Either the yoke, the crack or the inscription, or any combination of them, is sufficient to evoke, at least in a subconscious level, comfortable feelings" (1975, 35). He also said that there is an almost instant association between the Liberty Bell and the city of Philadelphia and the state of Pennsylvania.

One speech that is particularly adept at identifying the role of the Liberty Bell as a symbol was delivered by the Reverend H. M. J. Klein on November 19, 1903. The occasion was that of accepting a tablet from the Daughters of the American Revolution commemorating the role of the Zion Reformed Church in Allentown, Pennsylvania, for harboring and concealing the Liberty Bell during the time that the British occupied Philadelphia. In acknowledging this tablet, Klein asked, "Do men tell us that we have gathered here only to do honor to a symbol, only to give expression to a sentiment, only to record an episode of the past?" (Stoudt, 1927, 30). After asking, "Yet what is a symbol other than an object which stands for some great idea?" Klein compared the Liberty Bell to the flag and the cross. He further elaborated (Stoudt, 1927, 30):

> This independence bell is not a mere thing of cold metal. It has come through its history and associations to stand for the vast collective life of the American people. At the sight of it men are reminded of the birth and struggle of a great nation. Men would fight for it as they would fight for a flag, not because of what it is in itself, but because it stands for them as a symbol of that proclamation, which echoed throughout this land and unto all the inhabitants thereof.

Klein, in turn, added his own interpretation to the Bell by expressing the hope that the tablet he was helping to dedicate would "be a silent and eloquent expression for generations to come of the eternal truth that freedom without religion is but a mockery and that the eternal God is the refuge of men and nations" (Stoudt, 1927, 30).

See also: Eagles, Flags, the Statue of Liberty, and Related Symbols; Leviticus 25:10; Warwick, Charles F.

Further Reading

Bishop, David H. 1975. "Ascent to Significance: The Evolution of the Liberty Bell as a Cultural Symbol." American Studies senior thesis, Temple University, May 2. Located at National Independence Historical Park.

Callahan, Robey. 1999. "The Liberty Bell: From Commodity to Sacred Object." *Journal of Material Culture* 4 (1): 57–78.

Marcovitz, Hal. 2003. *The Liberty Bell. Part of American Symbols and Their Meaning.* Philadelphia: Mason Crest Publishers.

Matero, Frank G. 2013. "Housing the Bell: 150 Years of Exhibiting an American Icon." *Change over Time* 3 (Fall): 188–201.

Nash, Gary B. 2010. "Liberty Bell." *Philadelphia Encyclopedia.* http://philadelphiaen cyclopedia.org/archive/liberty-bell.

Sands, Robert W., Jr., and Alexander B. Bartlett. 2002. *Images of America: Independence Hall and the Liberty Bell.* Charleston, SC: Arcadia Publishing.

Stoudt, John Baer. 1927. *The Liberty Bell in Allentown and Allentown's Liberty Bell.* Allentown, PA: Berkemeyer, Keck.

Tafel, Jonathan Leigh. 1979. *The Historical Development of Political and Patriotic Images of America: A Visual Analysis of Fourth of July Cartoons in Five Newspapers.* PhD dissertation at Ohio State University.

Warwick, Charles Franklin. 1903. *Orations and Speeches of Charles F. Warwick.* R. Welch.

T

Taco Liberty Bell

One indication that the Liberty Bell remains fixed in American consciousness was the reaction that a prank ad on April 1, 1996, generated. Taco Bell, a fast food chain founded by Glen Bell that specializes in Tex-Mex cuisine, placed full-page advertisements announcing that "Taco Bell Buys the Liberty Bell." The ad included a picture of the Liberty Bell at the top and the following text: "In an effort to help the national debt, Taco Bell is pleased to announce that we have agreed to purchase the Liberty Bell, one of our country's most historic treasures. It will now be called the 'Taco Liberty Bell' and will still be accessible to the American public for viewing. While some may find this controversial, we hope our move will prompt other corporations to take similar actions to do their part to reduce the country's debt" ("The Taco Liberty Bell," n.d.). Below the text was the logo of Taco Bell, now with a crack resembling that of the Liberty Bell, as if confirming Robey Callahan's argument that "now the merest outline of a bell with a crack serves to call to mind the [Liberty] Bell" (Callahan, 1999, 72). Below the logo, in small print, were the words "Nothing Ordinary About It."

Fast-food chain Taco Bell's logo depicts a large bell. (Adrianadh/Dreamstime.com)

The company issued a separate press release indicating that the Bell would spend part of its time each year at the Taco Bell headquarters in Irvine, California. It bragged, "Now we've got the crown jewel of bells" ("The Taco Liberty Bell," n.d.).

For years, Americans have saved coins in small banks in the shape of the Liberty Bell, and it is possible that this practice may have lent credibility to the idea that Taco Bell's purchase of the Liberty Bell might have been a genuine attempt to pay down the national debt, which had risen sharply during the Ronald Reagan administration. Just the year before, a governmental shutdown precipitated by an impasse over the federal budget had briefly closed several national landmarks, including Independence Hall (Crockett, 2014).

However valid the budget concerns were, they did nothing to quell the thousands of phone calls that began pouring into the headquarters of the National Park Service by individuals who were concerned over such a corporate purchase. The service's spokespeople, who had been caught off guard, called a press conference to say that the advertisement was false. At noon, Taco Bell announced that its advertisement had been an April Fool Day's joke, but that it was donating $50,000 to the upkeep of the Bell.

Later in the day, White House press secretary Mike McCurry joined the fun by announcing, "We'll be doing a series of these. Ford Motor Co. is joining today in an effort to refurbish the Lincoln Memorial. It will be the Lincoln Mercury Memorial" ("The Taco Liberty Bell," n.d.). The next day, Taco Bell circulated a picture of its chief executive officer dressed as one of the founding fathers and posing with the Bell (Crockett, 2014).

The advertisement drew massive publicity and increased sales at Taco Bell, but it also led to some critical comments by individuals who believed that it was in bad taste. Even for those who may have been amused, the advertisement seemed to cross the line in blending the sacred (the Liberty Bell) with the profane (fast food). Law professor Ronald Collins questioned whether the next joke might involve a crucifix. Jonathan Blum, Taco Bell's vice president of public affairs, who had been part of the team that came up with the ploy, said, "For those who didn't get the joke and care about the bell, just think about how much more recognition we've given it in this one day. There's been a terrific response among people I talked to, and some of them even said, 'Hey, thanks for making me aware of how we need to take care of our monuments'" ("The Taco Liberty Bell," n.d.).

See also: Advertising and the Liberty Bell; Civil Religion and the Liberty Bell

Further Reading

Callahan, Robey. 1999. "The Liberty Bell: From Commodity to Sacred Object." *Journal of Material Culture* 4 (1): 57–78.

Crockett, Zach. 2014. "When Taco Bell 'Bought' the Liberty Bell." Priceonomics, July 14. https://priceonomics.com/when-taco-bell-bought-the-liberty-bell.

Nash, Gary B. 2010. *The Liberty Bell.* New Haven, CT: Yale University Press.

"The Taco Liberty Bell." n.d. Museum of Hoaxes. http://hoaxes.org/archive/permalink/taco_liberty_bell.

Tapping and Broadcasting the Sound of the Liberty Bell

Because it is cracked, the Liberty Bell is no longer suitable for ringing, but the desire to hear it, which is fed by its emotional appeal and its historic significance, remains powerful. For over a century, the bell has been tapped, and often broadcast, on historic occasions (Paige, 1988).

In 1915, prior to taking its trip to San Francisco, the Bell was struck three times. Its sound, and one from a bell struck in San Francisco, were transmitted across the country (Paige, 1988, 51). On Flag Day of 1917 (June 14), the Bell was struck again to mark the last day of the first Liberty Loan Campaign to help finance World War I. In 1925, 1926, and 1927, the Bell was tapped, and the sound carried by radio, to announce the new year (Paige, 1988, 58). It was also tapped for the sesquicentennial of the American Revolution, the birth of the nation, and the end of sesquicentennial celebrations (Paige, 1988, 58).

In 1931, the Bell was tapped on January 25 to mark the 225th anniversary of Benjamin Franklin's birth. After the radio transmission of the tapping of the Bell for George Washington's birthday the next year, authorities announced that this would end the practice for the next hundred years (Paige, 1988, 61).

Nonetheless, Admiral Richard E. Byrd was allowed to tap the Liberty Bell by sending an electronic impulse from Antarctica on July 4, 1934, and it was tapped again on Independence Day of the next year (Paige, 1988, 61). On April 22, 1936, the Bell was tapped by representatives of the Emergency Peace Campaign, and on June 23 by members of the Democratic National Convention, who were arguing for increased preparedness (Paige, 1988, 61–62).

On May 14, 1937, the Bell was tapped to mark the 200th anniversary of the opening of the Constitutional Convention of 1787, on July 4 for Independence Day, and on October 15 for the opening of the Second Annual Negro Congress. Although it was common to give 13 taps for the original colonies, this time the 13 taps were for the ratification of the Thirteenth Amendment, which abolished slavery. The next year, it was tapped on June 21 to mark the 150th anniversary of New Hampshire's ratification of the U.S. Constitution (Paige, 1988, 62)

On June 24, 1940, the Bell was tapped for the opening of the Republican National Convention in Philadelphia. That same year, many military enlistees took their oath in front of the Bell (Paige, 1988, 63).

On July 2, 1941, the Liberty Bell was tapped and the sound broadcast by radio to initiate a new campaign to sell defense bonds (Pagie, 1988, 63). At President Franklin D. Roosevelt's suggestion, it was further tapped and broadcast to stimulate support for World War II. Such a tapping was transmitted on June 17, 1942, on October 10 to signal the 31st anniversary of the Chinese Republic, with which the United States was allied against Japan, and on Thanksgiving Day to symbolize American gratitude for its freedoms (Paige, 1988, 66).

Tapping and broadcasting continued throughout the remainder of the war. In 1942, it was tapped for "I Am an American Day," which was May 16. It was also tapped on in July 4 and to open a bond drive on September 24 (Paige, 1988, 67). In 1944, it was tapped again to open another war bond drive (the fourth of its kind). That June 6, it announced the invasion of Normandy (by being tapped seven times to spell out the word *Liberty*). On June 9, it was tapped to announced Flag Week activities, and again on August 23, to be taped for radio stations to use when American allies secured victory in Europe (Paige, 1988, 67).

On March 9, 1945, the Bell was tapped to announce the liberation of the Philippines. One month later, on April 9, it was tapped to launch another Liberty Bond campaign. On May 20, it was tapped once again for "I Am an American Day" (Paige, 1988, 68). On V-J Day, August 15, 1945, the Bell was tapped to celebrate the Japanese surrender (Dollman, April 20, 2018). The war ended formally in 1945, but the Bell was tapped again on "I Am an American Day" in 1946 (Paige, 1988, 68).

In 1947, representatives of the U.S. International Women's Conference had their chance to tap the Liberty Bell. On November 1, 1951, a descendant of Andrew McNair, who had been the bell ringer in 1776, rang it to commemorate the 200th anniversary of its casting (Paige, 1988, 69–70).

In 1952, the same year that President Dwight D. Eisenhower visited the Bell, it was tapped to begin a television broadcast entitled *We the People* (Paige, 1988, 70). Two years later, the Bell, which was being increasingly used to symbolize American liberty versus foreign communism, was tapped on Abraham Lincoln's birthday to call for freedom in Eastern European nations under the sway of the Soviet Union, as it would be again on George Washington's birthday the next year (Paige, 1988, 71).

Abba Eban, Israel's ambassador to the United States, tapped the Bell in 1955, and then again for the next two years, to mark his nation's seventh anniversary and its close ties to the United States (Paige, 1988, 71).

On November 9, 1959, the Columbia Record Company and the Philadelphia Orchestra successfully recorded the tapping of the Liberty Bell (Paige, 1988, 73). In 1962, it was tapped on August 13 to protest the construction of the Berlin Wall, and to express hope for individuals in communist countries. Later that year, it was tapped to mark the opening of a new home office for the Independence Life and Accident Company in Louisville, Kentucky, which used the Liberty Bell as its insignia (Paige, 1988, 74–75).

In 1963 and 1964, the Bell was tapped on July 4, and the following year, a recording of the sound was used (Paige, 1988, 75).

On July 4, 1976, the Centennial Bell, in the Liberty Bell Tower, pealed out 13 times (Martin, 1976).

In recent years, the Pennsylvania Society of the Sons of the Revolution (PSSR) sponsored a "Let Freedom Ring" ceremony. During this event, descendants of the original signers of the Declaration of Independence are permitted to tap the Bell.

Although most tapping has been done with a small mallet, a picture of Rosa Parks and Philadelphia mayor W. Wilson Good show them gently striking the Bell with their fists on January 18, 1988, to honor Dr. Martin Luther King, Jr.'s birthday (a tradition that had begun two years earlier and continues to this day). West Germany's chancellor, Helmut Schmidt, apparently tapped the Bell with his knuckles on a visit during July 17 of the U.S. bicentennial year (Sands and Bartlett, 2012, 119, 126).

See also: Crack in the Liberty Bell; Liberty Loans; Occasions for Ringing the Liberty Bell; Presidents and Foreign Dignitaries at the Liberty Bell; Silence of the Liberty Bell

Further Reading

Dollman, Darla Sue. 2018. "The Liberty Bell: International Symbol of Freedom." Owlcation, April 20. https://owlcation.com/humanities/The-Liberty-Bell-Symbol -of-American-Independence.

"How to Be a Bell Tapper." 2015. Society of the Descendants of the Signers of the Declaration of Independence, May 3. http://www.dsdi1776.com/members-only-how-to-be -a-bell-tapper.

Martin, Harold H. 1976. "Liberty Bell to Clunk—Softly." UPI Archives, June 30. https://www.upi.com/Archives/1976/06/30/Liberty-bell-to-clunk-softly/4374500 289137.

Paige, John C. 1988. *The Liberty Bell of Independence National Historical Park: A Special History Study*, ed. David C. Kimball. Denver: Denver Service Center, National Park Service, Department of the Interior.

Sands, Robert W., Jr., and Alexander B. Bartlett. 2002. *Images of America: Independence Hall and the Liberty Bell*. Charleston, SC: Arcadia Publishing.

Tokyo, Japan, Replica of the Liberty Bell

After World War II, U.S. forces occupied Japan. General Douglas MacArthur headed the Supreme Command of Allied Powers (SCAP) in Japan from 1945 to 1952. During this time, the United States donated a replica of the Liberty Bell, which remains on display at the Hibiya Park in Tokyo. It appears to have been one of the bells that the Paccard Bell Foundry in Annecy, France, cast for states and territories in connection with a savings bond drive.

The plaque on the bell, which is in English, was photographed by the blog *Lost Tokyo*. It reads as follows ("Hibiya Park Liberty Bell," 2014):

DEDICATED TO YOU, A FREE CITIZEN IN A FREE LAND
THIS REPRODUCTION OF THE FAMOUS LIBERTY BELL IN INDEPENDENCE HALL PHILADELPHIA, WAS PRESENTED TO THE PEOPLE OF JAPAN BY A GROUP OF AMERICAN COMPANIES AT THE SUGGESTION OF GENERAL DOUGLAS MacARTHUR. THIS PRESENTATION WAS ARRANGED BY THE HONORABLE JOHN W. WNYDER, SECRETARY OF THE UNITED STATES TREASURY.

ITS DIMENSIONS AND TONE ARE IDENTICAL WITH THOSE OF THE ORIGINAL LIBERTY BELL WHEN IT RANG OUT THE INDEPENDENCE OF AMERICAN IN 1776, BECOMING THEREBY A SYMBOL OF FREEDOM TO NOT ONLY AMERICANS BUT ALL MANKIND.

IN STANDING BEFORE THIS SYMBOL, YOU HAVE THE OPPORTUNITY TO DEDICATE YOURSELF, AS DID THE FOUNDING FATHERS OF THE UNITED STATES, TO THE PRINCIPLES OF FREEDOM WHICH YOU SHARE WITH FREE CITIZENS EVERYWHERE.

This plaque was indicative of American efforts, which have largely succeeded, to direct Japan away from authoritarian to democratic rule.

See also: Global Significance of the Liberty Bell; State Liberty Bell Replicas

Further Reading
"Hibiya Park Liberty Bell." 2014. *Lost Tokyo* (blog), June 18. http://lost-tokyo.blogspot.com /2014/06/hibiya-park-liberty-bell.html.

Tourism and the Liberty Bell

The idea of using the Liberty Bell to promote tourism does not appear nearly as exalted as using it to impart patriotism, to fight for the abolition of slavery, or to argue for women's suffrage. Still, there can be little doubt that many of the celebrations that have featured the Bell have been designed to lure visitors, and not always to Philadelphia.

From 1885 to 1915, the Liberty Bell took seven trips out of the state of Pennsylvania to be part of expositions, fairs, and commemorations. Although these trips undoubtedly promoted patriotism, especially as the train that carried it made stops along the way, they also lured people to the events who otherwise might not have attended. The trips to the South had the additional advantage of promoting national unity in the aftermath of the U.S. Civil War.

For most of its history, however, the Liberty Bell has remained in Philadelphia. Originally located in the steeple, it was taken from there as it decayed and was displayed throughout the nineteenth century in various spots within the building. As

Visitors observe the Liberty Bell. (Lei Xu/Dreamstime.com)

the bicentennial of the Declaration of Independence approached, the Bell was moved to a pavilion not far from the building, which served until it was moved again in 2003 to a new center, which provided more interpretative panels for visitors. The first of these moves was explicitly made because of fears that Independence Hall would be unable to accommodate the crowds that were expected for the bicentennial celebrations.

The centennial exhibition in 1876, which celebrated the city's historic role in the American Revolution, was generally considered to be a success. One of the highlights of the year was the completion of a large Centennial Bell, which was placed in the tower of Independence Hall. The sesquicentennial celebrations that were held 50 years later, and that prominently highlighted the Liberty Bell, were not nearly so successful, with only 6.4 million people attending, falling well short of the projected 30 million (Wilson, 2000, 93). This seems to have largely been because of Philadelphia's own lackluster support for the event, which stemmed from its conception of itself as a manufacturing town rather than as a tourist destination.

By 1976, this mindset had largely changed, and the city was making tourist dollars a much higher priority. Philadelphia vied vigorously against Boston to lure a World's Fair to the city. Disputes over where such an exposition would be held, as well as increasing estimates of the cost of such an exhibition, eventually scuttled such plans, as directors for the bicentennial celebrations scheduled events throughout the nation to commemorate this anniversary. Apparently, estimates of huge numbers of tourists actually ended up deterring individuals who might otherwise have visited but who did not want to deal with large crowds. Indeed, of the 20,000 visitors who came each day in June, less than a third visited Independence Hall or the Liberty Bell (Wilson, 2000, 219). Cities like Boston, Williamsburg, Virginia, and Washington, D.C., also reported smaller crowds than anticipated (Wilson, 2000, 220).

However disappointing the crowds may have been, Philadelphia was among the cities that had come to recognize the value of tourist dollars. Writing in 2002, Charlene Mires observed that about 800,000 people tour Independence Hall each year, and that about twice that many see the Liberty Bell. She largely attributed this to the fact that the lines and the tour were both shorter. By comparison, she noted that about 5.5 million people visited the Statue of Liberty, about 2.5 million visited Mount Rushmore in South Dakota, and about 1.4 million visited the *U.S.S. Arizona* memorial in Hawaii (Mires, 2002, 273–274). In 2016, more than 5 million people visited the Independence National Historical Park, which was a 17 percent increase from the previous year; as of 2017, the highest number of visitors to the park was 7.3 million, who visited in 1987, the centennial of the U.S. Constitution (Kopp, 2017).

Since 1976, the city has witnessed the construction of the National Constitution Center (NCC), which opened on July 4, 2003; and the Museum of the American Revolution, which opened on April 19, 2017. Both of which are located near Independence Hall and the Liberty Bell Center. Linda Loyd calls Independence National Historical Park an "economic juggernaut" and notes that the Park Service has plans to restore the First Bank, as well as other financial landmarks in the city, to their original splendor (Loyd, 2017).

Of course, many people are drawn to the National Archives in Washington, D.C., which houses the original, engrossed copy of the Declaration of Independence, as well as original copies of the U.S. Constitution and the proposed Bill of Rights, all of which were created in Philadelphia. The Declaration was lent to the city of Philadelphia for the centennial and sesquicentennial celebrations.

See also: Centennial Exposition of 1876; Declaration of Independence and the Liberty Bell; Journeys of the Liberty Bell; Liberty Bell Center; Liberty Bell Pavilion; Sesquicentennial International Exposition

Further Reading

Kopp, John. 2007. "Visitors Come in Droves to See Independence Hall, Liberty Bell in 2016." *Philly Voice,* January 18. https://www.phillyvoice.com/visitation-soars-independence-national-park.

Loyd, Linda. 2017. "The Economic Juggernaut That Is Independence National Historical Park." *The Inquirer,* June 30. http://www2.philly.com/philly/business/tourism_casinos/big-crowds-expected-at-independence-national-historical-park-20170630.html.

Mires, Charlene. 2002. *Independence Hall in American Memory.* Philadelphia: University of Pennsylvania Press.

Wilson, Martin W. 2000. *From the Sesquicentennial to the Bicentennial: Changing Attitudes Toward Tourism in Philadelphia, 1926–1976.* PhD dissertation at Temple University, January.

Two-Hundred-and-Fiftieth Anniversary Liberty Bell

In 2002, USA Renaissance decided to celebrate the 250th anniversary of the original casting of the Liberty Bell by asking the Whitechapel Foundry in England, which had cast the original, to cast another replica. This version included headstock and fittings and an engraved crack to imitate the one on the current Liberty Bell ("Another Liberty Bell"). This bell is now displayed under a pagodalike structure in Green Bay, Wisconsin.

See also: Replicas of the Liberty Bell; Whitechapel Foundry

Further Reading

"Another Liberty Bell." n.d. *Whitechapel Bell Foundry News.* http://www.whitechapelbellfoundry.co.uk/newsf.htm.

U

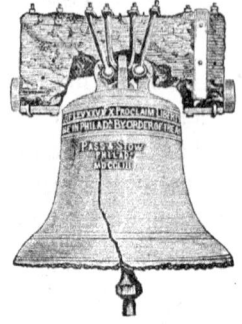

Union "Liberty Bell" Polka (Song, 1860)

Although the Liberty Bell appears to have received its present name not only from its inscription, but also from abolitionists, who sought to use it as a symbol of emancipation, it can and has been used for other purposes and causes.

Although the presidential election of 1860 largely featured the Republican Abraham Lincoln against the Democrat Stephen A Douglas, both of Illinois, it also featured another Democrat, C. Breckinridge of Kentucky, and the Constitutional Union candidate, John Bell of Tennessee. The latter candidate and his party sought to ignore the issue of slavery in preference to emphasizing national unity.

The year of this election featured the publication of a piece of sheet music entitled "The 'Union Bell' Polka." Composed by Charles Grobe (1817–1879), it was published by Lee and Walker in Philadelphia, James A. McClure in Nashville, and McClure, Hurlbut & Co. in Memphis. The cover features an oval picture of John Bell, appearing quite stern.

Although the score did not contain lyrics, the music was preceded by the words: "THE UNION BELL POLKA," and by the following poem (Grobe, 1860, 3):

Hark! The Union Bell is ringing,
   All the land its echoes hear,
Listen what the notes are telling;
   Free men hark! For Peace is near.
All unworthy passions buried
   By the voice of this great BELL:
Brothers rise, and live as brothers,
   And loud the Union chorus swell.

Is seems clear that the polka title is playing on the last name of the Constitutional Union Party candidate. Because the music does not contain a picture of the Liberty Bell, it is impossible to tell with certainty whether it intended to refer specifically to the bell in Philadelphia. Whether it intended to refer specifically to this Bell or to the general conception of a bell of harmony, the Liberty Bell would later be employed, especially in its journeys to various fairs and expositions, as a symbol of reconciliation of North and South.

Interestingly, as he entered the presidency, Abraham Lincoln viewed his primary responsibility as that of preserving the Union rather than that of freeing the slaves. Constitutional Unionists split their allegiances during the Civil War. John Bell supported the Confederacy, but many of his Northern counterparts, including his vice presidential candidate, Edward Everett, supported the Union.

See also: Abolitionists and the Liberty Bell; Journeys of the Liberty Bell; Music and the Liberty Bell; Political and Social Movements and the Liberty Bell; Reconciliation and the Liberty Bell; Symbolism of the Liberty Bell

Further Reading

Grobe, Charles. 1860. *The Union Bell Polka.* Lee & Walker, Philadelphia. Notated Music. https://www.loc.gov/item/ihas.200000206.

United States v. Marcavage (2010)

The original home of the Liberty Bell, designated as the State House, was a place for the Pennsylvania Assembly to gather. In addition to calling legislators to work, the Bell was often rung to gather people for political protests, particularly in the period leading up to the American Revolution. Just as the Bell later became a symbol for abolitionists and advocates of women's suffrage, the grounds that surround its displays have been popular gathering spots for protestors, especially from the civil rights era forward.

On October 6, 2007, Michael Anthony Marcavage led an antiabortion protest on a sidewalk on 6th Street in front of the Liberty Bell Center, which is managed by the National Park Service. Marcavage had a bullhorn that he used to preach to passersby, and some other demonstrators were holding pictures of aborted fetuses. A city code outlined a process for obtaining a permit, but Marcavage and approximately 20 other demonstrators had not obtained one. Park rangers several times asked Marcavage to move, at one point granting him a "verbal permit" to a nearby "grassy area," but he refused to move and was eventually arrested for the misdemeanors of violating the terms of a permit and interfering with an agency function. Despite Marcavage's arguments that this conviction violated the free speech provisions of the First Amendment to the U.S. Constitution, a magistrate convicted Marcavage of both offenses and sentenced him to 12 months of probation, which he appealed. He lost his appeal in a U.S. District Court, but that decision was overturned by the Third U.S. Circuit Court of Appeals.

The appellate court decision, written by Judge Mike Fisher, decided that the conviction for violating a verbal permit was invalid because applicable law specifically referred to a permit as "a written authorization," and the verbal permit was therefore invalid. This left the court to decide whether the conviction for interfering with agency function could survive Marcavage's First Amendment challenges.

Deciding that this was an "as-applied," rather than a "facial" challenge, the court applied forum analysis. It decided that the sidewalk in question was a traditional public forum rather than one created specifically by governmental designation or a nonpublic forum. The fact that the sidewalk in question was paved with Belgian blocks and bordered by chain-linked metal bollards did not distinguish it from other sidewalks that courts had designated as public fora. Although this sidewalk was used to enter the Liberty Bell Center, it was also used for other purposes.

Identifying the sidewalk as a traditional public forum meant that any governmental restrictions on speech must be limited to "time, place, and manner" restrictions that were content neutral and narrowly tailored to serve significant governmental interests. Moreover, if the restrictions were "content-based," then the government had to establish that "they were necessary to serve a compelling governmental interest, were narrowly drawn to achieve that interest, and were the least restrictive means of achieving that interest" (Unruh, 2010, 280).

The court determined that the restrictions were content based by making several observations, some of which differed from the conclusions of the lower court. The rangers had not attempted to subject individuals demonstrating nearby on behalf of breast cancer awareness, pictures did not show that traffic on either the sidewalk or nearby roads was blocked, and rangers indicated that they acted in part to shield visitors from pictures of aborted fetuses that they considered to be disturbing.

Precedents clearly established, however, that any regulations based on the content of speech were presumptively invalid and that they were therefor subject to strict scrutiny. In this case, the actions of the rangers were neither "narrowly tailored," nor had they used the "least restrictive means." The alternative that the ranger posed to Marcavage to go to another side posed a stark alternative that he was not obligated to accept. If they were simply concerned about obstructing the flow of visitors, they could have ordered him to move a short way up or down the block. Nor did they inform him that he could simply continue moving (as the breast cancer awareness demonstrators were doing), rather than remaining stationary.

Although acknowledging that the rangers "on the whole treated Marcavage and his group with courtesy and respect and comported themselves with no small amount of restraint and patience," the court observed that "First Amendment jurisprudence requires a far more nuanced approach designed to strike the right balance between competing interests" (*United States v. Marcavage,* 609 F.3d 264 2010).

See also: Political and Social Movements and the Liberty Bell

Further Reading

United States v. Marcavage, 609 F.3d 264 (2010).

Unruh, Bob. 2010. "Free Speech Restored at Liberty Bell Display." *World Net Daily,* June 18. https://www.wnd.com/2010/06/167845.

V

Verdin Company

The Verdin Company in Cincinnati boasts that it was in business in 1842. It was founded by two brothers, Francis De Sales and Michael Verdin, who arrived in Ohio from Alcase, France, in 1825 and originally established a tower clock business. The company website (Verdin, n.d.) notes, "Six generations and 175 years later, The Verdin Company has grown from that modest beginning to become the industry leader in bells, bell equipment, restoration, digital carillons, and clocks."

A timeline on the site indicates that the company installed the clock and bell equipment for Old St. Mary's Church in Cincinnati in 1842, that Alois Nicholas Verdin invented a "continuous mechanical winder for tower clocks" in 1910, that Theopholis Verdin invented the first electric bell ringer in 1927, that it acquired the VanBergen Bell Foundry in 1997, that it created the 66,600-pound Peace Bell in 1999, and that in 2001, it created a mobile foundry in order to cast a bell for each of the 88 counties in Ohio in celebration of the state's bicentennial. As of its 175th anniversary in 2017, Verdin boasts having "55,000 installations worldwide" and as being "the oldest privately-held manufacturing business in Ohio."

Current family members included James Verdin, Bob Verdin III, and Tim Verdin. In addition to selling and maintaining bells, the company does the same with church organs and sells handbells.

It is still possible to purchase a replica of the Liberty Bell from the company.

See also: American Legion Freedom Bell; World Peace Bell

Further Reading

Verdin. n.d. https://www.verdin.com/about.

Williams, Peter W. 1997. "'The Heart of It All': The Varieties of Ohio's Religious Architecture." *U.S. Catholic Historian* 15 (Winter): 75–90.

Veterans Stadium Liberty Bell

Just as the singing of "The Star Spangled Banner" is often associated with the opening of sporting events in the United States, the Liberty Bell has had a special place in at least one sports venue—namely, Veterans Stadium in Philadelphia, which served as home to the Philadelphia Phillies baseball team and the Philadelphia Eagles football team. The stadium opened in April 1971, closed in September 2003, and was demolished on March 21, 2004.

A distinctive feature of the park was that it included a replica of the Liberty Bell that was approximately 20 feet tall and 15 feet wide. Originally described as being "on the façade of the 400 level at Veterans Stadium . . . it was moved to a permanent location on top of the upper bowl in center field" (Tobaggan, 2018). The bell was lined with lights and lit up any time the home team got a home run.

When Veterans Stadium was demolished and the bell sat for some time in a warehouse, C. W. Dunnet and Company, a food distributor, purchased the bell, which it originally planned to place on its headquarters' roof. After these plans proved to be too ambitious and the Phillies expressed renewed interest in the bell, the company sold it back to the team. It then refurbished it and placed it in its new Citizens Bank Park in March 2019, near the entrance at Pattison Avenue and 11th Street and the "Pass and Stow area," featuring a beer garden (Campitelli, 2019). This stadium already had another large mechanical bell over center field, which chimes every time a run is scored.

In a somewhat related development, a number of Division I colleges created what they called the "Liberty Bell Classic" in 1992. They initially played their games at Veterans Stadium and now play their championship at Citizens Bank Park (Phillies.com, n.d.).

These were not the only teams to capitalize on their location and feature a bell. The Philadelphia 76ers, whose name already emphasizes the date of American independence and whose logo is red, white, and blue, purchased a 350-pound bell on eBay and begin incorporating it into its rituals in 2013. After one team member refused to touch the bell upon entering the court, management instead began striking it three times prior to the game, often enhancing the ceremony by inviting local celebrities to participate. Joel Embiid, a star basketball player for the 76ers, donned a white Phantom of the Opera mask as he struck the bell in the first playoff game against the Miami Heat (Fischer, 2018).

See also: Advertising and the Liberty Bell; Pennsylvania

Further Reading

Campitelli, Enrico. March, 21, 2019. "Vet Stadium Bell Back with New Life: A First Look at the Old Vet Stadium Liberty Bell Now Outside of Citizens Bank Park." https://www.nbcsports.com/philadelphia/the700level/first-look-old-vet-stadium-liberty-bell-now-outside-citizens-bank-park.

Coggin Toboggan. 2018. "Stadium Liberty Bell at CBP by 2019." Crossing Broad.com, February 23. https://www.crossingbroad.com/2018/02/phillies-plan-to-refurbish-and-display-veterans-stadium-liberty-bell-at-cbp-by-2019.html.

Fischer, Jake. 2018. "Liberty at Last: The Process Behind the 76er' Bell-Ringing Ceremony." SI.com, May 4. https://www.si.com/nba/2018/05/04/76ers-nba-playoffs-joel-embiid-sam-hinkie-meek-mill.

Parent, Andrew. 2018. "15 Years Later, Phillies Plan to Bring Veterans Stadium Bell to Citizens Bank Park." *Philly Voice,* February 24. https://www.phillyvoice-com/15-years-later-phillies-plan-bring-veterans-stadium-bell-citizens-bank-park.

Phillies.com. n.d. "Liberty Bell Classic." https://www.mlb.com/phillies/community/youth-baseball-softball/liberty-bell-classic.

Virginia Liberty Bell

The Liberty Bell in Philadelphia was once called the "Independence Bell" because it was so closely associated with the announcement of American independence. Even though it is now almost certain that the bells in Philadelphia did not ring until July 8, when the Declaration of Independence was publicly read, rather than on July 4, when the Second Continental Congress adopted the Declaration of Independence, and it is uncertain whether the steeple holding the Liberty Bell was secure enough for it to be rung even on the latter date, the Bell was certainly witness to some of the most extraordinary events in the nation's early history. Still later, it became a symbol in the movement for wider liberty among African Americans and women.

It is important to keep in mind that long before modern mass media, bell ringing accompanied important announcements throughout the 13 colonies at a time when bells often conveyed news of danger, alarm, and joy. One bell that is known to have participated in a number of such events is the one that is located in the steeple of the Bruton Parish Church in Williamsburg, Virginia, which was the capital of the colonies during the Revolutionary War, as well as the home of the College of William and Mary, where Thomas Jefferson was educated. As in Boston, support for independence in Williamsburg actually preceded that in Philadelphia, where Quakers were particularly reluctant to engage in such armed conflict.

Bruton Parish Church in Williamsburg, Virginia. The steeple houses the Virginia Liberty Bell. (Library of Congress)

Like the original casting of the Liberty Bell, the bell at Bruton Parish was cast by the Whitechapel Foundry in England. It was made in 1761, and installed in a new brick tower and steeple in 1769. Apparently, its only inscription reveals that it was the gift of James Tarpley, a prominent local merchant. The bell is known to have pealed in 1775 for the return of Peyton Randolph after he served as president of the Continental Congress, in 1776 for independence, and in 1783 for the proclamation of peace with Britain. It was apparently rung so frequently that the vestry expressed concern that it might crack (Springer, 1976, 76).

In publishing transcriptions from the church's first *Vestry Book* in 1855–1856, the Reverend John C. McCabe observed (Springer 1976, 76):

> A new bell and a new steeple were to usher in a new order of things, and his Sacred Majesty George III was to be decidedly "rung out" of all authority, right, title or interest in these Colonies; colonies destined in a very few years to bind themselves into a glorious league against oppression and tyranny, civil, military, or religious, and to endure, as we trust, as "THESE UNITED STATES," when kingcraft shall be remembered only among the stories of the past.

The Bruton Parish Church, the third such structure with that name, is a brick building laid out in the form of a cruciform. It was built between 1710–1715, enlarged in the 1750s, and restored in 1907 and again in 1937–1938, the latter time with the help of the Colonial Williamsburg Foundation.

In 2002, a group of students from the Canterbury Episcopal campus ministry helped clean the bells and coat them with conservator's wax. Chalk and soapstone signatures from members of the college choir in the 1890s remained visible (Erickson, 2012). The church remains a prominent landmark in Colonial Williamsburg and continues to serve the local parish.

Another church with a similar storied history is the First Baptist Church of Williamsburg, which dates its founding to 1776. It was the first such church to be organized solely by African Americans (Blakemore, 2016). Its 500-pound Freedom Bell, which was cast in 1886, fell in disrepair, but it was restored, in part by the Colonial Williamsburg Foundation, for Black History Month in 2016. It subsequently helped ring in the opening of the National Museum of African American History and Culture in Washington, D.C., after which it was rehung it its church.

See also: African Americans and the Liberty Bell; Declaration of Independence and the Liberty Bell; Names for the Liberty Bell

Further Reading

Blakemore, Erin. 2016. Smithsonian.com, September 21. https://www.smithsonianmag.com/smithsonian-institution/historic-bell-helps-ring-new-african-american-history-museum-180960545.

"Bruton Parish Church." Colonial Williamsburg. http://www.history.org/almanack/places/hb/hbbruch.cfm.

Erickson, Mark St John. 2012. "Historic Bruton Parish Church Gets Bell Cleaned." *Daily Press,* November 4. http://www.dailypress/com/news/williamsburg/dp-nws-bruton-bell-20121104-story.html.

Mason, George Carrington. 1945. "Historic Parishes of America: Bruton Parish." *Historical Magazine of the Protestant Episcopal Church* 14 (December): 276–293.

Springer, L. Elsinore. 1976. *That Vanishing Sound.* New York: Crown Publishers.

"Voice of Liberty, The" (Song, 1917)

One of the songs that dates from early into America's entry into World War I was written by Ervin Biddle, with music by Maurice Stretch, entitled "The Voice of Liberty." A colorful cover sketched in blue portrays the Liberty Bell, with the crack facing the reader and the dates "1776" and "1917" on the Bell. It is swinging from a yoke in a stone tower and is apparently being rung by a giant eagle sitting on it. The inside cover, just above the title, indicates that the song is "Dedicated to Our President Woodrow Wilson."

The song consists of two verses and a chorus. The first verse, which does not actually mention the Liberty Bell, says that the nation will "fight 'till vict'ry's won," as George Washington and his men did back in 1776. The second verse indicates that "America . . . Is not too proud to fight" against tyrants, and it follows the first verse's reference to Washington with a new reference to Woodrow Wilson.

Consistent with the title of the song, the chorus indicates that "the voice of liberty is ringing" and hopes for victory by the Star Spangled Banner. It notes that "our Eagles [sic] not a lamb," and, as if to reinforce images of 1776, the flag, the Bell, and two presidents, indicates that "We're off to fight for Uncle Sam."

See also: Eagles, Flags, the Statue of Liberty, and Related Symbols; Music and the Liberty Bell

Further Reading

"Voice of Liberty, The." 1917. Words by Ervin Biddle, music by Maurice Stretch. Camden, NJ: Biddle & Stretch Publishers. Accessed at the Library of Congress at https://www.loc.gov/item/2009371916.

"Voice of the Old Bell, The" (Song, 1876)

Throughout much of its history, today's Liberty Bell was designated as the "Old Bell" because it had been hung in the State House steeple prior to the purchase of a second, newer bell that was connected to a clock.

Although abolitionists had dubbed the Bell "the Liberty Bell," the old usage continued. Thus, in what he described as "The most popular centennial song out," Wellesley Bradshaw published a song, with Julia S. Thompson arranging the music, called "The Voice of the Old Bell" for the centennial of the Declaration of Independence, which was celebrated in Philadelphia in 1876.

The first verse began with the words, "Ring out, ring out, you dear old Bell" and recounted how heroes of the Revolutionary War died to secure American freedom. In the aftermath of the Civil War, the second verse expressed the hope that the "loud voice" of the Bell would ring through North and South and East and West "[t]o welcome Peace again!"

The final verse, perhaps in anticipation of the words that that would later adorn the base of the Statue of Liberty, gave the Bell an international dimension. After Americans join in chorus around the Bell, they will (Bradshaw, 1876):

Then send your voice to other lands,
    To tell them o'er the sea,

We'll welcome them with outstretch'd hands,
   To share our Liberty!

See also: Centennial Exposition of 1876; Music and the Liberty Bell; Names for the Liberty Bell; Statue of Liberty

Further Reading

Bradshaw, Wellesley. 1876. *History and Legends of the Old Liberty Bell in Independence Hall, at Philadelphia. To Which is Added That of the New Bell*. Philadelphia: C. W. Alexander.

W

Wallace, William Ross

William Ross Wallace (1819–1881) was a Kentucky-born American poet who was educated at Hanover College, studied law in Lexington, Kentucky, and practiced in New York. He began writing poetry in 1837 and was highly regarded by such contemporaries as Edgar Allan Poe and William Cullen Bryant. His best-known lyric is probably the phrase, "For the hand that rocks the cradle is the hand that rules the world," from the poem named after this line.

In 1862, Wallace published a poem as a book, illustrated by John A. Howe. It featured a beautiful title page with a colorful graphic that pictured the Bell being wrapped in a U.S. flag. The fact that it was published in New York and that it featured the U.S. flag, rather than its Confederate counterpart, suggests that it was written to rally support for the Union cause.

The primary emphasis of the poem, however, was the American Revolution. The opening lines, which are printed below an outdoor sketch with the poem's title, proclaimed (Wallace, 1862):

A sound like the sound of a tempest rolled,
  And the heart of a people stirred,
    For the bell of freedom at midnight tolled,
      Through a fettered land was heard.
        And the chime still rung
        From its iron tongue,
      Steadily swaying to and fro;
        And to some it came
        As a breath of flame,
  And to some as a sound of woe.

An asterisk noted that the Bell was "Rung in Philadelphia upon the announcement of the Declaration of Independence, July 4th, 1776" (Wallace, 1862).

As the poem continues, attention shifts focus from the Bell to the flag. Stanza III, which is illustrated by the sketch of a ship upon the sea, thus notes (Wallace, 1862):

Along the tall mountain, along the tost wave,
  Swept the ranks of the bond, swept the ranks of the brave;
    And a shout as of waters went up to the dome,
    And a sun-drinking banner unfurled,

Like an Archangel's pinion flashed out from his home,
Uttered freedom and hope to the world.

The final stanza seeks to unite the images of the Bell and the flag. Above the
stanza is a picture of a city flying multiple flags, whereas at the bottom of the page
is a stone bell tower (which does not really resemble the tower at Independence
Hall) with "The Liberty Bell" inscribed over it (Wallace, 1862):

That old bell is still seen by the patriot's eye,
  And he blesses it ever when journeying by:
  Long years have passed over it, and yet every soul
    Must thrill in the night to its deep, solemn roll;
    For it speaks in its belfry when kissed by the blast,
    Like a broad blessing breathed from the lips of the Past.
    Long years will roll o'er it, and yet every chime
    Must unceasingly tell of an era sublime.
    And more splendid, more dear than the rest of all Time.
      Oh, yes! If the flame on our altars should pale,
    Let its voice but be heard, and the freeman will start
      To rekindle the fire, while he sees on the gale
    All the stars, all the stripes of the flag of his heart.

John Stoudt (1930, 67–68) records the lines above under the title "The Old Bell."

See also: Declaration of Independence and the Liberty Bell; Eagles, Flags, the Statue of
Liberty, and Related Symbols

Further Reading

Stoudt, John Baer. 1930. *The Liberty Bells of Pennsylvania*. Philadelphia: William J.
    Campbell.
Wallace, William Ross. 1862. *The Liberty Bell*. New York: James C. Gregory.

Warwick, Charles F.

In 1898, Charles F. Warwick (1852–1913), the mayor of Philadelphia, gave a speech
in response to a prompt, "What does the Liberty Bell say about it?" He delivered
the speech at a banquet held in Atlanta on the occasion of the "Peace Jubilee" on
December 15, 1898. It was later published as part of a larger collection in 1903.

Warwick began by recalling the trip that the Liberty Bell had made to the Atlanta
Exposition and the hospitality with which it had been received, but he then turned
to the recent American victory in the Spanish-American War and what the Liberty
Bell might have to say about it. He observed, "To-day although its voice be husky
and a lisp be on its tongue, it has lost none of the old eloquence of sentiment and
association, and in this year of Jubilee it speaks to the children, as it once did to
the Fathers" (Warwick, 1903, 275). As he reviewed American history, Warwick saw
a history of great progress, in which "[w]e stand in the front rank among the nations
of the earth, and we are the only great exemplification in all time of pre-eminent
success in popular institutions and government" (1903, 275).

Observing that the war with Spain had joined North and South together in a common cause, Warwick said, "When the old bell first rang for liberty our fathers stood in defence of their rights; a century and a quarter later their sons stood united in defence of the liberty of an oppressed and a suffering people of another race and nation" (1903, 277). Summarizing U.S. victories during the war, Warwick observed, "We are one people with one flag, one country and one destiny" (1903, 279).

Having come to take Cuba, the Philippines, and other territories, Warwick thought it was inconceivable that the United States would give them back to Spain, which he portrayed as despotic and administratively incompetent. Countering arguments that such a policy was imperialistic, Warwick said, "There is no pride of conquest raging in our hearts, we are not bent on destruction, for we represent a civilization, Christian in character, humane in purpose, which labors for the uplifting of the human race; a civilization without a 'Ghetto,' that is liberal and tolerant, that protects every citizen in his personal, political and religious rights" (1903, 285). Whatever the final disposition of the territories, he argued that the United States could not give them back to Spain.

As he neared the end of his speech, Warwick returned again to the Liberty Bell. Noting that the Bell had from the beginning "watched the nation grow and expand," he said that "before I left home it requested me to say that we must proceed slowly and cautiously, one step at a time, and then we will avoid the danger, sure to result from a hasty leap in the dark; that we must consider the questions that confront us with an eye single to the future welfare and stability of our popular institutions, and then all will be well" (1903, 289). He ended by commending President William McKinley's call for the nation to begin to join in caring for the Confederate dead.

This speech is a good example of the way that the Liberty Bell was increasingly used as a sign of unity. Just as in his speech, he described how the Bell had spoken to him, in a book that he later wrote on Pennsylvania, Warwick further personified the Bell. He observed, "It has rejoiced and wept with our fathers, has often rung a paean for our victories and has silently tolled a monody [a lament] for our defeats." Noting that the time of Reconstruction that had followed the Civil War had been "a trying period," he stated that "the bell, as if it still had a great mission to perform, came out from its resting place, hallowed with sacred memories, and once more united the children of those fathers whom it had so often served and for whom it had so often spoken" (Warwick, 1903). He said, "So eloquent in its silence, it became, as it were, a tie to united in a common sentiment those sections of the country that had been only a few years back engaged in fratricidal strife" (Rosewater, 1926, 204–205).

See also: Atlanta Cotton States and International Exposition of 1895; Reconciliation and the Liberty Bell

Further Reading

Rosewater, Victor. 1926. *The Liberty Bell: Its History and Significance.* New York: D. Appleton.

Warwick, Charles Franklin. 1903. *Orations and Speeches of Charles F. Warwick.* Philadelphia: Rees Welch.

Washington Monument Fund, In re (1893)

The case of *In re Washington Monument Fund*, decided by the Pennsylvania Supreme Court in 1893, involved a petition by trustees of a Washington Monument Fund to erect a statue of George Washington on Independence Square. The decision, which involved determining the successors to the original trustees and giving them authority to place the statue where they wanted, is most notable for Justice (later Chief Justice) James T. Mitchell's comments on Independence Hall and the Liberty Bell.

Mitchell observed that the city of Philadelphia had title to Independence Square "in fee simple" [meaning with no encumbrances on it] (*In re Washington Monument Fund*, 154 Pa. 621 at 634). The city obtained this title from the state by an act of 1816, which allowed the city to purchase the property for $70,000; had it decided against the purchase, the state was going to sell the land for $150,000 to be divided into individual lots.

Mitchell observed, "The act apparently regarded the state house itself as old material, for it makes no reservation of it, and in fact only mentions it incidentally, in directing that 'the large clock, now remaining within the state house' shall be removed to Harrisburg if the commissioners think it of value enough to warrant the expense, but, if not, they are to sell the same 'either separately or with the house and lot to which the same is attached.' That is all the description of which the historic state house was thought worthy" (*In re Washington Monument Fund*, 154 Pa. 621 at 636).

Mitchell goes on to indicate, however, that appreciation for Independence Hall had subsequently increased. Noting the Liberty Bell's trip to the World's Columbian Exposition of 1893 in Chicago, he thus observed that (*In re Washington Monument Fund*, 154 Pa. 621 at 636):

> Notably does it illustrate the growth of national and patriotic sentiment that while I am writing this review of the act of 1816 the Liberty Bell, which was not thought worth mention in it, but left to be sold as old lumber, with the walls and rafters of Independence Hall, is making a triumphant journey, in a special train, with a special guard, to the gathering of nations at Chicago, and at every stopping place, by day or by night, meeting a spontaneous outpouring of love and pride and veneration not accorded to any ruler in the world. That our people were patriotic they had proved before 1816 by two wars, but their sense of historic veneration was small. Fortunately, it was not altogether wanting in Philadelphia, and the vandalism of the act was averted.

Mitchell had observed earlier in his opinion that historical interest in Independence Hall had previously been revived by the visit to Philadelphia by Lafayette in 1824.

The statue was eventually erected in 1897, not on the Independence Mall, but rather at the Green Street entrance to Fairmont Park. It was moved in 1928 near the stairs of the Philadelphia Museum of Art and was restored on its 100th anniversary.

See also: Ownership of the Liberty Bell; World's Columbian Exposition in Chicago (1893)

Further Reading

Gudehus, E. R. 1915. *The Liberty Bell: Its History, Associations and Home*. Philadelphia: Dunlap Printing Company.

In re Washington Monument Fund, 154 Pa. 621 (1893).

Whitechapel Foundry

The original Liberty Bell, as well as its "sister" bell, which was ordered later and a recasting of which is currently at Villanova University, was cast by Thomas Lister, of Whitechapel, London, in 1752. The replacement for the original Bell, which is now an American icon, was recast from medal from the first of these bells, to which additional copper was added.

There is continuing dispute as to why the original Liberty Bell cracked. It is possible that the original bell was too brittle because it had a higher ratio of tin to copper than was proper. Some Americans believed that the Bell was either defective from its manufacture or that it was improperly packed and shipped, while Whitechapel suggests that it was improperly struck when it got to the American colonies. In 1976, the year of the bicentennial of the Declaration of Independence, Americans purporting to be from the Procrastinators Society of America showed up outside the foundry carrying signs saying "WE GOT A LEMON" and "WHAT ABOUT THE WARRANTY?" Foundry owners responded, tongue firmly in cheek, that they would replace the Bell if it were returned in its original packaging ("The Story of the Liberty Bell," n.d.). They also might have suggested simply turning the Bell so that the crack was on the other side (Steel, 2011). Or, they could have pointed out that they had offered to recast the Bell in December 1944 as a symbol of Anglo-American friendship, but that Americans had come to cherish their own cracked recasting (Paige 1985, 68).

The Whitechapel Foundry, which is sometimes listed as the oldest manufacturer in Britain, began in Elizabethan England in 1570, moved to Whitechapel Road in 1739, and remained there until it was sold for 5.1 million pounds in 2017—and resold the same day for 7.9 million pounds (Williams, 2018). Although there have been reports that the foundry would move elsewhere, or even be bought back because of its historic significance, neither has happened to date, apparently leaving John Taylor & Co. of Loughborough in Leicestershire as the only remaining such company in England.

At a time when churches routinely called parishioners to

The historic shopfront of the Whitechapel Bell Foundry in London, England. The Liberty Bell was cast at this foundry in 1752. (Leklek73/ Dreamstime.com)

worship, competition was much stiffer. Barnaby J. Feder quoted one of the Whitechapel Foundry owners, who observed that "There were over 30 bell-founders in Britain in the 17th century," at which time Britain was sometimes called "the ringing isles" (Feder, 1983). Business declined during the twentieth century, but it was helped in part by widespread use of handbell choirs.

Beginning in 1968, the foundry began casting up to 2,400 numbered replicas of the Liberty Bell at one-fifth the size of the original. Each was mounted on an oak stand and, like the original, was tuned to E flat (Springer, 1976, 69).

During its long history, in addition to designing and casting numerous church bells, like the Great Bell of Montreal Cathedral and the Clock Bells of St. Paul's Cathedral, Whitechapel cast Big Ben, the bell in the tower of the British Parliament. It also designed a 23-ton bell (actually cast in the Netherlands) for the 2010 London Olympics (Farrell, 2016).

See also: Composition of the Liberty Bell; Crack in the Liberty Bell; Sister to the Liberty Bell

Further Reading

Farrell, Sean. 2016. "Whitechapel Bell Foundry to Ring in New Era as Owner Sells Site." *The Guardian,* December 2. https://www.theguardian.com/business/2016/dec/02/whitechapel-bell-fou7ndry-to-ring-in-new-era-as-owner-sells-site.

Feder, Barnaby J. 1983. "British Bell Maker Sees Better Times." *The New York Times Archives,* July 4. https://www.nytimes.com/1983/07/04/business/british-bell-maker-sees-better-times.html.

Paige, John C. 1988. *The Liberty Bell: A Special History Study,* ed. by David C. Kimball. Denver: Denver Service Center, National Park Service, United States Department of the Interior.

Springer, L. Elsinore. 1976. *That Vanishing Sound.* New York: Crown Publishers.

Steel, Piers. 2011. "The Greatest Procrastinator in History Still Alive: Puts Off Death." *Psychology Today,* March 7. https://www.psychologytoday.com/us/blog/the-procrastination-equation/201103/the-greatest-procrastinator-in-history-still-alive-puts.

"The Story of the Liberty Bell." n.d. Whitechapel Bell Foundry. http://www.whitechapelbellfoundry.co.uk/liberty.htm.

Williams, Hattie. 2018. "Whitechapel Bell Foundry May [Be] Brought Back from Developers and Reopened by Royal Charity." *Church Times,* July 6. https://www.churchtimes.co.uk/articles/2018/6-july/news/uk/whitechapel-bell-foundry-may-bought-back-from-developers-and-reopened-by-royal charity.

"Who Knocked a Crack in the Liberty Bell?" (Song, 1976)

Of all the musical lyrics connected to the Liberty Bell, none could be more bizarre than those that were included in a children's record released in 1976 called *Ali and His Gang vs. Mr. Tooth Decay.* Having become the world heavyweight champion of boxing, Muhammad Ali joined singer Frank Sinatra, sports announcer Howard Cosell, and others in a project designed to teach healthy eating habits and fight tooth decay among children.

Ali's featured song, not surprisingly, focused more on himself than on tooth decay. Asking "Who Knocked the Crack in the Liberty Bell?" the song responds, "Ali, Ali." The song also credits him with making the ride with Paul Revere and dumping the tea in Boston Harbor.

Although the song portrays the boxer as someone who eats railroad spikes for breakfast, and of murdering a rock, injuring a stone, and hospitalizing a brick, it reminds listeners that "Ali's always getting blamed for things he didn't do." Jason Heller observes that the recording has "charm, for all its corniness and clunkiness" (Heller, 1976). He further observes that it earned the American Dental Association's seal of approval and "was nominated for a Grammy in the Best Recording for Children category" (Heller, 1976).

Muhammad Ali, celebrated American boxer, stands over an opponent in the boxing ring. (Library of Congress)

See also: Crack in the Liberty Bell; Music and the Liberty Bell

Further Reading

Heller, Jason. 2016. "Remembering Muhammad Ali's Trippy, Anti-Cavity Kids' Record." *Rolling Stone,* June 6. https://www.rollingstone.com/music/music-news/remembering-muhammad-alis-trippy-anti-cavity-kids-record-64027.

Wilbank, John

John Wilbank operated the Wilbank Foundry in Germantown, Philadelphia, which is known to have operated from 1822 to 1837 (Goeppinger, 2016, 167). In 1828, as it was renovating the State House (Independence Hall), Philadelphia ordered a bell from Wilbank for 45 cents a pound. The first bell, weighing 4,275 pounds, was placed in the steeple in September 1828. However, that December it was replaced with another of Wilbank's bells, which had a better tone (Rongione, 1976, 12). In 1876, it was in turn replaced by the 13,000-pound Centennial Bell, given by Henry Seybert and cast by Meneely and Kimberly of Troy, New York. The Wilbank bell that it replaced was installed in the Town Hall in Germantown prior to the centennial celebration of the Battle of Germantown (Rongione, 1976, 13).

Citing the *Register of Pennsylvania* (I:153; 2:144), Rongione reports that Wilbank (but Nash 2010, 26, says it was William Meredith) was supposed to take "the bell that the clock now strikes upon"—presumably the clock constructed by Thomas Stretch on the side of the building—for a $400 credit, but apparently found that it would be more costly to remove the Bell than to leave it where it was. He has also been quoted as saying, "I cannot destroy the bell . . . your children and my children will some day value it, so I let it stand" (Rongione, 1976, 12). This has led some scholars to believe that the bell he was saving is what we today call the Liberty Bell (Codon, 1996). However, the preponderance of the evidence suggests that it was the bell connected to the clock, which was being removed during the renovation of the State House (Griffin, 1908, 82). In a subsequent lawsuit, Wilbank was not forced to remove the bell, which remained with the city of Philadelphia, but he was assessed court costs (Rongione, 1976, 12).

See also: Centennial Bell; Sister to the Liberty Bell

Further Reading

Condon, Tom. 1996. "Ring One Up for Savior of Liberty Bell." *Courant,* July 4. http://articles.courant.com/1996-07-04/news/9607040405_1_new-bell-pound-bell-ringing.

Goeppinger, Neil. 2016. *Large Bells of America: History of Church Bells, Fire Bells, School Bells, Dinner Bells and Their Foundries.* Sarasota, FL: Suncoast Digital Press.

Griffin, Marlin. 1908. "The Liberty Bell. Historian Griffin Offers a Correction." *American Catholic Historical Researches* 4 (January): 82.

Rongione, Louis A. 1976. "Sister to the Liberty Bell." *Records of the American Catholic Historical Society of Philadelphia* 87 (March–December): 3–32.

Women's Suffrage and the Liberty Bell

The Liberty Bell has alternatively been the symbol of independence, of republican government, and of abolitionism. It has also served as a symbol for other causes, including equal rights for African Americans, women, and members of the lesbian, gay, bisexual, transgender, and queer/questioning (LGBTQ) community.

As John Adams was seeking independence, his wife, Abigail, urged him to "remember the ladies," but New Jersey was the only one of the original 13 colonies that vested some unmarried women with the right to vote (Vile, 2015b, 89–93). This movement was still considered to be quite novel when delegates to the Seneca Falls Convention of 1848 drew up its Declaration of Rights and Sentiments, which it patterned after the Declaration of Independence, but which proclaimed that "all men and women are created equal."

Many women were active abolitionists and hoped that they would gain political rights along with the newly freed slaves. Instead, the Fourteenth Amendment (1868) became the first to introduce the word "male" into the Constitution by limiting penalties to states that attempted to restrict the right to vote to such individuals. The controversy over whether women should support the rights of African Americans while their own rights went unrecognized led to a division between individuals like Elizabeth Cady Stanton and Susan B. Anthony, who had opposed ratification of the Fourteenth Amendment and formed the National Woman Suffrage Association, and individuals like Henry Ward Beecher and Lucy Stone, who favored the amendment and formed the American Woman Suffrage Association (Kraditor, 1981, 3–4). The two groups did not merge until 1890, when they became the National American Woman Suffrage Association (NAWSA).

As Western states began to increase in population, some of them, beginning with Wyoming in 1869, began to grant women the right to vote, partly in the hope that they would have enough voting members to gain statehood. A women's suffrage amendment gained increasing support in the U.S. Congress. However, some individuals supported the Shafroth-Palmer Amendment, which would have allowed each state to have a referendum on the subject if requested to do so by 8 percent or more of the voters, rather than setting a single national standard (Vile, 2015a, 329).

Pennsylvania was one state that decided to hold such a referendum on its own. As this vote was pending, Katharine Wentworth Ruschenberger, who was a member of the Pennsylvania Woman Suffrage Association (PWSA), commissioned the Meneely Bell Company of Troy, New York, to cast a replica of the Liberty Bell and to add the words "Establish Justice." It thereafter became known either as the "Justice Bell" or the "Liberty Bell of Suffrage" (Leach, 1984, 207). Advocates of women's suffrage loaded the bell on a flatbed truck and visited all 67 counties of the state in what still proved to be a referendum defeat. The women chained the bell's clapper so that it would not be rung until women got the vote in all states, as eventually occurred on September 25, 1920, with the adoption of the Nineteenth Amendment. Ruschenberger touted this "completion of democracy" as a continuation of the "creation of democracy" initiated by American revolutionaries. The Bell was rung 48 times, in recognition that suffrage would now extend to women in all 48 states of the existing union.

The Bell is now installed in the rotunda of the carillon at the Washington Memorial Chapel at Valley Forge National Park. It was temporarily displayed at the Visitor's Center at the Independence Historical Park on the 75th anniversary of the ratification of the Nineteenth Amendment in 1995.

See also: Abolitionists and the Liberty Bell; Declaration of Independence and the Liberty Bell; Democracy and the Liberty Bell; Justice Bell; Political and Social Movements and the Liberty Bell

Further Reading

"The Justice Bell Story." n.d. Justice Bell Foundation. http://www.justicebell.org/the-justice-bell-story.

Kraditor, Aileen S. 1981. *The Idea of the Woman's Suffrage Movement, 1890–1920*. New York: W. Norton.

Leach, Roberta J. 1984. "Jennie Bradley Roessing and the Fight for Woman Suffrage in Pennsylvania." *Western Pennsylvania Historical Magazine* 67 (1984): 189–211.

Roessing, Jennie Bradley. 1914. "The Equal Suffrage Campaign in Pennsylvania." *Annals of the American Academy of Political and Social Science* 56 (November): 153–160).

Vile, John R. 2015a. *Encyclopedia of Constitutional Amendments, Proposed Amendments, and Amending Issues, 1789–2015*. 4th ed., 2 vols. Santa Barbara, CA: ABC-CLIO.

Vile, John R. 2015b. *Founding Documents of America: Documents Decoded*. Santa Barbara, CA: ABC-CLIO.

World Peace Bell

Although Americans chose freedom over peace when declaring their independence from Great Britain in 1776, Americans consider themselves to be a peaceful people who believe that liberty and justice contribute to such a condition.

As the year 2000 approached, many people undoubtedly recalled the biblical portrayal of a millennial kingdom of peace and prosperity. Indeed, early American pictures by Edward Hicks often depicted a "Peaceable Kingdom" in which, consistent with biblical portrayals of a millennial kingdom, carnivores and herbivores (lions, oxen, and children) live together in peace. The paintings typically also portray William Penn and Native Americans in the background.

As the new millennium approached, plans were laid to create a massive World Peace Bell, patterned after the Liberty Bell, which would commemorate the 50th anniversary of the Universal Declaration of Human Rights, as well as the new millennium. It replaced the "Big Joe" bell that hangs in the tower of St. Francis de Sales Roman Catholic Church in Cincinnati, which weighs 27,390 pounds, as the largest such swinging bell in the United States ("The Story of 'Big Joe,'" n.d.).

Like the state replicas of the Liberty Bell that were cast in 1950, the World Peace Bell was cast in Nantes, France, by the Paccard Bell Foundry in conjunction with the Verdin Bell Company of Cincinnati. It was 12 feet in height, weighs 66,000 pounds, and, at the time it was created, was the largest swinging bell in existence (Lucas, 1999). The Bell's clapper weighs 6,878 pounds, and its yoke another 16,512 ("The Millennium Monument World Peace Bell," n.d.).

Cast on December 11, 1998, and rung in Nantes on March 20, 1999, the Bell was transported to New Orleans, where it participated in Independence Day celebrations. It then traveled by boat up the Mississippi and Ohio rivers, stopping (as the Liberty Bell had done on the trips that it took to various fairs and expositions between 1885 and 1915) at 14 cities along the way. The Bell was officially opened on September 21, 1999, on the International Day of Peace and rang in the new millennium on New Year's Eve in 1999.

The bell is located in front of the courthouse in Newport, Kentucky; plans to place it within a 1,200-foot Freedom Tower have yet to be realized (Wartman, 2016). The World Peace Bell Plaza does contain two miniature World Trade Center towers constructed after the infamous terrorist attacks of September 11, 2001. The World Peace Bell is one of more than 20 bells worldwide that are designated as peace bells (Munteanu and Ene, 2011, 60).

See also: Annecy Liberty Bell Replica; Journeys of the Liberty Bell; State Liberty Bell Replicas

Further Reading

Lucas, Ken. 1999. "In Honor of the World Peace Bell and the City of Newport, Kentucky." U.S. House of Representatives. *Congressional Record:* August 5, 1999 (Extensions of Remarks), E1798.

"The Millennium Monument World Peace Bell." n.d. Southbank Partners. http://www.southbankpartners.com/world-peace-bell/what-is-it.aspx.

Munteanu, Sorin Ion, Ioan Cilbanu, and Viorel Ene. 2011. "The Heaviest Cast Bells Existing in the World—Art of Casting." *Metalurgia International* 16: 56–62.

"The Story of 'Big Joe.'" n.d. The Verdin Company. https://www.verdin.com/big-joe.

Wartman, Scott. 2016. "What Will Be Built on World Peace Bell Site?" *Cincinnati Inquirer,* February 27. https://www.cincinnati.com/story/news/2016/02/27/what-built-world -peace-bell-site/80987738.

World's Columbian Exposition in Chicago (1893)

From 1885 to 1915, the Liberty Bell took seven trips outside Philadelphia. The first was to the World's Industrial and Cotton States Industrial Exposition in New Orleans, motivated in part by the desire to help heal the divisions between North and South that had led to the Civil War. The second trip was taken in 1893 to the Columbian Exposition being held in Chicago, one year belatedly, to commemorate the 400th anniversary of Christopher Columbus's "discovery" of America.

The Bell left Philadelphia on April 25, 1893, aboard a car with the words "Philadelphia—Pennsylvania—Chicago" on either side. It sat on a wooden frame with a crossbeam that had "Proclaimed Liberty" on one side and "Throughout the Land" on the other, each under the date "1776." Rosewater further notes that the Bell was surrounded by a railing and that "[o]n the thirteen posts of the railing were thirteen globes, lettered each with the name of one of the original thirteen states. Pennsylvania's globe bore a miniature reproduction of the Old Liberty Bell with these words around its rim, 'Philadelphia, 1776—Columbian Exposition, Chicago, 1893'" (1926, 159). It traveled by train through Harrisburg, Erie, Corry, Oil City, and Pittsburgh, Pennsylvania; through Cleveland and Columbus, Ohio; and through Indianapolis before arriving in Chicago on April 28 or 29 (Paige, 1988, 38, 104). On April 26, the day that the train passed through their city, Josephine and William Cooper gave birth to a daughter, whom they named Liberty Bell Cooper in the Bell's honor (Mires, 2002, 147).

At the exposition, the Bell was again suspended from a yoke, with the words "Proclaim Liberty" just below the date "1776," and was exhibited in a room in the Pennsylvania building designed to replicate a room in Independence Hall. It was surrounded by what appears to have been a brass railing (Sands and Bartlett, 2012, 80).

Concern was expressed that the trip may have resulted in a lengthening of the crack in the Bell. This report resulted in an editorial in the *Philadelphia Public Ledger* of May 1, 1893, which John C. Paige described as "the first expression of concern by Philadelphians of allowing the bell out of the city" (1988, 38).

Chicago had constructed a virtual alabaster city (which partially inspired the words of the song "America the Beautiful") consisting of a Court of Honor built around a large reflecting pool that contained a giant statue of a female figure called "Republic" and a Columbian fountain. The buildings, composed of iron structures, were encased with wood and covered with staff, a material made largely of cement, plaster of Paris, and hemp, that resembled marble (Weller, 2014, 71). The exposition, which helped launch the "city beautiful" movement, was also the debut of the Ferris wheel, which is now a standard feature of carnivals, circuses, and amusement parks.

In 1871, a great fire swept through Chicago, destroying much of the city, but it had rebounded, with its 1870 population of 300,000 rising to almost 1.1 million people, as recorded in the 1890 census (Weller, 2014, 83). In 1886, the city had been the site of violence in the Haymarket affair, in which eight people were killed in a confrontation between police and labor organizers, which resulted in the execution of four anarchists.

Although the buildings were all of classical design, the exposition was designed to highlight the city's and the nation's progress. The congressional resolution of April 30, 1890, that had authorized the exposition had envisioned "an exhibition of the resources of the United States of America, their development, and the progress of civilization of the new world" (Davis, 1892, 308). Weller has observed, "It is not easy today to recapture the sense of exuberance, the optimism, and the euphoria that seemed to pervade American life in the 1890s. Universal peace, the triumph of democracy, the brotherhood of man, the supremacy of the United States—all seemed to be conceivable goals and the Exposition was the crowning expression of these aims and ideals" (2014, 83).

On a less positive side, the exposition had numerous anthropological exhibits that portrayed Native American Indians as uncivilized—although an exhibit by the federal government portrayed their children as being educated (LaPier and Beck, 2015, 23). When Chief Red Cloud visited Buffalo Bill's Wild West Show, he observed, "This big show all about pale face who found red men over here. Ugh! Bad medicine" (Lapier and Beck, 2015, 23). Moreover, toward the end of the event, Mayor Carter Harrison was assassinated.

After the Bell arrived in Chicago, it was loaded onto a float drawn by 13 horses and escorted to the exposition grounds in a popular parade. A Committee of Arrangements had observed "as the Independence Bell was and is the people's bell, so the procession should be a procession of the people in its honor" (Nash, 2010, 89). On its way, President Grover Cleveland delivered a brief address, and about 25,000 people visited the Liberty Bell on May 1, the opening day (Rosewater, 1926, 160–161).

Independence Day celebrations on July 4 were the highlight of the fair, with extraordinary displays of fireworks. Hampton L. Carson, who had headed the centennial celebrations of the U.S. Constitution, offered a tribute on that occasion to the Columbian Liberty Bell, a 13,000-pound bell cast from a variety of historical artifacts and copper coins contributed by schoolchildren, patterned after the Liberty Bell, and designed to give it a voice (Carson, 1894). A band also played "The Liberty Bell March," which John Philip Sousa had composed for the occasion. Harriet Stafford, of Massachusetts, draped the Paul Jones Flag, or Serapis Flag, of alternating red, white, and blue stripes, which was reputed to have been flown over the British frigate *Serapis* after its capture during the Revolutionary War (Rosewater, 1926, 161).

The designation of a "Colored American Day" stimulated debate between journalist Ida B. Wells and statesman Frederick Douglass as to whether this was a chance to highlight the progress of their race or whether it was patronizing and offensive (Hudson, 2010, 36).

The Columbian Exposition, like others that would follow, churned out its fair share of souvenirs. A particularly beautiful example is a small copper bell souvenir with the words of the Liberty Bell and the dates "1776" and "1892" (Nightingale, 2016).

On its return trip, the train carrying the Liberty Bell left Chicago on October 31 and traveled through Richmond, Indiana; Eldorado, West Manchester, Dodson, Brookville, Stillwater Junction, Miami City, Dayton, Xenia, Waynesville, Morrow, Loveland, Cincinnati, Cedarville, London, and Columbus, Ohio; Pittsburgh, Irwin, Greensburg, Johnstown, Latrobe, Derry, Altoona, Tyrone, Huntingdon, Mifflin, Duncannon, Perryville, Lewistown Junction, Harrisburg, Reading, Allentown, and Bethlehem, Pennsylvania, before arriving in Philadelphia on November 5 (Paige, 1988, 104).

Crowds gathered throughout the Bell's trips, with smaller towns, where the train was not scheduled to stop, lighting bonfires so people could see it as it passed (Rosewater, 1926, 159–1760). On the return trip, the stop in Allentown, where the Bell had been hidden at the Zion Reformed Church in 1777, was particularly dramatic. The Bell had been moved to a trolley car and escorted to the church, and the city put on a dramatic display of lighted houses and fireworks that was the subject of many news stories (Rosewater, 1926, 162). It has been estimated that as many as 20 million people (almost a third of the nation's population) had viewed it from the time it departed from Philadelphia to the time that it returned (Rosewater. 1926, 163).

See also: Allentown; Columbia Liberty Bell; Journeys of the Liberty Bell; "Liberty Bell March, The" (Song, 1893); Zion Reformed Church

Further Reading

Carson, Hampton L. 1894. "Oration Delivered at the Invitation of the City of Chicago and of the World's Fair Commission, on the Fourth Day of July, 1893, in Jackson Park, Chicago." *Pennsylvania Magazine of History and Biography* 17: 49–55.

Davis, George R. 1892. "The World's Columbian Exposition," *North American Review* 154 (March): 305–318.

Hudson, Lynn M. 2010. "'This Is Our Fair and Our State': African Americans and the Panama-Pacific International Exposition." *California History* 87: 26–45; 66–68.

LaPier, Rosalyn, and David R. M. Beck. 2015. *City Indian: Native American Activism in Chicago, 1893–1894.* Lincoln: University of Nebraska Press.

Mires, Charlene. 2002. *Independence Hall in American Memory.* Philadelphia: University of Pennsylvania Press.

Nash, Gary B. 2010. *The Liberty Bell.* New Haven, CT: Yale University Press.

Nightingale, Claudine. 2016. "Sweet Liberty: World's Fairs' Love Affair with the Liberty Bell." Adam Matthew, February 5. https://www.amdigital.co.uk/about/blog/item/sweet-liberty.

Paige, John C. 1988. *The Liberty Bell of Independence National Historical Park: A Special History Study*, ed. David C. Kimball. Denver: Denver Service Center, National Park Service, Department of the Interior. Accessed through pubs.etic.nps.gov.

Rosewater, Victor. 1926. *The Liberty Bell: Its History and Significance.* New York: D. Appleton.

Sands, Robert W., Jr., and Alexander B. Bartlett. 2002. *Images of America: Independence Hall and the Liberty Bell*. Charleston, SC: Arcadia Publishing.

Weller, Allen Stuart. 2014. "The World's Columbian Exposition." In *Lorado Taft: The Chicago Years,* ed. Robert G. La France and Henry Adams with Stephen P. Thomas. Champaign: University of Illinois Press, 65–85.

World's Industrial and Cotton Exhibition in New Orleans (1885)

From the time that the Liberty Bell came to Philadelphia from England, it remained in the city except for a brief period, along with its recastings. This period of time was when it and other bells were hauled to Allentown to prevent their capture by British troops who were occupying the town, in case they would want to melt them down into shot and cannon.

Although the Bell was becoming an icon of the United States as a whole, it might be considered especially sacred to Pennsylvania, the 50th anniversary of whose charter it was thought to commemorate. Therefore, it took considerable persuasion to persuade Philadelphia's founders, who had proudly highlighted the Bell at the Centennial Exposition of 1876 (the first World's Fair held on U.S. soil), to allow the Bell to leave the city. It did so largely as a symbol of national reconciliation in the wake of the Civil War (1861–1865) and the end of congressional Reconstruction (1877).

Although the fair, which was designed to mark the 100th anniversary of the first American shipment to cotton to Europe in 1784, opened on December 16, 1884, the Liberty Bell did not arrive until January 1885. It was carried on a flat car with wooden railings and suspended from a yoke that read "1776—Proclaim Liberty"; streamers on the sides of the car had the words "Philadelphia—New Orleans" and with what Rosewater describes as "the emblem of clasped hands at the center" (1926, 152). On its way, the train carrying the Bell stopped in four Pennsylvania cities; in Columbus and Cincinnati, Ohio; in Louisville, Kentucky; in Nashville, Tennessee; and in Birmingham, Montgomery, and Mobile, Alabama (Shepherd, 1985, 284). The Bell appears to have been greeted enthusiastically along its journey. Apparently, publicists for the fair sought to increase public interest by circulating a false story that a mob overpowered the police escort, loaded the Bell onto a truck, and dumped it over the side of a levee ("The Taco Liberty Bell," n.d.).

When the train stopped in Biloxi, Mississippi, it picked up Jefferson Davis, the former president of the Confederate States of America, who continued to New Orleans. Consistent with the theme of reconciliation, Davis, who consistently referred to "this glorious old bell" rather than the "Liberty Bell," observed: "I think the time has come when reason should be substituted for passion and when men who have fought in support of their honest convictions, shall be able and willing to do justice to each other" (Liberty Bell: Journey to New Orleans, *Daily Picayune*, January 27, 1885). Not surprisingly, he chose to associate the Bell with the American Revolution rather than with the cause of emancipation—while substituting "property" (possession of slaves?) for "the pursuit of happiness": "Yon sacred organ that gave voice to the proudest declaration that a handful of men ever made when they faced the greatest military power on the globe; when a handful of men declared to all the world their inalienable right, and staked life, liberty and property in defense of their declaration. It was with your clear tones you sent notice to all who were willing to live or die for liberty and felt that the day was at hand when every patriot must do a patriot's duty" (*Daily Picayune*, January 27, 1885). Similarly, he observed, "Glorious old Bell, the son of a revolutionary soldier bows in reverence to you, worn by time, but increasing in sacred memories" (Liberty Bell: Journey to New Orleans. *Daily Picayune*, January 27, 1885).

According to a story in the *New Orleans Daily Picayune* the next day, January 28, 1885, Davis may have been upstaged by his granddaughter, who, after being lifted to touch the Bell, chose instead to embrace it. Moreover, the *Philadelphia Evening Bulletin* of January 27, 1865, noted, "Of anything more ridiculous could be imagined than that a cracked bell—no matter what its history—could make men better or worse, friends or foes, by being hippodromed from State to State, it is the actual spectacle of the late President bombastically apostrophizing this same cracked bell as 'Yon, sacred organ!'" (Liberty Bell: Journey to New Orleans).

Although the Bell was supposed to arrive on a Tuesday, its entrance had to be delayed for a day, during which there was controversy as to whether it should be kept on the specially built train car that had brought it or hoisted by a derrick onto another one. Although the World's Exposition got off to a slow and rainy start, at which many exhibits remained unfinished and to which rail travel proved to be expensive, just over one million visitors are believed to have attended, and the Liberty Bell itself was an attraction that pointed to reconciliation (Shepherd, 1985, 278). The return trip took a different route, again going through Mobile and Montgomery, but also going through Atlanta, the Carolinas, and Maryland before reaching Philadelphia on June 17 (Nash, 2010, 82), which would in time accede to six additional requests to send it on tour.

On the Bell's return to Philadelphia, a broadside circulated in Philadelphia entitled "PHILADELPHIA'S WELCOME to the glorious OLD LIBERTY BELL." It featured a sketch of the Liberty Bell, as well as a scene picturing Independence Hall and a poem by Edward J. Virtue. The last stanza of that poem struck the chord of unity that had largely motivated the trip (Virtue, 1885):

Welcome! Welcome back to thy hallowed resting place,
From whence thou proclaimed Liberty to every race!
Forever may the North, the South, the East, the West,
As brothers and Patriots, guard thee in thy rest.

When the Liberty Bell returned from the Panama-Pacific Exposition of 1915 (the last of its trips), it revisited New Orleans, which was described as "a particularly gala event" (Rosewater, 1926, 188).

In an interesting footnote to the original visit, in *Bayle v. City of New Orleans*, a New Orleans taxpayer was able to get an injunction against a $5,000 city expenditure for the mayor and other dignitaries to accompany the Bell back to Philadelphia, on the basis that this exceeded the municipality's powers.

See also: Bayle v. City of New Orleans (1885); Journeys of the Liberty Bell; Pennsylvania; Reconciliation and the Liberty Bell

Further Reading

"Liberty Bell: Journey to New Orleans." Independence Hall in American Memory. [Contains reports from major newspapers of the day]. http://www.independencehall-americanmemory.com/the-liberty-bell/liberty-bell-journey-to-new-orleans.

Nash, Gary B. 2010. *The Liberty Bell*. New Haven, CT: Yale University Press.

Rosewater, Victor. 1926. *The Liberty Bell: Its History and Significance*. New York: D. Appleton.

Shepherd, Samuel C., Jr. 1985. "A Glimmer of Hope: The World's Industrial and Cotton Centennial Exposition. New Orleans, 1884–1885." *Louisiana History: The Journal of the Louisiana Historical Association* 26 (Summer): 271–290.

"The Taco Liberty Bell." n.d. The Museum of Hoaxes. http://hoaxes.org/archive/permalink/taco_liberty_bell.

Virtue, Edward J. 1885. "Philadelphia's Welcome to the Glorious Old Liberty Bell." Broadside.

Wreath-Laying at the Liberty Bell

One of the most solemn of any state ceremonies is the laying of a wreath of flowers, typically at a grave or other national monument. There are extensive protocols for such ceremonies, especially during state visits (Miliccia, 2016, 197–199). Although such ceremonies generally honor martyrs or war dead, they may also mark national holidays.

One of the largest wreath-laying ceremonies may also have been one of the earliest. On May 15, 1919, Philadelphia held a parade to honor veterans of World War I. On that occasion, the Liberty Bell was moved in front of Independence Hall for the ceremony, in which 67 wreaths were laid at the foot of the Bell to represent each of the counties in Pennsylvania (Sands and Bartlett, 2002, 100).

There does not appear to be a complete list of these ceremonies in which the Liberty Bell has been used, but there have been numerous instances. Many have been by private citizens or groups seeking to commemorate a historic date or cause, rather than by foreign dignitaries.

A former slave who later became a college president and a banker, Richard Robert Wright, began laying wreaths yearly from 1942 forward, on February 1 (Nash, 2010, 164; note that Paige, 1988, consistently cites the day as February 2, perhaps confusing it with the date of news stories published about the events). He did this in an effort, which ultimately proved successful, to establish a National Freedom Day to commemorate President Abraham Lincoln's signing of legislation that led to the Thirteenth Amendment (Nash, 2010, 164). When Wright laid the wreath in 1946, he observed that he did so "in commemoration of the soldiers and sailors of both races who died for the preservation of freedom in all wars through the World War II" (Kachum, 2004, 294). Dr. Martin Luther King, Jr., placed the wreath there in 1959 (Paige, 1988, 72).

John Paige has further identified a number of such occasions. These have included January 27, 1943, when the Philadelphia Committee for the Freedom of India placed a wreath by the Bell; January 1948, when the Italian ambassador left a wreath; in 1954, during Americanization Week (the last week of April); on March 26, 1959, when Aristide N. Pilavakis, general consul of the Greek Embassy, laid a wreath to mark the 138th anniversary of Greek independence of Turkey; and in June 1963, at the opening of the 74th annual convention of the Central Conference of America Rabbis (Paige, 1988, 67, 69, 71, 73, 75). As he reached the 1970s, Paige observed, "Various wreath laying ceremonies by countries allied with the United States and by patriotic organizations continued to take place at the Liberty Bell to symbolize loyalty and shared ideals with the United States" (1988, 78).

In a related tradition, wreaths are typically laid at the statue of Commodore John Barry, outside Independence Hall, each Memorial Day (Sands and Bartlett, 2002, 44).

See also: National Freedom Day; Symbolism of the Liberty Bell

Further Reading

Froideville, Gilbert Monod de, and Mark Verheul. 2016. *An Expert's Guide to International Protocol.* Amsterdam: Amsterdam University Press.

Katchun, Mitch. 2004. "'A Beacon to Oppressed Peoples Everywhere': Major Richard R. Wright Sr., National Freedom Day, and the Rhetoric of Freedom in the 1940s." *Pennsylvania Magazine of History and Biography* 128 (July): 279–306.

Nash, Gary B. 2010. *The Liberty Bell.* New Haven, CT: Yale University Press.

Paige, John C. 1988. *The Liberty Bell of Independence National Historical Park: A Special History Study*, ed. David C. Kimball. Denver: Denver Service Center, National Park Service, Department of the Interior.

Sands, Robert W., Jr., and Alexander B. Bartlett. 2002. *Images of America: Independence Hall and the Liberty Bell.* Charleston, SC: Arcadia Publishing.

Y

Year of Jubilee

The inscription on the Liberty Bell, which is taken from Leviticus 25:10, to "proclaim liberty throughout all the land unto all the inhabitants thereof," comes from a passage that also refers to a Year of Jubilee, or celebration. During this year, the 50th anniversary (and subsequent multiples of 50) of entering the land of Canaan, designated as the "Year of Jubilee," the Israelites were instructed to return all familial lands and to free slaves.

Although both the original and recast Liberty Bells are designated a year or two later, 1751 marks the 50th anniversary of the year that William Penn granted his Pennsylvania Charter of Privileges, a type of constitution, to the colony. This suggests that Isaac Norris II might have chosen the inscription for the Liberty Bell from Leviticus as a way of commemorating this.

In his 1825 inaugural address, President John Quincy Adams noted that 1824 had marked the 50th anniversary of the First Continental Congress. He proceeded to say, "The year of Jubilee, since the first formation of Our Union, has just elapsed; that of the Declaration of our Independence, is at hand" (Burstein, 2001, 4). This second anniversary, with which the ringing of bells is so frequently associated, was further hallowed in the popular mind when two of the leading lights of the Revolution, Thomas Jefferson and John Adams, both of whom played a role in the writing of the Declaration of Independence, died on July 4, 1826.

African American spirituals are sometimes known as *jubilees,* but the meaning of the term apparently varies. William Tallmadge has observed that "[i]t has been used to designate those black spirituals whose texts refer to freedom—freedom in death from the hardships of life, followed by the attainment of heavenly bliss, and freedom from slavery. The term has also been used to specify those spirituals having a joyous character, as it has been used to refer to the entire body of black spirituals" (Tallmadge, 2008, 229). He notes that the Fisk Jubilee Singers from Fisk University in Nashville, which was begun with a number of former slaves, took their name from the biblical Year of Jubilee.

One study of African American religion observes that the two primary themes that dominated conversation during and after the American Civil War were Exodus (the story of the Israelites' travels from bondage in Egypt to freedom in the land of Canaan) and Jubilee. The author observes that the former emphasized the need to leave Southern states for Liberia or for states in the American North or West, whereas the latter was based on (ultimately false) hopes that former slaves would be given some of the plantation property that they had worked and become economically self-sufficient (Harper, 2016, 65–97).

There is further evidence that the nation's centennial celebrations in 1876, which included celebrations in Philadelphia, further marked renewed interest in the Liberty Bell, which, as a result of abolitionist literature, had become increasingly associated with emancipation. As he looked forward to this celebration, John Shoemaker, who was chair of the Philadelphia Centennial Committee, stated (Paige, 1988, 85):

> This is true, there appears to have been no first jubilee to all the inhabitants on our fiftieth anniversary—too many millions of our inhabitants were then in slavery—we then could not fully carry out the text and proclaim liberty to all. But now upon the second fiftieth year we are able to do so. Cracked and shattered as the bell may be the base upon which that motto is cast remains firm and solid, and shaken as has our country been with the din of battle and bloody strife, that principle remains pure and perfect for all time to come and the whole text, Liberty Jubilee, will be literally carried out in 1876. "Liberty can now be proclaimed throu all the land to all inhabitants thereof."

In later advocating for a National Freedom Day, to honor Abraham Lincoln's signing of the congressional joint resolution that led to the Thirteenth Amendment abolishing slavery, Richard R. Wright began in 1942 to lay a wreath in front of the Liberty Bell each February 1.

See also: Abolitionists and the Liberty Bell; Leviticus 25:10; National Freedom Day; Norris, Isaac, II

Further Reading

Burstein, Andrew. 2001. *America's Jubilee*. New York: Alfred A. Knopf.

Harper, Matthew. 2016. *The End of Days: African American Religion and Politics in the Age of Emancipation*. Chapel Hill: University of North Carolina Press.

Paige, John C. 1988. *The Liberty Bell of Independence National Historical Park: A Special History Study*, ed. David C. Kimball. Denver: Denver Service Center, National Park Service, Department of the Interior.

Tallmadge, William. H. 2008. "Fisk Jubilee Singers." In *New Encyclopedia of Southern Culture*, ed. Bill C. Malone. Chapel Hill: University of North Carolina Press, 228–229.

"You're a Grand Old Bell" (Song, 1919)

Throughout World War I, the Liberty Bell was used as a key symbol in the drive to sell Liberty Bonds to finance the conflict. As the war ended, J. E. Dempsey composed the words and Johann C. Schmid composed the music to a song called "You're a Grand Old Bell." The words clearly reflect George M. Cohan's earlier 1906 song, from the popular musical *George Washington, Jr.* "You're a Grand Old Flag."

Notably, although the cover pictures the Liberty Bell, a line across the top of the music notes that "THE RED, WHITE AND BLUE SHARES ITS GLORY WITH YOU."

In the first verse of the song, a son asks his father why people cheer "[f]or a bell that is old and broken" The father explains that the Bell had proclaimed that the nation was free. In language that comes close to that which a Christian believer might associate with Jesus, the second verse observes that "One can tell to gaze at the wound in your side that your fond heart is bro–ken, Not with pain, but with joy 'tis plain, for your work was, in deed, well done." Evoking other bells, the chorus ends by observing, as had the cover sheet, "For the Red, White and Blue, Shares its glo-ry with you. You're a Grand Old Bell" ("You're A Grand Old Bell," n.d.). The music was originally published by H. A. Weymann & Son.

See also: Eagles, Flags, the Statue of Liberty, and Related Symbols; Liberty Loans; Music and the Liberty Bell

Further Reading

"You're a Grand Old Bell." n.d. Historic American Sheet Music, David M. Rubenstein Rare Book & Manuscript Library, Duke University. https://library.duke.edu /digitalcollections/hasm_a2267.

Z

Zion Reformed Church

The Zion Reformed United Church of Christ in Allentown, Pennsylvania, is a very historic church. It is believed to be the spot where the Liberty Bell and other bells from Philadelphia were taken and hidden under the floorboards between September 25, 1777, and June 25, 1778, to keep them from being captured and melted down by the British who occupied Philadelphia.

As news that General William Howe would soon be occupying the city was announced, the Pennsylvania Assembly voted on June 16, 1777, "That the president and council be authorized and empowered to remove as soon as they may think proper, all the bells belonging to the several churches and other public buildings and also all the copper and brass in this city, to some place of safety" (Stoudt, 1927, 12). On September 14, 1777, the Second Continental Congress adopted a further resolution "That the Board of War be directed to order the Commissary General of military stores, to apply to the Supreme Executive Council of the States of Pennsylvania, to a place of security, upon a near approach of the enemy to the city" (Stoudt, 1927, 12). Although the Reverend Jacob Duche of the Christ Church in the city (who ultimately sided with the Tories) expressed confidence that the bells would not be endangered, they were nonetheless removed with other bells, including the bell in the State House now designated as the Liberty Bell.

The bells were moved in a caravan that is believed to have included some 700 wagons; the one carrying the Liberty Bell broke down in Bethlehem and had to be moved to another. There is an ongoing dispute as to whether the teamster who drove the carriage was a gentleman named Frederick Leaser or someone named John Jacob Mickley (Stoudt, 1927, 33–46). A likely possibility is that Mickley carried the bell to Bethlehem, and that, when his wagon broke down, Leaser completed the journey (Kramer, 1975, 68). There are also rumors, possibly part of an original disinformation campaign designed to keep the Bell hidden, that it was sunk in the Delaware River.

The current Zion Church is the third to be built in Allentown. The first was constructed in 1762 and was shared between the Reformed congregation and a Lutheran congregation now known as St. Paul's Lutheran Church. A second church, completed in 1776 and built of stone, housed the bells from Philadelphia the following year. A third Federal style brick church replaced this building in 1838, and it was, in turn, replaced in 1888 by the current neo-Gothic building designed by Lewis Shelly Jacoby, with an interior of dark wood and beautiful stained glass windows. It contains a large bell, purchased in 1790, with a German inscription inviting parishioners to worship. An earlier bell, cast in 1769 and believed to have announced independence, was exhibited at the Sesquicentennial Exposition in Philadelphia in 1926; it is sometimes called "Allentown's Liberty Bell" (Stoudt, 1927, 60).

The basement of the church includes a Liberty Bell Museum, which houses Allentown's Liberty Bell, as well as a replica of the Liberty Bell. It also houses a mural painted by Edwin Howland Blashfield, originally for the Liberty Trust Company, showing the unloading of the Liberty Bell at the Zion Reformed Church (the mural is dominated by an angel with outstretched wings holding a banner with the words, "Proclaim liberty throughout all the land"), and exhibits on colonial America and the Revolutionary War.

After being exhibited at the World's Columbian Exposition in Chicago in 1893, the Liberty Bell stopped for a time in Allentown, where it was met by a demonstration what was described by the *Philadelphia Record* as "the most remarkable ever made in the Lehigh Valley city." The paper noted, "The town was a blaze of red fire when the train arrived, and every whistle shrieked out a welcome which re-echoed from the throats of thousands of people who packed in and around the station" (Stoudt, 1927, 28).

In 1908, the Reverend H. M. J. Klein gave a speech while accepting a tablet presented to the church by the Daughters of the American Revolution, in which he explained that the Liberty Bell has become a symbol that stood "for the vast collective life of the American people" (Stoudt 1927, 30).

See also: Museums of the Liberty Bell; Security for the Liberty Bell; Symbolism of the Liberty Bell; World's Columbian Exposition in Chicago (1893)

Further Reading

"History's Headlines: Allentown's Zion Reformed UCC Church Prepares to Honor Its 125-Year-Old Sanctuary and Its Architect." 2013. WFMZ.com, June 17. http://www .wfmz.com/fetures/historys-headlines/historys-headlines-allentowns/zion -reformed-ucc-church-prepares-to-honor-its-125 -year old-sanctuary-and-its-architect /18980737.

Kramer, Justin. 1975. *Cast in America: The Historically Accurate, Exciting Story of the Liberty Bell*. Los Angeles: Justin Kramer Incorporated.

"Our Heritage." History in Allentown, PA/ Zion's Reformed UCC. http://libertybellchurch .org/our-heritage.

Stoudt, John Baer. 1927. *The Liberty Bell in Allentown and Allentown's Liberty Bell*. Allentown, PA: Berkemeyer, Kick.

Appendix

CITIES AND STATES WHERE LIBERTY BELL HAS BEEN DISPLAYED

Atlanta, Georgia, Atlanta Cotton States and International Exposition (1895)

Boston, Massachusetts, Bunker Hill Monument Anniversary (1903)

Charleston, South Carolina, South Carolina Interstate and West Indian Exposition (1902)

Chicago, Illinois, World's Columbian Exposition (1893)

New Orleans, Louisiana, World's Industrial and Cotton Exposition (1885)

San Diego, California, Panama-California International Exposition (1915)

San Francisco, California, Panama-Pacific Exposition (1915)

St. Louis, Missouri, Louisiana Purchase Exposition (1904)

OTHER STATES AND CITIES WHERE LIBERTY BELL TRAVELED THROUGH AND/OR MADE TRAIN STOPS

	Arrival Date	Scheduled Arrival Time
Alabama		
Birmingham	January 25, 1885	3:00 p.m.
Montgomery	January 25, 1885	6:00 p.m.
Montgomery	June 1885	
Arizona		
Bowie	November 16, 1915	8:25 a.m.
Maricopa	November 16, 1915	2:00 a.m.
San Simon	November 16, 1915	8:55 a.m.
Tucson	November 16, 1915	5:30 a.m.
Willcox	November 16, 1915	7:35 a.m.
Yuma	November 15, 1915	8:30 p.m.

California

Anaheim	November 1914	Return trip
Bakersfield	November 11, 1915	10:15 p.m.
Chico	July 16, 1915	11:55 a.m.
Colton	November 15, 1915	2:50 p.m.
Dinaba	November 11, 1915	6:55 p.m.
Exeter	November 1915	Return trip
Fresno	November 11, 1915	5:50 p.m.
Fullerton	November 2015	Return trip
Loma Linda	November 2015	Return trip
Los Angeles	November 15, 1915	6:00 a.m.
Marysville	July 16, 1915	1:30 p.m.
Oceanside	November 1915	Return trip
Ontario	November 1915	Return trip
Orange	November 1015	Return trip
Pomona	November 1915	Return trip
Porterville	November 11, 1915	8:30 p.m.
Red Bluff	July 16, 1915	10:25 a.m.
Sacramento	July 16, 1915	3:30 p.m.
San Diego	November 12–14, 1915	
San Juan Capistrano	November 2015	Return trip
San Francisco	July 16, 1915	9:30 p.m.
Santa Ana	November 1915	Return trip

Colorado

Denver	July 10, 1915	8:00 a.m.
Greeley	July 10, 1915	1:50 p.m.
La Salle	July 10, 1915	1:30 p.m.

Connecticut

Bridgeport	June 15, 1903	6:55 p.m.
Hartford	June 16, 1903	9:25 a.m.
New Haven	June 15, 1903	7:35 p.m.
New London	June 19, 1903	5:10 p.m.
Stonington	June 19, 1903	4:30 p.m.
Willimantic	June 16, 1903	11:25 a.m.

Delaware

Wilmington	October 4, 1895	8:53 a.m.

Georgia

Dalton	October 7, 1895	8:50 a.m.
Gainesville	January 29, 1896	
Rome	October 7, 1895	10:45 a.m.

Idaho

Boise	July 12, 1915	7:00 a.m.
Caldwell	July 12, 1915	9:00 a.m.
Pocatello	July 11, 1915	9:00 p.m.
Wesler	July 12, 1915	10:45 a.m.

Illinois

Altamont	November 1915	Return trip
Anna	November 20, 1915	8:20 p.m.
Arcola	November 17, 1904	8:25 a.m.
Cairo	November 20, 1915	7:00 p.m.
Carbondale	November 20, 1915	9:00 p.m.
Chicago	June 5, 1904	4:45 a.m.
	July 6, 1915	5:40 p.m.
Decator	June 17, 1904	7:00 a.m.
East St. Louis	November 21, 1915	11:20 a.m.
Effingham	November 1915	Return trip
Galesburg	June 7, 1904	2:15 p.m.
Geneseo	July 7, 1915	10:48 a.m.
Greenville	November 21, 1915	12:40 p.m.
Highland	November 1915	Return trip
Marshall	November 1915	Return trip
Molene	July 7, 1915	11:28 a.m.
Mound	November 1915	Return trip
Murphysboro	November 20, 1915	10:00 p.m.
Oakland	November 17, 1904	9:00 a.m.
Paris	November 17, 1904	9:35 a.m.
Peoria	June 7, 1904	3:55 p.m.
	July 7, 1915	7:00 a.m.
Rock Island	June 6, 1904	12:00 p.m.
	July 7, 1915	11:55 a.m.
Springfield	June 7, 1904	6:25 p.m.
	June 16, 1904	3:15 p.m.

St. Louis	November 21, 1915	1:00 a.m.
Vandalla	November 21, 1915	1:30 p.m.

Indiana

Columbus	November 21, 1915	2:30 a.m.
Brazil	November 21, 1915	5:35 p.m.
Edinburg	November 1915	Return trip
Fort Wayne	July 6, 1915	12:18 p.m.
Gary	July 6, 1915	4:34 p.m.
Indianapolis	April 28, 1893	5:00 p.m.
	November 17, 1904	5:40 p.m.
	November 21, 1915	7:30 p.m.
Plymouth	July 6, 1915	2:53 p.m.
Richmond	October 31, 1893	
	November 17, 1904	1:50 p.m.
Scottsburg	November 22, 1915	4:00 a.m.
Sullivan	November 17, 1904	11:40 a.m.
Terre Haute	November 17, 1904	10:20 a.m.
	November 21, 1915	4:40 p.m.
Vincennes	November 17, 1904	1:00 p.m.

Iowa

Davenport	July 7, 1915	12:20 p.m.
Des Moines	July 7, 1915	10:00 p.m.
Dubuques	June 7, 1904	8:00 a.m.
Grinnell	July 7, 1915	4:47 p.m.
Iowa City	July 7, 1915	2:20 p.m.
Marengo	July 7, 1915	3:44 p.m.

Kansas

Atchison	July 8, 1915	5:05 p.m.
Leavenworth	July 8, 1915	4:00 p.m.
Topeka	July 8, 1915	8:30 a.m.

Kentucky

Anchorage	November 22, 1915	10:30 a.m.
Campbellsburg	November 1915	Return trip
Fuilton	November 20, 1915	2:40 p.m.
Lagrange	November 22, 1915	10:50 a.m.
Latonia	November 1915	Return trip

Louisville	January 24, 1885	6:00 p.m.
	November 22, 1915	6:00 a.m.
Paducah	November 30, 1915	4:50 p.m.
Pewee Valley	November 1915	Return trip
St. Matthews	November 1915	Return trip

Louisiana

Crowley	November 19, 1915	5:05 a.m.
Franklin	November 19, 1915	7:10 a.m.
Jennings	November 19, 1915	4:25 a.m.
Lafayette	November 19, 2015	5:45 a.m.
Lake Charles	November 19, 1915	3:20 a.m.
Morgan City	November 19, 1915	7:45 a.m.
New Iberia	November 19, 1915	6:25 a.m.
New Orleans	January 26, 1885	12:00 a.m.
Raceland	November 1915	Return trip
Schriever	November 19, 1915	8:35 a.m.

Maryland

Baltimore	June 1885	
	October 1895	10:44 a.m.
Elkton	October 1895	9:22 a.m.

Massachusetts

Attleboro	June 19, 1903	2:35 p.m.
Boston	June 16, 1903	3:50 p.m.
Middleboro	June 19, 1903	1:15 p.m.
Plymouth	June 18, 1903	7:30 p.m.
Taunton	June 19, 1903	2:05 p.m.

Mississippi

Brookhaven	November 19, 1915	6:25 p.m.
Crystal Springs	November 1915	Return trip
Durant	November 19, 1915	11:30 a.m.
Hazelhurst	November 19, 1915	7:10 p.m.
Jackson	November 19, 1915	8:30 p.m.
McComb	November 1915	Return trip

Missouri

Kansas City	July 8, 1915	12:00 p.m.
St. Joseph	July 8, 1915	6:25 p.m.
St. Louis	June 8—November 16, 1904	

Nebraska

Hastings	July 9, 1915	6:30 p.m.
Lincoln	July 9, 1915	12:45 p.m.
McCook	July 9, 1915	10:30 p.m.
Omaha	July 9, 1915	5:00 a.m.

New Jersey

Elizabeth	June 15, 1903	1:20 p.m.
Jersey City	June 15, 1903	1:45 p.m.
	June 20, 1903	11:45 a.m.
Lambertville	November 25, 1915	12:45 a.m.
New Brunswick	June 15, 1903	12:40 a.m.
Newark	June 15, 1903	1:45 p.m.
Phillipsburg	November 25, 1915	11:35 a.m.
Princeton	June 15, 2903	11:27 a.m.
Trenton	June 15, 1903	11:00 a.m.
	November 25, 1915	1:15 p.m.

New Mexico

Deming	November 16, 1915	11:40 a.m.
Lordsburg	November 16, 1915	9:55 a.m.

New York

Albany	November 24, 1915	8:30 p.m.
Amsterdam	November 24, 1915	7:10 p.m.
Auburn	November 24, 1915	2:00 p.m.
Batavia	June 4, 1904	11:35 a.m.
	November 24, 1915	10:00 a.m.
Bergen	November 1915	Return trip
Buffalo	June 4, 1904	11:40 a.m.
	November 24, 1915	7:00 a.m.
Canandaigua	June 4, 1904	9:35 a.m.
	November 24, 1915	12:20 p.m.
Canastota	November 1915	Return trip
Clifton Springs	November 1915	Return trip
Dunkirk	June 4, 1904	1:05 p.m.
Elmira	June 4, 1904	7:00 a.m.
Geneva	November 24, 1915	1:00 p.m.
Harlem River	June 15, 1903	4:20 p.m.
	June 20, 1903	10:00 a.m.

Herkimer	November 24, 1915	5:35 p.m.
Little Falls	November 1915	Return trip
Mayville	November 1915	Return trip
Oneida	November 24, 1915	4:15 p.m.
Oneonta	November 1915	Return trip
Penn Yan	June 4, 1904	8:45 a.m.
Phelps	November 1915	Return trip
Rochester	June 4, 1904	10:15 a.m.
	November 24, 1915	10:55 a.m.
Rome	November 24, 1915	4:40 p.m.
Schenectady	November 24, 1915	7:40 p.m.
Seneca Falls	November 24, 1915	1:30 p.m.
Syracuse	November 24, 1915	2:50 p.m.
Utica	November 24, 1915	5:15 p.m.
Waterloo	November 1915	Return trip
Watkins	June 4, 1904	8:00 a.m.

North Carolina

Charlotte	January 1896
Greensboro	January 1896
Salisbury	January 1896

Ohio

Ashtabula	June 4, 1904	3:30 p.m.
Brookville	1893	
Bucyrus	July 6, 1915	8:19 a.m.
Cedarville	1892	
	1915	Return trip
Cincinnati	January 24, 1885	10:30 p.m.
	1893	
	November 22, 1915	1:30 p.m.
Cleveland	April 27, 1893	12:00 a.m.
	June 4, 1904	5:15 p.m.
	November 23, 1915	6:00 a.m.
Columbus	January 24, 1885	5:30 p.m.
	April 27, 1893	8:00 p.m.
	November 18, 1904	6:00 p.m.
	November 22, 1915	9:11 p.m.
Crestline	July 6, 1915	7:53 a.m.

Dayton	1893	
	November 18, 1904	3:10 p.m.
	November 22, 1915	6:30 p.m.
Dennison	November 18, 1904	10:15 p.m.
Dodson	1893	
Eldorado	1893	
Hamilton	November 22, 1915	5:15 p.m.
Hudson	November 1915	Return trip
Lima	July 6, 1915	10:12 a.m.
London	1893	
	November 18, 1904	5:05 p.m.
	November 1915	Return trip
Loveland	1893	
Mansfield	July 6, 1915	7:15 a.m.
Miami City	1893	
Middleton	November 22, 1915	5:56 p.m.
Morrow	1893	
Niles	November 23, 1915	12:11 p.m.
Ravena	November 23, 1915	11:15 a.m.
Sandusky	June 4, 1904	6:55 p.m.
South Charleston	November 18, 1904	4:40 p.m.
	November 1915	Return trip
Steubenville	November 18, 1904	
Stillwater Junction	1893	
Toledo	June 4, 1904	8:15 p.m.
Upper Sandusky	July 6, 1915	8:53 a.m.
Van Wert	July 6, 1915	11:18 a.m.
Waynesville	1893	
West Manchester	1893	
Wyoming	1915	Return trip
Xenia	1893	
	November 18, 1904	4:05 p.m.
	November 22, 1915	7:27 p.m.
Youngstown	November 23, 1915	12:34 p.m.

Oregon

Baker	July 12, 1915	12:10 p.m.
Cayuse	1915	

Huntingdon	July 12, 1915	11:20 a.m.
La Grande	July 12, 1915	2:30 p.m.
Pendelton	July 12, 1915	5:25 p.m.

Pennsylvania

Allentown	November 1893	
Altoona	January 23, 1885	5:00 p.m.
	November 1893	
	November 19, 1904	6:35 a.m.
	July 5, 1915	11:20 p.m.
Bethlehem	November 1893	
Carbondale	November 1915	Return trip
Chester	October 4, 1895	8:31 a.m.
Corry	April 26, 1893	1:30 p.m.
Derry	November 1893	
Duncannon	November 1893	
Erie	April 26, 1893	4:00 a.m.
	June 4, 1904	2:20 p.m.
Ford City	November 1915	Return trip
Gouldsboro	November 1915	Return trip
Greensburg	November 1893	
Harrisburg	January 23, 1885	1:20 p.m.
	April 25, 1893	1:15 p.m.
	November 1893	
	November 19, 1904	10:50 a.m.
	July 5, 1915	6:30 p.m.
Huntingdon	November 1893	
Irwin	November 1893	
Johnstown	November 1893	
Kittanning	November 1915	Return trip
Lancaster	January 23, 1885	10:00 a.m.
	July 5, 2015	5:00 p.m.
Latroube	November 1893	
Lewistown Junction	November 1893	
Maunch Chunk	November 25, 1915	10:55 a.m.
Mifflini	November 1893	
New Kensington	November 1915	Return trip
Oil City	April 26, 1893	3:25 p.m.

Perryville	November 1893	
Pittsburgh	January 23, 1885	9:50 p.m.
	April 26, 1893	7:30 p.m.
	November 1893	
	November 19, 1904	2:35 a.m.
	July 6, 1915	3:00 a.m.
	November 23, 1915	4:40 p.m.
Pocono Summit	November 25, 1915	9:50 a.m.
Reading	November 1893	
Scranton	November 25, 1915	11:30 p.m.
Stroudsburg	November 25, 1915	10:25 a.m.
Tyrone	November 1893	

Rhode Island

Providence	June 16, 1903	1:35 p.m.
	June 19, 1903	2:50 p.m.

South Carolina

Blacksburg	January 1895	
Greeneville	January 1896	
Spartanburg	January 1896	

Tennessee

Athens	October 7, 1895	9:35 a.m.
Bristol	October 6, 1895	1:30 p.m.
Chattanooga	October 7, 1895	11:30 a.m.
Cleveland	October 7, 1895	10:25 a.m.
Dyersburg	November 20, 1915	1:30 p.m.
Greenville	October 6, 1895	7:00 p.m.
Johnson City	October 6, 1895	3:40 p.m.
London	October 7, 1895	8:50 a.m.
Memphis	November 20, 1915	6:00 a.m.
Nashville	January 25, 1885	8:00 a.m.

Texas

Alpine	November 16, 1915	11:20 p.m.
Arlington	November 18, 1915	11:25 a.m.
Austin	November 17, 1915	4:30 p.m.
Bartlett	November 17, 1915	7:45 p.m.
Beaumont	November 19, 1915	1:30 a.m.

Bremand	November 18, 1915	5:35 p.m.
Bryan	November 18, 1915	7:00 p.m.
Calvert	November 18, 1915	6:05 p.m.
College	November 18, 1915	7:12 p.m.
Corsicana	November 18, 1915	3:35 p.m.
Dallas	November 18, 1915	12:00 p.m.
Dalworth	November 1915	Return trip
Del Rio	November 17, 1915	3:20 a.m.
Denison	November 18, 1915	6:00 a.m.
Denton	November 1915	Return trip
El Paso	November 16, 1915	2:30 p.m.
Ferris	November 1915	Return trip
Fort Worth	November 18, 1915	10:00 a.m.
Grand Prairie	November 1915	Return trip
Granger	November 17, 1915	7:30 p.m.
Goresbeck	November 1915	Return trip
Hearne	November 18, 1915	6:22 p.m.
Hillsboro	November 18, 1915	12:01 a.m.
Hondo	November 1915	Return trip
Houston	November 18, 1915	9:45 p.m.
Liberty	November 1915	Return trip
Marfa	November 16, 2015	11:45 p.m.
Navasota	November 18, 1915	7:35 p.m.
New Braunfels	November 17, 1915	1:50 p.m.
San Antonio	November 17, 1915	11:00 a.m.
San Marcos	November 17, 1915	2:20 p.m.
Sanderson	November 17, 1915	2:15 a.m.
Temple	November 17, 1915	8:30 p.m.
Thornton	November 1915	Return trip
Uvalde	November 1915	Return trip
Waco	November 17, 1915	9:45 p.m.
Whitesboro	November 18, 1915	7:45 a.m.
Wortham	November 1915	Return trip

Utah

Ogden	July 10, 1915	7:55 a.m.
	July 11, 1915	4:10 p.m.
Salt Lake City	July 10, 1915	9:00 a.m.

Virginia

Alexandria	October 4, 1895	2:15 p.m.
Ashland	October 4, 1895	6:07 p.m.
Bedford	October 5, 1895	4:25 p.m.
Charlottesville	January 1896	
Christiansburg	October 6, 1895	9:10 a.m.
Crewe	October 5, 1895	11:40 a.m.
Danville	January 1896	
Doswell	October 4, 1895	5:52 p.m.
Farmville	October 5, 1895	12:35 p.m.
Fredericksburg	October 4, 1895	3:53 p.m.
Glade Springs	October 6, 1895	12:30 p.m.
Lynchburg	October 5, 1895	2:30 p.m.
	January 1896	
Milford	October 4, 1895	5:15 p.m.
Nottoway Court House	October 5, 1895	11:20 a.m.
Petersburg	October 5, 1895	11:20 a.m.
Richmond	June 1885	
	October 4, 1895	7:15 p.m.
Roanoke	October 5, 1895	5:40 p.m.
Quantico	October 4, 1895	3:10 p.m.
Wytheville	October 6, 1895	11:00 a.m.

Washington

Cottage Grove	July 15, 1915	5:55 p.m.
Eugene	July 15, 1915	5:00 p.m.
Everett	July 13, 1915	11:55 p.m.
Olympia	July 14, 1915	6:30 p.m.
Portland	July 15, 1915	6:00 a.m.
Roseburg	July 15, 1915	8:15 p.m.
Salem	July 15, 1915	2:00 p.m.
Seattle	July 14, 1915	9:15 a.m.
Spokane	July 13, 1915	8:00 a.m.
Tacoma	July 14, 2014	4:00 p.m.
Walla Walla	July 12, 1915	7:30 p.m.
Wenatchee	July 13, 1915	5:30 p.m.

Washington, D.C

| | October 4, 1895 | 12:15 p.m. |
| | January/February 1896 | |

Wisconsin

La Crosse	June 5, 1904	4:40 p.m.
Milwaukee	June 5, 1904	8:00 a.m.
Minneapolis	June 5, 1904	1:00 p.m.
Portage	June 5, 1904	1:45 p.m.
Red Wing	June 5, 1904	8:25 p.m.
Sparta	June 5, 1904	3:50 p.m.
St. Paul	June 5, 1904	9:35 p.m.
Wabasha	June 5, 1904	7:35 p.m.
Watertown	June 5, 1904	12:25 p.m.
Winoma	June 5, 1904	6:10 p.m.

Wyoming

| Cheyenne | July 10, 1915 | 4:30 p.m. |
| Laramie | July 10, 1915 | 6:15 p.m. |

Note: The material for this chart was compiled from Paige (1988).

Whereas Paige lists itineraries of each individual trip, I have chosen to organize materials under states, cities, dates, and times, in hope that teachers might find it particularly helpful to be able to know when and where the Bell visited within their states. It is quite likely that the train carrying the bells were not always able to adhere to this exact schedule. Large welcomes might well have encouraged the train to stay longer in some locales than in others. Weather could also have played a factor. The Bell was carried on the flatbed of a train car and illuminated at night, and there are reports that people often gathered along the tracks just to see the train go by.

Paige does not appear to have published an itinerary for the Liberty Bell's journey back from the South Carolina Interstate and West Indian Exposition of 1902 in Charleston, South Carolina, to Philadelphia.

I have relied on a letter from H. Y. Darnell of the Pennsylvania Railroad to William H. Ball of Philadelphia dated December 3, 1915, and contained in the Historic Note Card File of the Independence National Historical Park, to add a number of stops that the train made on its return from California to Philadelphia in 1915. Darnell observed that "many places with large populations were run through slowly as at Newport and Covington, Kentucky; numerous stops were made for watering and icing [the] train, watering engines, and for train orders, as at Yaleta, Clint, Fabens, Fort Hancock, Sierra Blanca, Hot Wells, Lobo, Valentine, Marathon and Spoffard, all in Texas; most of the other points where this was necessary were scheduled stops."

Glossary

Abolitionists
Individuals who favored the emancipation of American slaves. As much as any group, they appear responsible for branding the bell in Philadelphia as the Liberty Bell.

Bicentennial
A 200th anniversary.

Bronze
A metal, largely made of copper and tin, from which the Liberty Bell, as well as most other bells, are made.

Campanology
A term composed of the Latin word for *bell* and the Greek word for *word,* or *study,* which is used to designate the study of bells. It includes both the technology and history of the subject.

Cannon
The loops that are used to attach a bell to its yoke.

Casting
The process by which molten metal is poured into a mold to make bells and other objects.

Centennial
A 100th anniversary.

Clapper
A metal object that hangs inside a bell and strikes it to create sound.

Cope
The mold that shapes the outer surface of a bell during casting.

Core
During the casting of a bell, the core gives shape to its inner surface.

Crown
The top portion of a bell.

Declaration of Independence
A document, largely written by Thomas Jefferson and adopted by the Second Continental Congress on July 4, 1776, that declared that the 13 North American colonies were breaking away from their mother country of Great Britain.

Dumb
The Liberty Bell is sometimes referred to as dumb because its crack prevents it from being rung.

Exposition
A fair, often international, typically commemorating a historic event.

Foundry
A place where bells and other metal objects are cast.

Hum note
The sound that swells from a bell after being hit with its clapper.

Icon
A painting or object, originally of Jesus or one of the saints, that serves as a representation or symbol. The Liberty Bell is an icon because it stands for liberty and other American values.

Independence
Generally used to refer to a person's or nation's autonomy. When the 13 colonies revolted from Great Britain, they declared their independence.

Independence Bell
One of the early names used for the Liberty Bell, intended to stress its connection to the American Revolution.

Independence Hall
The name now given to the old State House in Philadelphia, where the Liberty Bell was housed throughout most of its history and where delegates signed both the U.S. Declaration of Independence and the U.S. Constitution.

Inhabitant
An individual who lives within a particular area or jurisdiction.

Inscription
Words that are written, or inscribed, on bells or other objects. The inscription on the Liberty Bell is from Leviticus 25:10 and says, "Proclaim LIBERTY throughout all the land to all the inhabitants thereof." It also includes the names of John Pass and John Stow, who recast the Bell

Jubilee Celebration
The Hebrew people were instructed to celebrate a Year of Jubilee every 50 years, during which land would be returned to the families to which it was originally allocated, and slaves would be freed.

Knell
The sound, typically associated with funerals or mourning, that a bell makes when it is tolled slowly.

Leviticus
The third book of Hebrew Scriptures (the Old Testament of Christians), attributed to Moses, that dealt with the laws governing matters related to the temple.

Liberty
A synonym for *freedom*, often with the connotation of freedom regulated by laws of the people's making.

Lip
The rim of a bell, which surrounds its sound-bow.

Muffle
To stifle the sound of a bell, usually on occasions of mourning, by attaching a piece of leather to the clapper as it strikes.

Old Bell
One of the original names given to the Liberty Bell, designed to distinguish it from the replacement that was used in conjunction with a clock.

Pass and Stow
The names of the two individuals, both with the first name of John, who recast the Liberty Bell after it cracked on its first ringing.

Peal
The sound of a bell. When bells are rung, they are said to have been *pealed*.

Pennsylvania
With a name literally meaning "Penn's Forest," Pennsylvania is one of the middle colonies. It was founded by William Penn, who received a grant from King Charles II of Britain and sought to establish a colony that would provide religious freedom.

Philadelphia
The city (whose name means "brotherly love" in Greek) founded by William Penn in the state of Pennsylvania; Independence Hall and the Liberty Bell are located here.

Proclaim
To tell or announce. The Liberty Bell contains an inscription from Leviticus 25:10, which begins with the words "Proclaim LIBERTY throughout all the land."

Profile
Another name for the shape of a bell; a bell's profile largely determines its sound, or timbre.

Relic
An ancient object, generally of historical interest, that evokes deep emotions.

Sesquicentennial
A 150th anniversary. The United States celebrated the sesquicentennial of its independence in 1926.

Sestercentennial
A 250th anniversary.

Shoulder
The rounded upper portion of a bell, on which any inscriptions are typically written.

Sound-bow
The large and thick bottom portion of a bell, against which the clapper strikes.

Spider
A device added to the inside of the Liberty Bell, with six arms designed to distribute the weight of the Bell to prevent further cracking.

State House
Name of the building, originally the home of the Pennsylvania Assembly, now known as Independence Hall. This is where the Declaration of Independence and Constitution were signed, and which, throughout most of its history, was the home of the Liberty Bell.

Steeple
A tall tower on top of a roof, typically found on churches, but also found on Independence Hall and some other governmental buildings.

Stickle board
Also known as a *crook,* this is a piece of wood that is used as a template to give shape to a bell before casting.

Strike note
The sound that a bell makes when hit with a clapper.

Suffrage
The right to vote.

Suffragists
Individuals who advocated the right of women to vote. American suffragists traveled with a replica of the Liberty Bell that also contained the words, from the preamble to the U.S. Constitution, "Establish Justice."

Symbol
A mark or object that represents an object or a concept. As its name has suggested, the Liberty Bell has been a symbol both of colonial independence from Britain and of individual liberty, especially for former slaves and women.

Talisman
An object that is thought to bring good luck.

Timbre
The sound of a bell.

Tocsin
A signal or alarm. The Liberty Bell has been called a "tocsin of liberty."

Venerable
Something or someone worthy of esteem.

Venerated
Revered and held in high esteem.

Waist
The tapering section of a bell just above the sound-bow, which extends to the shoulder.

Yoke
The name for a beam from which a bell is suspended. In the case of the Liberty Bell, it is made of American elm and reinforced with iron and still.

Bibliography

ARTICLES, CHAPTERS, AND SHEET MUSIC

Alexander, Mary D. 1925. "The Ringers of the Liberty Bell." *Journal of the Illinois State Historical Society* 18 (October): 658–667.

"American College Wants the Old Liberty Bell Home." 2003. *Philadelphia Business Journal,* October 9. https://www.bizjournals.com/philadelphia/stories /2003/10/06/daily25.html.

"American Freedom Bell + Spirit of Liberty Collection Exhibits." USS Midway Museum. https://www.midway.org/calendar-events/american-freedom-bell -spirit-of-liberty-collections-exhibits

"American Freedom Bell, Charlotte Museum of History—Bells on Waymarking .com." http://www.waymarking.com/waymarks/WM6WKK_American _Freedom_Bell_Charlotte_Museum_Of_History.

American Heritage Foundation. n.d. "The Story of the 1975–1976 American Freedom Train." http://www.freedomtrain.org/american-freedom-train-consist -041-childrens-bell.htm.

Anderson, Betsy. "The Liberty Bell in Philadelphia is onboard as the Honorary Bell of Peace." https://www.worldwar1centennial.org/index.php/communicate /press-media/wwi-centennial-news/5580-bells-of-peace-update-the -liberty-bell-is-onboard.html.

"Another Liberty Bell." n.d. *Whitechapel Bell Foundry News.* http://www .whitechapelbellfoundry.co.uk/newsf.htm.

Araiza, Victor. 2013. "Professor Sparks Project to Bring Liberty Bell Replica to Campus." *UHCL The Signal,* September 16. https://uhclthesignal.com /wordpress/2013/09/16/professor-sparks-project-to-bring-liberty-bell -replica-to-campus.

"ASM Historical Landmarks." n.d. https://www.asminternational.org/membership /awards/historical-landmarks.

"Auction In Melbourne To Help Raise Funds For Replica of Bell." 1976. *The Orlando Sentinel*, April 30, p. 14.

Backaitis, Stan. 2018. "Footprints of Lithuanians in America 1919–1945, Part II— Birth of a Self Reliant Ethnic Community and Watchful Guardians of their Ancestral Homeland." May 2. https://lithampedia.com/part-2-test-53b9e3a 5afea.

Backaitis, Stasys. 2018. "A Gift From the Heart—The American Lithuanian Liberty Bell." *Draugas News,* April 17. https://www.draugas.org/news/a-gift-from-the-heart-the-american-lithuanian-liberty-bell.

Batuman, Elif. 2009. "The Bells." *The New Yorker,* April 27. https://www.newyorker.com/magazine/2009/04/27/the-bells-6.

"Bells and Bell-Founding." 1854. *The Illustrated Magazine of Art.* 3 (15): 167–176.

Bergsma, John S. 2005. "Once Again, the Jubilee, Every 49 of 50 Years?" *Vetus Testamentum* 55 (January): 121–125.

Berkes, Howard. 2006. "Happy Fourth, in a Town Named Freedom." NPR, July 4. https://www.npr.org/templates/story/story.php?storyId=5533062.

Blakemore, Erin. 2016. Smithsonian.com, September 21. https://www.smithsonianmag.com/smithsonian-institution/historic-bell-helps-ring-new-african-american-history-museum-180960545.

Bland, Sidney R. 1993. "Women and World's Fairs: The Charleston Story." *South Carolina Historical Magazine* 94 (July): 166–184.

Bohlin Cywinski Jackson. n.d. "Liberty Bell Center." https://bcj.com/projects/liberty-bell-center.

Bosanac, Alexandra. 2014. "Canada's 'Liberty Bell' Comes Home After 150 Years on U.S. Soil." *Huffington Post,* June 30. https://www.huffingtonpost.ca/2014/06/30/canada-liberty-bell-charlottetown_n_5542988.html.

Branham, Robert James. 1996. "'Of Thee I Sing': Contesting America." *American Quarterly* 48 (December): 623–652.

Broder, John M. 1993. "Clinton Honors S. Africa Ex-Foes at Liberty Bell." *Los Angeles Times,* July 5. http://articles.latimes.com/1993-07-05/news/mn-10250_1_south-africa.

Brooks, Elbridge S. 1900. "The Liberty Bell." In *The School Speaker and Reader,* ed. William DeWitt Hyde. Boston: Ginn, 93–96.

Browne, Ryan. 2018. "Pentagon to Return Bells Captured in the Philippines over 100 Years Ago." *CNN Politics,* August 14. https://www.cnn.com/2018/08/14/politics/pentagon-philippines-balangiga-bells/index.html.

Bruno, Lee. 2016. "Let Freedom Ring: Buffalo Soldiers and the Liberty Bell." *Argonaut—Journal of the San Francisco Museum and Historical Society* (Winter): 6–15.

"Bruton Parish Church." Colonial Williamsburg. http://www.history.org/almanack/places/hb/hbbruch.cfm.

Bush, George W. 2001. "Remarks at an Independence Day Celebration in Philadelphia." The American Presidency Project, July 4. http://www.presidency.ucsb.edu/ws/?pid=73536.

Bush, George H. W. 1990. "Remarks in Prague, Czechoslovakia, at a Ceremony Commemorating the End of Communist Rule." November 17. The American Presidency Project. http://www.presidency.ucsb.edu/ws/?pid=19066.

"Bush Rings Liberty Bell in Prague." 1990. *The New York Times,* November 18.

Bykofsky, Stu. 1997. "Pistol-Packing Tourist." *Philadelphia Daily News,* February 28, 9.

Caconrad. 2015. "Poet in the Crack of Liberty: My Life with Christopher, 1988." Poetry Foundation. https://www.poetryfoundation.org/harriet/2015/06/poet-in-the-crack-of-liberty-my-life-with-christopher-1988.

Caine, Burton. 1997. "'The Liberal Agenda': Biblical Values and the First Amendment." *Touro Law Review* 14: 129–197.

"California Bell Legends: A Survey." 1945. Written by The Editors. *California Folklore Quarterly* 4 (January): 18–28.

Callahan, Robey. 1999. "The Liberty Bell: From Commodity to Sacred Object." *Journal of Material Culture* 4 (1): 57–78.

Campbell, Tom. 2018. "The Annecy Liberty Bell Replica." Tom Loves the Liberty Bell.com, June 19. http://tomlovestheliberty bell.com/2018/06/10/the-annecy -liberty-bell-replica.

Campbell, Tom. 2018. "National Treasury: The Case of DC's Missing Liberty Bell." Tom Loves the Liberty Bell.com, April 21. http://tomlovestheliberty bell.com /2018/04/21/national-treasury-the-case-of-dcs-missing-liberty-bell.

Campbell, Tom. 2017. "Phil Tovrea's Liberty Bell Replica: Phoenix Arizona." Tom Loves the Liberty Bell.com, November 30. http://tomlovestheliberty bell .com/2017/11/30/phil-tovreas-liberty-bell-replica-phoenix-arizona.

"The Canadian Liberty Bell." n.d. http://www.riches-lieux.com/wp-content/uploads /2018/05/The-Canadian-Liberty-Bell.pdf.

Carson, Hampton L. 1894. "Oration Delivered at the Invitation of the City of Chicago and of the World's Fairs Commission, on the Fourth Day of July, 1893, in Jackson Park, Chicago." *Pennsylvania Magazine of History and Biography* 17:49–55.

Carter, Katherine D. 1980. "Isaac Norris II's Attack on Andrew Hamilton." *Pennsylvania Magazine of History and Biography* 104 (April): 139–161.

"Casting the Liberty Bell." National Science Foundation. https://www.nsf.gov/news /special_reports/liberty/01_history_01.jsp.

Chapman, Maria Weston. 1839. "Sonnet." *The Liberty Bell*. The Friends of Liberty. Boston: Anti-Slavery Bazaar.

Chase, Malcolm. 1990. "From Millennium to Anniversary: The Concept of Jubilee in Late Eighteenth- and Nineteenth-Century England." *Past & Present* 129 (November): 132–147.

Cherveny, Tom. 2016. "Milan Dedicates New Liberty Bell." *West Central Tribune*, August 26. http://www.wctrib.com/news/4102857-milan-dedicates-new -liberty-bell.

Coggin Tobbogan. 2018. "Stadium Liberty Bell at CBP by 2019." Crossing Broad .com, February 23. https://www.crossingbroad.com/2018/02/phillies-plan-to -refurbish-and-display-veterans-stadium-liberty-bell-at-cbp-by-2019.html.

Condon, Tom. 1996. "Ring One Up for Savior of Liberty Bell." *Courant*, July 4. http://articles.courant.com/1996-07-04/news/9607040405_1_new-bell -pound-bell-ringing.

Coolidge, Calvin. 1926. "Speech on the 150th Anniversary of the Declaration of Independence." Teaching AmericanHistory.org, July 5. http://teachingamerican history.org/library/document/speech-on-the-occasion-of-the-one-hundred -and-fiftieth-anniversary-of-the-declaration-of-independence.

Cosecha. 2018. "Immigrant Youth Walking for DACA Rally at Philadelphia Liberty Bell." Popular Resistance.org, February 20. https://popularresistance .org/immigrant-youth-walking-for-daca-rally-at-philadelphia-liberty-bell.

Cress, Joseph. 2016. "Ringing in 1902: Local Residents Rang in 1902 by Admiring the Liberty Bell." *The Sentinel.* https://cumberlink.com/news/local /history/ringing-in-local-residents-rang-in-by-admiring-the-liberty/article _863b36c5-7879-557f-831b-a73de94c80ff.html.

Crockett, Zach. 2014. "When Taco Bell 'Bought' the Liberty Bell." Priceonomics, July 14. https://priceonomics.com/when-taco-bell-bought-the-liberty-bell.

"Cuban Stowaway Clings To His Own Liberty Bell." 1987. KNT News Service, January 9. http://articles.orlandosentinel.com/1987-01-09/news/0100100009 _1_hector-morales-clang-cuba.

Cumberland County, New Jersey. "Cumberland County Liberty Bell." http://www .co.cumberland.nj.us/libertybell.

Darling, Henry R. 1968. "Crackless Liberty Bell That Rings Coming Here from London in June." *Philadelphia Sunday Bulletin*, February 25, Section 1, 32.

Davis, George R. 1892. "The World's Columbian Exposition," *North American Review* 154 (March): 305–318.

Dawdy, Shelli. 2011. "On Loss of Belladier David Hall: Bells Must Be Ringing in Heaven." *OKG News,* October 12. http://okgrassroots.com/?p=22253.

De Groot, Kristen. 2018. "Philly Group Wants the City's Other Liberty Bell Put on Display," March 13. http://www.mcall.com/news/nationworld/pennsylvania /mc-nws-philadelphia-bicentennial-bell-20180331-story.html.

"Declaration of Common Aims of the Independent Mid-European Nations." October 16, 1918. http://www.carpatho-rusyn.org/fame/proc.htm.

"Declaration of Independence—Anniversary." June 26, 1963. S Con. Res. 25, 77 Stat. p. 944.

"Deere Helps Create 'Peace Plow' for Chicago World's Fair." 2015. *John Deere Journal,* November 11. https://johndeerejournal.com/2015/11/deere-helps -create-peace-plow-for-chicago-worlds-fair.

"Delaware Freedom Ways: The Quaker Idea of Reciprocal Liberty." n.d. https:// erenow.com/common/fourbritishfolkwaysinamerica1989/102.html.

Desbler, Charles D. 1892. "How the Declaration Was Received in the Old Thirteen." *Harpers New Monthly Magazine* 85 (July): 165–187.

Diggs, Morse. 1978. "He Dreams of Recasting Bell." *Akron Beacon Journal*, July 4.

Ditzel, Paul. 1968. "The Story of the Liberty Bell Since 1751." *American Legion Magazine* 85 (December): 24–27; 52–54.

Dollman, Darla Sue. 2018. "The Liberty Bell: International Symbol of Freedom." Owlcation, April 20. https://owlcation.com/humanities/The-Liberty-Bell -Symbol-of-American-Independence.

Doutrich, Paul. 1988. "From Revolution to Constitution: Pennsylvania's Path to Federalism." In *The Constitution and the States: The Role of the Original Thirteen in the Framing and Adoption of the Federal Constitution*, ed. Patrick T. Conley and John P. Kaminski. Madison, WI: Madison House, 37–54.

Ducibella, Jim. 2017. "The Inside Scoop on Ringing the Wren Bell." College of William & Mary, April 27. https://www.wm.edu/news/stories/2017/the-inside -scoop-on-ringing-the-wren-bell.php.

Duncan, Adam. 2013. "NPS Relocates the Bicentennial Bell," January 31. https:// www.nps.gov/inde/learn/news/nps-relocates-the-bicenteennial-bell.htm.

Durden, William G. 2010. "Remarks of President William G. Durden." May 23. http://www.dickinson.edu/news/article/252/remarks_of_president_william _g_durden.

Eaton, William J. 1992. "Clinton Asks Americans to Ring in His Inaugural." *Los Angeles Times,* December 19. http://articles.latimes.com/1992-12-19/news /mn-2132_1_inaugural-event.

Ehrenreich, Ben. 2010. "The End. Death in L.A. Can Be an Odd Undertaking." *LA Magazine.* http://origin-www.lamag.com/features/Story.aspx?id=1362579.

Emch, Dale. 2001. "Ohio Bicentennial: 88 County Bells an Appealing Memorial." *The Blade,* December 16. https://www.toledoblade.com/State/2001/12/16 /Ohio-bicentennial-88-county-bells-an-appealing-memorial.html.

Erickson, Mark St John. 2012. "Historic Bruton Parish Church Gets Bell Cleaned." *Daily Press,* November 4. http://www.dailypress/com/news/williamsburg /dp-nws-bruton-bell-20121104-story.html.

Eskenazi, Tamara Cohn, and Jacob L. Wright. 2013. "What the Liberty Bell Can Teach Us About America and the Fourth of July." Fox News, July 3. http:// www.foxnews.com/opinion/2013/07/03/what-liberty-bell-can-teach-us -about-america-and-fourth-july.html.

Evensen, Bruce J. 1993. "'Saving the City's Reputation': Philadelphia's Struggle over Self-Identity, Sabbath-Breaking and Boxing in America's Sesquicen-tennial Year." *Pennsylvania History: A Journal of Mid-Atlantic Studies* 60 (January): 6–34.

Farrell, Sean. 2016. "Whitechapel Bell Foundry to Ring in New Era as Owner Sells Site." *The Guardian*, December 2. https://www.theguardian.com/business /2016/dec/02/whitechapel-bell-fou7ndry-to-ring-in-new-era-as-owner -sells-site.

Feder, Barnaby J. 1983. "British Bell Maker Sees Better Times." *The New York Times Archives,* July 4. https://www.nytimes.com/1983/07/04/business /british-bell-maker-sees-better-times.html.

Feiler, Bruce. 2009. "How Moses Shaped America." *Time*, October 12. http://content .time.com/time/subscriber/article/0,33009,1927303-3,00.html.

Fendrick, Susan P. 2016. "The Bells That Still Can Ring: On Rest and Action (Parshat Behar, Leviticus 25: 1–26:2)." *Huffington Post,* May 24. https:// www.huffingtonpost.com/rabbi-susan-p-fendrick/the-bells-that-still-can -ring-on-rest-and-action-parshat-behar-leviticus-251-262_b_10120144 .html.

Ferguson, Kevin. 2012. "History Lesson: If You Don't Like the Olympics, Just Make Your Own." July 30. https://www.scpr.org/blogs/offramp/2012/07/30/9216 /history-lesson-if-you-dont-olympics-just-make-your

Fey, Marshall A. 1975. "Charles Fey and San Francisco's Liberty Bell Slot Machine." *California Historical Quarterly* 54 (Spring): 57–62.

Finkel, Ken. 2016. "Philadelphia Politics and the Presidential Campaign of 1932." Phillyhistory.org, October 10. https://www.phillyhistory.org/blog/index.php /2016/10/philadelphia-politics-and-the-presidential-campaign-of-1932.

Firstworldwar.com. n.d. "Vintage Audio: Liberty Bell (It's Time to Ring Again)." http://www.firstworldwar.com/audio/libertybell.htm.

Fischer, Jake. 2018. "Liberty at Last: The Process Behind the 76er' Bell-Ringing Ceremony." SI.com, May 4. https://www.si.com/nba/2018/05/04/76ers-nba -playoffs-joel-embiid-sam-hinkie-meek-mill.

"For Pope Francis, It's Imperative: Religious Liberty Is a Gift from God. Defend It." 2015. Catholic News Agency, September 26. https://www.catholicnews agency.com/news/for-pope-francis-its-imperative-religious-liberty-is-a -gift-from-god-defend-it-39467.

Ford, Gerald R. 1976. "Remarks of Gerald R. Ford in Philadelphia, Pennsylvania (Bicentennial Celebration)," July 4. Gerald R. Ford Presidential Library and Museum. https://www.fordlibrarymuseum.gov/library/speeches/760645 .asp.

Fosmoe, Margaret. 2015. "Notre Dame Grad Student Seeks Liberty Bell Fix." South Bend Tribune.com, February 20. https://www.southbendtribune.com/news /local/notre-dame-grad-student-seeks-liberty-bell-fix/article_d4fd733f -89f3-5aff-b780-25f1a14e0c74.html.

Frazier, Arthur H. 1974. "The Stretch Clock and Its Bell at the State House." *Pennsylvania Magazine of History and Biography* 98 (July): 287–313.

Freedman, M. Troy. 2018. "Bronze Age and Religious Roots of Modern Debtor-Creditor Law." *Pennsylvania Bar Association Quarterly* 89: 166–177.

"Freedom Bell." n.d. The Village of Mt. Morris. http://mtmorrisil.net/freedom-bell.

French, Mrs. Charles L. 1944. "The Last Years of Kaskaskia." *Journal of the Illinois State Historical Society* 37 (September): 229–241.

Frey, Carroll. 1951. "The Strange Fortunes of the Liberty Bell." *American Heritage*. New Series 3 (Fall): 46–49.

Fried, Stephen. 2017. "World War I: 100 Years Later. How the Liberty Bell Won the Great War." Smithsonian.com, April. https://www.smithsonianmag.com /history/how-liberty-bell-won-great-war-180962471.

Friedman, Leo, and Minnie Wilson. 1919. *Once More the Liberty Bell Shall Chime Liberty to All*. Monographic. North American Music Company, Chicago. Notated Music. https://www.loc.gov/item/2013565446.

Friends of Independence National Historical Park. n.d. "Other Bells at Independence NHP." http://friendsofindependence.org/other-bells-at-independence -nhp.

Fritz, Meaghan M., and Frank E. Fee, Jr. 2012. "To Give the Gift of Freedom: Gift Books and the War on Slavery." *American Periodicals: A Journal of History & Criticism*, 23: 60–82.

Frost, J. William. 2014. "Why Quakers and Slavery? Why Not More Quakers?" In *Quakers and Abolition*, ed. Brycchan Carey and Geoffrey Plank. Champaign, IL: University of Illinois Press, 29–42.

Frost, J. William. 1978. "The Origins of the Quaker Crusade Against Slavery: A Review of Recent Literature." *Quaker History* 67 (Spring): 42–58.

Garet, Ronald R. 2000. "Proclaim Liberty." *Southern California Law Review* 74: 145–168.

Gegan, Evangelos I. 1997. "International Arbitration and the Resolution of Cultural Property Disputes: Navigating the Stormy Waters Surrounding Cultural Property." *Ohio State Journal of Dispute Resolution* 13: 129–166.

"Georgia May Add MLK 'Liberty Bell' to Stone Mountain." Real-Time News from Al.com. AP. https://www.al.com/news/index/ssf/2015/10/georgia _may_add_mlk.html.

Giannini, Robert L., III. 1997. "A New Way to Look at 'Pass and Stow.'" Independence National Historical Park, May 1.

Gillett & Johnston (Croydon) Ltd. Our Freedom Bell. https://www.gillettjohnston .com.uk/gillett-johnston-croydon-ltd-our-freedom-bell.

Gopnik, Blake. 2014. "Jeff Koons' Art Rings a Bell." artnet News, September 15. https://news.artnet.com/exhibitions/jeff-koonss-art-rings-a-bell-102236.

Government Publishing Office. 1963. "Declaration of Independence—Anniversary." June 26. S Con. Res. 25, 77 Stat. p. 944. https://www.govinfo.gov/content/pkg /STATUTE-77/pdf/STATUTE-77-Pg944.pdf.

Gratz, Irwin. 2017. "It Aimed to Make the World 'Safe for Democracy': World War I and Its Aftermath." Maine Public Radio, February 3. https://www .mainepublic.org/post/it-aimed-make-world-safe-democracy-world-war-i -and-its-aftermath.

Griffin, Marlin. 1908. "The Liberty Bell. Historian Griffin Offers a Correction." *American Catholic Historical Researches* 4 (January): 82.

Grobe, Charles. 1860. *The Union Bell Polka.* Lee & Walker, Philadelphia. Notated Music. https://www.loc.gov/item/ihas.200000206.

Gustin, Kelsey. 2018. "The Anti-slavery Fair." August 8. https://www.bpl.org/blogs /post/the-anti-slavery-fair.

Gutierrez, Jason. 2018. "U.S. Returns Bells Taken as War Booty from Philippines in 1901." *The New York Times,* December 11. https://www.nytimes .com/2018/12/11/world/asia/balangiga-bells-united-states-philippines .html.

Hager, Frederick W. 1911. *Ring Out Liberty Bell Patriotic March Song.* Monographic. Notated Music. https://www.loc.gov/item/2013564757.

"The Hall-Harte Archive of Suffragist Photographs." n.d. https://www.swanngal leries.com/news/2014/12/hall-harte-suffragist-photographs.

Hanson, Victor F., Janice H. Carlson, Karen M. Papouchado, and Norman A. Nielsen. 1976. "The Liberty Bell: Composition of the Famous Failure." *American Scientist* 64 (November–December): 614–619.

Harris, Leslie J. 2009. "Motherhood, Race, and Gender: The Rhetoric of Women's Antislavery Activism in the *Liberty Bell* Giftbooks." *Women's Studies in Communication* 32 (Fall): 293–319.

Harrison, Richard S. 1991. "Irish Quaker Perspectives on the Anti-Slavery Movement." *Journal of the Friends Historical Society* 56 (1) (1991): 106–125.

Hartzell, Roy, and Mary A. Feldman. 1918. *The Liberty Bell.* Monographic. Howard Publishing Company, Washington, D.C. Notated Music. https://www .loc.gov/item/2014561560.

Harvey, Bruce. 1997. "Architecture for the Future at the Charleston Exposition, 1901–1902." *Perspectives in Vernacular Architecture* 7: 115–130.

Haspel, Paul. 2012. "Bells of Freedom and Foreboding: Liberty Bell Ideology and the Clock Motif in Edgar Allan Poe's 'The Masque of the Red Death.'" *Edgar Allan Poe Review* 13 (Spring): 46–70.

Hayes, Monica. 2007. "Local Group to Renew Ties to Canadian City Founded by Ex-slaves." *Pittsburgh Post-Gazette,* August 20. http://www.post-gazette .com/life/lifestyle/2007/08/20/Local-group-to-renew-ties-to-Canadian -city-founded-by-ex-slaves/stories/200708200198.

Hazeltine, Rachel C. 1918. *Make the Old Bell Ring.* Monographic. Sam-a-lam, Publisher, Sunnyvale, CA. Notated Music. https://www.loc.gov/item/2013564717.

Heartland Weekend. n.d. "Kaskaskia: Home to the Liberty Bell of the West." http://www.heartlandweekend.com/kaskaskia-home-to-the-liberty-bell-of -the-west.

Heller, Jason. 2016. "Remembering Muhammad Ali's Trippy, Anti-Cavity Kids' Record." *Rolling Stone,* June 6. https://www.rollingstone.com/music/music -news/remembering-muhammad-alis-trippy-anti-cavity-kids-record-64027.

Hennessey, Maureen Hart, ed. 1999. *Norman Rockwell: Pictures for the American People.* New York: Harry N. Abrams.

"Hibiya Park Liberty Bell." 2014. *Lost Tokyo* (blog), June 18. http://lost-tokyo .blogspot.com/2014/06/hibiya-park-liberty-bell.html.

Hill, Richard S. 1953. "The Mysterious Chord of Henry Clay Work." *Notes* 10 (March): 211–225 and 10 (June): 367–390.

Hilt, Eric, and Wendy M. Rahn. 2016. "Turning Citizens into Investors: Promoting Savings with Liberty Bonds During World War I." *RSF: The Russell Sage Foundation Journal of the Social Sciences* 2 (October): 86–108.

Hingston, Sandy. 2016. "10 Things You Might Not Know About the 1876 Centennial Exhibition." *Philadelphia Magazine,* May 10. https://www.phillymag .com/news/2016/05/10/centennial-exhibition-history.

"Historic Hand Signed Norman Rockwell Lithograph Entitled 'Celebration' and/ or 'Liberty Bell,'" n.d. https://worthingtongalleries.com/shop/art-subject /american-revolutionary-war/historic-hand-signed-norman-rockwell -lithograph-entitled-celebration-andor-liberty-bell.

Holst, Holly Jean. n.d. "Silent No More: The Justice Bell." http://philadelphiaen cyclopedia.org/archive/liberty-bell/justice-bell.

Hooks, Cindy. 2018. "Judge's Decision Draws Traveling Protest to Taos." *Taos News,* August 23. http://www.santafenewmexican.com/news/local_news /judge-s-decision-draws-traveling-protest-to-taos/article_41733308-a229 -5846-ba68-318fbe0b502f.html.

Horning, Timothy. 2010. "Touching Liberty (Literally)." *Discoveries from the City Archives,* August 23. https://www.phillyhistory.org/blog/index.php/2010/08 /touching-liberty-literally.

How I Met Your Mother (TV Series). "'The Sweet Taste of Liberty.' Quotes (2005)." https://www.imdb.com/title/tt0606117/quotes.

"How to Be a Bell Tapper." 2015. Society of the Descendants of the Signers of the Declaration of Independence, May 3. http://www.dsdi1776.com/members -only-how-to-be-a-bell-tapper.

Howell, Dave. 2018. "'Give Me Your Tired' . . . or Maybe Not: Allentown Exhibit Reveals Immigration Has Long Been a Thorny Issue." *Morning Call,* March 28. https://www.mcall.com/entertainment/mc-ent-liberty-bell -museum-immigration-exhibit-allentown-20180314-story.html.

Hudson, Lynn M. 2010. "'This Is Our Fair and Our State': African Americans and the Panama-Pacific International Exposition." *California History* 87: 26–45; 66–68.

Hydepark.org. n.d. "A Mystery from the Fair." *World's Columbian Exposition of 1893.* http://www.hydepark.org/historicpres/ColumbianExp.htm#mystery.

Hylton, John. 1991. "The Music of the Louisiana Purchase Exposition." *College Music Symposium* 31: 59–66.

Hyson, Jeffrey. 2004. "Exhibit Review." *Pennsylvania Magazine of History and Biography* 128 (July): 307–310.

"Independence Bell—July 4, 1776." n.d. https://www.ego4u.com/en/read-on -ligerature/poem-independence-bell.

Independence National Historical Park. n.d. "The Story of a Symbol." https://www .nps.gov/parkhistory/online_books/hh/17/hh17h.htm.

Jackson, Joseph. 1943. "Birthplace of a Nation." *Records of the American Catholic Historical Society of Philadelphia* 54 (March): 1–27.

Johnson, Herbert. Picture of cartoon printed between 1912 and 1941. "Ringing the Bell of World Democracy." Library of Congress. https://www.loc.gov /pictures/item/2016682469.

Jones, Jean. 1998. "Our Liberty Bell Has No Crack and a More Fascinating His-tory." *Bridgeton Evening News,* June 26. http://www.co.cumberland.nj.us /content/22596/23487/23597/24194.aspx.

Jones, Richard. 2013. "Residents Start Fund to Save Hamilton's Liberty Bell." *Journal-News,* October 13. https://www.journal-news.com/news/residents -start-fund-save-hamilton-liberty-bell/sMtzGJL8uNCFYXLONXBc1J.

Jones, Richard O. 2014. "Piece of Local History Restored; The Liberty Bell Rings Again!!!" Butler County Historical Society, April 23. http://bchistoricalsociety .com/main/2014/04/piece-local-history-restored-liberty-bell-rings.

Jordan, Gretchen Graf. 1964. "Hawthorne's 'Bell': Historical Evolution Through Symbol." *Nineteenth-Century Fiction* 19 (September): 123–139.

"The Justice Bell Story." Justice Bell Foundation. http://www.justicebell.org/the -justice-bell-story.

Kaiser, Daniel. 2017. "When the Liberty Bell Visited Grinnell." Grinnell Stories, May 6. http://grinnellstories.blogspot.com/2017/05/when-liberty-bell-visited -grinnell.html.

Kang, Sung Won, and Hugh Rockoff. 2015. "Capitalizing Patriotism: The Liberty Loans of World War I." *Financial History Review* 22: 45–78.

Katchun, Mitch. 2004. "A Beacon to Oppressed Peoples Everywhere': Major Richard R. Wright Sr., National Freedom Day, and the Rhetoric of Free-dom in the 1940s." *Pennsylvania Magazine of History and Biography* 128 (July): 279–306.

Kazek, Kelly. 2015. "Replicas of 12 World-Famous Things You Can See Right Here in Alabama." AL.com, February 24. https://www.al.com/living/index.ssf /2015/02/12_replicas_of_world-famous_si.html.

Kelly, Olivia. 2014. "Dublin's Freedom Bell to Be Restored." *Irish Times,* March 11. https://www.irishtimes.com/culture/heritage/dublin-s-freedom-bell-to-be -restored-1.1719697.

Kennedy, Dustin. 2013. "Revising the Public Sphere: George Lippard, Class, and U.S. Nationalism." *ESQ: A Journal of the American Renaissance* 59: 585–617.

Kevles, Daniel J. 2013. "A Primer of A, B, Seeds: Advertising, Branding, and Intellectual Property in an Emerging Industry." *U. C. Davis Law Review* 47: 657–678.

KGF Staff. 2016. "Bombing at Portland City Hall Still Unsolved 45 Years Later." KGW.com, January 12. https://www.kgw.com/article/news/investigations /bombing-at-portland-city-hall-still-unsolved-45-years-later/283-839117.

Kimball, Paige. n.d. "Justice Bell Article." Unpublished document provided by staff of the Independence National Historical Park in Philadelphia.

King, Martin Luther. 2008. "I Have a Dream Today." *The Guardian,* August 28. https://www.theguardian.com/commentisfree/2008/aug/28/uselections 2008.constitutionandcivilliberties.

Klein, Milton M. 1977. "Commemorating the American Revolution: The Bicentennial and Its Predecessors." *New York History* 58 (July): 257–276.

Koons, Jeff. Liberty Bell Artworks. http://www.jeffkoons.com/search/node /Liberty%20Bell.

Kopp, John. 2007. "Visitors Come in Droves to See Independence Hall, Liberty Bell in 2016." *Philly Voice,* January 18. https://www.phillyvoice.com /visitation-soars-independence-national-park.

"Korean Bell of Friendship." SanPedro.com—San Pedro, California. https:// sanpedro.com/san-pedro-area-points-interest/korean-bell-friendship.

"Koret Helps Renovate Jerusalem's Liberty Bell Park." n.d. *Jewish News of Northern California.* https://www.jweekly.com/1999/09/03/koret-helpspreno- vatepjerusalem-s-liberty-bell-park.

Korshak, Yvonne. 1987. "The Liberty Cap as a Revolutionary Symbol in America and France." *Smithsonian Studies in American Art* 1 (Autumn): 52–69.

Ku Lueven. n.d. "Carillon." Home Erfgoed—En Publiekswerking. https:www .kuleuven.be/junstenerfgoed/expo-events/carillon.

Kurjack, Dennis C. 1953. "The 'President's House' in Philadelphia." *Pennsylvania History: A Journal of Mid-Atlantic Studies* 20 (October): 380–394.

Lalinde, Jaime. 2014. "How to Make a Koons." *Vanity Fair,* June 6. https://www .vanityfair.com/culture/2014/06/how-to-make-akoons-liberty-bell.

Larned, Larry. 2006. "Birth of the Blue Bell Telephone Sign: The History of the Blue Bell Telephone Sign as Implemented by New England Telephone and Telegraph." https://www.belltelephonesigns.com.

Lawler, Edward, Jr. 2005. "The President's House Revisited." *Pennsylvania Magazine of History and Biography* 129 (October): 371–420.

Lawler, Edward, Jr. 2002. "The President's House in Philadelphia: The Rediscovery of a Lost Landmark." *Pennsylvania Magazine of History and Biography* 126 (January): 5–95.

Lazarus, Emma. 1883. "The New Colossus." NPS.gov, November 2. https://www .nps.gov/stli/learn/historyculture/colossus.htm.

Leach, Roberta J. 1984. "Jennie Bradley Roessing and the Fight for Woman Suffrage in Pennsylvania." *Western Pennsylvania Historical Magazine* 67 (1984): 189–211.

"Legazpi City Albay." 2017. Facebook, April 1. https://www.facebook.com /510888042351492/posts/the-72-year-old-liberty-bell-the-gift-given-by-the -americans-to-the-people-of-al/1301442873296001.

Leminski, Karen. 1995. "Picturing American History, 1770–1930." *The Historian* 57 (Spring): 567–572.

Leslie, J. P. 1853. "The Bell." In *The Liberty Bell*. Boston: National Anti-Slavery Bazaar, 304–315.

Levine, Art. 2014. "Behar: The 'Torah'—not 'Taco'—Liberty Bell." *Yerushatenu*, May 9. https://rabbiartlevine.com/Home/tablid/2652/ID/1104/Behar-The -Torah-not-Tac0-Liberty-Bell.aspx.

Levy, Dan. 2017. "Philly Export: The United States Actually Has More Than 50 Liberty Bells." Billy Penn.com, May 29. https://billypenn.com/2017/05 /29/philly-export-the-united-states-actually-has-more-than-50-liberty -bells.

"Liberty Bell." n.d. The Highground. https://www.thehighground.us/tributes_and _facilities/liberty-bell.

"Liberty Bell." n.d. Philadelphia Museum of Art. http://www.philamuseum.org /collections/permanent/302817.html.

"The Liberty Bell." 1918. Washington, D.C.: Howard Music Company. Accessed at https://www.oc.gov/item/2014561560.

"The Liberty Bell: An Apt Symbol for American Coinage." 2016. *Mint News Blog,* December 28. http://mintnewsblog.com/the-liberty-bell-an-apt-symbol-for -american-coinage.

Liberty Bell—at Bunker Hill, Boston, June. 1903. Photograph. Library of Congress. https://www.loc.gov/item/2003653808.

"The Liberty Bell, 1850—Buxton Settlement, Raleigh ON—Bells on Waymark- ing.com." n.d. http://www.waymarking.com/waymarks/WMJDN1_The -Liberty_Bell_1850_Buxton_Settlement_Raleigh_OH.

"Liberty Bell–Glover Park—Marietta, GA.—Exact Replicas on Waymarking.com." n.d. http://;www.waymarking.com/waymakrs/WM42V1_Liberty_Bell _Glover_Park_marietta_GA.

"Liberty Bell: Journey to New Orleans." Independence Hall in American Mem- ory. [Contains reports from major newspapers of the day]. http://www .independencehall-americanmemory.com/the-liberty-bell/liberty-bell -journey-to-new-orleans.

"Liberty Bell—St. Patrick's Park, Dublin, Ireland." n.d. http://www.waymarking .com/waymarks/WMQZ7D_Liberty_Bell_St_Patricks_Park_Dublin _Ireland.

"Liberty Bell and Bell Tower." n.d. http://www.cityofliberty.org/About?Liberty _Bell_and_Bell_Tower.aspx.

"Liberty Bell Brought to Allentown (mural study, Allentown, Pennsylvania Post Office)." n.d. Smithsonian American Art Museum. https://americanart.si .edu/artwork/liberty-bell-brought-allentown-mural-study-allentown -pennsylvania-post-office-1558.

"The Liberty Bell at Penn State." n.d. Penn State College of Engineering. https:// www.ime.psu.edu/department/liberty-bell.aspx.

"Liberty Bell Button with Attached American Flag and 'Votes for Women' Ribbon." n.d. Ann Lewis Women's Suffrage Collection. https://lewissuffrage collection.omeka.net/items/show/1050.

"Liberty Bell Cafe." n.d. *American Reform.* https://sites.google.com/a/nexgenacademy.com/more-than-laissez-faire/african-native-american/african-native-american-political-cartoons-1/liberty-bell-cafe.

"Liberty Bell in Boston." 1903. *The Sacred Heart Review* 19 (25), June 20. https://newspapers.bc.edu/?a=d&d=BOSTONSH19030620-01.2.13.

"Liberty Bell Made of Wheat." n.d. *RoadsideAmerica.* https://www.roadsideamerica.com/story/16559.

"Liberty Bell Memorial Museum." n.d. *Honor America.* http://honoramerica.org/liberty-bell-memorial-museum-2.

"Liberty Bell Memorial Museum (in Transition)." n.d. *RoadsideAmerica.* https://www.roadsideamerica.com/story/13865.

"The Liberty Bell Museum." Libertybellmuseum.org.

"Liberty Bell of Louvain." n.d. Roads to the Great War. http://roadstothegreatwar-ww1.blogspot.com/2016/05/liberty-bell-of-louvain.html.

"The Liberty Bell of the Old Northwest." 1910. *The American Catholic Historical Researches*, New Series, 6 (October): 379–380.

"The Liberty Bell Replica." n.d. Liberty Municipal Library. https://liberty.ploud.net/about-us-the-liberty-bell-replica.html.

"Liberty Bell Replica Goes on Display in Rapid City." 2014. Associated Press, June 1. https://www.panhandlepost.com/liberty-bell-replica-goes-on-display-in-rapid-city.

"Liberty Bell Replica Locations." http://tomlovesthelibertybell.com/liberty-bell-replica-locations.

"Liberty Bell Vigil of Women & Men in Black." 2001. The Shalom Center, September 8. https://theshalomcenter.org/content/liberty-bell-vigil-women-men-black.

"Liberty Belle." 2018. *DC Unofficial Guide to the Universe.* http://dcuguide.com/w/Liberty_Belle_(Libby_Lawrence).

"The Liberty Belles." 1901. *The New York Times*, September 29, 19.

"The Liberty Bells Are Ringing a Patriotic Song." Library of Congress. https://www.loc.gov/resource/ihas.200210016.0/?sp=1.

Lipp, Kenneth. 2013. "Watch About 200 People Smoke a Joint at the Liberty Bell." *The Philly Declaration,* March 17. https://phillydeclaration.org/2013/03/17/watch-about-200-people-smoke-a-joint-at-the-liberty-bell.

Little, Stuart J. 1993. "The Freedom Train: Citizenship and Postwar Political Culture 1946–1949." *American Studies* 34 (Spring): 35–67.

"A Look Back." 2014. Daughters of the American Revolution, March/April. https://www.dar.org/national-society/celebrate-125/look-back-marchapril-2014.

Lott, Travis. 2017. "Before Becoming a State, Illinois Had Its Own Liberty Bell." *Belleville News-Democrat,* December 3. https://www.bnd.com/news/local/article187812418.html.

Lowenthal, David. 1977. "The Bicentennial Landscape: A Mirror Held Up to the Past." *Geographical Review* 67 (July): 253–267.

Loyd, Linda. 2017. "The Economic Juggernaut That Is Independence National Historical Park." *The Inquirer,* June 30. http://www2.philly.com/philly/business /tourism_casinos/big-crowds-expected-at-independence-national-historical -park-20170630.html.

Lucas, Ken. 1999. "In Honor of the World Peace Bell and the City of Newport, Kentucky." U.S. House of Representatives. *Congressional Record*: August 5, 1999 (Extensions of Remarks), E1798.

Lukes, Zdenek. "My Prague." http://www.czech.cz/en/Turistika/My-Prague -%I2%80%93-Zdenek-Lukes.

Lynch, Matt. 2008. "For Whom Should John Brown's Bell Toll?" *Wicked Local Marlborough,* July 22. http://marlborough.wickedlocal.com/x1625323222 /For-whom-should-John-Browns-bell-toll.

Lyon, Jeff. 1994. "Humdinger of a Whodunit." *Chicago Tribune,* October 1. http:// www.chicagotirbune.com.

Machi, Vivienne. 2004. "Hamilton Celebrates Return of Liberty Bell." *Journal News,* April 27. https://www.journal-news.com/news/hamilton-celebrates -return-liberty-bell/v9VVU3axPdAFeWrmRkS0VO.

MacLeish, Archibald. 1962. "The American Bell." In *Let Freedom Ring: The Story of Independence Hall and its Role in the Founding of the United States.* New York: American Heritage Publishing, 49–60.

Madden, R. R. 1847. "The Liberty Bell." Friends of Freedom. *The Liberty Bell.* Boston National Anti-Slavery Bazaar.

"Mark O'Connor Sheet Music Titles." n.d. http://www.sitemason.com/site/kGwSPe /liberty.bell.orchestral.html.

Martin, Harold H. 1976. "Liberty Bell to Clunk—Softly." UPI Archives, June 30. https://www.upi.com/Archives/1976/06/30/Liberty-bell-to-clunk-softly /4374500289137.

Mason, George Carrington. 1945. "Historic Parishes of America: Bruton Parish." *Historical Magazine of the Protestant Episcopal Church* 14 (December): 276–293.

Matero, Frank G. 2013. "Housing the Bell: 150 Years of Exhibiting an American Icon." *Change over Time* 3 (Fall): 188–201.

Mathis-Lilley, Ben. 2016. "We Need to Make the Liberty Bell Way Bigger." *The Slatest,* July 26. http://www.slate.com/blogs/the_slatest/2016/07/26/the _liberty_bell_is_too_small.html.

Maule, Bradley. 2013. "Striking a Chord For Liberty." Hidden City Philadelphia, April 5. https://hiddencityphila.org/2013/04/striding-a-chord-for-liberty.

Maur, Louis. 1952. "Liberty Bell." Philadelphia: Grimes Music Publishers.

Maxwell, Tom. 2017. "A History of American Protest Music: How the Hutchinson Family Singers Achieved Pop Stardom with an Anti-Slavery Anthem." March. https://longreads.com/2017/03/07/a-history-of-american-protest -music-how-the-hutchinson-family-singers-achieved-pop-stardom-with -an-anti-slavery-anthem.

May, Isaac Barnes. "Religious Society of Friends (Quakers)." *Encyclopedia of Greater Philadelphia.* http://philadelphiaencyclopedia.org/archive/religious -society-of-friends-quakers.

"The McShane Bicentennial Commemorative of the Second Liberty Bell." American Bell Association. https://americanbell.org/aba-forum/topic/columbian-liberty-bell.

Meakin, Kate. "Wright, Richard R., Sr. (1855–1947)." *BlackPast.* http:www.blackpast.org/aah/wright-richard-r-sr-1855-1947.

Medhurst, Martin J. 1997. "Eisenhower and the Crusade for Freedom: The Rhetorical Origins of a Cold War Campaign." *Presidential Studies Quarterly* 27 (Fall): 646–661.

Meeser, Geo. F., and Francis Weiland. 1855. *The Old State House Bell.* Stayman and Brothers, Philadelphia. Monographic. Notated Music. https://www.loc.gov/item/sm1855.590180.

Menard, Drew. 2017. "Bells Installed Atop Freedom Tower." April 27. http://www.liberty.edu/news/index.cfm?PID=18495&MID=232358.

Mendte, Larry. 2013. "It's Time to Ditch Rocky Philadelphia." *The Philly Post,* July 7. https://www.phillymag.com/news/2013/07/05/time-ditch-rocky-philadelphia.

"The Mental Health Bell." n.d. Mental Health America. http://www.mentalhealthamerica.net/bell.

"The Millennium Monument World Peace Bell." n.d. Southbank Partners. http://www.southbankpartners.com/world-peace-bell/what-is-it.aspx.

Miller, Eileen. 1976. "The Liberty Bell." *Science and Children* 13 (January): 31–32.

Mires, Charlene. 1999. "In the Shadow of Independence Hall: Vernacular Activities and the Meanings of Historic Places." *The Public Historian* 21 (Spring): 49–64.

Mires, Charlene. 2009. "Invisible House, Invisible Slavery: Struggles of Public History at Independence National Historical Park." In *Culture and Belonging in Divided Societies: Contestation and Symbolic Landscapes,* Marc Howard Ross, ed. Philadelphia: University of Pennsylvania Press, 216–237.

"Mission Dolores Park—The Mexican Liberty Bell Gets a New Home." July 9, 2014. http://sfrecpark.org/mission-dolores-park-the-mexican-liberty-bell-gets-a-new-home.

Mitchell, Tia. 2018. "Senators Back Liberty Bell Monument Honoring MLK Atop Stone Mountain." AJC.com, April 4. https://www.ajc.com/news/local-govt—politics/senators-back-liberty-bell-monument-honoring-mlk-atop-stone-mountain/Wk6FuT9oiswR9jrJy8zndJ.

Morales, Tatiana. 2003. "Liberty Bell on the Move." CBS News, October 9. https://www.cbsnews.com/news/liberty-bell-on-the-move.

Morgan, Sue. 1990. "Dalai Lama Visits Liberty Bell." UPI, September 22. https://www.upi.com/Archives/1990/09/22/Dalai-lama-visits-Liberty-Bell/7587653976000.

Mowry, Duane. 1928. "An Address Which Was Not Delivered: Fourth of July Oration of Hon. James R. Doolittle." *Journal of the Illinois State Historical Society* 32 (July): 224–232.

"Mr. R. R. Madden." February 13, 1886. *British Medical Journal.* 1: 311.

Munteanu, Sorin Ion, Ioan Cilbanu, and Viorel Ene. 2011. "The Heaviest Cast Bells Existing in the World—Art of Casting." *Metalurgia International* 16: 56–62.

Museum of the Bible. 2016. "Museum of the Bible Installs First Exhibit Item: An Exact Replica of the Liberty Bell." Press release, August 16. https://www .museumofthebible.org/press/press-releases/museum-of-the-bible-installs -first-exhibit-item-an-exact-replica-of-the-liberty-bell.

Music Division, the New York Public Library. n.d. "The Bells of Fate." New York Public Library Digital Collections. http://digitalcollections.nypl.org/items /510d47de-05d1-a3d9-e040-e00a18064a99.

Music Division, the New York Public Library. n.d. "The Song of the Liberty Bell." New York Public Library Digital Collections. http://digitalcollections.nypl .org/items/510d47df-f216-a3d9-e040-e00a18064a99.

Nash, Gary B. 2010. "Liberty Bell." *Philadelphia Encyclopedia.* http://philadelphiaen cyclopedia.org/archive/liberty-bell.

Nash, Gary B. 2004. "For Whom Will the Liberty Bell Toll? From Controversy to Collaboration." *The George Wright FORUM* 21: 39–52.

National Park Service. 2015. *Bells Across the Land 2015.* Park Resource Packet. https://www.nps.gov/civilwar/upload/PARK-RESOURCE-PACKET-1.pdf.

Neale, Rick. December 22, 2017. Florida Today. "Liberty Bell Museum in Melbourne No Longer Open: Honor America in Limbo." https://www .floridatoday.com/story/news/2017/12/22/liberty-bell-museum-melbourne -no-longer-open-honor-america-limbo/923749001.

Neff, Craig. ". . . And Meanwhile in Philadelphia." 1980. SI.com Vault, July 28. https://www.si.com/vault/1980/07/28/824835/and-meanwhile-in -philadelphia-half-a-world-from-lenin-stadium-boycotting-athletes-some -of-whom-gave-olympian-performances-proved-theres-no-alternative-to -the-games.

Newman, Harvey K. "Atlanta's Hospitality Businesses in the New South Era, 1880– 1900." *Georgia Historical Quarterly* 80 (Spring); 53–76.

Nickels, Thom. 2014. "Philly Writer George Lippard, a Friend of Edgar Allen [sic.] Poe." Huffington Post blog, September 29. https://www.huffingtonpost.com /thom-nickels/philly-wirter-george-lipp_b_5633934.html.

Nighan, Michael J. 2017. "Big Bell, Big Bell and School Bells: An Ex-president, the Liberty Bell, and Several Thousand School Teachers Come to Town." *Talker of the Town,* August 7. http://talkerofthetown.com/2017/08/07/big-bill -big-bell-and-school-bells-an-ex-president-the-liberty-bell-and-several -thousand-school-teachers-come-to-town.

Nightingale, Claudine. 2016. "Sweet Liberty: World's Fairs' Love Affair with the Liberty Bell." Adam Matthew, February 5. https://www.amdigital.co.uk /about/blog/item/sweet-liberty.

Noe Hill. n.d. "Liberty Bell Slot Machine." https://noehill.com/sf/landmarks/cal0937 .asp.

"Normandy Liberty Bell." The Liberty Bell. http://www.ushistory.org/libertybell /normandybell.html.

Norris, George W. 1877. "Isaac Norris." *Pennsylvania Magazine of History and Biography* 1: 449–454.

Ogline, Jill. 2004. "'Creating Dissonance for the Visitor': The Heart of the Liberty Bell Controversy." *The Public Historian* 26 (Summer): 49–58.

"The Old State House Bell." Library of Congress. https://www.loc.gov/resource
    /sm1855.590180.0/?sp=1.

"Old Hickory Liberty Bell At Brussels World's Fair." 1958. *The Observer*, July 14,
    13. Located at the Independence National Historical Park in the Historical
    Note Card File under the Date 14 July 1958.

"Once More the Liberty Bell Shall Chime Liberty to All." 1919. Words by Minnie
    Wilson, Music by Leo Friedman. Chicago: North American Music Company.
    Accessed at Library of Congress https://www.loc.gov/item/2013565446.

O'Neil, Tim. 2014. "Look Back 250. World's Fair of 1904 Was St. Louis's Biggest
    Show." *STL Today,* August 31. https://www.stltoday.com/news/archives/look
    -back-world-s-fair-of-was-st-louis-biggest/article_42cfb7bc-121d-5aa3
    -86a2-6df0b4f70da5.html#12.

Paine, Thomas. 1775. "Liberty Tree—Poem by Thomas Paine." *Poem Hunter.*
    https://www.poemhunter.com/poem/liberty-tree.

Parent, Andrew. 2018. "15 Years Later, Phillies Plan to Bring Veterans Stadium
    Bell to Citizens Bank Park." *Philly Voice,* February 24. https://www
    .phillyvoice-com/15-years-later-phillies-plan-bring-veterans-stadium-bell
    -citizens-bank-park.

Parker, H. 1911. *Ring It Again! The Call of the Liberty Bell*. Monographic. Notated
    Music. https://www.loc.gov/item/2014563357.

"Peace Bells Around the World." Peace Bell Foundation. https://peacebellfoundation
    .org/peace/peace-bells-around-the-world.

Pelland, Dave. 2010. "World War Memorial, Norfolk." CTMonuments.net, Octo-
    ber 11. http://ctmonuments.net/20-10/10/world-war-memorial-norfolk.

Pelling, Kirstie. 2018. "The Bell That Tolls for Democracy." May 3. The Family
    Adventure Project. https://www.familyadventureproject.org/leipzig-bell
    -democracy-bell.

Penn, William. 1701. "Pennsylvania Charter of Privileges." UShistory.org. http:www
    .ushistory.org/documents/charter.htm.

"Perot Purchases a Copy of Magna Carta." 1984. *The New York Times,* Septem-
    ber 27. https://www.nytimes.com/1984/09/27/us/perot-purchases-a-copy-of
    -magna-carta.html.

Petzsch, Edward. 1885. *The Liberty Bell*. Blackmar, A. E. & Co., New Orleans,
    monographic. Notated Music. https://www.loc.gov/item/sm1885.27891.

Philadelphia Museum of Art. May 17, 2003–July 27, 2003. "Museum Studies 7:
    Christian Marclay, The Bell and the Glass." https://www.philamuseum.org
    /exhibitions/2003/61.html.

"Philadelphia, United States 1926, Sesqui-Centennial International Exposition."
    n.d. America's Best History. https://americasbesthistory.com/wfphiladel
    phia1926.html.

"Philadelphia's 1920 Celebration of the 19th Amendment." n.d. Justice Bell Foun-
    dation. http://www.justicebell.org/philadelphial-celebration.

Phillies.com. n.d. "Liberty Bell Classic." https://www.mlb.com/phillies/community
    /youth-baseball-softball/liberty-bell-classic.

"Piece of Historic Liberty Bell Recovered on Sand Island." 2015. KNON2 Staff,
    November 20. https://www.khon2.com/news/local-news/piece-of-historic
    -liberty-bell-recovered-on-sand-island_2018030911415441/1025654071.

"Police Charge Man over Liberty Bell Threat." 2013. CNN, January 27. https://www
.cnn.com/2013/01/27/justice/pennsylvania-liberty-bell-threat/index.html.

Pope, Kitty J. 2011. "Liberty Bell, Originally a Symbol for the Abolishment of Slavery, Also Has Ties to Black History." October 10. https://www.african
america.org/topic/liberty-bell-originally-a-symbol-for-the-abolishment-of
-slavery-also-has-ties-to-black-history.

Portes, Jacques, and Marie-Jeanne Rossignol. 2009. "Celebration and History: The
Case of the Louisiana Purchase." *Empires of the Imagination: Transatlan-
tic Histories of the Louisiana Purchase*, ed. Peter J. Kastor and Francois
Weil. Charlottesville: University of Virginia Press, 327–364.

"Portuguese Man Acquitted in Liberty Bell Threat." 2013. AP, October 22. https://
www.apnews.com/42ae1b07528146d1bcc9e0203585c442.

Protest Song Lyrics. n.d. "Get Off the Track! (A Song for Emancipation), Lyrics."
http://www.protestsonglyrics.net/Freedom_Songs/Get-Off-The-Track
.phtml.

Raymond, Aurelia F. 1858. "The Liberty Bell." *The Liberty Bell*. The Friends of
Liberty. Boston: Anti-Slavery Bazaar.

Read, Allen Walker. 1931. "'Liberty' in Iowa." *American Speech* 6 (June):
360–367.

Reinberger, Mark, and Elizabeth McLean. 1997. "Isaac Norris's Fairhill: Architecture, Landscape, and Quaker Ideals in a Philadelphia Colonial Country
Seat." *Winterthur Portfolio* 32 (Winter): 243–274.

"Replica of the Liberty Bell of Mexico." n.d. John F. Kennedy Presidential Library
and Museum. https://www.jfklibrary.org/asset-viewer/archives/JFKSG
/JFKSG-MO-1963-1179/JFKSG-MO-1963-1179.

Reyes, Jessica. 2016 "Robbers Who Stole Millions in Jewelry Sentenced." *The News
Journal,* April 25. https://www.delawareonline.com/story/news/crime/2016
/04/25/smash-and-grab-jewelry-robbers-get-20-years-prison/83494108.

Richter, Jan. 2009. "The Bells of Prague." Czech Radio, December 26. https://www
.radio.cz/en/section/special/the-bells-of-prague.

"Right Out Liberty Bell Patriotic March Song." Library of Congress. https://www
.loc.gov/resource/ihas.200204747.0/?sp=1.

Riley, Edward M. 1953. "The Independence Hall Group." *Transactions of the American Philosophical Society* 43 (1953): 7–42.

"Ring the Bell, Watchman!" https://www.fresnostate.edu/folklore/ballads/DTringbe
.html.

"Ring the Normandy Liberty Bell at National Constitutional Center." National Constitution Center, July 22.

"Ring Those Bells: Paul Revere, Bell Maker." n.d. Massachusetts Historical Society. https://www.masshist.org/object-of-the-month/objects/ring-those-bells
-paul-revere-bell-maker-2011-07-01.

"Robinson's Liberty Bells." n.d. Atlas Obscura. https://www.atlasobscura.com
/places/robinson-s-liberty-bells.

Robles, Frances. 2013. "A Daughter of the Cuban Revolution Visits the Liberty
Bell." *The New York Times,* May 3. https://thelede.blogs.nytimes.com/2013
/05/03/liberty-bell-visit-by-fidel-castrtos-sexologist-niece-angers-cuban
-americans.

Roessing, Jennie Bradley. 1914. "The Equal Suffrage Campaign in Pennsylvania." *Annals of the American Academy of Political and Social Science* 56 (November): 153–160.

Rongione, Louis A. 1976. "Sister to the Liberty Bell." *Records of the American Catholic Historical Society of Philadelphia* 87 (March–December): 3–32.

Rosen, Jeffrey. 2018. "America Is Living James Madison's Nightmare." *The Atlantic,* October. https://www.theatlantic.com/magazine/archive/2018/10/james-madison-mob-rule-568351.

Rossen, Jake. 2017. "When the Liberty Bell Went on a National Tour." Mental Floss, May 8. http://mentalfloss.com/articles/500549/when-liberty-bell-went-nationa-tour.

Royles, Dan. 2016. "Civil Rights (LGBT)." *Encyclopedia of Greater Philadelphia.* http://philadelphiaencyclopedia.org/archive/civil-rights-lgbt.

Rozhlas, Česky. 2017. "My Prague." January 4. http://www.czech.cz/en/Turistika/My-Prague-%E2%80%93-Zdenek-Lukes.

Rybczynski, Witold. 1998. "Moving the Bell." *The Atlantic*, June. https://www.theatlantic.com/magazine/archive/1998/06/moving-the-bell-377128.

Saltz, Jerry. 2015. "Zombies on the Walls: Why Does So Much New Abstraction Look the Same? And Taking in Jeff Koons, Creator and Destroyer of Worlds and Post-Macho God: Matisse's Cut-Outs Are World-Historically Gorgeous." In *The Best American Magazine Writing 2015*, ed. Sid Holt. New York: Columbia University Press, 344–361.

Saramago, Jose. 2002. "From Justice to Democracy By Way of the Bells." *Terra Incognita,* January 22. http://www.terraincognita.50megs.com/saramago.html.

Schlesinger, Arthur M. 1952. "Liberty Tree: A Genealogy." *New England Quarterly* 25 (December): 435–458.

SchoolhouseRock! "Trip to Philly II: The Liberty Bell—You Tube." https://www.youtube.com/watch?v=8GsAF4mXYv4.

Segal, Rick. 2015. "Fare Well, Liberty Bell." desiringGod, July 4. https://www.desiringgod.org/articles/fare-well-liberty-bell.

Shallit, Joseph. 1942. "Reporter Taking Snapshot of Liberty Bell Arrested; You Can Buy One for 5c." *Philadelphia Record*, July 4, 1.

Shattuck, Charles E. "The True Meaning of the Term 'Liberty' in Those Clauses in the Federal and State Constitutions Which Protect 'Life, Liberty, and Property.'" *Harvard Law Review* 4 (March 15): 365–392.

Shepherd, Samuel C., Jr. 1985. "A Glimmer of Hope: The World's Industrial and Cotton Centennial Exposition. New Orleans, 1884–1885." *Louisiana History: The Journal of the Louisiana Historical Association* 26 (Summer): 271–290.

"Sheriff Has Liberty Bell: It Was Seized on Attachment by the Firm Which Cast It." 1896. *The New York Times*, November 11, 3.

Shoemaker, Metta J., Genevieve Irene Nevin, and Marks Probasco. 1917. *The Liberty Bells Are Ringing: A Patriotic Song.* Monographic. Marks Probasco Publisher, Mishawaka, IN. Notated Music. https://www.loc.gov/item/2009371604.

Siebert, Karen. 2003. "Advancing Democracy by Conquering Space." *Portrait of Freedom: The 250th Anniversary of the Liberty Bell*. Clearwater, FL: Belmont International, 94–101.

Simon, Katrina. 2015. "Re-casting the Past: Re-instating Once Broken and Tuneless Bells and the Recalling of Past Urban Landscapes." *Environment, Space, Place* 7 (Spring): 28–46.

Simpson, Pamela H. 2010. "A Vernacular Recipe for Sculpture—Butter, Sugar, and Corn." *American Art* 24 (Spring): 23–26.

Skelton, Olive M. 1918. *Our Liberty Bell*. Monographic. Olive M. Skelton, Exeter, Canada. Notated Music. https://www.loc.gov/item/2009371952.

"Slavs Proclaim Independence Shrine." 1918. *Evening Public Ledger*, October 26, 1.

Smelser, Marshall. 1970. "The Glorious Fourth—or, Glorious Second? Or Eighth?" *History Teacher* 3 (January): 25–30.

Smith, James G. 1976. "A Report on 'The New Liberty Bell.'" *Choral Journal* 16 (March): 19–25.

Smyth, William D. 1987. "Blacks and the South Carolina Interstate and West Indian Exposition." *The South Carolina Historical Magazine* 88 (October): 211–219.

Sneff, Emily. "Presenting the Facts: National Treasure." Course of Human Events. December 19, 2016. https://declaration.fas.harvard.edu/blog/facts-national treasure.

"So-Called Dollars. U.S. Centennial Exposition 1876 Philadelphia, PA." https://www.so-calleddollars.com/Events?US?Centennial.html.

"The Song of the Liberty Bell." 1904. Music Supplement to the *Boston Sunday Herald*, August 14.

Spaid, Arthur R. 1896. "Our Liberty Bell." *Journal of Education* 43 (June 18): 416.

Spikol, Liz. 2015. "How Philadelphia Helped Give Birth to the LGBT Rights Movement." *Philadelphia Magazine*, June 28. https://www.phillymag.com/g-philly-2015/06/28/annual-reminder-lgbt-philadelphia.

"Spirit of the Liberty Bell." n.d. Providence Forum. https://providenceforum.org/project/spirit-liberty-bell

Stamp-Collecting-World. n.d. "West Berlin Stamps Freedom Bell Issues 1951–1956." https://www.stamp-collecting-world.com/westberlin_bells.html.

Stathis, Stephen W. 1978. "Returning the Declaration of Independence to Philadelphia: An Exercise in Centennial Politics." *Pennsylvania Magazine of History and Biography* 102 (April): 167–183.

Statue of Liberty—Ellis Island Foundation, Inc. n.d. "Statue History." https://www.libertyellisfoundation.org/statue-history.

Steel, Piers. 2011. "The Greatest Procrastinator in History Still Alive: Puts Off Death." *Psychology Today*, March 7. https://www.psychologytoday.com/us/blog/the-procrastination-equation/201103/the-greatest-procrastinator-in-history-still-alive-puts.

Stewart, J. A. 1915. "The Liberty Bell's Great Trip." *Journal of Education* 82 (June 15): 48–49.

Stille, Charles J. 1889. "Pennsylvania and the Declaration of Independence." *Pennsylvania Magazine of History and Biography* 13 (January): 385–429.

Stockmeyer, Norman Otto, Jr. 1992. "The Liberty Bell Award—Symbol of Law Day." *Michigan Bar Journal* 71 (January): 20–21.

Stoddard, Christine. 2015. "The Liberty Bell in Papal Visit Graphics." *Arlington Catholic Herald,* September 24. https://www.catholicherald.com/news/the_liberty-bell_in_papal_visit-graphics.

"The Story of 'Big Joe.'" n.d. The Verdin Company. https://www.verdin.com/big-joe.

"The Story of the Liberty Bell." n.d. Whitechapel Bell Foundry. http://www.whitechapelbellfoundry.co.uk/liberty.htm.

Strauss, Valerie. 2016. "Is July 2 America's True Independence Day? John Adams Thought So." *Washington Post,* July 1. https://www.washingtonpost.com/news/answer-sheet/wp/2016/07/01/is-july-2-the-true-independence-day-john-adams-thought-so/?utm_term=.ebec6b8eef99.

Szynkowski, Joe. 2004. "Liberty Bell of the West." TheSouthern.com, November 12. https://thesouthern.com/liberty-bell-of-the-west-article_bd64bb58-6a83-11e4-8c7e-d76b93e7d0a0.html.

"The Taco Liberty Bell." n.d. The Museum of Hoaxes. http://hoaxes.org/archive/permalink/taco_liberty_bell.

"Take a Tour of Lady Liberty's Torch (Right This Second)." 2018. *The New York Times,* November 13. https://www.nytimes.com/interactive/2018/11/13/nyregion/statue-of-liberty-torch-ar-ul.html?action=click&module=Top%20Stories&pgtype=Homepage.

Tallmadge, William. H. 2008. "Fisk Jubilee Singers." In *New Encyclopedia of Southern Culture,* ed. Bill C. Malone. Chapel Hill: University of North Carolina Press, 228–229.

Tamony, Peter. 1968. "The One-Armed Bandit." *Western Folklore* 27 (April): 117–124.

Tauber, Michelle. 2016. "'Mr. President, It Was Muskrats': Toni Tennille on the Time She Sang 'Muskrat Love' for Queen Elizabeth—in the White House!" *People,* March 19. https://people.com/royals/toni-tennille-on-the-time-she-sang-muskrat-love-for-queen-elizabeth.

Taylor, Blaine. 2003. "A History of the Liberty Bell, 1701–2003." 37–39. *Portrait of Freedom: The 250th Anniversary of the Liberty Bell.* Clearwater, FL: Belmont International.

Teunissen, John J., and Evelyn J. Hinz. 1974. "The Attack on the Pieta: An Archetypal Analysis." *Journal of Aesthetics and Art Criticism* 33 (Autumn): 43–50.

Thomas, Lara. August 2005. "Liberty Bell Replica Sails to States." Military Sealift Command. http://www.msc.navy.mil/sealift/2005/August/libertybell.htm.

Thompson, Ralph. 1934. "The Liberty Bell and Other Anti-Slavery Gift-Books." *New England Quarterly* 7 (March): 154–168.

Tiedemann, Joseph S. 2010. "A Tumultuous People: The Rage for Liberty and the Ambiance of Violence in the Middle Colonies in the Years Preceding the American Revolution." *Pennsylvania History: A Journal of Mid-Atlantic Studies* 77 (Autumn): 387–431.

TowerBells.org. n.d. "Garden City: USA—NY." http://www.towerbells.org/data/NYGDNCTY.HTM.

Townsend, Jen, and Renee Zettle-Sterling. 2017. "Liberty Cast and Recast." *CAST* (blog). July 4. https://www.castartandobjects.com/blog/2017/7/4/liberty-cast-and-recast.

Tremel, Andrew. "Presidents of the United States (Presence in the Region)." Encyclopedia of Greater Philadelphia. http://philadelphiaencyclopedia.org/archive/presidents-of-the-united-states.

"Truman Campaign Button." n.d. Truman Library. https://www.trumanlibrary.org/photographs/view.php?id=20596.

Truman, Harry S. "Address in Independence at the Dedication of the Liberty Bell." Public Papers Harry S. Truman 1945–1953. https://www.trumanlibrary.org/publicpapers/index.php?pid=1440.

Trump, Donald J. 2002. "Portrait of Freedom." In *Portrait of Freedom: The 250th Anniversary of the Liberty Bell*. Clearwater, FL: Belmont International.

Turtledove, Harry. *Liberty Bell: The Liberty Bell In the Presence of Mine Enemies*. Harry Turtledove Wiki. http://turtledove.wikia.com/wiki/Liberty_Bell.

Unruh, Bob. 2010. "Free Speech Restored at Liberty Bell Display." *World Net Daily,* June 18. https://www.wnd.com/2010/06/167845.

UPI. "31 U.S. Towns Have 'Liberty.'" 2011. July 4. https://www.upi.com/31-US-towns-have-liberty/18521309802360.

USS Bowfin Submarine Museum and Park. December 2, 2015. https://www.facebook.com/bowfinpark/posts/welcome-americas-the-freedom-bell-to-hawaiiwe-are-proud-that-spirit-of-liberty-f/10153766257139839.

"Voice of Liberty, The." 1917. Words by Ervin Biddle, music by Maurice Stretch. Camden, NJ: Biddle & Stretch Publishers. Accessed at the Library of Congress at https://www.loc.gov/item/2009371916.

Walton, Hanes, Jr., Roosevelt Green, Jr., Willie E. Johnson, Kenneth A. Joran, Leslie Buri McLemore, C. Vernon Gray, and Marion Orr. 1991. "R. R. Wright, Congress, President Truman and the First National Public African-American Holiday: National Freedom Day." *PS: Political Science and Politics* 24 (December): 685–688.

Warfield, Patrick. 2011. "The March as Musical Drama and the Spectacle of John Philip Sousa." *Journal of the American Musicological Society* 64 (Summer): 289–318.

Warnock, Kae. 2016. "That Rings a Bell!" National Conference of State Legislatures Blog, July 1. http://www.ncsl.org/blog/2016/07/01/that-rings-a-bell-.aspx.

Warren, Charles. 1945. "Fourth of July Myths." *William and Mary Quarterly* 2 (July): 237–272.

Warschawsky, Steven. 2007. "Visiting the Liberty Bell." *Real Clear Politics,* March 18. https://www.realclearpolitics.com/articles/2007/03/visiting_the_liberty_bell.html.

Wartman, Scott. 2016. "What Will Be Built on World Peace Bell Site?" *Cincinnati Inquirer,* February 27. https://www.cincinnati.com/story/news/2016/02/27/what-built-world-peace-bell-site/80987738.

Washington, Booker T. "Booker T. Washington Delivers the 1895 Atlanta Compromise Speech." History Matters. http://historymatters.gmu.edu/d/39.

Welch, Diane. 2015. "Idea for 'Freedom Bell' Rings Out, Thanks to Rancho Santa Fe Resident." *Rancho Santa Fe Review,* June 14. http://www.ranchosantafereview.com/sdrsf-Freedom-bell-armed-forces-2015jun14-story.html.

Werber, Cassie. 2016. "'There Is a Crack in Everything, That's How the Light Gets In': The Story of Leonard Cohen's 'Anthem.'" *Quartz,* November 22. https://qz.com/835076/leonard-cohens-anthem-the-story-of-the-line-there-is-a-crack-in-everything-thats-how-the-light-gets-in.

Wertz, Marianna. 2005. "Friedrich Schiller's 'The Song of the Bell.'" *Fidelio* 14 (Spring–Summer): 36–45.

"Who Washes the Liberty Bell?" 2014. *Metro,* April 1. https://www.metro.us/local/who-washes-the-liberty-bell/tmWncE—41MI6YEnO7HDs.

"Who? What? Where?" 1976. *American Legion Magazine,* September, 30.

Wiggins, Michael. 2015. "Independence Hall and Liberty Bell Exhibit." Indegogo, May 12. https://www.indiegogo.com/projects/independence-hall-and-the-liberty-bell-exhibit#.

Williams, Hattie. 2018. "Whitechapel Bell Foundry May [Be] Brought Back from Developers and Reopened by Royal Charity." *Church Times,* July 6. https://www.churchtimes.co.uk/articles/2018/6-july/news/uk/whitechapel-bell-foundry-may-bought-back-from-developers-and-reopened-by-royal charity.

Williams, Peter W. 1997. "'The Heart of It All': The Varieties of Ohio's Religious Architecture." *U.S. Catholic Historian* 15 (Winter): 75–90.

Williams, Thomas. 1918. *Ring Out Ye Bell of Liberty.* Monographic. The Songwriters Bureau, Philadelphia. Notated Music. https://www.loc.gov/item/2014564543.

Willis, Paul. 2004. "The Liberty Bell: A Meditation on Labor, Liberty, and the Cultural Mediations That Connect or Disconnect Them." *Annals of the American Academy of Political and Social Science* 595 (September): 223–248.

Wilson, Ryan. 2015. "Celebrating the Founders of the LGBT Movement in Philadelphia." Human Rights Campaign, July 9. https://www.hrc.org/blog/celebrating-the-founders-of-the-lgbt-movement-in-philadelphia.

Windhausen, John D. 1967. "Quaker Pacifism and the Image of Isaac Norris, II." *Pennsylvania History: A Journal of Mid-Atlantic Studies* 34 (October): 346–360.

Wolf, Stephanie Grauman. 2013. "Centennial Exhibition (1876)." *Encyclopedia of Greater Philadelphia.* http://philadelphiaencyclopedia.org/archive/centennial.

Work, Henry C. 1865. *Ring the Bell, Watchman!* Root & Cady, Chicago. Notated Music. https://www.loc.gov/item/ihas.200002355.

"World War I Memorial—Norfolk, CT—U.S. National Register of Historic Places on Waymarking.com." n.d. http://www.waymarking.com/waymarks/WMGM97_Norfolk_World_War_I_Memorial_Norfolk_CT.

"You're a Grand Old Bell." n.d. Historic American Sheet Music, David M. Rubenstein Rare Book & Manuscript Library, Duke University. https://library.duke.edu/digitalcollections/hasm_a2267.

BOOKS AND PAMPHLETS

Abshire, Joan. 2008. *The John Brown Bell: The Journey of the Second-Most Important Bell in American History, from Harpers Ferry, West Virginia, to Marlborough Massachusetts.* Marlborough Historical Society. www .HistoricMarlborough.org/resources/John+Brown_Bell.pdf

Aden, Roger C. 2015. *Upon the Ruins of Liberty: Slavery, the President's House at Independence National Independence Historical Park and Public Memory.* Philadelphia: Temple University Press.

Alexander, Mary D. 1929. *Andrew McNair and the Liberty Bell 1776.* Chicago: University of Chicago Press.

Aron, Paul. 2013. *Why the Turkey Didn't Fly.* Williamsburg, VA: The Colonial Wiliamsburg Foundation.

Bailyn, Bernard. 1967. *The Ideological Origins of the American Revolution.* Cambridge, MA: Belknap Press of Harvard University Press.

Becker, Carl. (1922) 1970. *The Declaration of Independence: A Study in the History of Political Ideas.* New York: Vintage Books.

Belisle, D. W. 1959. *History of Independence Hall: From the Earliest Period to the Present Time, Embracing Biographies of the Immortal Signers of the Declaration of Independence, with Historical Sketches of the Sacred Relics Preserved in That Sanctuary of American Freedom.* Philadelphia: John Challen & Sons.

Bernstein, Andrew. 2001. *America's Jubilee: How in 1826 a Generation Remembered Fifty Years of Independence.* New York: Alfred A. Knopf.

Bishop, David H. 1975. "Ascent to Significance: The Evolution of the Liberty Bell as a Cultural Symbol." American Studies senior thesis, Temple University, May 2. Located at National Independence Historical Park.

Blockson, Charles L. *The Liberty Bell Era: The African American Story.* St. Louis, MO: Regent Publishing.

Boland, Charles Michael. 1973. *Ring in the Jubilee: The Epic of America's Liberty Bell.* Riverside, CT: Chatham Press.

Bradshaw, Wellesley. 1876. *History and Legends of the Old Liberty Bell in Independence Hall, at Philadelphia. To Which Is Added That of the New Bell.* Philadelphia: C.W. Alexander.

Branham, Robert James, and Stephen J. Hartnett. 2002. *Sweet Freedom's Song: "My Country 'Tis of Thee" and Democracy in America.* New York: Oxford University Press.

Casey, Janet. G. 2015. *Teaching Tainted Lit: Popular American Fiction in Today's Classroom.* Iowa City: University of Iowa Press.

Chesterton, G. K. 1922. *What I Saw in America.* New York: Dodd, Mead, and Company.

Clark, Justin T. 2018. *City of Second Sight: Nineteenth Century Boston and the Making of American Visual Culture.* Chapel Hill: University of North Carolina Press.

Clark, Luther A., and Mary E. Glasgow. *America's Liberty Bells.* Monographic, 1911. Notated Music. https://www.loc.gov/item/2013564337.

Coates, Florence Earle. "The Liberty Bell." *Poems*. Boston: Houghton, Mifflin, and Company, 1898.

Conway, Adaline May. 1914. *A Silent Peal from the Liberty Bell*. Philadelphia: George W. Jacobs.

de Bolla, Peter. 2007. *The Fourth of July and the Founding of America*. Woodstock, NY: Overlook Press.

Eberlein, Harold Donaldson, and Cortland Van Dyke Hubbard. 1939. *Portrait of a Colonial City, 1670–1838*. Philadelphia: J. B. Lippincott Company.

Eckhardt, George H. 1955. *Pennsylvania Clocks and Clockmakers: An Epic of Early American Science, Industry, and Craftsmanship*. New York: Devin-Adair Company.

El-Khoury, Rololphe, ed. 2006. *Liberty Bell Center: Bohlin Cywinski Jackson*. 2006. New York: ORO Editions.

Fischer, David Hackett. 2005. *Liberty and Freedom*. New York: Oxford University Press.

French, Francis, and Colin Burgess. 2007. *Into That Silent Sea: Trailblazers of the Space Era, 1961–1965*. Lincoln: University of Nebraska Press.

Friends of Freedom. 1844. *The Liberty Bell*. Maria Weston Chapman, ed. Boston: Massachusetts Anti-Slavery Fair.

Friends of Freedom. 1843. *The Liberty Bell*. Maria Weston Chapman, ed. Boston: Boston-Anti-Slavery Society.

Friends of Freedom. 1839. *The Liberty Bell*. Maria Weston Chapman, ed. Boston: Boston-Anti-Slavery Society.

Froideville, Gilbert Monod de, and Mark Verheul. 2016. *An Expert's Guide to International Protocol*. Amsterdam: Amsterdam University Press.

Gardella, Peter. 2014. *American Civil Religion: What Americans Hold Sacred*. New York: Oxford University Press.

Gerenson, Edward. 2012. *The Statue of Liberty: A Transatlantic Story*. New Haven, CT: Yale University Press.

Gilbert, James. 2009. *Whose Fair? Experience, Memory, and the History of the Great St. Louis Exposition*. Chicago: University of Chicago Press.

Goeppinger, Neil. 2016. *Large Bells of America: History of Church Bells, Fire Bells, School Bells, Dinner Bells and Their Foundries*. Sarasota, FL: Suncoast Digital Press.

Gordon, Tammy S. 2013. *The Spirit of 1976: Commerce, Community, and the Politics of Commemoration*. Amherst: University of Massachusetts Press.

Green, Steven K. 2015. *Investing a Christian America: The Myth of the Religious Founding*. New York: Oxford University Press.

Greiff, Constance M. 1987. *Independence: The Creation of a National Park*. Philadelphia: University of Pennsylvania Press.

Gudehus, E. R. 1915. *The Liberty Bell: Its History, Associations and Home*. Philadelphia: Dunlap Printing.

Guerra, Lillian. 2018. *Heroes, Martyrs, and Political Messiahs in Revolutionary Cuba, 1946–1958*. New Haven, CT: Yale University Press.

Hall-Quest, Olga W. 1965. *The Bell That Rang for Freedom: The Liberty Bell and Its Place in American History*. New York: E. P. Dutton

Hamilton, Alexander, James Madison, and John Jay. 1961 [orig. 1787–1788]. *The Federalist Papers*. New York: New American Library.

Harper, Matthew. 2016. *The End of Days: African American Religion and Politics in the Age of Emancipation*. Chapel Hill: University of North Carolina Press.

Heintze, James R. 2007. *The Fourth of July Encyclopedia*. Jefferson, NC: McFarland

Hieronimus, Robert, with Laura Cortner. 2008. *The United Symbolism of America: Deciphering Hidden Meanings in America's Most Familiar Art, Architecture, and Logos*. Franklin Lakes, NJ: New Page Books.

Horwitz, Elinor Lander. 1976. *The Bird, the Banner, and Uncle Sam: Images of America in Folk and Popular Art*. Philadelphia: J. P. Lippincott.

Howard, Hattie. 1887. *Later Poems*. Hartford: Lockwood & Brainard.

Independence National Historical Park. n.d. *The Liberty Bell: A Symbol for "We the People": A Teacher Guide with Lesson Plans*. https://www.nps.gov/inde /learn/education/upload/The%20Liberty%20Bell%20Teacher%20 Guide%20Feb%202010.pdf.

Kashatus, William C., III. 1992. *Historic Philadelphia: The City, Symbols & Patriots, 1681–1800*. Lanham, MD: University Press of America.

Keels, Thomas H. 2017. *Sesqui! Greed, Graft, and the Forgotten World's Fair of 1926*. Philadelphia: Temple University Press.

Keyser, Charles S. 1893. *The Liberty Bell, Independence Hall, Philadelphia. A Complete Record of All the Great Events Announced by the Ringing of the Bell*. Philadelphia: Allen, Lane & Scott's Printing House.

Keyssar, Alexander. 2009. *The Right to Vote: The Contested History of Democracy in America*. New York: Basic Books.

Kimball, David. 1989. *The Story of the Liberty Bell*. Fort Washington, PA: Eastern National.

Kirschbaum, Eric. 2014. *Burning Beethoven: The Eradication of German Culture in the United States During World War I*. New York: Berlinica Publishing.

Kraditor, Aileen S. 1981. *The Idea of the Woman's Suffrage Movement, 1890–1920*. New York: W. Norton.

Kramer, Justin. 1975. *Cast in America: The Historically Accurate, Exciting Story of the Liberty Bell*. Los Angeles: Justin Kramer Incorporated.

Krythe, Maymie R. 1968. *What So Proudly We Hail: All About Our American Flag, Monuments and Symbols*. New York: Harper & Row, Publishers.

LaPier, Rosalyn, and David R. M. Beck. 2015. *City Indian: Native American Activism in Chicago, 1893–1894*. Lincoln: University of Nebraska Press.

Leopold, George. 2016. *The Supersonic Life and Times of Gus Grissom*. West Lafayette, IN: Purdue University Press.

Lippard, George. 1847 *George Washington and His Generals: or, Legends of the Revolution*. Philadelphia: G. B. Zieber.

Longshore, Jos. S., and Benjamin L. Knowles. 1876. *The Centennial Liberty Bell. Independence Hall; Its tradition and Associations. The Declaration of Independence and Its Signers. With an Appendix Embracing the Opening Ceremonies of the International Exhibition, and of the Centennial Celebration of July 4th, 1876*. Philadelphia: Claxton, Remsen & Haffelfinger.

Lubig, Joseph M. 2011. *Maltese in Michigan*. East Lansing: Michigan State University Press.

Maier, Pauline. 1997. *American Scripture: Making the Declaration of Independence*. New York: Alfred A. Knopf.

Malone, Dumas. 1943. *The Story of the Declaration of Independence*. New York: Oxford University Press.

Marcovitz, Hal. 2003. *The Liberty Bell. Part of American Symbols and Their Meaning*. Philadelphia: Mason Crest Publishers.

McShane Bell Foundry. n.d. *The McShane Bell Foundry*. Baltimore.

Meacham, Jon. 2018. *The Soul of America: The Battle for Our Better Angels*. New York: Random House.

Mires, Charlene. 2002. *Independence Hall in American Memory*. Philadelphia: University of Pennsylvania Press.

Moreno, Barry. 2000. *The Statue of Liberty Encyclopedia*. New York: Simon & Schuster.

Morris, Madge. 1885. *Poems*. San Francisco: The Golden Era.

Nash, Gary B. 2010. *The Liberty Bell*. New Haven, CT: Yale University Press.

Nash, Gary B. 2006. *First City: Philadelphia and the Forging of Historical Memory*. Philadelphia: University of Pennsylvania Press.

Paige, John C. 1988. *The Liberty Bell of Independence National Historical Park: A Special History Study*, ed. David C. Kimball. Denver: Denver Service Center, National Park Service, Department of the Interior. Accessed through pubs.etic.nps.gov.

Peck, Robert S. 1992. *The Bill of Rights and the Politics of Interpretation*. St. Paul, MN: West Publishing.

Perdue, Theda. 2010. *Race and the Atlanta Cotton States Exposition of 1895*. Athens, GA: University of Georgia Press.

Peterson, Russell L. *Strange Bedfellows: How Late-Night Comedy Turns Democracy into a Joke*. New Brunswick, NJ: Rutgers University Press.

Randel, William Peirce. 1969. *Centennial: American Life in 1876*. Philadelphia: Chilton Book.

Rees, Thomas. 1906. *Spain's Lost Jewels: Cuba and Mexico*. Springfield: Illinois State Register.

Report of the Proceedings of a Convention composed of Delegates from the Thirteen Original United States Held in Independence Hall on Monday the Fifth, and Tuesday the Sixth of July, 1852, for the Purpose of Considering the Propriety of Erecting One or More Monuments I Independence Square, Philadelphia in Commemoration of the Declaration of Independence, July 4, 1776, and in Honor of the Signers Thereof . . ." 1852. Philadelphia: Crissy & Markley, Printers.

Robbins, Trina. 1996. *The Great Women Superheroes*. Northhampton, MA: Kitchen Sink Press.

Rosewater, Victor. 1926. *The Liberty Bell: Its History and Significance*. New York: D. Appleton.

Rydell, Robert W. 1984. *All the World's a Fair: Visions of Empire at American International Expositions, 1876–1916*. Chicago: University of Chicago Press.

Sands, Robert W., Jr., and Alexander B. Bartlett. 2002. *Images of America: Independence Hall and the Liberty Bell*. Charleston, SC: Arcadia Publishing.

Sandoz, Ellis, ed. 1991. *Political Sermons of the American Founding Era, 1730–1805*. Indianapolis: Liberty Fund.

Shalev, Eran. 2014. *American Zion: The Old Testament as a Political Text from the Revolution to the Civil War*. New Haven, CT: Yale University Press.

Siebert, Karen. 2003. "Advancing Democracy by Conquering Space, Liberty Bell 7." In *Portrait of Freedom: The 250th Anniversary of the Liberty Bell*. Clearwater, FL: Belmont International, 94–101.

Simpson, Pamela. H. 2012. *Corn Palaces and Butter Queens: A History of Crop Art and Dairy Sculpture*. Minneapolis: University of Minnesota Press.

Springer, L. Elsinore. 1976. *That Vanishing Sound*. New York: Crown Publishers.

Stoudt, John Baer. 1930. *The Liberty Bells of Pennsylvania*. Philadelphia: William J. Campbell.

Stoudt, John Baer. 1927. *The Liberty Bell in Allentown and Allentown's Liberty Bell*. Allentown, PA: Berkemeyer, Keck.

Tafel, Jonathan Leigh. 1979. *The Historical Development of Political and Patriotic Images of America: A Visual Analysis of Fourth of July Cartoons in Five Newspapers*. PhD dissertation at Ohio State University.

Tomek, Beverly C. 2014. *Pennsylvania Hall: A "Legal Lynching" in the Shadow of the Liberty Bell*. New York: Oxford University Press.

Van Loon, Hendrik Willem. 1943. *Thomas Jefferson*. New York: Dodd, Mead, and Company.

Vile, John R. 2019. *The Declaration of Independence: America's First Founding Document in U.S. History and Culture*. Santa, Barbara, CA: ABC-CLIO.

Vile, John R. 2018. *The American Flag: An Encyclopedia of the Stars and Stripes in U.S. History, Culture, and Law*. Santa Barbara, CA: ABC-CLIO.

Vile, John R. 2017. *The Jacksonian and Antebellum Eras, Documents Decoded*. Santa Barbara, CA: ABC-CLIO.

Vile, John R. 2016. *The Constitutional Convention of 1787: A Comprehensive Encyclopedia of America's Founding*, rev. 2nd ed., 2 vols. Clark, NJ: Talbot Publishing.

Vile, John R. 2015. *Encyclopedia of Constitutional Amendments, Proposed Amendments, and Amending Issues, 1789–2015*, 4th ed., 2 vols. Santa Barbara, CA: ABC-CLIO.

Voorhis, Harold V. B. and Ronald E. Heaton. 1976. *Loud and Clear: The Story of Our Liberty Bell*. Revised ed. Norristown, PA: Ronald E. Heaton.

Wallace, William Ross. 1862. *The Liberty Bell*. New York: James C. Gregory.

Watson, Henry C. 1852. *The Old Bell of Independence; or, Philadelphia in 1776*. Philadelphia: Lindsay and Blakiston.

Weller, Allen Stuart. 2014. "The World's Columbian Exposition." In *Lorado Taft: The Chicago Years,* ed. Robert G. La France and Henry Adams with Stephen P. Thomas. Champaign: University of Illinois Press, 65–85.

Whipple, Wayne. 1910. *The Story of the Liberty Bell*. Philadelphia: Henry Altemus.

Williams, R. [Ranson] G. 1835. *Anti-Slavery Record*, vol. I. New York: R.G. Williams for the American Anti-Slavery Society.

Wilson, Martin W. 2000. *From the Sesquicentennial to the Bicentennial: Changing Attitudes Toward Tourism in Philadelphia, 1926–1976.* Dissertation at Temple University, January.
Winsett, R. E., ed. 1941. *Liberty Bells.* Dayton, TN: R. E. Winsett.

SELECTED CHILDREN'S BOOKS

Bailey, R. J. 2017. *Liberty Bell.* "Hello, America!" series. Minneapolis: Bullfrog Books.
Binns, Tristan Boyer. 2001. *Symbols of Freedom: The Liberty Bell.* Chicago: Heinemann Library.
Firestone, Mary. 2007. *The Liberty Bell (American Symbols).* Matthew Skeens, illustrator. Picture Window Books.
Jango-Cohen, Judith. 2004. *The Liberty Bell.* Pull Ahead Books.
Magaziner, Henry Jonas. 2007. *Our Liberty Bell.* John O'Brien, illustrator. New York: Holiday House.
McDonald, Megan. 2005. *Saving the Liberty Bell.* Marsha Gray Carrington, illustrator. New York: Atheneum Books for Young Readers.
Milhous, Katherine. 1964. *Through these Arches: The Story of Independence Hall.* Philadelphia: J. B. Lippincott.
Moore, Ruth Nulton. 1968. *Hiding the Bell.* Philadelphia: Westminister Press.
Steen, Sandra, and Susan Steen. 1994. *Independence Hall.* New York: Dillon Press.

COURT DECISIONS

Bayle v. City of New Orleans, 23 F. 843 (1885).
In re Washington Monument Fund, 154 Pa. 621 (1893).
Morton v. City of Philadelphia, 4 PA. D. 523 (1895).
Plessy v. Ferguson, 163 U.S. 537 (1896).
United States of America, Appellee, v. Walter Augustus Bowe, Robert Steele Collier, and Khaleel Sultarn Sayyed, Defendants, 360 F.2d 1 (2d Cir. 1966).

Index

Note: Page numbers in **bold** indicate main entry for term.

About the Author

John R. Vile, PhD, is a professor of political science and dean of the University Honors College at Middle Tennessee State University. He has written and edited a variety of books on legal issues, the U.S. Constitution, and the American founding period. They include the following: *More Than a Plea for a Declaration of Rights: The Constitutional and Political Thought of George Mason of Virginia* (2019); *The Declaration of Independence: America's First Founding Document in U.S. History and Culture* (2019); *The American Flag: An Encyclopedia of the Stars and Stripes in U.S. History, Culture, and Law* (2018); *The Civil War and Reconstruction Eras* (2018); *A Constellation of Great Men: Exploring the Character Sketches by Dr. Benjamin Rush of Pennsylvania of the Signers of the Declaration of Independence* (2018); *Essential Supreme Court Decisions,* 17th ed. (2018); *Constitutional Law in Contemporary America,* 2 vols. (2017); *Encyclopedia of the First Amendment,* rev. online ed. (2017); *The Jacksonian and Antebellum Eras* (2017); *American Immigration and Citizenship* (2016); *The Constitutional Convention of 1787: A Comprehensive Encyclopedia of America's Founding,* 2 vols., 2nd ed. (2016); *Conventional Wisdom: The Alternative Article V Mechanism for Proposing Amendments to the U.S. Constitution* (2016); *The Early Republic* (2016); *A Companion to the United States Constitution and Its Amendments,* 6th ed. (2015); *Encyclopedia of Constitutional Amendments, Proposed Amendments, and Amending Issues, 1789–2015,* 4th ed. (2015); *Founding Documents of America: Documents Decoded* (2015); *The United States Constitution: One Document, Many Choices* (2015); *The Wisest Council in the World: Restoring the Character Sketches by William Pierce of Georgia of the Delegates to the Constitutional Convention of 1787* (2015); *Re-Framers: 170 Eccentric, Visionary, and Patriotic Proposals to Rewrite the U.S. Constitution* (2014); *Encyclopedia of the Fourth Amendment* (2013); *The Men Who Made the Constitution: Lives of the Delegates to the Constitutional Convention of 1787* (2013); *The Writing and Ratification of the U.S. Constitution: Practical Virtue in Action* (2012); *James Madison: Founder, Philosopher, Founder and Statesman* (2008); *Encyclopedia of Civil Liberties in America* (2005); *Great American Judges: An Encyclopedia* (2003); *Great American Lawyers: An Encyclopedia* (2002); *History of the American Legal System: Interactive Encyclopedia* (CD-ROM, 2000); *Tennessee Government and Politics* (1998); *Constitutional Change in the United States* (1994); *Contemporary Questions Surrounding the Constitutional Amending Process* (1993); *The Theory and Practice of Constitutional Change in America* (1993); *The Constitutional Amending Process in American Political Thought* (1992); and *Rewriting the United States Constitution* (1991).

www.ingramcontent.com/pod-product-compliance
Lightning Source LLC
Chambersburg PA
CBHW080410270326
41929CB00018B/2975